**NorthJersey
MediaGroup
BOOKS**

To Elda
with best wishes
Richard Muti

Cent'Anni

---

the
Sinatra
LEGEND
at 100

RICHARD MUTI

**NorthJersey
MediaGroup
BOOKS**

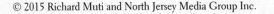

Published by North Jersey Media Group Inc.

Amre Youssef, *Publishing Coordinator*
Glenn Garvie, *Designer and Manager of Production*
Kim Kline, *Editor*
Maggie Grande, *Marketing Supervisor*
Zhanna Gitina, *Photo Editor*

Cover Photo: © Getty Images
Author photo: Christopher Ottaunick

ISBN 978-0-9909889-4-6

Library of Congress Control Number: 2015915681

Printed in the United States of America

First printing November 2015

North Jersey Media Group Inc.
1 Garret Mountain Plaza
Woodland Park, N.J. 07424

For Mauro Richard Muti and

Mafalda Stella Muti, née Milano,

my parents,

and for Sergio Muti and

Rosaria Muti, née Potenza,

and for Giuseppe Milano and

Pia Milano, née Remia,

my grandparents.

O for a Muse of fire, that would ascend
The brightest heaven of invention…

William Shakespeare, *Henry V*

The only thing you owe the public
is a good performance.

Humphrey Bogart, to Frank Sinatra

CONTENTS

PREFACE

"He considers himself the greatest vocalist in the business."

Understanding the Frank Sinatra phenomenon, even now — 100 years, or *cent'anni*, after his birth — remains an elusive goal, because there were so many renditions of the man, so many different Frank Sinatras.

Four years after Sinatra won a well-deserved Oscar for Best Supporting Actor, in 1953, for his portrayal of Army Private Angelo Maggio in *From Here to Eternity*, Joanne Woodward received the Oscar for Best Actress for her role in *The Three Faces of Eve*, based on a true story about a woman with multiple personalities. Just three of those personalities appeared in the motion picture, but the actual patient exhibited signs of 22 different women inhabiting her. I don't suggest that Frank Sinatra suffered from a mental disorder, or that the various aspects of his personality and character were blocked from his consciousness. There's no doubt about one thing, however. These diverse facets of the man — some brilliant in their eye-catching allure and some darkly flawed and foreboding, best kept from public view — tell a story of the most fascinating entertainer of the 20th century.

The Sinatra beloved by millions of fans — the bobby-soxer heartthrob of the 1940s, before becoming "The Voice" and, later, "The Chairman of the Board" and "Ol' Blue Eyes" — is the well-known version and, probably, the easiest to like. Writer John McPhee, in a piece for *The New Yorker*,[1] introduced me, fittingly, to an obscure Italian word that may offer the best description of this particular Frank Sinatra.

The word is *sprezzatura*, coined by Baldassare Castiglione, a formidable author, diplomat, and courtier among the city-states of Renaissance Italy. McPhee, with the help of one of his Princeton University students and a daughter residing in Italy, defined the term thusly: "effortless grace, all easy, doing something cool without apparent effort" and having "nonchalance," although that word implies an indifference or lack of warmth, attributes entirely absent from and opposite to the unique way Sinatra delivered the lyrics of just about every song he sang, over a career spanning 60 years.

There are offshoots of this user-friendly image of Frank Sinatra. He could be tremendously generous and compassionate, quick to assist performers down on their luck and, in some instances, help complete strangers in the throes of misfortune. Watching television one night with his daughter Tina, Sinatra saw a news clip about an impoverished family that had just lost everything as a result of a Christmas tree fire. Sinatra picked up a phone and called an employee, telling him to "send them a nickel" — Sinatra parlance for $5,000.[2]

Buddy Rich — the flashy drummer Sinatra often feuded with, like cock roosters in a barnyard turf war, when the two worked together in Tommy Dorsey's band — battled illness and financial turmoil through much of his professional life. During one such period, Sinatra paid for Rich's hospital bills. In another, when Rich visited Sinatra backstage after a concert and talked about forming a band, Sinatra wrote him a check for $25,000 on the spot to help him get started.[3]

When Sammy Davis, Jr., then part of a minor Las Vegas act called the Will Mastin Trio, lost an eye in a terrible car crash in November 1954, the young entertainer was despondent. Dancing was a big part of his performing life, and he worried that with one eye, he'd never be able to regain the balance that enabled him to execute his intricate routines. Sinatra visited Davis in his hospital room and hugged the sobbing young man.

"You're gonna be fine," Sinatra said. "Charlie [a favorite Sinatra nickname for his pals], you gotta be strong. You'll come out of this thing bigger than ever. You're alive, man. *You're alive."*[4]

Sinatra took Sammy under his wing, brought him to his Palm Springs home to recuperate, then took him to his mother's house in New Jersey for an Italian dinner. When Davis was fully recovered, Sinatra helped get him a booking at Ciro's, a Hollywood club, and packed the room with a star-studded audience, including Bogart and Bacall, James Cagney, Cary Grant, Edward G. Robinson, and Spencer Tracy. They gave Sammy a thunderous reception. Sinatra was right — Davis did become "bigger than ever."

Frank Sinatra was a fierce champion of racial equality and an implacable foe of intolerance, at a time when there was a risk to such advocacy, especially for an entertainer. In 1945, he made a film short for RKO Studios called *The House I Live In*. In it, Sinatra, already a big star, talked to a gang of boys about showing respect and understanding toward those of different religious backgrounds. The film short received a special Academy Award, and Sinatra got a standing ovation from the Hollywood crowd when he accepted it. On October 23, 1945, he went to Benjamin Franklin High School in Harlem to plead for racial tolerance and to help quell violence that had erupted between Italian-American and African-American students. In November, he went on a similar mission to Gary, Indiana, where he told students, "I can lick any son of a bitch in the joint." His attempt to connect with the students on their level was unsuccessful — they just wanted to hear him sing. But he made the attempt, which was more than other entertainers were doing.[5]

Sinatra's work in this regard also brought him unwanted scrutiny from those who were trying to tie him to the Communist Party in America. The Federal Bureau of Investigation maintained a file on the singer, but was never able to plausibly connect Sinatra to the Communist Party or to any of its front organizations. Sinatra was left-leaning during the 1940s, certainly, but a Commie? Never.

Up to the early 1960s, the entertainment business was still segregated in many of its venues, including Las Vegas. Black performers often could not occupy the rooms, guest elevators, or restaurants in the very hotels in which they were performing or even join the white folks in losing money in the casinos. Sinatra fought that mindset wherever he performed, using his celebrity as clout and insisting on equal treatment for every black member of his entourage. While on tour later in his career, Sinatra was still sensitive to racial issues. At one concert, he saw that the musicians hired for the event were predominantly white — there were just three black faces among the 40 members of the orchestra.

"What the fuck is this snow-white orchestra you got here?" Sinatra demanded of the concert promoter, who replied that it was too late to change, that it would be too expensive.

"I want at least 30 percent black musicians," Sinatra ordered. Later, when Sinatra returned to the concert hall for rehearsal, the orchestra included 15 black musicians.[6]

For every admirable trait Sinatra exhibited over his lifetime, there seemed to be a more sinister, less appealing flip side. Sincere in his attitude toward race and religion, Sinatra would nevertheless pepper his nightclub act with ethnic slurs, drawing laughs from the audiences of the 1950s, '60s and '70s. Sammy Davis, Jr. was a favorite target at gatherings of the Rat Pack "Summit" in the early 1960s, when Dean Martin and Peter Lawford joined in the "fun."[7] Sinatra's nickname for his personal valet, a black man he paid very well and seemed genuinely affectionate toward, was "spook."[8] Some of the epithets he delivered offstage, among cronies, were even more egregious, especially when he was drunk or sensed a breach of loyalty.

During World War II, Sinatra appeared regularly at bond rallies in the States and made musical recordings, called V-Discs, for the servicemen fighting around the globe, yet he never went near a war zone to entertain them, as did Bob Hope, Bing Crosby, Phil Silvers, and dozens of other male and female Hollywood stars, at great risk to their safety. It wasn't until May and June of 1945, after the shooting in Europe had ended, that Sinatra performed for troops still stationed in Italy. Even then, he damaged his image by making a fuss over the hotel accommodations the Army had arranged for his troupe in war-torn Rome — they weren't grand enough. Sinatra was classified 4-F during the war, but many considered that to be a manufactured arrangement to keep him out of uniform. It was not, according to a secret FBI investigation, which didn't become public until many years later.

Sinatra was adored by millions of women, yet he was an unfaithful husband, to put it mildly, and an absent father. George Jacobs, his valet for 15 years, called him "the best telephone father there ever was."[9] He could lavish attention and expensive gifts on the woman of the moment, then drop her with little or no explanation. Lauren Bacall found that out soon after Sinatra took up with her.

In the 1950s, Frank was close friends with Humphrey Bogart and his wife, Lauren Bacall, leaders of the Holmby Hills Rat Pack, a group of celebrities who gathered periodically in the Bogart home, in an elite area of Los Angeles that gave this group its name, to drink, play silly practical jokes on one another, exchange *civilized* witticisms, and revel in each other's company — sort of an Algonquin Round Table West, though less literary.[10] Bacall, who was the first to use the term "rat pack," described membership criteria this way: "One had to be addicted to non-conformity, staying up late, drinking, laughing, and not caring what anyone said or thought about us."[11] Among the charter members were Spencer Tracy and Katharine Hepburn, David Niven and his wife, restaurateur Mike Romanoff, Judy Garland and husband Sid Luft, screenwriter Nunnally Johnson, and Hollywood agent Irving "Swifty" Lazar.

Sinatra, who idolized Bogart and Spencer Tracy, drifted into the group's orbit in 1952, in the pre-*From Here to Eternity* days, during an estrangement from second wife Ava Gardner. "He was alone and not happy," Bacall recalled, "neither work nor his personal life had been going well."[12]

Throughout Bogart's career, the tough-guy actor had a cigarette dangling from his mouth in just about every movie scene. More than an actor's prop, it was part of a hard-drinking, chain-smoking lifestyle that caught up with Bogie in 1956, when he was diagnosed with cancer of the esophagus. As Bogart's condition worsened, Frank Sinatra was frequently on hand to comfort "Betty" — Lauren Bacall's real name and the one all her friends used — and help her through the hard times. One observer said that Frank and Betty became intimate even before Bogart passed,[13] but soon afterwards, their relationship went public. They made plans to marry, which someone — Bacall or a friend — leaked to gossip columnist Louella Parsons. Sinatra was furious and broke off the engagement with a brief phone call. And then he simply stopped talking to his former fiancée . . . for six years.

Drunk or sober, but mostly drunk, Sinatra could be the nastiest, most ill-tempered person to be around. He would pick a fight at the slightest provocation, often using a chair or other handy object as a weapon or projectile. He once drove a golf cart into a plate-glass window at the Sands Hotel in Las Vegas, with his third wife, actress Mia Farrow, seated beside him, because of a perceived slight by a Sands executive inside the casino. He then piled chairs together and tried to set them on fire with his cigarette lighter. Fortunately, no one was seriously injured.[14]

Standing just 5 feet, 7½ inches tall (when not in elevator shoes) and weighing about 120 pounds for most of his adult life, Sinatra's muscle power and pugilistic skills did not always rise to the occasion, despite early publicity shots at Stillman's Gym in New York City showing him attired in boxing trunks and gloves.[15] No matter — the singer always had several brawny bodyguards in his entourage, including his friend Jilly Rizzo and road manager Hank Sanicola, ready to finish whatever physical altercation their boss started.

Performance contracts never meant much to Frank Sinatra, even as a singer in the Harry James band. Seven months after James discovered the 23-year-old at the Rustic Cabin, a roadhouse in Englewood Cliffs, New Jersey, and signed him to a two-year contract, rival bandleader Tommy Dorsey offered him $50 a week more and greater national exposure. Sinatra asked the lesser known James to be let out of his contract, and James goodheartedly acceded to his singer's wishes, not wanting to stand in the way of a kid he recognized as a future star. Sinatra would later quit the Dorsey band, in 1942, to go out as a solo act, but *that* broken contract proved more costly to the singer and fueled speculation about Mafia-style tactics used to persuade Dorsey to let him go.

Willie Moretti, a North Jersey crime boss and Hasbrouck Heights neighbor to the young Sinatra family (wife Nancy, two-year-old Nancy Jr., and the Voice himself) in the early 1940s, bragged to one intimate about his role in getting Dorsey to release Sinatra from his contract. Dan Lewis, entertainment editor for the *Bergen Evening Record* in the 1940s, once asked his gangster friend Willie Moretti about those rumors — years later, but before Moretti was gunned down in a Cliffside Park, New Jersey, restaurant in October 1951 by confederates of Albert Anastasia, head of Murder, Inc., the Mafia's enforcement arm.

"Well, Dan," Moretti told Lewis, "let's just say we took very good care of Sinatra." Moretti didn't elaborate on who the "we" was meant to represent in that statement, but no elaboration was necessary.[16]

Sinatra's mob connections may actually have started when he was a youth in Hoboken, his birthplace. Dolly and Marty Sinatra, Frank's parents, owned a saloon in Hoboken during Prohibition, where young Frankie first began singing in front of an audience, on a tabletop in his father's bar. Waxey Gordon, one of the area's top bootleggers, was a bar patron and, most likely, its liquor supplier. Frank's paternal grandfather came from the same village in Sicily that gave us Salvatore Lucania, better know as Lucky Luciano — someone Frank Sinatra would rub elbows with at various intervals during his career, along with a *Who's Who*-worthy list of organized crime figures that, besides Luciano and Moretti, included Meyer Lansky, Benjamin "Bugsy" Siegel, Frank Costello, Sam "Momo" Giancana, Joe Fischetti, Johnny Roselli, Carlo Gambino, Abner "Longy" Zwillman, Vito Genovese, and Angelo "Gyp" De Carlo, who was related to the Sinatra family through marriage.

Confidential sources once told law enforcement officials that Sinatra was a bagman for Luciano, delivering millions in cash to the exiled mobster in Cuba and Italy on three separate occasions. FBI files offered no corroboration for those claims, which Sinatra vehemently denied. But comedian Jerry Lewis made a similar assertion. He said Sinatra almost got caught while carrying $3.5 million in cash through U.S. Customs in New York,[17] information he could only have gotten from Sinatra, or someone close to him. Obviously, there was insufficient evidence to warrant prosecution, but the taint of mob association plagued Sinatra, fairly or unfairly, throughout his career.

The most famous manifestation of that rumor-filled, gossip-fed association, of course, was the Johnny Fontane character in Mario Puzo's book *The Godfather* and in the motion picture of the same name. Fontane got a career-changing role in a movie — read, Private Angelo Maggio in *From Here to Eternity* — when his godfather, Don Vito Corleone, arranged to have a Sicilian calling card, in the form of a horse's head, placed in the fictional movie producer's bed. Mario Puzo, for the rest of his life, would deny any connection between characters in his book and Frank Sinatra, but that didn't stop Sinatra's wrath from being visited upon the author when they ran into each other. It didn't help that Puzo's fictional godfather was said to be based, in part, on real-life Mafia boss Frank Costello, one of Sinatra's principal mob benefactors.[18] But Sinatra had another benefactor, one more important than any mobster.

Dolly Sinatra was clearly the driving force in the family, a not uncommon occurrence in the often matriarchal Italian culture. Her influence on Sinatra's life and career cannot be overestimated. James Farina, city clerk of Hoboken for the past 31 years, knew Dolly and called her "the engine that drove Frank Sinatra."[19] She was feisty, foul-mouthed, smart, ambitious, conniving, ruthless, and demanding — in short, all the traits one finds in her son and only child, the very essence, aside from his natural talent, of what made Sinatra Sinatra.

* * *

What was it, then, about Frank Sinatra? His beginnings hardly presaged the success he would later achieve. As a teenager, he'd sometimes burst into song, uninvited, at neighborhood gatherings, only to be viewed as a pest. Older boys once tossed him and his ukulele (the do-it-yourself accompaniment of the day) out of a pool hall, so they wouldn't have their game disturbed.[20] Frankie persisted, though, singing at every social club and church-basement dance that would have him, mostly for no payment. At first, he used a megaphone to project his voice, in the style of earlier singing sensation Rudy Vallee, but it wasn't a device that suited the young man's thin, reedy voice. After Dolly finally accepted that her son wouldn't be happy with any career choice but singing, she bought him a $65 microphone and public address system, which set Frankie apart from other local singers. It got him more gigs and more experience — exactly what he needed.

At 19, Sinatra sang as part of the Hoboken Four, contestants on Major Edward Bowes' Amateur Hour, a top radio show in the 1930s. The group was hastily formed by the Major himself after Frank and a Hoboken trio, the Three Flashes, had auditioned. Bowes introduced them as the "singing and dancing fools." They actually won that competition and went on to tour, briefly, with one of Bowes' theatrical groups. It didn't last, and Frank returned home, undeterred but with no prospects.

The ultimate goal for a singer in those days was to become part of an established band, as the featured vocal artist. But few professionals paid Sinatra much attention back then, despite his efforts at self-promotion. He even had the effrontery to approach bandleader Glenn Miller to ask for a job, but Miller turned him down. Sinatra, at the time, had no formal training as a singer, although he would later hire a voice coach for a short while, at a dollar per lesson. His politically connected mother called in favors to get her Frankie his first paid singing jobs as a solo performer, at a local Hoboken club and at the Rustic Cabin, where he had to do double duty as a waiter when not on stage. The log-cabin-style roadhouse was a popular watering hole for travelers going to and from New York City, including an occasional celebrity.

One night, while Sinatra was performing at the Rustic Cabin, a musician in the band told him songwriter Cole Porter was in the audience — the music genius who practically wrote the American songbook on his own. Sinatra dedicated his next number to Porter, but was so nervous he forgot the lyrics to a song he had sung many times, Porter's own "Night and Day."

Tommy Dorsey was also unimpressed the first time he heard Sinatra sing, or, as it turned out, *not* sing. Sinatra was auditioning in Manhattan for a job with Bob Chester's band when Dorsey, a friend of Chester's, walked into the studio to watch. "We were all in awe of him in the music business," Sinatra would tell biographer Robin Douglas-Home in the early 1960s. Just 22 or 23 at the time of the Chester audition, Sinatra froze when he saw Dorsey. "Not a sound came out," he later recalled. "It was terrible."[21] Dorsey teased Sinatra about it a year later, after Dorsey had recognized the younger man's talent and installed him as his own "boy singer," as male band singers were called in those days.[22]

Before the Dorsey job, though, there was bandleader Harry James, who hired Sinatra away from the Rustic Cabin in June 1939, at $75 a week — a good salary when the average family breadwinner, if lucky enough to have a job, was bringing home $25 a week. It was Sinatra's first big break. That same year, James commented about his new singer to a reporter from *DownBeat*, one of the music industry's top magazines.

"He considers himself the greatest vocalist in the business," James said. "Get that! No one ever heard of him. He's never had a hit record. He looks like a wet rag. But he says he's the greatest."[23]

Harry James' characterization was right on the money. He'd also hit upon the secret to the legend that Frank Sinatra became, which can be summed up in one word: *attitude*. Sinatra possessed unshakeable confidence in himself and faith in his ultimate rise to the heights of the entertainment world — it showed in every performance he gave. He was the original Jersey boy, if you will. People in a position to help liked his cockiness, and so did audiences.

It was an attitude forged in the rough-and-tumble world of the entertainment industry, by way of Hoboken, New Jersey.

Richard Muti
RAMSEY, NEW JERSEY
SEPTEMBER 2015

1

"Niccolò Machiavelli would have loved Dolly Sinatra."

Around 1 a.m. on December 1, 1983, Frank Sinatra and sidekick Dean Martin approached an empty, $25-minimum blackjack table at the Golden Nugget Hotel & Casino in Atlantic City, New Jersey, where Sinatra and Martin were then performing their brand of Rat Pack entertainment. In Sinatra's wake were the usual hangers-on, including a couple of formidable bodyguards, never more than a hard right-cross away from finishing any physical altercation their boss might start or, a bit more gently, blocking adoring fans from invading their idol's space or intruding on his thoughts.

Sinatra threw down $2,200 in hundreds, the only denomination he ever carried, and asked for chips. Each bill was crisp and clean, as though it had just been printed. The singer, who took three or four showers a day, changed his underwear a bunch of times, and washed his hands 20 or 30 times a day, never liked having used bills in his pocket, even in the late 1930s, when he was just starting out and when one- and five-dollar bills were his more likely forms of folding money.

For a casino dealer — in Atlantic City, Las Vegas, or anywhere in the world — having Frank Sinatra at your table, a gambler who played free and loose with his money, was a mixed blessing. If he won, or lost only a little but was in a good mood, Sinatra lavished tips on his dealer far in excess of what the usual player might give. But if he lost, or was in a foul mood to begin with, look out.

On this night in December 1983, Mr. Hyde was in attendance, not Dr. Jekyll.

Blackjack dealers in New Jersey are mandated by law to deal from a *shoe*, a box-like device that holds up to eight standard decks of cards simultaneously and dispenses them, one at a time, in a way that eliminates bottom- or second-card dealing and most other cheating opportunities. It also speeds up the game, allowing more hands to be dealt without the inconvenience of frequent card shuffling that single-deck dealing requires.

Sinatra didn't like playing blackjack from a shoe, and he barked at the table's South Korean-born dealer to use a single deck and deal by hand. When she politely refused, not wanting to violate the law or jeopardize her license to work in a casino, Sinatra lashed out at her.

"Go back to China!" he shouted.[1] Sinatra, throughout his career, had been an outspoken champion of ethnic and racial tolerance in America, even when it wasn't easy or profitable to be upfront about such issues. But that didn't stop him from peppering his everyday conversations, verbal confrontations, and nightclub act with frequent barbs of this type.

A pit boss, hovering nearby, caught the exchange and tried to intercede on the dealer's behalf, but Sinatra would not be mollified. He threatened to walk out on his nightclub engagement at the Golden Nugget, along with Dean Martin, unless his demands were met, then and there, at the blackjack table.[2]

For the pit boss and two levels of supervisor above him, no further threats were necessary. They ordered the dealer to do things Mr. Sinatra's way and deal from a single deck. Sinatra also wanted both his cards facedown instead of one down and one up, and he wanted to personally cut the cards each time. All of Sinatra's demands were met and all were violations of state gaming regulations, something the singer should have known.

Eye-in-the-sky cameras recorded every detail, and on August 1, 1984, the Golden Nugget was fined $25,000 by the New Jersey Casino Control Commission for the three infractions.[3] In sworn statements, the casino employees involved said they feared that Sinatra would have them fired if they refused his demands. No charges were brought against Sinatra — as the customer and not the house, he didn't violate any law, except, perhaps, an unwritten code of civility toward people just trying to do their jobs. One of the commissioners, Joel Jacobson, was so incensed at Sinatra's behavior that, on the record, he called the singer "an obnoxious bully,"[4] an epithet that would have repercussions for the singer and for his home state of New Jersey.

Jacobson said Sinatra had "forced working men and women to commit infractions because of the fear of losing their jobs." But Steve Wynn, owner of the Golden Nugget, unconditionally backed Sinatra, blaming the media for blowing things out of proportion, as well as blaming his own employees.[5]

Less than a month after the Casino Control Commission's report was made public, Sinatra attorney Milton Rudin, claiming that his client had been treated like "a punching bag,"[6] issued a statement on his client's behalf.

"Frank Sinatra has asked me to announce," Rudin said, "that after much personal reflection he has made a personal decision not to appear in the State of New Jersey."[7] No reason was given for the decision, but a close confidant of the singer, New York radio personality William B. Williams (WNEW), the man who first referred to Sinatra as "the Chairman of the Board," would later comment: "I believe he [Sinatra] made this decision because no one in New Jersey spoke up for him [after Joel Jacobson's verbal attack]."[8]

A New Jersey legislator would later offer a resolution proposing that "an official apology" be made to Sinatra, practically begging him to reconsider his ban on performing there. If adopted, it would have been an embarrassing moment in history, putting the sovereign state of New Jersey in the role of Frank Sinatra sycophant. Fortunately, wiser heads prevailed, and the legislature let the matter die.[9]

The December 1983 incident at the Golden Nugget would have been just a footnote in the Frank Sinatra story, if it were not so emblematic of the man's persona. Sinatra once said that the two people who most influenced his career were his mother and Tommy Dorsey. The Dorsey experience certainly made Sinatra into a better singer, but one could argue, convincingly, that Dolly Sinatra's imprint on her son's life overrode every other dynamic.

In 1951, just before Ava Gardner and Sinatra were to be married, Ava insisted on visiting with his parents. She and Frank, in New York City at the time, made the short trip to Hoboken, New Jersey, where Ava was warmly received by her future parents-in-law. In her 1990 memoir, Ava described her first, favorable impression of the city where Sinatra had been born and raised, "a city of narrow streets, outdoor markets, small shops and factories, a crowded, vigorous, bustling place." She noted that the elder Sinatras' home, purchased for them by their son a few years earlier, was spotlessly clean, perhaps obsessively so, which brought to Gardner's mind her fiancé's own obsession with cleanliness. Her observation of Mama Sinatra was equally perceptive: "I took one look at Dolly and saw where Frank got it all from: the blue eyes, the fair hair, the smile, the essential charm, cockiness, and determination."[10]

Shirley MacLaine, a charter member of the Sinatra Rat Pack and platonic friend of the singer for the last 40 years of his life, had her own reflections on the mother-son relationship, based in part on what friends had told her. Dolly was "opinionated, emotionally intractable, unstable, foulmouthed, overbearing, and seriously unpredictable," she wrote. "Frank told me that he feared and emulated his mother simultaneously. 'She was a pisser,' he'd say, 'but she scared the shit outta me. Never knew what she'd hate that I'd do.'"[11] According to MacLaine, "Frank never questioned his ability to succeed at anything. His mother saw to that. Sometimes, his methods were without conscience. His mother had seen to that, too."[12]

Pete Hamill, a Sinatra drinking buddy when the singer was in New York City, wrote several affectionate but honest profiles of the singer over the years. Hitting the mark squarely with his own take on Sinatra mère, Hamill may have put it best:

"Niccolò Machiavelli," Hamill wrote, "would have loved Dolly Sinatra."[13]

* * *

Natalie "Dolly" Garaventa,[14] not yet 17, and boyfriend Antonino "Marty" Sinatra, older by two years, ran away from their respective Hoboken homes to get married . . . but didn't go far. They eloped to Jersey City, about two miles away, and were married in a civil ceremony on Valentine's Day, 1913. It wasn't a marriage of necessity — Dolly wouldn't give birth to Frank, her only child, until late 1915 — but it still had some people wondering at the quickness of the courtship.

Marty was a bantamweight boxer, fighting under the name Marty O'Brien. It was common practice in those days for Italian boxers to take on Irish ring names, to appeal to a wider audience. Family lore has it that diminutive, blue-eyed Dolly, less than 5 feet tall and weighing just 90 pounds, hid her strawberry-blond tresses under a hat and dressed like a boy to sneak into an arena and watch Marty fight her older brother, Dominick "Champ" Garaventa, who also went by an Irish moniker in the boxing ring. Women weren't allowed into boxing matches at the time, but rules didn't stop Dolly, then or later. The fight supposedly ended in a draw, but Marty would soon more than meet his match. For the next 56 years, as long as he and Dolly were together (he died in 1969), it would be Dolly over the mild-mannered Marty, by a knockout.

Dolly's parents had been against Marty as a prospective husband for their daughter, ever since she and Marty began seeing each other. He was a nice enough young man, docile even, compared with Dolly's volatile temperament, but he couldn't read or write Italian, let alone English. And he was unlikely to provide much in the way of material comforts for Dolly, given his mediocre skills as a boxer and, without a trade, his apparent lack of earning power outside the ring. They should have known their opposition would not stop their willful daughter, who usually got what she wished, when she wished it.

The Garaventas had emigrated from the north of Italy, near Genoa, just before the turn of the century; the Sinatras came from Sicily a few years later. Northern Italians looked down on their Southern compatriots in the same way that the Irish looked down on Italians in general and that the Germans looked down on the Irish — in Hoboken, as well as in every other immigrant community in melting-pot America. Prejudice against Southern Italians was an actual policy of the United States government, which maintained, at its Ellis Island reception center, a separate classification for such immigrants: "Italy South," a geographic delineation reserved for no other nationality. In 1911, a House Committee on Immigration questioned the very premise of "the South Italian as a full-blooded Caucasian."[15]

Francesco Sinatra, Frank's grandfather, arrived at Ellis Island on July 6, 1900, aboard the *Spartan Prince*, a British vessel. Like most immigrants, especially those from the poorer regions of Europe, he traveled in steerage, the lowest class. He was 43 and came alone, with just $30 in his pocket, to pave the way for his wife and five children. Two older sons came next, in 1902. Then, on December 21, 1903, the entire family was reunited. Wife Rosa Saglimbeni Sinatra, age 46, Antonino (later, "Marty"), age 9, Angela, age 7, and Dorotea, age 5, arrived at Ellis Island on the *Città di Milano*. The ship's manifest listed their ultimate destination as 53 E. 105th Street in New York City, where Francesco and the older boys lived. The family eventually moved to Hoboken, where Francesco found work as a boilermaker and, later, in a pencil factory.

Dolly and Marty's first marital domicile was at 415 Monroe Street, in the Italian section of Hoboken.[16] The four-story building, a wooden structure built just 10 years earlier, had two cold-water flats on each floor, both sharing a bathroom at the end of the hallway.[17] It was there, at 415 Monroe Street on December 12, 1915, that Frank Sinatra suffered the first trauma of his life: his birth

Dolly's small frame would have made the delivery of any size baby difficult, but the women attending Dolly, as she lay on the kitchen table where the birthing would take place, soon realized that the task was beyond their skills . . . and they sent for a doctor. At-home deliveries, performed by midwives, were common among immigrants who could not afford the luxury of a hospital. Indeed, Rosa Garaventa, Dolly's mother, often acted as a midwife herself and was there to assist her daughter through the ordeal. It was fortunate for baby Frank that she was present.

By the time the doctor wrested the 13½-pound baby[18] from the birth canal, using pincer-like forceps with such force that the boy's left ear would be torn and his eardrum punctured, it appeared to all — all but Rosa Garaventa — that the child was stillborn. Putting the lifeless baby aside, the doctor and midwives gave their attention to the mother, whose survival was in doubt. (Dolly lived, of course, but she would be bedridden for months afterwards and would never be able to have more children.) Rosa saw to the child, holding his still form under the water tap until, finally, the cold water brought him around.[19] The baby let out a cry, to the relief of his grand-mother and the others in the room, as they continued to work anxiously to save Dolly. Frank Sinatra, later to be known as "The Voice that Thrilled Millions," had just given his first vocal performance, to a small but appreciative audience.

* * *

Still another Sinatra family myth arose about the naming of the new baby, a myth that would gain credence over the years in fan magazine articles and other fluff pieces, but it was just one more made-up biographical detail in the campaign to foster an everyman/regular guy image for Frank's rising star.

The choosing of a baby's godfather is an important ritual in the Italian culture.[20] A child destined for greatness — as, in Dolly's mind, her only child undoubtedly was — needed a godfather who could open doors, smooth the way. There were plenty of uncles as possibilities; Frank was the first grandchild on either side of the Garaventa-Sinatra families, so one can imagine the eagerness to fill the godfather role. Not good enough for Dolly, though, who probably perceived, correctly so, that the male candidates within the family were no great shakes.[21] Dolly would eventually become a woman to be reckoned with in Hoboken, but her political clout and personal power were yet to be achieved.[22] Choices for her son's godfather were limited, so she did the best she could.

Marty had a friend, Frank Garrick, who worked for a Hoboken news-paper, a prestigious job in those days, and who also was connected to the Irish power structure in the city. His uncle, Thomas Garrick, was a captain in the Hoboken Police Department,[23] which, like the local fire department, was dominated by the Irish. For a kid growing up in Hoboken on the wrong side of Willow Avenue — that is, in the Italian section, west of Willow — it wasn't a bad idea to have an "in" with the cops. And so Dolly chose young Frank Garrick to be the boy's godfather. That's the *true* part of the story. The myth had its origin in the baby's actual christening ceremony, on April 2, 1916, in St. Francis Roman Catholic Church on Jefferson Street in Hobo-ken.[24] Still incapacitated by the birthing ordeal almost four months earlier, Dolly did not attend.

Supposedly, the baby was to be named Martin, after his father, or, in another version of the story, was to be called Albert. But Garrick was nervous; when the priest asked him for the baby's name, a question usually put to the godfather, he got confused and gave his own name, Frank, instead of the name intended by the parents.

That part of the tale is nonsense, of course. Babies are named well before they get to the baptismal font, as was baby "Frank Sinestro," the name on his birth certificate, filed on December 17, 1915, five days after his birth.[25] One Sinatra biographer asserted that "Sinestro" was the real family name and even went so far as to connect the name to the Italian word *sinistra*, meaning "left" or "sinister," but such was not the case. The family name is, indeed, "Sinatra," as the Ellis Island record of Francesco's arrival attests. Non-Italian clerks and bureaucrats often mangled the spelling of Italian names, which seems to be what happened here. As to the origin of "Frank" on the birth certificate, it may have been given in honor of the godfather, or perhaps it was simply an Americanized version of Francesco. It was common practice among Italians to name a first-born son after the paternal grandfather, as well as to use Americanized versions of the Old Country names. Dolly finally got around to correcting the birth certificate almost 30 years later, on May 28, 1945, after her son had become famous. The name on the corrected document is "Francis A. Sinatra," for Francis Albert — the formal name young Frankie had used, even back in his school days.[26]

Dolly Sinatra, regaining her strength after the difficult childbirth, wasted no time in making her own mark in the world. Perhaps under the tutelage of her mother, Rosa, Dolly learned the trade of midwifery, which required no special education or certification in those unregulated times. And with it, she learned to do what some midwives, if willing, were called upon to do: abortions. Dolly's history as an abortionist was first revealed in Kitty Kelley's devastatingly blunt but extensively researched book *His Way: The Unauthorized Biography of Frank Sinatra*, published by Bantam Books in 1986.[27] In Dolly's mind, she was performing a necessary service in the Italian immigrant community, where a moment's indiscretion by a young girl could ruin her reputation and spoil all chances for a happy married life, if the problem weren't taken care of, quietly and safely.

The super-ambitious Dolly wasn't satisfied with one income. She worked part-time at an ice cream and candy store, as a chocolate dipper. The young babysitter she hired to take care of Frank would be partially paid with free candy, at the store owner's expense. Dolly also worked as an interpreter, in and around city hall. Speaking several dialects fluently, she put that knowledge to work whenever an Italian needed assistance in navigating the courts or the bureaucracy. She gained not only recognition as a leader (and a fixer) within her own immigrant community but also the notice of Hoboken mayors — Patrick Griffin (1915-1926), Gustav Bach (1926-1929), and Bernard McFeely (1930-1947) — all of whom needed a go-getter among the Italians to help supplement their Irish and German electoral support. (Dolly had been instrumental in helping many of those same Italian immigrants to get their American citizenship.) In time, Dolly was able to deliver 600 or more votes, reliably in every election, to the local political machine, as well as to the Hudson County Democratic machine, run by Frank "I Am the Boss" Hague. Writer Gay Talese described Dolly as "a kind of Catherine de' Medici of Hoboken's Third Ward,"[28] a reference not only to her scheming ways but also to the political power she amassed by getting out the Italian vote, first on behalf of the Irish politicos who dominated city hall, then for the Italian-American leaders who supplanted them.

One of those Italian-American mayors of Hoboken, Steve Cappiello (1973-1985), spoke of Dolly Sinatra in admiring terms.

"She was ahead of her time," Cappiello told one Sinatra biographer. "Unlike women of today, who speak of women's rights but do nothing about them, she was a woman of action." Grateful for Dolly's help early in his own political career, Cappiello added, "She could speak with a longshoreman's vocabulary, if necessary, or be eloquent if she had to impress the political hierarchy in order to make a point."[29]

In 1926, Marty had to give up boxing after breaking both his wrists. He tried working as a boilermaker, but an asthmatic condition forced him to give that up, too, and for a while he was without a job. Fortunately, Rosa Sinatra, Marty's mother, operated a little grocery store, so Dolly always had food for the table, even when things were tight. A Sinatra cousin, Vincent Mazolla, came over from Italy and lived with Marty and Dolly, becoming another compliant male figure in the household. Dolly got him a job on the docks, and he dutifully turned over every weekly paycheck to her. Finally, though, Dolly determined to put her clout to work at city hall. She demanded that Marty be hired as a fireman. When the mayor's top deputy told her there were no openings, she responded in typical Dolly fashion. "*Make* an opening!" she told the startled bureaucrat. Marty was appointed a Hoboken fireman on August 1, 1927, at a starting annual salary of $2,000, good money in those days. And he did not have to take what would ordinarily have been required: a written test. A good thing, he being illiterate.[30]

Around this same time, during Prohibition, Marty and Dolly opened a bar at 333 Jefferson Street, on the corner of Fourth Street. They called it "Marty O'Brien's," after Marty's ring name, but, curiously, the lettering on the saloon's window read "M.O.B ASSN. of ALL NATIONS"[31] — M.O.B standing for Marty O'Brien, but strangely prophetic of young Frankie's future association with a different kind of mob. The place wasn't really a speakeasy, because there was no need for secrecy. It operated in the open, as did dozens of other bars. The 18th Amendment was not a priority in Hoboken, reinforcing for young Frank, if any reinforcing was needed, that rules were made to be broken.

Like the newly affluent family in Norman Lear's 1970s sitcom *The Jeffersons*, the Sinatra family, its future now secure, was ready to "move on up to the East Side" in late 1927 — or, at least, 10 blocks farther east, out of Hoboken's Italian section and closer to where the rich folks lived — to a three-bedroom apartment at 703 Park Avenue. It was just the first in a series of moves "on up," for Dolly and Marty Sinatra . . . and for Frankie, then just turning 12.

2

"Your father finds out, he's gonna kick your ass."

The familiar Sinatra back story — that of a tough, if undersized, scrapper of a kid struggling to overcome his slum upbringing — was, in truth, a press agent's fabrication, initially crafted during World War II partly to offset the skinny, almost effeminate image that Sinatra projected onstage and partly to blunt criticism the singer was then receiving for his 4-F draft status and non-service in that war. If it could be shown that Sinatra was just a regular guy, who rose above the harsh circumstances of his youth . . . well, that might lessen the disparagement. And so, a fictional childhood was created.

The fawning treatment Sinatra initially got from fan magazines and gossip columnists, before he turned reporters into his own personal pariahs, fueled the deception. In 1943, Louella Parsons, the grande dame of Hollywood writers, gushed over "the American Italian boy" who loved spaghetti so much he would "get up in the middle of the night to eat it."[1] (The dark side of Frank's *Italian-ness* wouldn't emerge until 1947, after he was tied to Mafioso Lucky Luciano, among others.) The image-making progressed to a higher level under the expert guidance of publicist George R. Evans, whose initial goal, after being hired by the singer in late 1942, was to paint a glowing picture of Frank Sinatra as the typical all-American boy.

According to a bio that Evans made up in 1943, Frank's parents had hoped he would become a "civil engineer" — quite a stretch for an indifferent student whose highest academic achievement was a junior high school diploma and who completed just 47 days of high school[2] before being tossed out. Evans invented a sterling high school career for his client, who, in addition to being a good student, sang with the band and started up the school glee club. This amazing young man also won a swimming trophy, played on the "championship basketball team," and was "an outstanding member of the track team." Frank's early goal, according to the story, was "to become a newspaperman," and, after studying "shorthand and journalism for a year at Drake Institute, hoping to further his newspaper ambitions," he landed a job at the *Jersey Observer* as a "cub sports reporter." When Sinatra and "best girl Nancy," who would become his wife and the mother of his children, saw Bing Crosby perform at a nearby theater, Frank quit his newspaper job and resolved to become a singer.[3]

Almost all of that early fluff was hogwash, but even so, it didn't go far enough. There needed to be a harder edge to the story — an alternative "bad boy" aspect of Sinatra that would not only endear him further to the teen and preteen girls who made up the majority of his fan base, but also bolster his masculinity for the males in the audience, especially those in uniform. The fact that Sinatra was ineligible for service was enough of a blow to his popularity among members of the armed forces; to also have him perceived as a "girly-man," to use Arnold Schwarzenegger's coinage, would only have added to his problems. Except for when he went off message, Sinatra's early public statements about his background appear to have been carefully scripted, most likely by George Evans.

In a spoken introduction to a World War II V-Disc, Sinatra feigns a humble, low-class image for the troops he's about to sing for, purposely belittling himself to curry favor: "Gentlemen of the Armed Forces, this is the *hoodlum from Hoboken*," Sinatra says at the start of the V-Disc. (Emphasis added.) "I'd like to sing a tune for you and I hope *youse* like it, hey."[4]

When he was courting 19-year-old Mia Farrow in the 1960s, Sinatra, who was 30 years older than the woman who would become his third wife, told the gullible young actress about his beginnings, which she would later describe in her autobiography. "He had grown up in Hoboken, New Jersey," Farrow wrote, "in one of the toughest neighborhoods in the country — maybe the world."[5]

Around the same time, Sinatra characterized his old neighborhood this way: "It was a semi-slum area and it was pretty rough," he said. "There weren't gang wars, but there were beefs and there were battles about position and who should cross the line into where we lived and cross the line into where they lived. And I must say there were times when I skirted certain areas because the cry went up, 'Kill the dago,' in certain parts of town."[6]

In reality, once multiple streams of income started coming into the Sinatra household — from Dolly's midwife activities and translating services, Marty's salary as a fireman, the saloon business, and cousin Vincent's paychecks — the family was viewed by neighbors, friends, and acquaintances as rather well off. They had a car and took vacations, to the Jersey Shore and Catskill Mountains of New York State, at a time when such luxuries were out of reach for most immigrant families. Only-child Frankie was the best-dressed kid around — not surprising, given that his mother had opened a charge account for him at Geismer's, a local department store.[7] He had so many pairs of trousers that his friends nicknamed him "Slacksey O'Brien," honoring not only his snazzy wardrobe but also his pseudo-"upper-class Irish" heritage. A reputation as a sharp dresser certainly pleased Sinatra and his publicists as the fictional life story took hold, and it was repeated often; but there were other, less flattering descriptions applied to the young Sinatra, by people who knew him growing up.

One Hoboken neighbor remembered young Frankie, who suffered through two mastoid operations and an emergency appendectomy before he was 12, as "kind of a mama's boy, a bit of a sissy."[8] But as Sinatra got older, he became a mischief-maker and prankster (a trait that carried into adulthood), often getting himself into fixes he couldn't get out of on his own.

"Frank couldn't fight at all," another neighbor recalled. "He was an arrogant kid, though, and would go looking for trouble. Then, he couldn't defend himself, so [his friend] Tony [Macagnano] would have to do it for him."[9] Dolly instilled in Frank the notion that friendship and loyalty could be bought — a concept he practiced his entire life, consciously or unconsciously. She made sure he always had enough pocket money to treat friends to a movie or to a soda at the local drugstore fountain. When Frank and some of his friends formed a baseball club called the Turk's Palace, Dolly got them "flashy black and orange outfits, with a half-moon and dagger motif on the back."[10] Orange and black would remain Sinatra's favorite colors throughout his life, and one has to wonder if this might have been the origin of that preference.

On January 28, 1931, "Francis Albert Sinatra" was graduated from David E. Rue School (junior high) in Hoboken,[11] whereupon he entered A.J. Demarest High School. Nancy Sinatra, in her 1995 book, had her father at Demarest until his senior year, but most other biographers measure his high school career as being much briefer. One had him lasting into his sophomore year,[12] but author Kitty Kelley's research seems the most reliable. She has him being expelled from high school after just 47 days for "general rowdiness" and quotes his high school principal and one of his teachers on the subject:

"Frankie showed no real talent for anything," Principal Arthur Stover said. "It was possible for a student to leave school before sixteen in those days, provided he had permission from an authorized person. I had that authority." Teacher Macy Hagerty remembered Frank as "a lazy boy," with "absolutely no ambition at all when it came to school . . . ."[13]

Frank Sinatra himself appears to confirm Kelley's account of his school years rather than his daughter's version. He was in his late seventies at the time of Nancy's book and clearly saw no need for further puffery regarding his school years, six decades past.

"In my crowd," Sinatra said, "school was very uninteresting, and homework was something we never bothered with. The few times we attended class, we were rowdy. So it isn't surprising that a bunch of us were expelled."[14] One of Sinatra's friends from those early years provided a more detailed account of the incident that finally provoked Frank Sinatra's expulsion from high school.

Tony Consiglio, who called himself Frank Sinatra's "closest and most trusted friend," kept every confidence he was privy to (Frank called him "the Clam"), until he finally agreed, while in his eighties and years after Sinatra's death, to collaborate on an "as told to" book with writer Franz Douskey.[15]

Consiglio was raised in New Haven, Connecticut, but often visited family members in Hoboken while in his mid-teens, after he, too, had been asked to leave school. And that's how he met Sinatra, who was the only other kid Consiglio saw hanging around in Hoboken during the school day. They became friends, and Frank told him the story about how he came to be expelled.

"Frank got kicked out of school because of pigeons," Consiglio said. "He and three other kids bought pigeons for twenty-five cents apiece, put them under their jackets, and went to see a school play called *Cleopatra*. During the most serious part of the play, Frank and his pals opened their jackets and the pigeons went flying. They flew all over the auditorium while kids ducked and screamed. That was the end of the play and the end of high school for Frank."[16]

Tony Consiglio went on to become Sinatra's "body man" and general factotum for 30 years, off and on, while the singer was performing on the road — the person responsible for fulfilling the singer's every need, from seeing to the laundering of his shirts (they had to be precisely done, down to the pressed crease in a French cuff, or Sinatra would fly off the handle) to making excuses to wife Nancy Sinatra for the otherwise romantically engaged Sinatra. In the early 1940s, when Frank didn't return with Consiglio to the marital home in Hasbrouck Heights, New Jersey, after performing just across the Hudson River in New York City, Nancy asked, "Where's Frank?" Tony replied that Sinatra had remained in the city to consult with some people about an upcoming show. Not fooled, and not expecting a truthful answer from the loyal Consiglio, Nancy remarked, "Were the *people* blonde or brunette?"[17]

For the longest time, Frank's interest in a singing career did not sit well with Dolly and Marty Sinatra. It was okay for the preteen Sinatra to get up on a table in his father's saloon and sing to amuse the customers, but making a living in that fashion was the furthest thing from the parents' minds, especially when Frank became obsessed with the idea.

Radio was the primary entertainment medium in those days, and the Sinatras had the best radio available for young Frank to listen to his idol, Bing Crosby, then the biggest vocal artist in the country. Frank kept a picture of the crooner on his bedroom wall, and when his adulation for Crosby got too intense, Dolly wasn't hesitant about reproaching him. But it soon became apparent that Frankie wasn't cut out for anything else. Marty put it this way to his son: "Do you want to get a regular job? Or do you wanna be a bum?"[18]

As usual, Dolly Sinatra took the initiative in getting her son a job after he left school. She went to see Frankie's godfather, Frank Garrick, who was circulation manager for the *Jersey Observer*, a Hoboken newspaper. This was a year into the Great Depression, it must be remembered, when unemployment was in the 20 percent range and jobs were scarce. But Garrick came through for Dolly and his godson. He got Frank a job bundling newspapers for the delivery trucks, at a decent salary for a high school dropout, $12 a week. Predictably, it did not end well.

Frank soon tired of the physical labor, but then a chance arose for a more prestigious position on the paper's staff. A junior sports writer died in an accident, and even before the funeral, Dolly was pushing young Frank to go to his godfather and ask for the man's job — a position that Sinatra, given his meager academic achievements, was clearly unqualified to fill. Following his mother's instructions, Frankie went to speak to Garrick, who was not at work on that particular day. Not finding his godfather, the 15-year-old took the initiative and sat at the dead reporter's empty desk. He began going through the man's notes and files. The editor came in and, seeing Frank ensconced at the sports reporter's desk, asked him what he thought he was doing. Frank told the editor that Frank Garrick had given him the vacant job. Garrick was summoned and asked about his godson's assertion. When he denied knowing anything about it, the editor ordered him to fire the boy.[19]

Kitty Kelley interviewed Frank Garrick some 50-odd years later, and the incident still weighed heavily on the old man's mind.

"I had no choice," Garrick told Kelley. "I went over to Frankie and said, 'Why'd you do this, Frankie? This isn't right. If you'd come to me in the first place, I could have gotten you the job. Now my hands are tied. I have to let you go.'"[20]

Frank Sinatra learned many things in his youth by observing the most important person in his life, his mother. One of those learned skills was the ability to launch a blistering verbal attack against anyone who crossed him.

"Oh, the temper and the words and the filthy names he called me," Garrick said. "You have no idea of what that temper was like in those days. Murderous. Like he was going to kill me. He flared up something terrible, cursing and swearing and so vulgar. The words he used were hateful, awful. He called me every terrible name in the book and then stormed out."[21]

Dolly Sinatra, taking her son's side as expected, never spoke to Frank Garrick for the rest of her life. Garrick had been closer to Marty Sinatra, of course, but even Marty was subdued in all his future interactions with the newspaperman, obviously afraid of incurring the wife's wrath if he remained too close to Garrick. A few years after Dolly died, in a tragic plane crash in 1977, Sinatra finally called his godfather, after 50 years of silence, wanting to talk and reminisce with one of the few remaining links to his youth. In June 1982, Sinatra made the trek to Hoboken and visited the 85-year-old man, accompanied by sidekick and confidant Jilly Rizzo and by personal secretary Dorothy Uhlmann. It was an emotional reunion; Sinatra brought a fruit basket and, when he left, handed Garrick an envelope containing five crisp hundred-dollar bills. The two would continue to meet from time to time, until the old man's death. Sinatra would also send gifts — photos, pictures, and watches for Garrick and his wife. And, when he was performing in the New York-New Jersey area, Sinatra would invariably provide tickets for Garrick and arrange a limo for his transportation to an event.

It is telling that Sinatra waited until after his mother's death before reaching out to Frank Garrick, almost as though he, like his father, were afraid of Dolly's disapproval for letting the spirit of kindness and forgiveness govern his actions. There were many such instances of Sinatra shutting out those who acted in a way the singer perceived to be disloyal, no matter how slight or insignificant the offense. Jilly Rizzo, Phil Silvers, and Lauren Bacall, three of his closest friends, experienced it, as did fellow Rat Packers Sammy Davis, Jr., Peter Lawford, and Joey Bishop. No one, other than godfather Frank Garrick, suffered a 50-year banishment.

"My son is like me," Dolly Sinatra would boast, years after the Garrick incident but not necessarily in response to that particular matter. "You cross him, and he never forgets."[22]

* * *

Frankie went through several jobs after the *Jersey Observer* experience, none of which lasted for long. He worked in the local shipyard, catching hot rivets, but that ended after three days. Next, a job unloading books for a company in New York City, just a cheap ferry ride across the Hudson from home. Understandably, he found that boring. Then it was back to the Hoboken docks for one more brief stint at gainful employment. In the meantime, the family made another change in residence, in 1932, this time to a house of their own at 841 Garden Street, a three-story, four-bedroom house in one of the better parts of town, farther away still from the Italian section. The saloon had been sold by then, giving Dolly the funds to buy up to this new house, which cost $13,400, equivalent to $230,000 today.

It soon became apparent to Dolly and Marty Sinatra that Frankie would not be dissuaded from a singing career, no matter how improbable the chances for his successful attainment of that dream. Frank began singing at dances, social clubs, and political rallies — anywhere he could, really. At first, he used a megaphone to project his voice,[23] but Dolly would soon buy him a microphone and sound system, giving him an advantage over other aspiring singers in the area and enabling him to attract more interest from local bandleaders. Dolly also bought her son a 1929 Chrysler convertible,[24] helpful not only in getting around to singing jobs but also in the enhancement of his burgeoning love life.

The car was probably the impetus to Frankie's getting involved with the Three Flashes, a local singing group that was slightly more established in the business than he was. Fred Tamburro was the trio's leader; he and James Petrozelli were from the old neighborhood, just a few blocks from Frankie's first home in the Italian section of Hoboken. The third member, Pat Principe, lived in West New York, New Jersey, a nearby town. Tamby, Skelly, and Patty were a bit older than Frankie, who began pestering them to let him sing as part of their group. When the Flashes needed to get to a gig not easily reachable by public transportation, Frankie was there to offer a ride. Soon, Dolly was pressuring Tamby, whose family she knew, to let Frank sing with them. The trio got a chance to audition for Major Edward Bowes' Amateur Hour, a national radio talent competition emanating from the Capitol Theatre in New York City, and Frankie went along with them, hoping to get his own audition.

Bowes liked what he saw and heard, but wasn't about to devote the time to broadcast two separate acts from, essentially, the same hometown. So the trio became a quartet. The program card for the group's September 8, 1935, appearance on the show, when Sinatra was 19, is revealing. (The performance can still be heard on YouTube.) The act was originally listed as "Frank Sinatra and the 3 Flashes," but Bowes wrote above that entry "Hoboken Four," the name that would become part of the Sinatra legend. The address for the act was listed as "841 Garden St Hoboken, NJ," Frank's address. The Sinatra family phone number was their contact: "Hob. 3-0985." The type of act was given as "singing, dancing & comedy."[25]

Frank was suddenly transformed into the leader of a group he was only peripherally attached to, to the displeasure of the other three members. When Bowes asked them, on stage, who would speak for the group, Sinatra, never bashful, piped in immediately.

"I'm Frank, Major. We're looking for jobs," Sinatra said. "How about it? Everybody that's ever heard us likes us. We think we're pretty good."[26]

They sang "Shine," a song made popular by both Bing Crosby and the Mills Brothers. The rendition was exuberant, if a bit amateurish — it *was*, after all, an "amateur" hour — but they actually amassed one of the highest vote totals in the show's history, from both the theater and broadcast audiences. The Major was pleased and hired them to appear in two film shorts — *The Nightclub* and *The Big Minstrel Act* — he was making at Biograph Studios in The Bronx.[27] Frank did not have a singing role in either film, but that didn't stop him from carrying on about his movie debut.

"The way Frankie flipped about . . . you'd think he was already a star," Fred Tamburro would recall. "All he had was a walk-on. He kept haunting the theaters here, asking when they were going to play his pictures — *his pictures*."[28]

The film shorts became part of *Major Bowes Theater of the Air* and were shown in October 1935 at Radio City Music Hall, one of the showplace venues in New York City. The Hoboken Four singers were invited to join a Bowes theatrical touring group, with each man getting $50 a week, plus meals.[29]

Bowes had several collections of variety acts touring the country at the same time, and the Hoboken lads made their share of stops along the grueling circuit. Frankie's superior voice soon moved him, permanently, into the lead-singer spot in the quartet, as did his growing popularity with their audiences, especially females. The greater attention being paid to Frank on the tour created tension, and Tamby and Skelly often resorted to physical abuse of the smaller Sinatra to make their displeasure known. Patty did not join in, not wanting to pile on, but he later described the scene, which he attributed to jealousy over the girls Sinatra was attracting.

"Sometimes it got pretty bad for Frank," Patty said. "After all, he was a skinny little guy, and the two picking on him were older and bigger . . . and Frank couldn't fight back."[30]

Sinatra reached a point where he could no longer tolerate the living conditions on tour — a far cry from what he would later demand as his due — or the abuse. The act became the Hoboken Trio when its lead singer left the tour in Ohio and went home.[31]

Part of Frankie's motivation in quitting the Bowes tour may have been a cute 18-year-old named Nancy Barbato, the daughter of a Jersey City plasterer. Sinatra met Nancy a couple of years earlier when both were vacationing with their families at the Jersey Shore. Dolly liked Nancy at first and encouraged her son's interest in the girl. But there was a living to be made as a singer before anything serious could develop between them, and Frank, back home in Hoboken, threw himself into that effort.

He took any gig he could get, whether it paid or not. He sang for free on WAAT in nearby Jersey City and on WNEW in New York City, two radio stations willing to give him a chance. The price was right, even if the voice had not yet become "The Voice." Another radio gig on Fred Allen's popular *Town Hall Tonight* show added to his experience, but produced no breakthrough. Bandleader Ray Sinatra, Marty's cousin, fronted the NBC Radio orchestra and got Frank a few singing spots, but nothing permanent developed there, either.[32] The Hoboken Elks Club and Cat's Meow were two local venues at which he appeared, but any wedding or political rally would also do nicely. Still, no momentary setback seemed to dampen the young man's enthusiasm for the path he had chosen. Biographer Donald Clarke explained the process well: "[Sinatra] was learning the ropes. He pestered musicians, bandleaders and club owners, as well as song publishers for the latest tunes and arrangements, and whereas he'd been described as 'pushy like his mother,' now somebody described him as 'pushy, but polite.'

He was teaching himself more about how to charm people, something he never learned from Dolly . . . ."[33]

* * *

Hoboken's Union Club, at Hudson and Sixth streets, was one of the classiest venues in the city. It was owned by Joseph Samperi, an Italian immigrant who had risen from hotel messenger boy to become one of the leading citizens of Hoboken. Frankie had performed at catered affairs at the Union Club, weddings and such, but had never appeared in the club's Castle Bar Lounge, a showroom that featured some of the best female singers then active in the New York metropolitan area. For some reason, Joe Samperi had never booked a male singer into the Castle Bar Lounge. Dolly Sinatra changed that, in the early spring of 1938.

Dolly was a friend and benefactor of Samperi, steering many of her political events to his club, especially in the difficult early days of the Depression. When she asked Samperi, politely, to give her son a steady singing job, he could hardly refuse, although he was not especially impressed by Frankie's talent at that stage of his career. It would become Frank's first full-time gig as a solo act, at $30 a week. Later, after Frank became famous, Samperi was asked about his first impressions.

"Frank was a quiet person, perhaps a little shy; he was sincere and anxious to do his best," Samperi recalled. "Perhaps some would call him a perfectionist. He dressed well, always in a clean shirt, pressed suit, and shined shoes. He made a good appearance, even though he was rather thin. He liked to sing, but his voice was not so appealing as it is today. It was good, but lacked the style he [later developed]."[34] Displaying what may have been the first example of Sinatra's uncanny ability to make the correct career choice when it mattered, Frank quit the Union Club after two weeks to take a job that paid half of what he was already earning. And he had to wait on tables, to boot, as a singing waiter at the Rustic Cabin on Route 9W in Englewood Cliffs, New Jersey, about 15 miles north of Hoboken.

The Rustic Cabin looked exactly as its name implied — a structure of rough-hewn logs, with white cement filling the chinks, situated along a wooded, almost desolate stretch of roadway. Its wider dimension faced one of the busiest highways feeding into the George Washington Bridge, the span that had connected New Jersey with New York City for the previous seven years. It was a perfect spot for travelers, at either the end or the beginning of a long trip, to stop off for a drink and music. The roadhouse had a band and employed singers who doubled as waiters when they were not onstage.[35] It also had one more important feature, the thing that attracted Frank to this new singing opportunity. The Rustic Cabin, like a number of entertainment venues during the golden age of radio, had a live hookup to a radio station, called a "wire," that enabled its entertainment to be broadcast to a much larger audience, as large as the audience the radio station itself could reach. This not only served to draw customers to the nightspot; it also allowed the performers to achieve wider exposure for their talents. The Cabin's radio station partner was WNEW in New York City, which was fast becoming one of the top regional stations in the country.[36]

When Frankie learned from a Rustic Cabin band member that management was looking for a new male singer, he didn't hesitate in heading there for an audition. Frankie had already sung on WNEW, for free, when he was trying to build a name for himself. Now, if he could land the job at the roadhouse, he could put himself in position for even better things down the line. It turned out to be a big "if."

Bandleader Harold Arden was not impressed with Sinatra's audition and declined to offer the young singer a job. When a dejected Frankie returned home and headed to his bedroom to be alone (a means of crisis-coping that Sinatra would employ his whole life), Dolly sprang into action. She phoned Harry Steeper, the mayor of North Bergen, New Jersey, another stronghold of the Hudson County Democratic machine. She knew that Harry was also president of the New Jersey musicians union, as well as an assistant to James Petrillo, president of the American Federation of Musicians, the most powerful union in the entertainment business. Years later, Dolly recalled her conversation with Steeper.

"Frankie wants to sing at the Rustic Cabin," she told Steeper, "and the bandleader doesn't like him." She asked Steeper "to see to it that Frankie got another tryout and this time . . . see to it that he gets the job." Steeper wasted no time in assuring Dolly. He would take care of things, he said, adding: "Tell Frankie he is as good as hired."[37]

Harold Arden succumbed to the pressure. Leaving the Union Club in the spring of 1938, Frankie started immediately at the Rustic Cabin. Eager to please, he agreed to Arden's suggestion that he change his *too-Italian* name. Together they came up with "Frankie Trent," and Sinatra had fliers printed with that new stage name to help build a following at the road-house. He made the mistake of leaving one on the kitchen table at home.

"What's this," Dolly said, confronting her son with the incriminating evidence. "Get ridda that. Don't you change your name. Your father finds out, he's gonna kick your ass."[38]

And so, thank God, the world was deprived of the song stylings of "Frankie Trent." Or, more to the point, thank Dolly Sinatra.

3

"Whatever he stirred beneath our barely budding breasts, it wasn't motherly."

Fifteen dollars a week didn't go far, even in 1938. The *waiter* part of the Rustic Cabin job brought tips, but Frank's generosity toward Hoboken friends who came to hear him sing often meant picking up their bar tabs, so he was left with little for himself at the end of each week. He was still seeing Nancy Barbato on a steady basis, but his financial condition made marriage out of the question, at least for the time being. Besides, while on tour with Major Bowes' theatrical company, Sinatra had developed not just a roving eye, but a realization that he had a special allure for women — one that ensured he'd never be wanting for bed partners.

Sometime in the late spring of 1938, Frank started two-timing Nancy and seeing another woman — Antoinette Della Penta, or "Toni" — on a regular basis. Toni was 25, three years older than Frank, and lived with her parents in Lodi, New Jersey, a blue-collar town in southern Bergen County with a heavy concentration of Italian-Americans. The relationship took on a serious tone when Dolly and Marty Sinatra were invited to dinner at the Della Pentas' home.

Dolly decided almost immediately that Toni would not be a good match. She had a worn-out, used look — the Sinatras wouldn't learn until later that Toni was still married to a man named Francke, but separated at the time of her involvement with Frank.

The get-acquainted dinner didn't go well, thanks largely to Dolly's persistently negative remarks about the relationship between Toni and her son.

Dolly's dislike of the girl may have stemmed from her sense that Toni would be more difficult for her to control, compared with the mousier Nancy. Frank's road-tour womanizing was unknown to his mother, so Dolly probably thought the older and more experienced Toni would lead her son astray. And astray the young couple did go.

At some point, Frank bought a cheap ring and proposed to Toni, the object likely being a hotel room tryst rather than a lifetime of wedded bliss. (It wouldn't be long before Frank learned that marriage proposals were unnecessary to his amorous conquests. Within two years, Hollywood starlets would be lining up for his attention.) He began alternating dates at the Rustic Cabin between chaste Nancy one night and loose Toni the next. Nancy must have gotten wind of the deception. As she and Frank were sharing a table between sets on November 25, 1938, a waiter brought a telephone to the table and told Frank there was a call for him. Nancy grabbed the receiver and heard Toni on the other end of the line.

"He's my boyfriend," Nancy told the startled Toni, "and I don't know why you are calling him." As one might expect, an argument ensued before Nancy slammed down the phone. Frank was in full defensive mode, telling Nancy that the other woman meant nothing to him and was just a passing thing. Whether or not Nancy bought Frank's lies soon became immaterial: Within a half-hour, Toni showed up at the Rustic Cabin, and the two women immediately became embroiled in a full-fledged catfight, during which Nancy's dress was torn. Frank managed to pull Toni aside and told her another lie — that Nancy was pregnant and her father was forcing him to do the right thing. Toni stormed out of the club, but Dolly had judged the young woman accurately. She was not about to go quietly.[1]

As Frank was performing that next night, Saturday, November 26, two officers of the law showed up and placed him under arrest, in front of all the patrons at the Rustic Cabin on the busiest night of the week. Toni Della Penta had signed a criminal complaint against him, alleging that "on the second and ninth days of November 1938 in the Borough of Lodi . . . under the promise of marriage [Frank Sinatra] did then and there have sexual intercourse with the said complainant, who was then and there a single female of good repute . . . ."[2]

Sinatra was taken to the Bergen County Jail, where, in the early-morning hours of November 27, he was fingerprinted and photographed. (His mug shot would become famous when a blowup of it was seen gracing the wall of Tony Soprano's hangout in HBO's mob hit, *The Sopranos*.)

Frank's one phone call went to his mother, of course, and he cooled his heels in a jail cell until she could arrange for a bondsman to put up the $1,500 bail money, about $25,000 in today's dollars. The complaint was withdrawn 11 days later when authorities learned that Toni Della Penta was, in fact, married.[3] The particular offense she'd charged Frank with required that the complainant/victim be "a single female of good repute." But that was not the end of this particular tale. Author Kitty Kelley interviewed Toni Della Penta Francke on three separate occasions for her Sinatra biography and relates that Toni became frustrated when Frank did not call her after his release. She drove to the Sinatra home "to have it out with that awful Dolly."[4]

Toni and Dolly got involved in a shouting match, and police were summoned to 841 Garden Street in Hoboken. Since this was Dolly's turf, it's not surprising that Toni was the one arrested this time, for disorderly conduct. In retaliation, she signed a new criminal complaint against Frank the next day, December 22, 1938, this one charging him with adultery — committing the same two acts of sexual intercourse, but with "a married woman." (Both the charges lodged against Sinatra, on November 26 and December 22, were rarely used at the time and are no longer considered criminal offenses.) Sinatra made bail again and was released, but the resulting Hoboken newspaper headline was especially damaging to the young singer's reputation: "Songbird held in morals charge."[5]

In what may be the first heated skirmish in Frank Sinatra's lifelong war against the Fourth Estate, Sinatra telephoned the newspaper that ran the story and exploded.

"I'm coming over there," Sinatra told the hapless person who answered the phone, "and I'm going to beat your brains out, you hear me? I'm going to kill you and anyone who had anything to do with that article. And I ain't no fucking songbird."[6]

A Bergen County grand jury heard evidence on this new complaint on January 17, 1939, and refused to indict Sinatra. All charges against him were dismissed.[7] Frank was represented by an attorney who would soon be elected to the U.S. Congress — another political favor likely collected by Dolly Sinatra, who knew the importance of influence, no matter the issue.

One can only imagine the verbal abuse Frank had to endure from his mother over the Christmas holidays that year. Dolly surely had had enough of her son's bachelor shenanigans, whether he liked it or not. Arrangements were hastily made for a wedding. Frank would marry Nancy Barbato, who truly loved him and was still willing, despite the disastrous happenings of the two previous months. Even more astonishing was the fact that the Rustic Cabin not only continued to employ Frank after the disruptions in their place of business, but also gave him a raise, to $25 a week. Nancy was working and earning as much on her own, so the new marriage would at least have a secure start, from a financial standpoint.

On February 4, 1939, Mr. Francis A. Sinatra and Nancy Rose Barbato exchanged wedding vows in Jersey City, at the Church of Our Lady of Sorrows[8] — an ironic setting for a marriage that would have more than its fair share of sorrows over its 12-year duration. Marion Bush Schreiber, Frank's friend from their mid-teen years, was a guest at the wedding reception in the Barbato home. Her memory of Frank would be lasting.

"I'll never forget him that day," Schreiber recalled years later. "He looked like the saddest man I'd ever seen."[9]

* * *

Four years after his humiliating encounter with the criminal justice system in Bergen County, New Jersey, courtesy of Toni Francke, Frank Sinatra would experience one of his greatest triumphs — his blockbuster appearance, on December 30, 1942, at the Paramount Theatre in New York City, the event that launched the bobby-soxer phenomenon and transformed an above-average band singer into America's biggest entertainment attraction. The journey to that career pinnacle was not without its rough spots, the first of which greeted the newlyweds soon after their return from a brief honeymoon in North Carolina.[10]

On February 27, 1939, Dolly traveled to nearby Jersey City, the Hudson County seat, where she was arraigned in court on a criminal charge of performing an abortion. She pleaded *non vult contendere* to the complaint — a plea that accepted responsibility but didn't admit guilt. This occurred when Dolly was at a high point in her political power, and she received five years' probation as her sentence. Still, the matter made the local papers, and Nancy admitted to a friend that she felt shamed.

Frank tried to supplement the couple's modest income by working during the day with Nancy's father, a plasterer. But once again, his affinity for manual labor proved to be non-existent. He lasted just a few weeks and, thereafter, devoted his full attention to singing, at the Rustic Cabin every night and at whatever other gig he could generate. His big break — the first of several career-turning points he would experience over the years — came a few months later, in June 1939.

Louise Tobin, an accomplished band singer in her own right and the wife of trumpet player Harry James, was listening to WNEW radio in the couple's New York City hotel suite. The program was being broadcast from the Rustic Cabin in New Jersey, and the male singer she heard sounded like just the right match for the new band Harry was forming. James had been lead trumpeter in the Benny Goodman orchestra, but was looking for talented musicians to start up his own band. One of the spots he had to fill was boy singer. Louise called to her husband, who came into the room to listen. He liked what he heard and decided to go to Jersey the next night to catch the young singer's act in person.[11]

Bill Henri and His Headliners had replaced the Harold Arden band at the Rustic Cabin earlier in 1939, and Frank was in fine voice the night Harry James showed up to take his measure for a spot in the new band. Years later, James recalled how he felt only a few minutes into listening to Frank's rendition of Cole Porter's "Night and Day."

"I felt the hairs on the back of my neck rising," James said. "I knew he was destined to be a great vocalist."[12]

James made an offer to Sinatra that very night — $75 a week to start, triple what the singer was then earning — and asked Frank when he could start. "How about now?" was Sinatra's reply.

There's just one thing, James said at the time. What can we do about your name? He suggested that Frank use the stage name "Frankie Satin." It was a name that calls to mind every forgettable lounge lizard who ever performed in Las Vegas, rather than a future superstar. With the "Frankie Trent" memory still fresh in his mind, including the wrath of Dolly Sinatra it had inspired, Frank put to rest forever the idea of singing under any name but his own. "No way, baby," he told James. "The name is Sinatra. Frank *fucking* Sinatra."[13]

Sinatra joined the James band in July at its next booking — the Hippodrome Theatre in Baltimore, Maryland. From there they moved to the Roseland Ballroom in New York City for a stay that lasted the rest of the summer.[14] Ever hungry for personal recognition, Sinatra begged the band's manager, while at Roseland, to get him a mention in George T. Simon's influential column in *Metronome* magazine. Simon was accommodating, if not gushing. In his review of the Harry James band, he noted "the very pleasing vocals of Frank Sinatra, whose easy phrasing is especially commendable."[15] But 25 years later, in a *Billboard* article, Simon came clean as to his true impression of Sinatra that night at the Roseland Ballroom. "He sounded somewhat like a shy boy out on his first date," Simon wrote, "gentle, tender, but frightfully unsure of himself."[16]

Nineteen thirty-nine was a pivotal year, not just for Sinatra's career but also for the entertainment industry as a whole and for the entire world, once the war in Europe began. Some of the greatest motion pictures ever to grace the silver screen had their debut in 1939 — films like *Gone With the Wind*, *The Wizard of Oz*, *Mr. Smith Goes to Washington*, *Wuthering Heights*, *Goodbye, Mr. Chips*, and *Stagecoach*. It was also the year of the New York World's Fair, in Flushing Meadows, Queens, and the James band would perform there that summer, a daytime gig on August 27, as well as play at the famous Steel Pier in Atlantic City, before embarking on a national tour. Nancy joined her husband on tour, with the young married couple often hosting the entire band for a cheap spaghetti dinner to help with the band's financial situation. One West Coast gig had to be canceled when the nightclub burned down. At another club, the manager complained they were too loud and disturbed the customers. Still, it was a happy time. Nancy became pregnant with the couple's first child, a road baby who would grow up to become a singer herself.

Sinatra made six records with the Harry James band. But as with most Big Band recordings of the day, the singer got little of the glory. Boy singers were considered part of their band's sound, "just another instrument."[17] None of the records with James sold particularly well, although the best of the bunch — "All or Nothing at All" — would enjoy greater success later.[18] The conditions were not yet right for Sinatra's star to rise. He was still learning his trade, to be sure, but the collective emotions that his singing would eventually touch in his mostly female fan base — the longing for an absent boyfriend or husband, the sweet ecstasy of love denied — were still months, if not years, away. And it would take a war to kindle them. But there was also the growing realization, for Sinatra, that the Harry James band might not be the vehicle to take him on the career journey he envisioned.

✳ ✳ ✳

Tommy Dorsey was in the market for a boy singer. His male vocalist, Jack Leonard, the voice behind one of Dorsey's signature songs, "Marie," had abruptly quit the band in late 1939 after an argument with the temperamental leader. Dorsey was a hard-nosed taskmaster, sometimes when drunk but just as often when sober, and Leonard, who had been with the band for four years, took issue with one particular tirade that Dorsey launched against a couple of musicians.

The Tommy Dorsey band would soon be recognized as one of the best in the country, a rival to the Glenn Miller orchestra, but it was still finding its footing in 1939. Its sound needed freshening, and Dorsey started that process even before Leonard left. To jazz up his repertoire, Dorsey hired arranger Sy Oliver away from the trendier Jimmie Lunceford band, and soon added the great drummer Buddy Rich to join other talents, musicians like Bunny Berigan, Ziggy Elman, Joe Bushkin, and Jo Stafford and the Pied Pipers. Knowing that Dorsey needed a replacement boy singer, Jimmy Hilliard, a friend who worked at CBS Radio, made what turned out to be a fateful suggestion. "Have you heard the skinny kid who's singing with Harry James?" Hilliard asked. "He's nothing to look at, but he has a sound."[19]

Dorsey was interested, despite Sinatra's attack of nerves while auditioning with the Bob Chester band in Dorsey's presence a year or so earlier. When both his band and Harry James' were performing in Chicago, in late

1939, Dorsey sent an underling to slip Sinatra a note and set up a meeting. Nick Sevano, a Hoboken crony and Sinatra's valet at the time, would later comment: "I couldn't believe it when Frank showed it to me. The note was written on a torn-off piece of paper bag."[20]

The next afternoon, Sinatra showed up in Dorsey's hotel room at the appointed time and suffered through Dorsey's reminder of his nervous choke with the Chester band. But Dorsey was kind and invited the younger man to call him Tommy. He wanted Frank to audition, and so they adjourned to the hotel ballroom, where a couple of Dorsey's musicians were standing by. The song Dorsey picked for Frank to sing? "Marie," a song Frank had heard Jack Leonard sing on records dozens of times; he knew it cold, and nailed the audition. Dorsey offered Sinatra the job, and $125 per week, if Harry James would let him go.

James had a two-year contract with Sinatra, but when Sinatra approached him to ask to be let go, after fulfilling barely six months of the deal, the bandleader was magnanimous. He knew his band was struggling financially and correctly saw Sinatra's move to Dorsey as the right career choice for the young singer, whom he considered a friend. Sinatra would never forget James' unselfish gesture.

Frank's first appearance with Dorsey was at Shea's Buffalo Theatre in January 1940 — not the most pleasant month for a tour stop in Buffalo, New York. A young comedian by the name of Red Skelton was on the same bill.[21] The Dorsey-Sinatra collaboration would last through early September 1942. Sinatra always considered his time with the Dorsey band as the period in which he sustained his greatest growth as a professional singer, and every expert assessment of the Sinatra musical phenomenon is in accord with that opinion. The hit records cut by the Tommy Dorsey band during this time, with Frank Sinatra as the featured vocalist — backed by Connie Haines, who moved from Harry James' band to Dorsey's in April 1940,[22] and by Jo Stafford with the Pied Pipers — are impressive. Some of the sides are a bit sappy, in keeping with the style of that period, but others are timeless standards: "I'll Never Smile Again" (No. 1 on the charts for 12 weeks), "Star Dust," "Oh, Look at Me Now," "Dolores," "Let's Get Away From It All," and "Violets for Your Furs" were among the best. Dorsey had a second arranger, Axel Stordahl, whose style with ballads was a perfect match for Sinatra's voice; together, they produced "The Night We Called It a Day," "The Song Is You," and "Night and Day" — all hits.[23]

Sinatra's breath control — something Harry James had urged him to work on — vastly improved, as did his phrasing of a song's lyrics, thanks to the singer's observation of Tommy playing the trombone. Frankie Sinatra was every teacher's nightmare as a schoolboy back in Hoboken, but the young professional Frank Sinatra went to school on Tommy Dorsey and became a *summa cum laude* graduate less than three years later. But off the bandstand, it was rough going.

Drummer Buddy Rich and Frank hit it off nicely soon after Frank joined the band. They were rivals from the start, but friendly rivals, sitting next to each other on the band bus between tour stops and even rooming together on the road. Dorsey considered them his "two prima donnas."[24] But their cozy relationship would deteriorate as competition for preeminence in the band hierarchy intensified. Rich had joined the Dorsey band a few weeks before Sinatra, lured by Tommy's promise of a jazzier repertoire—just the thing for a drummer to showcase his stuff. Sy Oliver's arrangements suited Buddy Rich perfectly, and he reveled in the second billing that Dorsey had given him on theater marquees, program bills, and other promotional materials.

Sinatra's arrival and the growing effect he had on audiences soon led Dorsey to mix more ballads into a night's program. Dorsey played to that reaction by having band musicians feign their own swoons, echoing those of the more impressionable young ladies on the dance floor. On March 9, 1940, while the band was performing at one of Dorsey's favorite venues, Frank Dailey's Meadowbrook on Route 23 in Cedar Grove, New Jersey, Dorsey put Frank in the second spot on the bill, over Buddy Rich.[25] It didn't take long for Sinatra to let that attention go to his head. He began lording it over band mates, especially Buddy Rich and Connie Haines.

Haines had a beautiful voice but was a Southern country girl, something Sinatra constantly needled her about. Singing a duet with Haines on one particular night, Sinatra did his piece, then stepped back from the microphone as Haines moved forward to sing her part. Before she could begin, Frank said, sotto voce, "Do your thing, Cornball." The girl singer broke down in tears from the cumulative effect of this badgering, and

Tommy Dorsey immediately took her side, firing Sinatra. It would be a brief parting — Dorsey was no fool — and Frank soon returned to the fold, after offering Haines an apology.[26]

The Sinatra-Rich rift started when the Dorsey band had its first gig at the Paramount Theatre in New York City, in the spring of 1940. The two usually shared a dressing room at theaters, but on this occasion, Sinatra informed Rich that he wouldn't be able to do that. His reason? Frank's fans would be coming backstage after the shows, and it would be too crowded in the dressing room with Rich there, too. Rich was understandably miffed. Onstage, he began to throw Sinatra off during his ballads by talking to other band members, loud enough to be noticed, or by using his base drum or high-hat cymbal to screw with the beat.[27]

After the initial Paramount engagement, Dorsey added "East of the Sun" and "I'll Never Smile Again" to Frank's performance repertoire, causing Buddy to grouse even more. With each new slow-tempo ballad that Dorsey gave to Frank, an up-tempo instrumental featuring Buddy had to be cut.[28]

The band went on the road briefly before returning to New York City for an eight-week stint, beginning May 21, 1940, at one of the city's most prestigious venues, the Astor Roof, atop the hotel of the same name. They drew record crowds, and their engagement was extended.[29]

Frank and Nancy Sinatra were living in Jersey City during this time, a six-mile commute from New York, but Frank would mostly stay in the city with the band, at the Astor Hotel. He'd use Nick Sevano, his valet and Hoboken crony, and Hank Sanicola, a burly guy who was simultaneously Frank's rehearsal pianist, road manger, and bodyguard, to run interference for him with Nancy.[30] Frank was not in attendance when his first child, Nancy Sandra, forever to be known as Nancy Jr., was born at Margaret Hague Memorial Hospital in Jersey City, on June 8, 1940. Tommy Dorsey became her godfather.

The dam finally burst between Sinatra and Buddy Rich, backstage at the Astor on a hot muggy night in late August. Reportedly, Rich called Sinatra a "wop bastard,"[31] which triggered the clash. Singer Jo Stafford, who was friendly with both men, had a ringside seat to what happened next.

"Across the hall was another table with three or four of those big, tall glass pitchers full of ice water," Stafford related years later. "Frank was there. Buddy was in the doorway of the room, across from me. They were yelling at each other, about what I don't know. I wasn't even listening. Suddenly, out of the side of my eye, I saw Frank pick up one of those pitchers and hurl it at Buddy. It crashed into the wall, just over my head."[32]

The two men exchanged blows until other band members stepped in and broke up the fight. It wasn't clear who got the best of whom, but a truce was called and Rich and Sinatra would continue to work together for the remaining two years that Sinatra would be with the Dorsey band.

There's an old Italian proverb that counsels on the subject of revenge. "It is a dish best served cold," the saying goes. In Frank Sinatra's case, three days was cold enough.

Buddy Rich was having dinner alone at Child's Restaurant, a popular bistro near the Astor Hotel. He paid the check and had started the short walk back to the hotel when, as friend and biographer Mel Tormé would later say, "he felt a tap on his shoulder." Rich turned, but was immediately struck in the face. He would be unable to identify his attackers — two men who beat him severely ("Buddy Rich gets face bashed in" was the headline in a *DownBeat* story on September 1, 1940) but took nothing from him. His money and wallet were untouched. One of the men pummeled Rich while he was down on the sidewalk. Rich described the beating as "coldly efficient and professional," a "put-up job."[33] No arrests were made, but Rich's suspicions as to the instigator behind the attack were confirmed, two years later.

Here's how Tormé reported the incident.

"One night, just before Sinatra left Dorsey [on September 3, 1942], he [Rich] quietly approached Frank and asked him, point blank, if the mugs who had flattened him two years before had done so at Frank's request." Rich assured Sinatra that he wasn't holding a grudge, that it was "water under the bridge." He said that he had "no hard feelings," but "just wanted to know."[34]

"Sinatra hesitated," according to Rich, "but then admitted that he had asked a favor of a couple of Hoboken pals." Rich and Sinatra shook hands, and Rich wished him good luck, as Sinatra was about to embark on his solo career.[35]

Sinatra had signed a three-year contract with Dorsey but was growing impatient to begin his breakout as a solo act. In yet another example of Sinatra's canniness when it came to his singing career, as opposed to often clueless actions in his personal life, he recognized that for any singer to achieve individual fame and fortune, he or she had to go it alone, and not as one part of a 20- or 30-piece orchestra. Sinatra was afraid that other prominent band singers, like Perry Como with the Ted Weems band and Bob Eberly with the Jimmy Dorsey band, would beat him to the punch and suck up all the attention. At the time, Bing Crosby had the solo-performer field all to himself.

In May 1941, *Billboard* named Sinatra the "top male band singer." By the end of 1941, a *DownBeat* poll had him in the No. 1 spot, over the perennial title holder for that position, Bing Crosby.[36] By that time, Frank had already given Dorsey notice that he was leaving. Dorsey tried to ignore him on that subject — he had a contract, after all — but the pressure would grow for an end to the relationship. Finally, in August 1942, Dorsey agreed to let Sinatra out of his contract, for a price.

Dorsey sensed that Frank was willing to sign anything to obtain his freedom, and the "anything" in this case was an unconscionable deal that would probably be unenforceable today. Dorsey gave Sinatra $17,000 in a lump-sum payment, to provide the singer and his family with some financial security until he could get himself established. Sinatra agreed to pay Dorsey one-third of his gross earnings for the next 10 years, plus another 10 percent of gross earnings to Dorsey's personal manager, who had negotiated a record deal for Frank with Columbia Records.[37] On top of those payments, Sinatra would also have to pay the growing entourage that accompanied him everywhere. It's hard to understand how he thought those numbers worked for him.

Frank had built up a head of steam with Dorsey, but he was on his own now, just as he wanted to be. That meant hiring an arranger, retaining an agent and a publicist — in short, doing a host of things that had never been his responsibility. Dorsey and his manager had always worried about such things. But the young singer, just 26 at the time, would prove to be as shrewd a judge of talent as he was of the music he chose to sing. He started by stealing arranger Axel Stordahl away from Tommy Dorsey, offering to pay Stordahl $650 a week — five times what Dorsey was paying him.[38] The hits Stordahl arranged for Sinatra in the Columbia Records years underscore the wisdom of that move, songs like "If You Are But a Dream," "There's No You," "I Fall in Love Too Easily," and "Saturday Night (Is the Loneliest Night of the Week)," to name a few.[39]

Sinatra's first job after leaving Dorsey was in an otherwise forgettable movie, *Reveille With Beverly*, but his only on-screen presence was to sing "Night and Day,"[40] his seemingly go-to Cole Porter song for auditions and other special occasions. Then Manie Sacks, head of Columbia Records, managed to get Frank a radio show on the CBS Radio Network at $150 a week. The show proved to be such a success that, four weeks later, Sinatra was able to land a spot on the premier radio musical show of the day, *Your Hit Parade*, at $1,000 a week.[41] And that was just the beginning. In mid-1943, Sinatra got to sing one of his own hits on the show: "All or Nothing at All," his 1939 flop with Harry James, was rereleased and climbed rapidly in the charts to No. 1.[42]

Sinatra signed with General Amusement Corporation as his agent, and they were able to book him into the Mosque Theater in Newark. His success there, thanks, in part, to the draw of a home-state boy, would lead to the much more spectacular success across the Hudson River. After watching Sinatra's performance for a few shows and seeing the crowd's reaction, Harry Romm, one of Frank's GAC agents, pitched Sinatra to Robert M. Weitman, executive director of the Paramount Theatre. Weitman agreed to give Frank a try, as an "added attraction" to a show he'd already lined up — the Benny Goodman orchestra. Frank would receive $1,000 a week, for a four-week engagement.[43]

Sinatra made his solo Paramount debut on December 30, 1942. The 3,600-seat venue was standing room only. After the Goodman band finished its first set, the bandleader announced to the audience, "And now, Frank Sinatra." The ensuing noise blast caught Goodman by surprise, as he exclaimed, "What the hell was that?"[44] It was Frank Sinatra, and the birth of the bobby-soxers.

Singer Peggy Lee, on the same bill for that engagement, with the Benny Goodman band and Sinatra, described the chaotic scene: "We used to lean out the windows of the dressing room to see the crowds of swooners [as the

Sinatra fans were called], like swarms of bees down there in the street, just waiting for the sight of Frankie."[45]

George R. Evans, Sinatra's newly hired publicist, was accused of salting the crowd with a collection of demonstrative young ladies, as an inducement to general pandemonium — a charge he repeatedly denied right up to his premature death in 1950. Jack Keller, Evans' partner, came clean years later.

"The dozen girls we hired to scream and swoon did exactly as we told them," Keller admitted. "But hundreds more we didn't hire screamed even louder. It was wild, crazy, completely out of control."[46]

Sociologists and other experts in American culture would analyze and over-analyze the factors that motivated a whole generation of teen and pre-teen girls to turn into wild, crazy, out-of-control creatures. Did they want to "mother" the emaciated singer they saw onstage? He was hardly anyone's image of the ideal male, so perhaps that was the instinct he inspired. One pundit called the demonstrations "a bonding experience for young women."[47] Another citizen complained to FBI Director J. Edgar Hoover about the eroding morals of American womanhood, as exemplified by the bobby-soxers. Hoover wrote back, "Sinatra is as much to blame as the moronic bobby-soxers."[48]

One former member of the bobby-soxer brigade later did a piece on the subject for *The New York Times*. Martha Weinman Lear put it this way: "Whatever he stirred beneath our barely budding breasts," she wrote, "it wasn't motherly. The thing we had going with Frankie was *sexy*. It was exciting. It was terrific."[49]

4

"I certify that Frank Albert Sinatra is physically and/or mentally disqualified for military service."

In 1944 — around the time that more than 60,000 American GIs, most of them draftees, were being killed or wounded on the beaches and among the hedgerows of Normandy, France, and around the time that more than 100,000 Allied soldiers were being killed or wounded at Monte Cassino and Anzio, in Italy, and around the time that more than 30,000 troops, mostly U.S. Marines, were being killed or wounded taking Kwajalein, Saipan, Guam, and Peleliu in the Pacific, making way for even bloodier battles at Iwo Jima and Okinawa — Frank Sinatra was signing a five-year, $1.5 million contract with entertainment giant Metro-Goldwyn-Mayer, making him one of the highest-paid performers in the world.[1]

The controversy over Sinatra's 4-F Selective Service classification during World War II dogged the singer/actor throughout his career, especially when so many of his movies (at least 12 of 60), from *Anchors Aweigh* to *Von Ryan's Express*, cast him in military roles — either someone engaged in active-duty heroics or veterans just back from the war.[2] Playacting at being a hero did not make him a hero in the eyes of many military families; yet, through extremely effective press-agentry, Sinatra escaped the censure that a lesser public figure might have received. Women of all ages, from bobby-soxers to more matronly types, simply didn't care that Sinatra was not in uniform during the war. He was there, on stage or on the silver screen or on the radio or record player, to awaken or rekindle their romantic feelings while boyfriends or husbands were away. That's all that mattered to them, even as the country geared up to meet the challenges of wartime.

Isolationist policies of the United States after the Great War, before it became necessary to use Roman numerals to distinguish world wars, had allowed our Army to wither. According to Roosevelt Institute historian David Woolner, the U.S. Army had about 180,000 men in uniform as of June 1939. Just three months before Europe would become embroiled in war, we ranked 19th among the world's armies, right behind Portugal. Only after the Nazi Blitzkrieg rolled through Poland and the Low Countries, and forced France to capitulate, did Congress begin to remedy the situation. It passed, in September 1940, the Selective Service and Training Act, the first peacetime draft in American history.

The new law required all men between the ages of 18 and 65 to register, but contemplated military service only by those 36 and younger. In December 1940, when the Act became effective, 25-year-old Frank Sinatra, along with 16 million other eligible American men, registered for the draft. Sinatra, who was married and already the father of Nancy Sandra Sinatra, born June 8, 1940, received a legal exemption at that time because he was the sole support of his two dependents, Nancy Sr. and Nancy Jr.

On the day the Japanese attacked Pearl Harbor, Sinatra was at a Hollywood party, at Lana Turner's home. The drunken revel had started Saturday night and lasted well into Sunday, December 7, 1941, with passed-out guests strewn all about the place. (Nancy Sinatra was back in Hasbrouck Heights, New Jersey, with the couple's daughter.) Still employed by Tommy Dorsey, Sinatra was already pestering the bandleader to be let out of his contract; he wanted to become a solo performer, a move he rightly saw as key to his future success. Dorsey had raised his salary to $250 a week and was footing the bill for a love nest that Sinatra maintained on the West Coast (the better to take advantage of the plentiful supply of young starlets he attracted), but the bandleader's generosity did nothing to dampen the young singer's eagerness to go out on his own. When a late-arriving guest burst into Lana Turner's home and urged the bleary-eyed partygoers to turn on the radio, Sinatra and the others learned about the devastating attack on the American naval base and other military installations.

"As we listened [to the radio]," Turner would later say, "I looked around at the stunned young men in my living room, and thought how drastically our lives were going to change."[3]

Things did change for Frank Sinatra . . . for the better. In August 1942, Dorsey relented, finally allowing the singer to go off on his own, for a price that one could easily relate to Shylock's pound of flesh. Within five months, Sinatra appeared as a solo act at the mecca of the entertainment world, New York's Paramount Theatre, smashing all records for attendance and introducing into the American culture a new phenomenon: the bobby-soxer. But already there were rumblings in the press and grumblings on the streets of Hoboken, and elsewhere, about Frank Sinatra — not as to his newfound star status but as to his status as a "draft dodger," also newly acquired.

The day after Pearl Harbor saw the greatest number of voluntary sign-ups for the armed forces in the history of our nation. Millions of young men across America stood in line that Monday morning, waiting for the doors of their induction centers to open. Dozens of Sinatra's peers in the entertainment business eventually joined the throng, including Dorsey band stalwarts Joe Bushkin, Buddy Rich, Ziggy Elman, Sy Oliver, Paul Weston, and Bobby Burns. Jack Leonard, the Dorsey boy singer Sinatra replaced, would earn a Bronze Star in the war. Artie Shaw and Eddy Duchin, musical standouts in their own right, joined the Navy. Rudy Vallee, the singing sensation of the generation preceding Sinatra's, joined the Coast Guard. Actor Wayne Morris flew combat missions in the Pacific as a Navy pilot. Clark Gable rose to the rank of major in the Army Air Corps and flew in combat. Jimmy Stewart may have compiled the bravest record of all, as a bomber pilot in the European theater. Glenn Miller, too old to be drafted, volunteered for the Army Air Corps and formed a military band to entertain the troops, right in the thick of things. Miller would die in a plane crash just six months after D-Day (his single-engine transport plane went missing and was presumed lost), heading from England to France to put on still another show for the boys.

Frank Sinatra was experiencing stress of his own in the early war years. He professed to not care about going into the Army; it was the *not knowing* that got to him. "I'm dying," he told The Associated Press, "it's the uncertainty. I don't care whether I'm in the Army or not, but I'd like to know one way or another. It's embarrassing and it's annoying."[4] Sinatra was to soon find out his status, but *knowing* would not end the embarrassment.

In 1943, as the war heated up and the need for conscripts increased, dependency exemptions from the draft ended. On October 22, Sinatra reported to a draft board facility in Jersey City, New Jersey, where, in a response to a questionnaire, he stated that he had no "physical or mental defects or diseases." (He had answered similarly in a December 17, 1940, questionnaire, when he first registered for the draft.) Sinatra was given a preliminary physical examination by Dr. A. Povalski, a civilian physician, and found to have no disqualifying defects. He received a 1-A classification, marking him "available for service" in the armed forces.[5] Two months later, Sinatra was given another physical examination, this time by an Army doctor in Newark. It's unclear what precipitated this second physical, but the results differed dramatically from the earlier exam.

On December 11, 1943, one day before his 28th birthday, Frank Sinatra received the best birthday present imaginable for his burgeoning singing and movie career: He was reclassified 4-F, "rejected for service for physical, mental, or moral reasons." As he left the Army facility, Sinatra was met by reporters, to whom he gave the following explanation. Doctors found "a hole in my ear I didn't know about," he said, and "a few things I better take care of right away." When told about the finding, a former Hoboken schoolmate said, "Sinatra has no more ear trouble than General MacArthur."[6]

One newspaper headline at the time expressed the frustration, if not anger, that many felt over a celebrity like Sinatra avoiding the draft, justified or not: "Sinatra 1-A With U.S. Girls, Rated 4-F by Army Doctors."[7] Sinatra tried, unsuccessfully, to manage the public's reaction to his 4-F status. "I'm unhappy about it," he said, "because I've been bragging to friends that I'd get through."[8]

The reason for Sinatra's punctured eardrum has been most often reported to be the result of a botched delivery, during which the attending doctor used forceps to manhandle the oversize baby (13½ pounds) into the world, puncturing his left tympanum, tearing that ear, and permanently scarring that side of his face. Those scars remained throughout Sinatra's life, sometimes covered by makeup when he performed, and attested to the trauma he suffered at birth; indeed, careful examination of any full-face shot of the singer, especially in old age, clearly shows a deformed left ear. Still, Sinatra's own publicity people stirred the pot of controversy by also attributing the draft-preventing eardrum injury to a more macho reason. It occurred, they said, when Sinatra was hit in the head with a bicycle chain during a boyhood gang fight in Hoboken.

Although unknown to the public at the time, the controversy over Sinatra's draft status actually became one of the precipitating factors that caused the Federal Bureau of Investigation to open a file on Frank Sinatra — a file that would eventually grow to 1,275 pages within the locked cabinet where FBI Director J. Edgar Hoover kept his confidential records on Sinatra and on dozens of other celebrities and prominent leaders, like Dr. Martin Luther King, Jr.[9] This compilation of information about Sinatra — both reliable investigatory information and flat-out rumors and innuendo not worth the paper they were written on — was made available to the public for the first time in December 1998, more than six months after the singer's death, as a result of a Freedom of Information Act request.[10] Although some entries were redacted, to remove from public scrutiny any names and identifying information that might still have been sensitive, the files provided an interesting historical perspective to the Sinatra saga that might not have otherwise come to light.

Nationally syndicated gossip columnist and popular radio host Walter Winchell was, during his heyday (the early 1930s through late 1950s), one of the most powerful figures in the entertainment world, someone who could make or break careers with a single column item or a sentence or two in his radio broadcasts, which reached 20 million listeners each week. He was also a friend and secret source to J. Edgar Hoover and often supplied the nation's chief law enforcement officer with information about the mobsters Winchell liked to associate with in his nightly prowls around the New York City club scene.

Ironically, Walter Winchell was one of the few newspapermen that Frank Sinatra liked, perhaps out of respect for his power or, just as likely, because of the reporter's closeness to underworld figures, a status Sinatra also aspired to. And it was Winchell who gave Hoover the tip that led to the full-blown investigation of Frank Sinatra's draft status.

In late December 1943, less than three weeks after Sinatra got his 4-F ticket out of the draft, Winchell received an anonymous letter, which he forwarded to J. Edgar Hoover. The letter writer, claiming that his job would be in jeopardy if he revealed his identity, told Winchell that the FBI "is said to be investigating a report that Frank Sinatra paid $40,000.00 to the doctors who examined him in Newark recently and presented him with a 4-F classification. The money is supposed to have been paid by Sinatra's Business Manager. One of the recipients is said to have talked too much about the gift in a beer joint recently and a report was sent to the FBI."[11]

In reality, the FBI was not investigating Sinatra's draft status at the time, although a file had been opened on the singer, arising out of what the prudish Hoover considered the undue influence the entertainer was having on America's youth — namely, the bobby-soxers.

Hoover, no fan of Sinatra, whom he considered to be the at-fault party for the hysterical way in which young female fans were acting, was quick to pounce on Winchell's information. A Hoover lieutenant ordered Sam K. McKee, special agent in charge of the bureau's Newark office, to investigate the matter. McKee later advised his superiors, in a report on February 10, 1944, that "Sinatra's classification [4-F, as of December 11, 1943] appears to be regular and that he was disqualified because of a perforated eardrum and chronic mastoiditis and that his mental condition was one of emotional instability."[12] The agent acknowledged the earlier physical examination, which reported none of those defects, as well as Sinatra's denial of any such defects in his answers to questionnaires. McKee also questioned Mrs. Mae Jones, chief clerk for Local Draft Board No. 19. Mrs. Jones told him that "the local board had been particularly careful not to afford Sinatra special treatment and where any question of importance arose, the Board would immediately communicate with the State Headquarters for advice in view of the 'position' held by Sinatra." Mrs. Jones also expressed a personal opinion that Sinatra probably had had a private physician examine him before the Army doctor did his examination on December 11. Sinatra seemed to know he would be rejected, she said.[13]

The examining doctor, Capt. J. Weintrob, assistant chief medical officer for the induction center, certified that "Frank Albert Sinatra is physically and/or mentally disqualified for military service by reason of: 1. chronic perforation (left) tympanum; 2. chronic mastoiditis." In his report, Dr. Weintrob elaborated on his findings: "Chronic perforation lt. drum. Hist. of repeated discharge from ear — mastoid areas show coating in remaining cells and deformity of canal. Marks sclerosis in mastoid area."[14]

One side note to the draft status inquiry is interesting only for its exposure of the press-agent puffery about Sinatra's physical prowess that had been circulated in these early years of his career. According to George R. Evans, Sinatra's chief P.R. guy, the crooner was a former high school athlete who stood at 5 feet, 11 inches and tipped the scales at 140 pounds. The Army's examination showed a different physical specimen: "Height: 67½ inches; Weight: 119 lbs."[15]

On February 23, 1944, SAC McKee directed one of his subordinates to interview Dr. Weintrob, whose official report on file with the draft board had not gone into detail about what Sinatra told an examining psychiatrist regarding his mental condition. Those admissions by Sinatra were never made public. His physical defects alone were sufficient to disqualify him from service, so why embarrass the man publicly with those other disclosures — anyway, that was the thinking. There were no HIPAA rules in effect at the time, of course, but this courtesy was often extended to well-known subjects, whose careers or lives might be damaged by such details. Weintrob informed the interviewing special agent that Sinatra's draft status file actually received a lot closer scrutiny than anyone else's. The Army doctor had discussed his findings with two superior officers, both medical doctors, and then sent a certified copy of the entire file to their commanding general.

During the physical examination, according to Dr. Weintrob, Sinatra discussed the injuries he had received at birth to his left ear, probably from the use of forceps in the delivery. Sinatra said that "in his early childhood he had several mastoid operations and subsequently has had frequent and repeated attacks of 'running ear' on the left side . . . . He also stated that he often suffered from 'head noises' on the left side." Weintrob's physical examination backed up every one of Sinatra's statements regarding his ear. The doctor found evidence of "much post auricular scarification" and an auditory canal that was "narrowed" and "somewhat deformed." The eardrum was perforated — "not a result of an incision by human hands," but a condition that appeared to have gradually occurred by disease — secretions in the ear pushing to get out and eventually perforating the tympanum. X-rays backed up the diagnosis.[16]

What Sinatra told the psychiatrist about his mental problems was revealing. Here is how Weintrob reported it, up the chain of command.

"During the psychiatric interview, the patient stated that he was 'neurotic, afraid to be in crowds, afraid to go in elevator, makes him feel that he would want to run when surrounded by people. He has somatic ideas and has been very nervous for four or five years. Wakens tired in the A.M., is rundown and undernourished.' The examining psychiatrist concluded that this selectee suffered from psychoneurosis and was not acceptable material from the psychiatric viewpoint."

The report went on to state that because Sinatra would be rejected on the basis of his physical condition — "perforation of his left tympanum and chronic mastoiditis, left" — there would be no need to include "the diagnosis of psychoneurosis, severe" among the reported disqualifying factors. Instead, they called it "emotional instability," so as to "avoid undue unpleasantness for both the selectee and the induction service."[17]

Dr. Weintrob stated emphatically to the special agent who interviewed him that no one had tried to influence him in his decision to reject Sinatra for service, that no one spoke to him about the examination beforehand, and that he "was willing to stake his medical reputation on his findings."[18]

Any honest evaluation of the record has to conclude that Frank Sinatra was correctly disqualified from service in the armed forces as a draftee, despite lingering questions regarding the way the whole process was handled. Why hadn't Sinatra ever disclosed his ear problems on any prior questionnaire he was required to fill out? Why did the first physical examination, on October 22, 1943, result in a 1-A classification, with no mention of the ear problems? What precipitated a second physical exam less than two months later? Did Sinatra, between October 22 and December 11, get coached by a private physician on what information the singer should disclose during his physical, so as to ensure a 4-F classification? If so, and if it was clear that his ear condition would guarantee disqualification, why in the world did Sinatra go into such detail regarding his mental condition? There was nothing to be gained by that, and by doing so, Sinatra, ordinarily quite secretive about his private affairs, was risking serious damage to his reputation if any of the mental stuff ever got out. That was a real risk, because there is evidence that J. Edgar Hoover leaked other information about Sinatra's run-in with the law in late 1938, as well as the singer's mob ties, to favored reporters. Sinatra, in his draft induction interview with an Army psychiatrist, opened himself up to possible exposure as a certified nut case, which would have spelled doom for his public image, without question, especially if the gossip columnists Sinatra was openly feuding with got hold of those tidbits.

We'll never get definitive answers to any of these questions, but what we do have is a clear look at another aspect of Frank Sinatra's public-relations problem during the war years. Frank, the Voice, wasn't about to risk his well-being, or career, on any trip overseas to entertain troops, not while there was still shooting going on.

Nancy Sinatra — in her comprehensive and understandably supportive 1995 book about her famous father's life, *Frank Sinatra: An American Legend* — attributed the entertainer's failure to participate in USO tours to FBI reports naming the singer as a Communist sympathizer, thereby blocking him from getting necessary travel visas.[19] In Sinatra's FBI file, which Nancy Sinatra probably didn't have access to when she wrote her book, there is nothing that indicates any FBI involvement in Frank Sinatra's availability to participate in USO tours overseas, at least not during World War II.

Ms. Sinatra may have confused the timing of her father's efforts to perform overseas. After the Korean War ended, Sinatra did try to make a Far East trip with the USO during the 1954 Christmas holidays to entertain forces still stationed there, but was blocked by the Army. Sinatra actually met with three generals on September 7, 1954, in an attempt to get the Army to change its mind; the generals complimented Sinatra on his success in *From Here to Eternity* but refused to lift the ban, which they said was based on his being the subject of frequent stories in the left-wing press, including *The Daily Worker*, official paper of the American Communist Party, thereby identifying Sinatra "with the communist line."[20] Outrageous as it may seem today — that is, equating Sinatra's championing of tolerance and civil rights with the Communist line — such were the times, when McCarthyism, the House Un-American Activities Committee, and the Hollywood blacklist were in their heyday.

During the war years, and beyond, press agent George Evans' skills would be put to the test in protecting the reputation of his most important client. Even before the controversy over Sinatra's draft status arose, Evans, who began handling press relations for Sinatra soon after he left Dorsey's band to go out on his own, made sure that Frank would be available for any patriotic duty, including entertaining troops and selling war bonds, so long as the venues were stateside. It was actually George Evans who first put forth the story that Nancy Sinatra later repeated in her book — that Frank's enemies were spreading lies about non-existent Communist Party leanings, which caused the government to block his travel overseas to entertain troops.[21]

On May 16, 1943, Sinatra and other stars performed at a bond rally in New York's Central Park. Sinatra sang "God Bless America" on what was billed as "I Am an American Day." Two days later, he sang at Madison Square Garden on behalf of Greek war relief. On June 17, 1943, he sang on the Stage Door Canteen radio show, which was broadcast to troops around the world. In January 1944, Sinatra, Bob Hope, Bing Crosby, Ginger Rogers, and others traveled around the country entertaining servicemen and women, including a stop at the Hollywood Canteen, the movie industry's showcase for supporting U.S. troops. As to one Canteen appearance, Nancy Sinatra said: "At the end of his performance, it was reported that servicemen swarmed onto the stage, lifted him to their shoulders, and paraded him throughout the Canteen, cheering him so loudly that it could be heard blocks away."[22] Indeed, a photo does exist that backs up the exuberant reception Ms. Sinatra describes.[23] But three months earlier, on the other side of the continent, American servicemen had demonstrated a different opinion of Mr. Sinatra's patriotism.

Frank was making a second, triumphal appearance at the famed Paramount in New York City in mid-October 1943, this time receiving top billing, his giant-size image displayed above the marquee. At 4 a.m., thousands of teenage girls began lining up for his performances, despite curfews imposed by Mayor Fiorello La Guardia. By the time the theater doors opened, 20,000 young people were milling around Times Square, choking the world-famous landmark. The commotion was so pronounced that the event became known as the "Columbus Day Riot." At one point in that Paramount engagement, sailors on shore leave pelted Sinatra's image with rotten tomatoes, to show their displeasure over the singer's draft status. The event was recorded in photos for the local papers. Author William Manchester pulled no punches in expressing his view on the singer's standing in general within the armed forces: "I think Frank Sinatra was the most hated man of World War II."[24]

George Evans had his work cut out for him in dealing with Sinatra's public image during those years, when the most difficult obstacle to overcome was often his own client. After losing his temper on the set of *Anchors Aweigh* in 1944, Sinatra stormed off and threatened to quit. The movie, in which he and co-star Gene Kelly played sailors, would become one of Sinatra's most successful at MGM. Sinatra issued an apology the next day and explained his outburst this way: "It's easy for a guy to get hot under the collar, literally and figuratively, when he's dressed up in a hot suit of Navy blues and the temperature is a hundred and four degrees."[25] A statement like that gained the singer little sympathy among troops serving in war zones, where things getting "hot" took on greater meaning than discomfort in wearing the uniform on a movie set.

Evans finally landed Sinatra a chance to entertain troops overseas without putting himself in harm's way. V-E Day, May 8, 1945, quieted the guns in Europe, and Evans booked Sinatra into a USO tour to Italy, scheduled for May and June 1945. Still, Sinatra managed to bungle the public-relations purpose of the trip. He was on the West Coast and, to get to his tour departure point in New York, he bumped an Iwo Jima veteran off an eastbound plane.[26]

Evans recruited comedian Phil Silvers, a friend of Sinatra's and an old hand at USO tours, to manage this particular trip. Silvers — who wrote the words to one of Sinatra's most enduring hits, "Nancy (With the Laughing Face)," in honor of Nancy Jr.'s fourth birthday, in June, 1944[27] — was actually on his honeymoon when Evans approached him, but he readily agreed to take on the responsibility, as a favor to Sinatra. Together, Evans and Silvers, who achieved television fame in the 1950s as tough-talking but kind-hearted Sgt. Ernie Bilko, devised a plan to make 4-F Frank Sinatra less objectionable to military audiences: ridicule.

"There was no way I could just call him out on the stage and say to those grunts, 'Look, guys, here's Frank Sinatra,'" Silvers would later recall. "I mean he was not one of their favorite people, if you understand me.

"So I suggested — carefully — that we present him like a real *schmoe*, nobody the guys could possibly get jealous over. We put him in clothes two sizes too big to emphasize how skinny he was. I made jokes like where I looked Frank up and down and said, 'I know there's food rationing back home, but this is ridiculous,' that sort of thing. We kept it up until I felt the guys were warming up to him, sympathizing with him."[28]

The plan worked, despite *Stars and Stripes*, the servicemen's own Army newspaper, editorializing "Mice make women faint, too," an unflattering allusion to the behavior of Sinatra's female fans back home.[29] After watching the object of their animosity being put down by Silvers for an hour or so, the GIs started calling for him to sing. Sinatra obliged, with all the skill and emotion at his command. The USO tour began in triumphal fashion, but when the troupe moved on to other stops in Italy, Sinatra's temperamental side took hold. Always a stickler for precision and perfection in his stateside tours, Sinatra decided that the USO brass were not handling the arrangements in a way that suited him. He was right about the bungling, but he did himself and his reputation no favor when he complained about the hotel the Army booked for him in Rome, where the war had left little in the way of luxury accommodations. When the USO troupe returned to the States on July 6, 1945, Sinatra's rant to reporters did much to undo the good feelings he had engendered by making the tour in the first place.

"Shoemakers in uniform run the entertainment division," Sinatra complained, referring to the Army personnel who oversaw his trip. "Most of them have no experience in show business. They didn't know what time it was. They might just as well be out selling vacuum cleaners."[30]

Despite those imprudent remarks, which his enemies in the press made the most of, Frank Sinatra survived the war years with his reputation a bit tarnished but still viable, thanks to the enormity of his talent and the help of his publicist, George Evans. People were of a mind to forgive and forget in the exuberance of the post-war years. But Sinatra would soon precipitate more problems for himself, problems that made the draft-status controversy seem like a walk in the park, because of his association with certain individuals.

They were called *uomini rispettati* back home in Hoboken,[31] in the neighborhood where Sinatra grew up. Men of respect. J. Edgar Hoover and most Americans had another name for them: Mafia.

5

"He's the most fascinating man in the world, but don't stick your hand in the cage."

In the mid-1970s, writer Pete Hamill discussed with Frank Sinatra the possibility of their collaborating on a book about the singer's life. Sinatra had taken a liking to Hamill, the son of Irish immigrants, most likely attracted to the writer's Brooklyn street smarts, his hard-drinking ways, and the honest reporting he was known for. It didn't hurt that Hamill had also dated Shirley MacLaine, the official mascot of the Rat Pack during its heyday and a longtime Sinatra friend. Hamill told Sinatra that if they went ahead with the biography, he'd "have to discuss three subjects with him: his politics, his women, and the Mob."[1]

"[Sinatra] shrugged," according to Hamill, "and said that the first two were no problem." The singer went on to explain how the third subject — the Mob—might be cause for concern. "But if I talk about those other guys," Sinatra said, "someone might come knocking at my fucking door." Days after that initial book conversation, Sinatra called Hamill and gave the project his okay. "Hey, what the hell," Sinatra said. "All the guys I knew are dead anyway."[2] Unfortunately, the book never got written.[3]

There's no question that Frank Sinatra was friendly with dozens of organized crime figures and that his career received, from time to time, welcome assists from prominent Mafiosi and their Jewish counterparts. None of that help would have mattered if Sinatra hadn't had the requisite talent to begin with. But despite the many investigations — FBI wiretaps, state and federal government inquiries, and endless probing by news organizations, especially the far-right Hearst chain of newspapers — into that sordid aspect of the Sinatra story, no one ever proved that Sinatra had engaged in any *prosecutable* activity. He frequently lied or, to be more generous, shaded the truth about his relationships with mob figures, sometimes under oath, but no prosecutor was going to indict him for that, because no jury in the country would ever vote unanimously to convict a celebrity of Sinatra's stature on perjury charges alone.

In the entertainment business, as it was constituted in the days when Sinatra performed, close association with mob figures was inevitable: They ran the nightclubs — not openly, but behind the scenes, with appropriate frontmen to assume the public face of each enterprise. Deputy Chief Investigator Robert Buccino, of the New Jersey Division of Criminal Justice's Organized Crime and Racketeering Bureau, summed up the dilemma faced by Sinatra, Jimmy Roselli and Dean Martin, and just about every other nightclub performer, especially those of Italian heritage.

"All the Italian entertainers, in order to get ahead, had to deal with [the Mafia,]" Buccino said. "The restaurants, the bars, the clubs they would work in, all had some influence from the Cosa Nostra. So they buttered up to one another. It was both sides. For the Cosa Nostra, it was a badge of honor to be with entertainers and politicians. And the same with the entertainers: It was this moment of glory to be arm in arm with the Cosa Nostra — look at the old photos of Sinatra with Carlo Gambino. That was a trophy kind of thing."[4] As Sinatra put it to Hamill in their preliminary book discussions, he rubbed elbows with his fair share of mobsters.

"Did I know those guys?" Sinatra asked rhetorically. "Sure, I knew some of those guys. I spent a lot of time working in saloons. And saloons were not run by the Christian Brothers." Savoring the religious allusion, Sinatra added: "If Francis of Assisi was a singer and worked in saloons, he would have met the same guys."[5]

But the connection wasn't as inconsequential as Sinatra would have liked the public to believe. His relationship with mob figures stemmed not only from the unavoidable milieu in which he worked, but also from his lifelong infatuation with everything Mafia — the lifestyle, the alpha-male culture, the placing of loyalty and the code of silence above all else, and the power wielded by men with the same roots as his, men who pulled themselves up from nothing, using their natural talents, just as he had done. His talents, singing and acting, were the more acceptable in our culture; but theirs — monetizing every vice known to man and breaking legs when necessary to enforce their will — got them just as far.

The earliest eyewitness to Sinatra's fascination with the Mob may have been his own theatrical agent, Frank Cooper, who was then part of General Amusement Corporation, hired by Sinatra soon after he left the Dorsey band in September 1942. "I can tell you that Frank had a great love of gangsters," Cooper said, much later in life. "We would go out to dinner, and when I arrived at the restaurant to meet him, it wasn't just Frank; it was maybe six other guys. There were gangsters [around Sinatra] all the time I knew him. And I am sure he had relationships with those people."[6]

Actor Peter Lawford, an on-and-off Sinatra intimate, depending on the singer's mood, talked about Sinatra's relationship with Chicago mob boss Sam "Momo" Giancana (1908-1975), once described by police as "a snarling, sarcastic, ill-tempered, sadistic psychopath."[7] Giancana's criminal career started under Al Capone; by 1960, he'd been arrested 70 times and was implicated in 200 murders.[8]

"Frank idolized [Sam Giancana] because he was the Mafia's top gun," Lawford said. "Frank loved to talk about 'hits' and guys getting 'rubbed out.'"[9]

Actress Shirley MacLaine, who was close to Sinatra for the last 40 years of his life and had ample opportunity to observe the way he acted around wiseguys, characterized Frank as a Mafia "wannabe."[10] In 1958, MacLaine, Sinatra, and Dean Martin were on location in Madison, Indiana, filming *Some Came Running* when, as she put it, " 'The Boys from Chicago' visited Frank."[11] MacLaine didn't know who they were at first, but soon learned. "Frank's 'friends' — Sam Giancana, who seemed to be the boss, and various princes and consorts — were 'on the lam' (as they explained) from

Chicago," MacLaine said, "visiting their good friend, Francis Albert."[12]

George Jacobs was Sinatra's personal valet for 15 years (1953-1968) and knew the man better than most people did. In his memoir about the Sinatra years, Jacobs offered an opinion about the singer's attraction to the Mafia types, including Sam Giancana, that Jacobs often saw at his boss's Palm Springs home. "Because he grew up in a New Jersey subculture of godfathers, *padrones*, mob bosses, and such," Jacobs said, "Mr. S [as he called Sinatra] always seemed to need some power figures to look up to."[13]

If Frank Sinatra did indeed need powerful male figures in his life, his original home turf had its share. Five organized crime families divided up the northern New Jersey-New York City area, based sometimes on geography and sometimes on the nature of their illegal activities. Sinatra was most closely connected to the family controlled by Charles "Lucky" Luciano (1897-1962), and was related by marriage to two of its leaders. The other partners in this five-way criminal enterprise were the Carlo Gambino (1902-1976) family, the Giuseppe "Joe" Profaci (1897-1962)-Joseph Colombo (c. 1924-1978) family, the Tommy "Three-Finger Brown" Lucchese (1899-1967) family, and the Joseph "Joe Bananas" Bonanno (1905-2002) family.[14] There was also a "sixth family," based solely in New Jersey and headed by Simone "Sam the Plumber" DeCavalcante (1912-1997).[15] Its interaction with Sinatra was limited.

Lucky Luciano was born Salvatore Lucania in Lercara Friddi, a village in western Sicily, 28 miles from Palermo. Francesco Sinatra, Frank's paternal grandfather (a shoemaker, with no ties to organized crime), came from the same village.[16] Luciano was the mastermind who originally organized the five-family concept of mob cooperation, and under his leadership and that of Meyer Lansky (1902-1983), his Jewish partner (as a non-Italian, Lansky was ineligible for "official" Mafia membership), the crime syndicate thrived, initially as a result of running bootleg liquor while Prohibition was in effect.[17] Over the years, crime families in other metropolitan areas — notably, Chicago, Cleveland, New Orleans, Boston, Providence, Kansas City, Tampa, and Detroit — joined the "Five Families" to divvy up the spoils, from the skim in Las Vegas (raking in cash generated by the casinos off the top, before the IRS could account for the proceeds) to control of unions and their pension funds. Organized crime took on the face of a nationwide crime syndicate — one that held periodic summits to further its ends. If any of the syndicate's minions stepped out of line or became a potential risk to the organization's livelihood, or its survival, they were eliminated, with never a second thought.

In 1936, crime-busting Manhattan District Attorney Thomas Dewey convicted Luciano on multiple counts of compulsory prostitution. The mob boss received a 30- to 50-year prison sentence, but World War II would gain him a reprieve of sorts. In a deal with the government, Luciano promised to use his influence to root out Italian and German agents who might engage in sabotage in and around the New York-New Jersey waterfront. The Mob still controlled the docks during the war, and Luciano was seen as someone who could prevent a catastrophe by bringing information to the proper authorities. There's some question as to the actual worth of Luciano's efforts, but after the war, Dewey, then governor of New York, kept his word and commuted Luciano's sentence, on the condition that the mob leader accept deportation to Italy. Luciano reluctantly agreed (he'd been a resident here since he was 10 and considered the United States his home) and was deported in 1946.

One of Luciano's *capos*, Frank Costello (1891-1973), took over leadership of the family while his boss was in prison and after he was deported, but in 1957, Vito Genovese (1897-1969), another *capo*, or underboss, forced Costello out. The family then acquired the Genovese name as its identifier.[18] The Luciano/Costello/Genovese family would become the predominant organized crime influence in northern New Jersey, working through its three main lieutenants in that state: Abner "Longy" Zwillman (1899-1959), Guarino "Willie Moore" Moretti (1894-1951), and Ruggiero "Richie the Boot" Boiardo (1890-1984),[19] each of whom could claim some connection to the career of Frank Sinatra.

Longy Zwillman was the son of Jewish immigrants from Russia who settled in Newark, New Jersey, the state's largest city. Many considered him to be the second most powerful mob figure in the United States, after Lucky Luciano.[20] Some referred to Zwillman as "the Al Capone of New Jersey."[21]

Willie Moretti, as he was most commonly known, was probably Longy Zwillman's closest ally. Early on, Moretti was a muscleman for Frank Costello, his boyhood friend,[22] in Harlem, which had a heavy concentration of Italians in those days. In the early 1930s, Moretti moved to suburban Hasbrouck Heights, New Jersey, probably at Frank Costello's behest, to oversee gambling and bootlegging operations in that state. One of Moretti's *capos* was a cousin to Nancy Barbato,[23] whom Frank Sinatra married in 1939. The Sinatras — Frank, Nancy, and Nancy Jr. — would themselves move to Hasbrouck Heights in 1942 and take up residence in their first house (they'd previously lived in a Jersey City apartment), a Cape Cod at 220 Lawrence Avenue, around the corner from Willie Moretti's home.

Richie the Boot Boiardo (whose New Jersey crime family inspired HBO mob hit *The Sopranos*, according to David Chase, its producer) and Longy Zwillman were initially rivals for the bootlegging business in Newark and its environs, which included Hoboken. After Chicago boss Al Capone, a friend of Frank Costello's, tried and failed to broker peace between Boiardo and Zwillman, Lucky Luciano stepped in and arranged a truce. Among the top lieutenants in the Boiardo family was Angelo "Gyp" DeCarlo (1902-1973), who was born and raised in Hoboken and would figure prominently in Frank Sinatra's life.[24]

Gyp DeCarlo's sister-in-law, Loretta Riley, married Sam Sinatra, a nephew of Marty and Dolly Sinatra's (and Frank's cousin), in 1939. DeCarlo and Dolly were friends even before that marriage took place, organizing dances and working together in local politics,[25] but their association goes back even further. Dolly once told federal investigators that she was Gyp DeCarlo's babysitter when he was a boy (she was six years older).[26] Knowing Dolly's take-charge personality, it wouldn't be surprising if she had acted as matchmaker between her nephew Sam and Loretta, sister of Gyp's wife Agnes.

According to a 1951 magazine article by Lee Mortimer, a columnist for the Hearst chain's *New York Daily Mirror* and, perhaps, Sinatra's most relentless foe among members of the press, "The mob got Sinatra a job at the Rustic Cabin, a Jersey roadside retreat . . . ."[27] Taken alone, Mortimer's assertion might not carry much weight because of his longstanding feud with Sinatra, but four other sources give credence to the idea that Frankie's job at the Rustic Cabin was due, in particular, to Gyp DeCarlo's intercession. Although Dolly claimed credit for her son's getting the job, through her contacts with the musicians union, it may very well be that she used that scenario as a shield to keep Gyp out of it. She wouldn't have hesitated to seek DeCarlo's help in the matter or to use multiple sources of influence, like union officials, in addition to DeCarlo, in an all-out effort to aid her son's career.

Anthony Petrozelli, the brother of Hoboken Four singer Jimmy Petrozelli (Skelly), served prison time with Gyp DeCarlo and confirmed the close bond between the gangster and his brother's singing group, including Sinatra. Skelly's son also remembered a conversation with his father in which he expressed his opinion that DeCarlo was responsible for Sinatra's Rustic Cabin job. The Three Flashes — the predecessor group to the Hoboken Four — had played gigs at the Rustic Cabin before combining with Sinatra for the Major Bowes radio show, so Skelly would have been privy to DeCarlo's involvement with that roadhouse. Sam Sinatra's widow from a subsequent marriage, Rose, was of the same mind, based on conversations she'd had with Sam. And, finally, Robert Phillips, a former police officer familiar with organized crime in New Jersey, was unequivocal in his view: "Gyp DeCarlo was [Sinatra's] sponsor, his main man," Phillips said. "Sinatra was nowhere until Gyp DeCarlo put the okay on him."[28]

Sinatra had another angel within the New Jersey mob, one more powerful than DeCarlo. Even before Frank became Willie Moretti's neighbor, it appears that the North Jersey Mafia boss was taking an interest in him. Chico Scimone, an American-born pianist of Sicilian heritage, known for both his piano skills *and* his discretion, was often called upon to play at weddings and other occasions for New York-area mobsters, including Frank Costello, Carlo Gambino, and Willie Moretti. The musician had kept quiet about these command performances until after Joseph Bonanno, the last of the original Five Family dons, died in 2002; later, he related a story that had stuck in his mind, for obvious reasons.

In 1938 or 1939 (the pianist couldn't fix the time more precisely), Frank Costello telephoned Scimone and asked for his help. "The *amici* [friends] from New Jersey had contacted him [Costello] about a young fellow," Scimone recalled of his conversation with Costello. "They said he had a good voice and they wanted to test him . . . ."[29]

And so Scimone was called upon to play the piano for this "young fellow," who turned out to be Frank Sinatra. The timing of Costello's request would likely have coincided with Sinatra's Rustic Cabin gig, before Harry James "discovered" him there. Scimone described the session as "a little audition" and remembered Willie Moretti being in the room with Frank Costello. After Sinatra sang a few songs — one of which might have been "Night and Day" — he left. Costello and Moretti then asked Scimone what he thought about Sinatra's singing ability. "It's fine," the pianist replied — not gushing praise, but apparently enough to keep Costello and Moretti involved in Sinatra's career for years to come.[30]

* * *

Frank Sinatra landed his boy-singer jobs with the James and Dorsey bands on pure merit. No amount of mob influence (or Dolly influence, for that matter) could have pressured those two nationally known bandleaders to take on a singer they didn't believe had the talent to succeed with their bands. But mob pressure might have been involved in the decision by one of them to let Sinatra out of an onerous contract that he had impetuously agreed to, in August 1942.

When Tommy Dorsey came knocking at Sinatra's door in December 1939, after Sinatra had fulfilled just seven months of a two-year contract with Harry James, James was gracious in allowing the singer to take the job with the more prominent Dorsey band. He tore up his contract with Sinatra and wished him well, without getting a dime in compensation. Eileen Clancy Lorenzo, a Sinatra family friend, recalled the night when Frank, Harry James, Tommy Dorsey, and Martin Block, a WNEW radio personality, all showed up at Dolly and Marty's house at 841 Garden Street in Hoboken, to sign the Dorsey contract.

"It was a good holiday atmosphere," Lorenzo said. "Dolly made her famous dish: ravioli. Everyone loved it. And for once, Frank didn't sing."[31]

Sinatra's exit from the Dorsey band 2½ years after that festive occasion in Hoboken, to go out on his own as a solo act, was a different story. Dorsey had a valuable property in Sinatra, rated the No. 1 band singer in the country in 1941, along with an ironclad contract. Sinatra's popularity as the band's featured performer had continued to grow, and the ambitious singer knew instinctively that he needed to be free. He'd again given notice to Dorsey in February 1942 that he was leaving, which Dorsey continued to ignore; finally, with just five months left in a three-year contract, Sinatra couldn't, or wouldn't, wait any longer.[32] The fact that Sinatra was so anxious to get out of his contract only enhanced Dorsey's bargaining position. Frank Cooper, Sinatra's newly hired agent, was aghast at the deal his client had made to gain his freedom.

"He showed me the papers," Cooper related, "and then I saw that he gave Tommy Dorsey 33 percent of his gross earnings and 10 percent to Vannerson [Dorsey's agent, who got Sinatra a recording contract with Columbia Records] on top of that. Then, he had to pay 10 percent to me as his agent. I said [to Sinatra], 'We can't do this. This is crazy. You'll be broke all your life . . . .' "[33]

Sinatra's reply to Frank Cooper's concerns was succinct . . . and indicative, perhaps, of the singer's intention, at some point, to rely on mob help to rid himself of Dorsey's claim on his future earnings. "I wanted to get out," Sinatra told Cooper. "Don't worry. I'm not paying him a quarter. He can do whatever he pleases."[34]

After the release deal had been struck, Sinatra gave one farewell performance with the Dorsey band, on September 3, 1942, at which he introduced his replacement, Dick Haymes, who, ironically, had also replaced him as boy singer with the James band. Frank's final number was "The Song Is You."[35] As Sinatra left the stage, Dorsey was overheard muttering a remark that was clearly heartfelt, albeit against his own financial interests. "I hope he falls on his ass," Dorsey said.[36] Needless to say, that didn't happen, at least not right away.

Negotiations between the Dorsey and Sinatra camps to end the one-sided release deal began in early 1943, after it became abundantly clear that the young singer's career was turning into a cash cow. His solo engagement at the Paramount had been extended twice, with that venue's 3,600 seats sold out for every performance. A *Time* magazine review of Sinatra's Paramount appearance set the tone: "Not since [silent film star] Rudolph Valentino has American womanhood made such unabashed public love to an entertainer."[37] But, to that point, Sinatra's fans had been almost entirely bobby-soxers — hardly the flower of "American womanhood." The singer still had to prove himself in front of more mature audiences, and he wasted no time in meeting that challenge, willingly taking a cut from his Paramount paycheck.

On March 11, 1943, Sinatra began a four-week engagement at the Riobamba, an elegant nightclub at 151 E. 57th Street in New York City. Lyricist Sammy Cahn, who teamed up with Jimmy Van Heusen to write some of Sinatra's most memorable songs, described the Riobamba's clientele as "one of the most cosmopolitan, varied audiences as you can imagine — the kept girls, the rich, the famous, the infamous, sports figures, hoodlums . . . ."[38]

The club was owned, behind the scenes, by Louis "Lepke" Buchalter, head of Murder, Inc., the Mafia hit squad.[39] Buchalter was in prison at the time of Sinatra's engagement (and would eventually become the only mob boss ever executed for murder, in 1944), so Sinatra's agent wouldn't have dealt directly with the mobster. As was typical of nightclub bookings in those days, several acts were on the bill. Sinatra got second billing, at $750 a week. The headliner was Walter O'Keefe, an emcee and storyteller, whose fame has since vanished. As O'Keefe was ending his run at the club, on April 9, 1943, he made a surprise announcement to the audience, just before introducing Sinatra.

"When I came into this place," O'Keefe said, "I was the star and a kid named Sinatra was one of the acts. Then suddenly a steamroller came and knocked me flat. Ladies and gentlemen, I give you the rightful star . . . Frank Sinatra."[40] Sinatra had captivated the sophisticated Riobamba audience, and his run was extended, with a doubling of his salary.[41]

His immediate success as a nightclub performer was no fluke. In May, he went on to star at Frank Dailey's Meadowbrook in Cedar Grove, New Jersey, one of the top venues in that state in the 1930s and 1940s, and also one in which Willie Moretti had a silent interest. Then it was back to the Paramount on May 26, but this time as the headliner at $3,100 a week.[42]

Sinatra still hadn't paid Dorsey that "quarter," but pressure was growing to end the stalemate, helped along by Sinatra publicist George Evans. He hired bobby-soxers to picket the Tommy Dorsey band with signs reading "Dorsey Unfair to our Frankie" or the like.[43] Finally, the parties reached an agreement in August 1943, just as Sinatra was completing performances with four symphony orchestras around the country, including a sold-out Hollywood Bowl appearance with the Los Angeles Philharmonic on August

14, all arranged by Evans to further broaden his client's appeal.[44]

Music Corporation of America (MCA) already represented Tommy Dorsey, but that entertainment conglomerate also wanted to displace General Amusement Corporation (GAC) as the agent for Frank Sinatra. MCA would become an integral part of the negotiations to break Sinatra free from Dorsey, as would Manie Sacks of Columbia Records, whom Sinatra considered a close friend and mentor for the rest of the executive's life. Sacks brought in entertainment lawyer Saul Jaffe to represent Sinatra in the negotiations with Dorsey. Jaffe, who was also associated with the powerful American Federation of Radio Artists union, wasn't above using a bit of pressure himself. During the negotiations, Jaffe asked Dorsey if he wanted "to continue broadcasting on NBC," a not-so-thinly veiled threat that the attorney's union connections might make the NBC radio situation difficult. But Dorsey was a tough nut to crack. Despite the threat, or maybe in spite of it, he refused to budge.[45]

Nevertheless, a deal was eventually reached, rescuing Sinatra from his impetuous act of a year earlier. Dorsey would receive a lump-sum payment of $60,000, $35,000 of it to be paid by MCA, which became Sinatra's new agent. (GAC voluntarily stepped aside but received a small percentage going forward, as a reward for its success in managing Sinatra in the first year of his solo career.) Columbia Records, thanks to Manie Sacks, would pay Dorsey the remaining $25,000, as an advance against Sinatra's future royalties.[46]

This official version of how Frank Sinatra freed himself from Dorsey's claim on his future earnings is probably true, as far as it goes, but a more sinister influence may also have been at work. Dorsey was no slouch as a businessman, yet he gave up a contract that may have been worth millions to him, something he'd refused to do, even when Jaffe threatened him with union troubles. He certainly didn't need the $60,000 cash payment — not if it meant foregoing one-third of the gross earnings of the then-hottest performer in America. Even without clear proof that the Mob had a role in getting Sinatra from under Dorsey's thumb, logic, reason, and common sense argue in favor of that conclusion. So do various indications that emerged later.

We have Willie Moretti's response in the 1940s to a question from his friend Dan Lewis, the *Bergen Evening Record* entertainment editor, as to whether rumors about mob involvement in the Dorsey-Sinatra deal were true: "Well, Dan," Moretti told Lewis, "let's just say we took very good care of Sinatra."[47]

In a 1951 article for *The American Mercury*, writer Lee Mortimer, Sinatra's most persistent detractor, reported on a conversation he had with Tommy Dorsey about the release he eventually granted to Sinatra. "Shortly after the breakdown of negotiations," Mortimer relates, "Dorsey told me he was visited by three businesslike men, who told him out of the sides of their mouths to 'sign or else.'"[48] Mortimer had been investigating Sinatra's mob connections since 1947 and, as a result of his articles critical of Sinatra, was the victim of a Sinatra-administered beating on April 8, 1947, outside Ciro's restaurant in Hollywood; consequently, anything coming from the Hearst reporter has to be scrutinized. (Sinatra ended up paying Mortimer $9,000 in damages for the assault.[49]) Still, Dorsey lived until 1956 and never publicly challenged what Mortimer had written.[50] In fact, other sources reported similar assertions from Dorsey.

Ed Becker, a former Las Vegas casino executive, spoke to Sinatra biographers Anthony Summers and Robbyn Swan about a private conversation he'd had with Dorsey regarding the incident.

"Tommy told me it was true," Becker said, recalling Dorsey's specific words. "Three guys from New York City, by way of Boston and New Jersey, approached me," Dorsey had related to Becker, "and said they would like to buy Frank's contract. I said, 'Like hell you will.' . . . And they pulled out a gun and said, 'You wanna sign the contract?' And I did."[51]

It is notable that for the August 1951 article by Mortimer and in his conversation with Ed Becker, Dorsey never mentioned Willie Moretti by name. It may have been prudent for Dorsey to withhold the identity of his chief tormentor, even for a while after Moretti's rubout in October 1951, so as not to provoke a response from the gangster's confederates. But that reticence didn't hold. In a later conversation with a *Parade* magazine reporter, shortly before Dorsey's own death, the bandleader was more specific.

"I was visited by Willie Moretti and a couple of his boys," Dorsey told the *Parade* reporter. "Willie fingered a gun and told me he was glad to hear that I was letting Frank out of our deal. I took the hint."[52]

Dorsey's daughter Pat Hooker, who died in 2003, said her father had told her about a late-night phone call he'd received around this time, from someone threatening him and his children. Dorsey's actions soon afterward at his rural Bernardsville, New Jersey, home seem to support this story. He put barbed wire atop the brick walls surrounding his house, added searchlights and kept them on all night sweeping the property, and installed an electric fence at the entrance to his property.[53]

Writer Pete Hamill, Sinatra's drinking buddy, reported on an interesting twist to this story, without necessarily endorsing it. Given Hamill's closeness to Sinatra, one has to believe that if Sinatra had denied the substance of this tale in the initial book discussions between the two men, Hamill would not have included the story in his book, *Why Sinatra Mattered*, which, overall, cast Sinatra in a favorable light.

"In some versions of the tale," Hamill wrote, "Dolly Sinatra went personally to see Longie [sic] Zwillman at his mansion in New Jersey; in others, Sinatra made the visit himself. Zwillman was outraged at the injustice of it all and put Willie Moretti on the case," Hamill continued. "Moretti walked into Dorsey's dressing room, shoved a pistol into the bandleader's mouth, and told him to give Sinatra a release. Dorsey instantly agreed."[54]

Dolly again. The fact that she was the first choice among some storytellers to be the person who approached Longy Zwillman, "the Al Capone of New Jersey" . . . well, true or not, you gotta love her. Not only was she a mama bear, protecting her offspring with single-minded purpose; she was also a mama *fox* — at once artful, shrewd, and canny, her 90-pound, 4-foot-11 frame a match for anyone.

Sinatra and Tommy Dorsey would have a rapprochement of sorts when they appeared together, with Dorsey brother Jimmy, for a one-week engagement at the Paramount, August 15-21, 1956,[55] three months before Tommy's death at 51. Tommy summed up his lasting impression of his former boy singer this way: "He's the most fascinating man in the world," Dorsey said, "but don't stick your hand in the cage."[56]

6

"Frank, don't forget your galoshes."

F rank Sinatra became a California resident on January 1, 1944, establishing a domicile while filming RKO Radio Pictures' *Higher and Higher*, his debut in an actual acting role (he played himself). An earlier cameo appearance in *Reveille With Beverly* had Frank performing one song — the Cole Porter standby, "Night and Day." His second full-length feature, also a 1944 RKO release, was *Step Lively* — the movie in which he got his first on-screen kiss, from actress Gloria DeHaven.[1] Nancy Sinatra was back in New Jersey, meanwhile, where she gave birth, on January 10, 1944, to Franklin Wayne Emanuel Sinatra. As with Nancy Jr.'s arrival 3½ years earlier, Frank was absent for the happy event, too busy with his career and extracurricular affairs to be with his wife. But the ever-loyal George Evans, mindful of his client's growing image problems, arranged a photo op at Nancy's hospital bedside for the papers and movie magazines. Nancy was shown holding the new baby and dutifully smiling at a framed picture of her husband, the proud father. Frank did show up for the christening, but got into a flap with the priest over Frank's choice of Columbia Records executive Manie Sacks, a Jew, to be Frankie's godfather.

The kid from Hoboken had become enamored of the California lifestyle four years earlier, while he was still with Dorsey. In fact, if not for

Dolly Sinatra, Frank would have left Nancy Sr., Nancy Jr., and New Jersey far behind — about 3,000 miles behind. The band was in Hollywood in late October 1940 to play the sparkling new Palladium at night and to film *Las Vegas Nights* during the day.[2] Sinatra's salary had been bumped to $250 a week by Dorsey, in an effort to keep his boy singer happy.[3] It would work, for a while. The movie gig was just a cameo for the band — the musicians were paid as extras, and Frank, without getting any personal billing, would perform "I'll Never Smile Again," one of the Dorsey band's hit records. The director thought it would be a good idea to have Sinatra sing the song to a pretty girl, so he had starlet Alora Gooding, a "lissome, long legged, pert nosed"[4] blonde, take a seat in front of the bandstand as Frank and the Pied Pipers sang. Gooding was edited out of the final print of the film, but not from Sinatra's mind or his libido. She moved into the singer's hotel suite for the duration of the band's West Coast stay.

Nick Sevano was part of Sinatra's entourage at the time, performing every task imaginable for his hometown friend and enduring his share of abuse when things didn't measure up to Sinatra's exacting standards, friend or no friend. He would be fired in 1943, rehired years later, then fired again. But in the fall of 1940, Sevano was in a position to observe the Gooding affair firsthand.

"This was Frank's first big love away from home," Sevano would recall. "In fact, she was the first big love of his life after he married Nancy. He was crazy about her, really in love with her. She was his first brush with glamour and he was mad for her. The affair lasted a few years, and Frank even tried to leave Nancy because of it, but Dolly put the pressure on and wouldn't let him get a divorce."[5]

The supply of beautiful and willing Hollywood starlets — as well as established female stars, for that matter — was almost inexhaustible in those days. Frank may have been temporarily dazzled by the allure of Alora, as Sevano related, but he wasn't about to pass up the smorgasbord of pleasures available to him in the film capital by becoming a monogamous adulterer. Despite the distractions, Sinatra's career took precedence over his love life, at least for the moment. He broke free of his Dorsey contract in September 1942 and launched one of the most successful debuts of a solo singing act in history. With George Evans guiding his ascent, Sinatra made 1943 a banner year, but things were about to get even better.

In February 1944, he signed his biggest deal to date — a long-term contract with MGM that, along with his other earnings, made him one of the highest-paid entertainers in the world, according to gossip columnist Walter Winchell. In June, his motion picture career now secure, Sinatra moved Nancy, Nancy Jr., and baby Frankie from Hasbrouck Heights, New Jersey, to a new home — a pink Mediterranean-style house at 1051 Valley Spring Lane, formerly owned by actress Mary Astor. The house sat on an oversize lot fronting on Toluca Lake, an exclusive area of Los Angeles in the San Fernando Valley, just 10 miles from Hollywood. The Sinatras' neighbor down the block was Bob Hope. Nancy had been reluctant to leave New Jersey and her large family still residing there; but Frank, eager to make the move and wanting to keep Nancy happy at the same time, made arrangements for five of his wife's sisters, their husbands and children, and her two parents — almost the entire Barbato family—to uproot and relocate to Southern California. It made things easier for Nancy but would become a sore point and drive Frank, a man who craved his own space, free of outsiders, further away from home and hearth.

Frank started filming *Anchors Aweigh*, MGM's blockbuster musical co-starring Gene Kelly, in August 1944. The movie would be released in 1945 and become one of the studio's biggest moneymakers, solidifying Sinatra's place as not only the country's No. 1 singer, but also as one of its top actors, at least from the perspective of box-office receipts. It was said that upon taking over his star's dressing room on the MGM lot, Sinatra posted on the back of his door a list of the most desirable of MGM's starlets and veteran actresses, with the intent of checking off each name as she was added to Frank's score card of sexual conquests. By the time he left the studio in 1950, most of the names had been checked off.[6]

Nineteen forty-four also marked Frank Sinatra's entry into the heady world of national politics. As a kid, he'd been one of Dolly's Third Ward campaign workers — stuffing mailboxes with fliers, marching in parades, and cheering at rallies. He did whatever Dolly asked of him to help the local ticket she supported and the Hudson County Democrats. So it was a foregone conclusion that Frank would be behind Franklin Delano Roosevelt's 1944 re-election bid, the president's unprecedented run for a fourth term.

Sinatra had even named young Frankie after his political hero, not after himself. The use of celebrities in political campaigns was just coming into vogue, and Frank was eager to accommodate FDR in any capacity. But it was a thrilling moment when he was invited to the White House for tea.

The invitation came from an unexpected quarter — New York restaurateur Toots Shor. Shor's place, at 51 West 51st Street, was a world-famous hangout in Times Square and one of Sinatra's favorite drinking spots when he was back East, along with Jilly's Saloon on West 52nd Street, owned by Sinatra's close pal Jilly Rizzo.[7] Sinatra, an only child, once referred to Jilly Rizzo as "the brother he never had."[8]

One of the regulars at Toots Shor's was the chairman of the Democratic National Committee, who wanted to give FDR a lighter moment in the campaign by organizing a visit with the affable Shor, along with some of his celebrity cronies. Frank Sinatra was immediately asked to join the assemblage, which made its way to Washington on September 28, 1944.[9] The president was a charming host, but looked sickly. He'd win the election, of course, but would die five months later, just barely into that fourth term. Sinatra was ebullient when he left the White House, even as he kept up the "humble" façade that George Evans had perfected for the highest-paid entertainer in the world.

"I thought here is the greatest guy alive today," Sinatra told reporters, referring to the president, "and here's a little guy from Hoboken, shaking his hand. He knows about anything, even my racket."[10]

Later in the campaign, at a Madison Square Garden rally in New York City that was broadcast nationally, Sinatra doubled down on the "little guy" theme: "Since he [FDR] is good for me and my kids and my country," Sinatra said, "he must be good for all the other ordinary guys and their kids."[11] Sinatra was not an accomplished impromptu speaker, as his words demonstrate; still, his support for FDR was heartfelt, the conspicuous absence of any reference to wives and mothers notwithstanding. Nancy Sinatra did not command a lot of her husband's attention during this time.

George Evans labored mightily to limit, and cover up, his client's extramarital affairs. He lectured Sinatra about the deleterious effect the carousing was having on his image. In an attempt to add a little glamour to Nancy and make her more attractive for her husband, Evans arranged to have her teeth capped and her nose bobbed; he even got her makeup and hairstyling lessons. But Sinatra could not, or would not, contain himself. He was like the proverbial kid in the candy store, only this store was stocked with Hollywood women, and the kid had an appetite for sweets other than candy.

Among the early names crossed off Frank's dressing-room list was that of screen goddess Lana Turner.[12] Turner had been signed to an MGM contract at 17, in 1938,[13] and started off as the bad-girl distraction for Mickey Rooney in an Andy Hardy movie, before moving to meatier roles.[14] She starred in three noteworthy films before she was 20, all 1941 releases: *Johnny Eager*, opposite Robert Taylor; *Honky Tonk*, with Clark Gable; and *Ziegfeld Girl*, a musical with James Stewart, Judy Garland, and Hedy Lamarr. By that time, MGM had increased her salary to $1,500 a week,[15] making her one of its top-paid stars. Carrying over a sultry screen presence to her private life, Turner was one of the most promiscuous leading ladies of the day, with an appetite for musicians.

After a brief stint as one of bandleader Artie Shaw's eight wives, Lana started working her way through the Dorsey band. Drummer Buddy Rich fell hopelessly in love with her, much to the dismay of friends who knew her reputation — something Rich seemed oblivious to. She strung Rich along for a while, even visiting his parents and promising to marry him, all the while two-timing him whenever the urge struck her. She had a brief fling with Tommy Dorsey, who knew better than to get serious over someone whose morals were only a cut above those of the alley cats along the Sunset Strip. Among the other musicians and Hollywood stars to succumb to Lana Turner's beguiling charms were actor Victor Mature, singer Tony Martin, drummer Gene Krupa, actor Robert Stack, and actor Tyrone Power.[16]

In her memoir, Turner would claim that she and Frank Sinatra did not have a romantic relationship (Frank was "a friend, never a lover"),[17] but the overwhelming consensus says otherwise. An early draft of Turner's memoir supposedly contained the lurid details of her relationship with Sinatra, but Turner is said to have deleted them so as not to "give him [Sinatra] the satisfaction."[18]

In 1945, the name of another blond beauty started being linked to Sinatra. Marilyn Maxwell had also been a band singer before arriving in Holly-wood,[19] which may have made her more simpatico in Sinatra's eyes. But his eyes also could not have failed to contemplate what one commentator described as "every man's fantasy of a movie star: tall and voluptuous, with white porcelain skin, long platinum hair, and a smile so inviting that only monks could resist."[20] Another, equally alluring description went like this: "a stunning, corn-fed Iowa girl, bottle blond, with a body to kill for, a real brain in her head, and a truly sweet disposition."[21] All the while, Nancy Sinatra maintained a brave exterior, knowing of her husband's infidelities, but not wanting to know.

The Sinatras had started an annual tradition at their Toluca Lake home of hosting a grand New Year's Eve party, complete with homemade musi-cal-comedy productions starring their talented Hollywood guests. For years leading up to the 1945 holiday season, Nancy had weathered the pain of frequent gossip-column reports pairing her husband with first one gorgeous actress, then another. Despite it all, Frank kept coming home to her, and she let herself hope there was a chance for their marriage to hold together. Those hopes rose even higher when, a few days before Christmas, she used Frank's Cadillac to go to the beauty parlor.[22] Reaching into the glove com-partment for a comb, Nancy saw a blue jewelry case, tied neatly with a ribbon. Her curiosity getting the best of her, she undid the ribbon and opened the box, only to discover a diamond bracelet almost too dazzling to behold. It had to be Frank's Christmas gift to her, she thought, and it prob-ably cost a fortune — his way to make amends by giving her a truly spectacular present. She put the bracelet back the way she had found it and said nothing to her husband. On Christmas morning, however, her gift from Frank was a pair of pearl earrings — beautiful and costly in their own right, but not what she had expected. Still, she said nothing, even though the absent bracelet made her wonder.

The mystery would be solved eight days later, at the New Year's Eve party. Frank was greeting guests, while Nancy saw to food preparation in the kitchen. When she came out to the living room to mingle with their friends, her eyes were drawn to Marilyn Maxwell, seated on the sofa with husband John Conte. There, on Marilyn's wrist, was the same distinctive bracelet Nancy had found in the glove box of Frank's Caddy. Devastated, Nancy summoned a reservoir of courage she probably didn't know she possessed and ordered Maxwell out of her house. Later, when Nancy and Frank were alone, she let her husband have it: "How dare you shame me in my own home," she said, bitter tears filling her eyes. "But she doesn't mean anything to me," Frank pleaded. "No one could compare to you."[23] In a way, Frank's pathetic response was reminiscent of his attempt to cover his tracks when Nancy discovered him two-timing her with Toni Della Penta back in 1938, before their marriage. It's doubtful that Nancy believed his portrayal of the Maxwell affair, but she accepted her fate and allowed him to stay in the house . . . for the time being.

* * *

In the spring of 1946, Sinatra began work on *It Happened in Brooklyn*, co-starring Jimmy Durante, Kathryn Grayson, Gloria Grahame, and Peter Lawford.[24] It would be his first full-length feature since *Anchors Aweigh*, filmed two years earlier.[25] Aside from a couple of exceptional musical numbers — Frank singing the great Sammy Cahn/Jule Styne ballad "Time After Time" and then teaming up with Jimmy Durante for "The Song's Gotta Come from the Heart" — the picture was considered second-rate by most critics.[26] Sinatra played the role of Danny Miller, a veteran returning to his beloved Brooklyn, where he sings a paean to that borough's famous bridge and renews a friendship with the musically inclined custodian (Durante) of his old high school, who gives him the confidence to win a job as a song plugger in a music store. What the film lacked in dramatic flair, it made up for in behind-the-scenes turmoil. Sinatra had turned into a director's (and producer's) nightmare, perhaps as a result of the box-office success of *Anchors Aweigh* giving him a swelled head or, just as likely, his personal life taking its toll. He was often late to the set, when he wasn't a complete no-show, causing production delays and alienating the other actors, who frequently had to shoot around the absent star.

Nineteen forty-six hadn't started well, what with the humiliating scene at the Sinatras' New Year's Eve party. Despite his promises to Nancy, Frank remained very much involved with Marilyn Maxwell, as well as with Lana Turner — an almost unimaginable adulterous adventure, even in licentious Hollywood. After shooting the beginning scenes at MGM studios in Hollywood, production on the picture broke for a few months to get ready for location work in Brooklyn. Frank was able to maintain the pretense of a happy home life, while immersing himself in work and, when circumstances permitted, continuing his affairs with the two glamorous stars.

Sinatra would make more than 50 records for Columbia during the year, in Hollywood and New York City, including such classics as "Begin the Beguine," "That Old Black Magic," and "September Song."[27] And he kept up a hectic concert schedule as well, with appearances in San Francisco, Philadelphia, Detroit, Chicago (where he earned $41,000 for a one-week engagement — the equivalent of a half-million in today's dollars), and New York City. It would take Madison Square Garden, with its 20,000-seat capacity, to accommodate the demand for tickets. His weekly half-hour *Songs by Sinatra* radio show, sponsored by Old Gold cigarettes, followed him by remote broadcast from wherever he was performing at the time.[28] The New York appearance coincided nicely with the planned location shooting in June and July for *It Happened in Brooklyn*. It also provided Sinatra with an opportunity to see Marilyn Maxwell, whom he invited to share his suite at the Waldorf Astoria Hotel, as though a continent could shield the affair from the prying eyes of the tabloid press.

Toots Shor had ringside seats for the Joe Louis-Billy Conn Heavyweight Championship fight in Yankee Stadium on June 19 and invited Frank to join him. When Shor, who was going to have his wife with him, learned that Sinatra planned on bringing Maxwell to the event, he became upset. The fight would be covered by every major newspaper in the country, and pictures of Sinatra seated at ringside next to Marilyn Maxwell would have been the lead story in many of those papers, irrespective of the boxing match's outcome. Rather than confront the volatile Sinatra over the issue, Shor called Manie Sacks to see if the Columbia Records executive could talk sense into their mutual friend. Sacks also shied away from what surely would have been a nasty scene. He did not want to get into the middle of this and wisely decided to call publicist George Evans, the one person who seemed to have a modicum of control over Sinatra's womanizing. Even Evans saw the futility of a head-on discussion with Sinatra over the matter. Instead, he contacted Marilyn Maxwell directly, in an attempt to appeal not only to her better nature — she wouldn't want to be branded as a home wrecker — but also to her career instincts.

"Listen, you've got a morals clause in your studio contract that says you can't disgrace the studio by going out with a married man," Evans told the tearful Maxwell. "You ain't never seen bad publicity like the kind you're gonna see if you go out on the town with Sinatra."[29]

Evans' plan worked. Maxwell not only turned Sinatra down regarding the fight; she pulled up stakes, went back to California, and ended her affair with the singer. Sinatra was furious, with Evans and with Maxwell. He went to the fight alone, sitting with his pal, Yankee Clipper Joe DiMaggio, and DiMaggio's date, actress Marlene Dietrich. Sinatra was so angry that he hardly paid attention to Louis' stunning 8th-round knockout of the out-matched Conn. When he got back to the hotel in the early morning hours, he picked up the phone and called Lana Turner, who had stayed over in New York after the May premiere of *The Postman Always Rings Twice*, one of her best films. They would spend the rest of his time in New York together, before he headed back to the Coast in mid-July to resume studio shooting for *It Happened in Brooklyn*. He also had a concert engagement at the Hollywood Bowl in late July and August.

Production on the picture ground to a halt once again in September, when Sinatra received a call from comedian Phil Silvers, the man who had saved the singer's reputation a year earlier by guiding him through a successful USO tour in Italy, at a time when Sinatra's 4-F status was causing serious public-relations problems. This time, Silvers needed help. He and his comedy-team partner, Rags Ragland, had been booked to play the Copacabana, New York City's classiest venue, but the 40-year-old Ragland died suddenly of a heart attack on August 20, and Silvers was despondent — not only over the loss of a friend but also out of fear of laying an egg at the mob-controlled nightclub (Frank Costello owned the major share[30]). Ragland's role was to be Silvers' straight man, just as Sinatra had been during the USO tour. Silvers wondered if Frank could come to New York and help him out. Sinatra felt Silvers' pain — he had been friends with Ragland, too — and told the comedian not to worry. On September 9, 1946, opening night, Silvers did the first show on his own, and barely got through it. But when he returned to his dressing room, there was Sinatra.

"Hi," Frank said, "what do we open with?"[31]

Sinatra had left the filming in California, without permission and at the risk of a breach of contract lawsuit, to be with Silvers in New York. It was a gesture Silvers would never forget, and the comedian was able to finish the Copa engagement on his own, to rave reviews. Two days later Sinatra was back in Hollywood, where he picked up on the movie he'd been neglecting. He also picked up on other unfinished business: Lana Turner.

Frank and Lana began carrying on their affair openly — a dangerous game in Hollywood, where Hedda Hopper and Louella Parsons ruled, the two most powerful gossip columnists overseeing the motion picture industry. Each was syndicated in dozens of papers nationwide, with millions of readers. In the pre-television and pre-Internet age, newspapers held great sway over public opinion, for good or ill. Movie studios depended on the drawing power of their stars to generate a profit, and if the public turned thumbs down on any particular star, especially proven money makers like Sinatra and Turner, both in the MGM stable, that could prove disastrous. And so, the studios catered to these self-appointed arbiters of good taste and propriety, as did the stars themselves. The reporters and others of their ilk were fed tidbits by publicists, positive items about the stars they represented and negative ones about others who might be competitors for a role or an award. They also had stringers working the clubs and hot spots, looking for a juicy scoop. Strange as it may seem today, the gossip columns were often used by Hollywood types to communicate with one another — a kind of 1940s and '50s Facebook. Hopper and Parsons, masters of manipulation, were both aware of the often bludgeon-like power they wielded.

Like many stars, Lana Turner wasn't a fan of either of these two columnists, but she wasn't about to complain until long after both were dead. In her 1982 memoir, Turner let her true feelings show. "Hedda Hopper and Louella Parsons dominated Hollywood," Turner said, holding nothing back. "They took bribes and gifts and played favorites, and God help you if they ever got mad at you."[32]

Both Hedda and Louella belonged to the Hollywood Women's Press Club, which doled out annual citations to the movie industry. In November 1945, after Sinatra's triumph in *Anchors Aweigh* and his Academy Award for *The House I Live In*, the Press Club gave him the "Outstanding Achievement Award," for his "remarkable work in furthering racial tolerance and approaching the problem of juvenile delinquency."[33] One year later, it was a different story — that same group cited him as the "Least Cooperative Actor,"[34] with good reason.

Louella Parsons, who wrote for the Hearst chain and had a readership of 40 million Americans, was already down on Sinatra because of his behavior on the set of *It Happened in Brooklyn.* There were few secrets in Hollywood, and Parsons had her contacts in every studio. She knew about Sinatra's antics during the filming of that picture, as well as about his adulterous dalliances, and she wasn't about to let him get away with it. "I have always liked Frankie," Parsons wrote, "but I think right now he needs a good talking to."[35]

Sinatra fired back an ill-advised response to that particular column and, in what had to have been one of George Evans' rare missteps, dared Parsons to print it, which is exactly what she did. "In the future," Frank wrote, "I'll appreciate your not wasting your breath on any lectures because when I feel I need one, I'll seek advice from someone . . . who tells the truth."[36] Within a matter of months, he would be eating humble pie at Parsons' table.

The pressures on the Sinatra marriage reached almost unbearable proportions in the fall of 1946, not solely because of Frank's philandering but also because of his uncontrolled spending. He was making lots of money but spending it like . . . well, like a drunken sailor. Nancy had always been tight with a dollar, a necessity back in the Harry James and Tommy Dorsey days. When the money started pouring in, Frank opened the spigot wider, but Nancy still watched every penny. She got Sinatra's crony Nick Sevano fired because she didn't like the sloppy way he accounted for his expenses, which she scrutinized like an IRS auditor. Frank bought a new house for Dolly and Marty back in New Jersey, spending $22,000 in cash — more than a quarter of a million today, money that Nancy deemed wasted. When she complained about it, he retaliated by complaining about her sisters and family always being there in his home, when he wanted peace and quiet.

Things came to a head in early October, soon after shooting wrapped on *It Happened in Brooklyn.* Frank and Lana both attended a party at the home of ice-skater-turned-actress Sonja Henie on October 5. They may have arrived separately, but they were inseparable the whole night, and when the party ended, Frank didn't go home — at least not to his own home. The next morning he phoned Nancy and told her that he "wanted his freedom." Not a divorce, but a separation. Nancy's first reaction was to call George Evans in New York, to seek an ally in getting Frank back home, but her husband had already left town with Lana. They were in Palm Springs together. Evans issued a statement that the separation was "just a family squabble." He said that Frank had "gone to a desert resort for a little privacy" and that "there was no talk of a divorce"; rather, the couple was expected to "make up in a few days."[37]

Hedda Hopper, famous for her quirky hats and nasty commentary, had a readership of 32 million by the mid-1950s, 20 percent of the entire population of the United States.[38] The overriding theme in her columns was the sanctity of marriage and a good home life, and, in covering Hollywood hanky-panky, she invariably took the side of the wronged wife and against the intervening Jezebel.[39] In her first column after news of the Sinatras' separation became public, Hopper wrote, "Did you ever hear Frankie sing 'I'm not much to look at, nothing to see, but I've got a woman crazy for me'? That's a thing of the past, his wife Nancy told me yesterday." She'd go on to comment in this same vein in every column she wrote while the separation lasted, often including negative remarks from her readers.[40]

Not wanting to miss an opportunity to further her conservative agenda, Hopper, along with some of her readers, used the separation to blast Sinatra for his support of liberal causes. "Last year [1945]," Hopper wrote, "Frank Sinatra got an Academy Award for the song 'The House I Live In.' Evidently, that house wasn't big enough for Nancy and the children."[41]

In a private meeting with Lana Turner, MGM studio head Louis B. Mayer chastised his female star about her profligate ways and reminded her of the morals clause in her contract. "The only thing you're interested in," Mayer said, "is . . . " The words were left unspoken, but as he paused, Mayer pointed to his groin area to get the message across.[42]

Meanwhile, George Evans and Manie Sacks were working on Sinatra, who was holed up in a bachelor apartment he took when he moved out of the Toluca Lake house. He was destroying his career, they told him. If he knew what was good for him, he'd put an end to this mess and get back together with Nancy. Finally, it registered. Frank agreed to give the marriage another try, but there had to be a dramatic flair to the reconcilement, to overcome all the bad publicity the separation had created. Evans and Sacks came up with a plan, but they needed the aid of old reliable Phil Silvers to help them pull it off.

Following his successful run at the Copacabana, Silvers was then appearing at Slapsy Maxie's, a Hollywood nightclub run by Maxie Rosenbloom, an ex-prizefighter who became a lovable character actor in the 1940s and '50s.[43] In a perfect bit of staging on the night of October 23, the comedian called his pal Frank Sinatra to the stage to sing a song. The song was "Going Home," the lyrics of which had absolutely nothing to do with the situation at hand. It was the title of the song that mattered, along with the tremulous quality of Sinatra's voice as he sang it. When Frank finished, he started walking, amid the applause, toward his table on one side of the club, only to be intercepted by Phil Silvers, who guided him to the opposite side. There, at a table with Frank's friend, songwriter Jule Styne, sat Nancy. Frank took his wife in his arms and, as the nightclub audience cheered, kissed her.

Nancy and Frank left Slapsy Maxie's arm in arm and went back to his apartment, where they made love . . . and a baby. This was Hollywood, after all, the town that invented happy endings. But the Hollywood ending wouldn't last. Still unsure of her husband's intentions, Nancy eventually aborted the pregnancy, without informing Frank.

Soon after his return to Toluca Lake, Frank reached out to Louella Parsons, who duly published his act of contrition. "I have been so exhausted," Frank told the columnist in an exhibition of groveling almost too pathetic to witness, especially considering its insincerity. "I have been confused. I know I did many things I shouldn't have, things that I am now sorry for."[44]

Parsons granted him absolution, of a sort. "I'm going to quit picking on Frankie Sinatra," she wrote, "because I think he is a mixed up boy right now."[45]

✳ ✳ ✳

Writer Pete Hamill reported on an incident Frank cited as his moment of realization that his marriage to Nancy was not going to work, that she was stuck in a New Jersey mindset and would never make the transition to the sophisticated California world he craved. Sinatra was leaving the house one evening to attend a business meeting in Los Angeles (or so he said), and it was raining heavily. Nancy called after him, with nothing but love and concern in her voice: "Frank," she said, "don't forget your galoshes."[46]

7

"It was the dumbest thing I ever did."

Lucky Luciano, imprisoned from 1936 until his release from custody and deportation to Italy in early 1946, wasted no time in reasserting himself as a force in the crime syndicate he had created. In autumn of that year, with the paid-for acquiescence of dictator Fulgencio Batista, Luciano moved his base of operations to Cuba, just 90 miles from American shores. Early in 1947, he called for a "summit" in Havana — a gathering of bosses from across the United States, to map out the future of "their thing." A board of directors meeting, if you will, for an entity as vast as the largest corporations in America.

Meyer Lansky, who once famously declared, "We're bigger than U.S. Steel,"[1] was in attendance at the summit, as was Frank Costello, the titular head of the Luciano family in America. Vito Genovese, who would depose Costello in 1957 — he was there. The other leaders of the Five Families were there: Tommy Lucchese, Carlo Gambino, Joe Bonanno, and Joe Profaci, founder of what would turn into the Colombo family. Longy Zwillman, Willie Moretti, and Joseph "Doc" Stacher were there from New Jersey. In 1952, Stacher would oversee the mob's interests in the Sands Hotel and Casino in Las Vegas. Giuseppe "Joe Adonis" Doto, a Luciano associate with gambling and restaurant interests in New Jersey, was there.[2]

Carlos Marcello and Santo Trafficante were there, representing New
Orleans and Tampa, respectively. Detroit's Moe Dalitz was there. Tony
Accardo (1906-1992), whom Al Capone once dubbed "Joe Batters" for his
skill in putting a baseball bat to more lethal use, was there from Chicago,
along with Joe and Rocco Fischetti.[3]

Johnny Roselli, the Chicago mob's representative in Los Angeles,[4] was
there in Havana. Roselli was making inroads into the motion picture industry by controlling unions and bankrolling the right people. It was Roselli
who reportedly got Harry Cohn the money in the 1930s to take over
Columbia Pictures, the studio that would make *From Here to Eternity* —
the 1953 movie that would change Frank Sinatra's life.[5]

And there was one more, *unfortunate* attendee in Havana — Frank
Sinatra, fast becoming, if not already, the No. 1 motion picture, recording,
and nightclub star in America. And soon to become, thanks to his presence
in Havana at this time and his association there with this underworld rogues'
gallery, the target of every right-wing newspaper reporter and politician in
America, people who didn't like Sinatra's politics to begin with, his outspoken support of liberal causes, or his ethnic heritage. On February 11, 1947,
Sinatra was photographed as he walked from a Pan Am plane that had just
arrived from Miami. He was flanked by Joe and Rocco Fischetti and was
carrying a suitcase, at a time when commercial airline passengers did not
ordinarily have carry-on luggage.[6]

Robert Ruark, then working as a Scripps-Howard newspaper columnist,
spotted Sinatra in Havana and, sensing a scoop, made it his business to track
the singer's movements and interactions — at the Hotel Nacional, in its
casino, and at a racetrack — with known mob figures. These were clearly
not the chance encounters that Sinatra would later claim them to be. On
February 20, 1947, Ruark's article, "Sinatra Is Playing With the Strangest
People These Days," broke the story in the *New York World-Telegram*, *Washington News* and other Scripps-Howard papers.[7] More articles on the same
subject would follow.

"I am frankly puzzled as to why Frank Sinatra, the fetish of millions,
chooses to spend his vacation in the company of convicted vice operators
and assorted hoodlums," Ruark wrote. "He was here for four days last week
and his companion[s] in public [were] Luciano, Luciano's bodyguards, and

a rich collection of gamblers."[8]

Ruark showed his bias against the singer by denigrating Sinatra's espousal of liberal causes: "Mr. Sinatra," Ruark wrote, "the self-confessed savior of the country's small fry, by virtue of his lectures on clean living and love-thy-neighbor, his movie shorts on tolerance, and his frequent dabblings into the do-good department of politics, seems to be setting a most peculiar example."[9]

This was the first public disclosure of Sinatra's possible links to organized crime, and it was quickly picked up by Hearst columnists Westbrook Pegler and Lee Mortimer, both old Sinatra nemeses, as well as by other media sources. Mortimer would later claim that Sinatra was carrying $2 million cash in the suitcase he carried off the Miami plane, as a bagman for Lucky Luciano, but FBI files released in 1998 did not back up that allegation,[10] which Sinatra also denied. Because there were photos of Sinatra socializing with his disreputable friends,[11] he couldn't very well deny that he had been in Havana and had been in their company. Instead, he concocted a series of far-fetched stories that did little to dispel the furor.

Sinatra responded to Ruark's February 20 story in the *New York World-Telegram* this way: "I was brought up to shake a man's hand when I am introduced to him," Sinatra said, "without first investigating his past."[12] Later, he told gossip columnist Hedda Hopper that he "dropped by a casino one night" and that one of the casino hosts asked him to meet "a few people."[13]

"I couldn't refuse," Sinatra told Hopper, "so I went through some routine introductions without paying attention to the names of the people I was meeting. One happened to be Lucky Luciano. Even if I caught his name, I probably wouldn't have associated it with the notorious underworld character." Sinatra said he sat at Luciano's table "for about 15 minutes," then "got up and went back to the hotel."[14]

"When such innocent acts are so distorted," Sinatra lamented, "you can't win."[15]

Sinatra's presence in Havana that February may have, in fact, been "innocent." There's no suggestion that he sat in on any of the mobsters' "business" discussions, one of which authorized a hit on their errant colleague Benny "Bugsy" Siegel,[16] whom Sinatra had met in Los Angeles and admired greatly.[17] Clearly, Sinatra was there at Luciano's command, but it may have only been a carefully crafted "cover story" for the gathering of syndicate members: They could claim they were in Havana to see their favorite singer perform and to hang out with him for a few days. Sinatra was "a good kid and we was all proud of him," Luciano would later say.[18]

When Italian police raided Luciano's Naples home a few years after the Havana conference, they found a gold lighter with the following inscription: "To my dear pal Lucky from his friend Frank Sinatra."[19]

Although it is unlikely that Frank Sinatra engaged in any illegal activity in Havana during that infamous trip in February 1947, he would never escape the taint of mob affiliation that dogged him for the rest of his career — indeed, for the rest of his life.

"It was the dumbest thing I ever did," Sinatra acknowledged to Pete Hamill in the 1970s. That was all. About that startling admission from Sinatra, all Hamill would later say was, "He did not elaborate."[20]

* * *

There is a biblical cast to the life and career of Francis Albert Sinatra. Without stretching the metaphor, one can easily find parallels, from Joseph's prophecy to Pharaoh to the return of the Prodigal Son, Hollywood-style.

From 1940 through 1946, Frank Sinatra experienced seven years of unimaginable abundance. His swift rise to become the No. 1 band singer in the United States with Tommy Dorsey was quickly followed by the most spectacular launch of a solo act in entertainment history. He parlayed that celebrity into movie stardom, built not so much on his acting skill as on screen presence and a distinctive vocal style.[21] Women fell in love with him; men wanted to be like him. Sinatra had help, to be sure: Publicist George Evans, arranger Axel Stordahl, and Columbia Records executive Manie Sacks come to mind, as well as the mob bosses who took a liking to the brash young singer and gave him an occasional assist. But it was pure talent that formed the underpinning for this time of plenty, making it all the more difficult, then, to foretell the seven years of famine that followed.

It began, almost imperceptibly, with Sinatra's politics. His full-throated support of FDR in 1944, at a time when few celebrities got involved that way, brought him to the attention of Roosevelt haters, of which there were many, including the powerful William Randolph Hearst. Lee Mortimer, a columnist for the Hearst chain, would call Sinatra "one of Hollywood's leading travelers on the road to Red fascism." Earlier, Mortimer had dubbed Sinatra "the 4-F from Hasbrouck Heights,"[22] which triggered the feud between the two men. Westbrook Pegler, another Hearst writer, piled on in similar fashion. From 1945 to 1953, Frank Sinatra would be labeled a "Commie" 12 times by witnesses testifying before the House Un-American Activities Committee. Gerald L. K. Smith, head of the America First Party, a right-wing fringe group, claimed before that same Congressional committee, in 1946, that Sinatra "has been doing some pretty clever stuff for the Reds."[23] There was no evidence to support any of these allegations, unless one considers Sinatra's preaching of racial and religious tolerance — extremely brave positions for a celebrity to take at this time in American history — a mark of Communism.

Sinatra's disastrous four-day sojourn in Havana, Cuba, with Lucky Luciano and more than a dozen other organized crime figures in February 1947, coming as it did on the heels of well-publicized marital infidelities, contributed to the downward spiral. Then, on the night of April 8, 1947, Sinatra's frustration boiled over. As he and friends were dining at Ciro's, he spotted Lee Mortimer leaving the Hollywood nightclub and followed him outside. The Hearst writer had picked up on reporter Robert Ruark's exposé of the Havana affair and was needling Sinatra unmercifully in his *New York Daily Mirror* column. To compound Sinatra's anger, Mortimer had just given *It Happened in Brooklyn*, which premiered in March, a terrible review.[24]

Outside the club, Sinatra reportedly struck Mortimer from behind as he was about to enter a cab, knocking him to the ground; then, with crony Sam Weiss, a 6-foot, 200-pound song plugger, holding the diminutive columnist down, according to witnesses, Sinatra continued the beating.[25] The fight was broken up, but Sinatra would later be charged with battery — that is, harmful or offensive contact with another person. Investigators assigned to the Los Angeles District Attorney's Office investigated and later issued a report.

"We are convinced," the report concluded, "that Sinatra, with a gang behind him and with the active assistance of one man, made an unexpected and unprovoked assault on Mortimer."[26]

Sinatra would claim that Mortimer, as he was leaving the club, passed by Sinatra's table and referred to him as "that dago." Later, he changed his story, saying that Mortimer gave him "a sneering look." No one in Sinatra's dinner party was willing to testify in his behalf, but before the case came to trial, Sinatra wisely decided to settle, no doubt encouraged by MGM studio head Louis B. Mayer.[27] He paid $9,000 in damages directly to Mortimer and an additional $15,000 or more in costs. Sinatra admitted that he was mistaken about the "dago" comment, and, after his attorney addressed the court and expressed his client's "regret over the whole episode," the case was dismissed.[28]

William Randolph Hearst would not be so forgiving. In retaliation for the attack on Mortimer, the publishing tycoon issued a "don't use" decree, meaning that the name of Frank Sinatra was banned from Hearst newspapers. In the Hollywood world of the 1940s, *no* publicity was often a worse fate than *bad* publicity. The ban would hold for almost a year, until March 1948, when Louis Mayer was finally able to orchestrate a face-to-face meeting between the 84-year-old Hearst and Sinatra, facilitated through the intercession of actress Marion Davies, Hearst's longtime mistress but also a big fan of Sinatra's.[29] Thanks to his frequent obnoxious behavior and undisciplined verbal outbursts, Sinatra had honed his groveling skills to a fine edge by this time, at least with respect to people having power over his career. (He almost never apologized to friends or employees he may have hurt with his actions or words.)

John Hearst, Jr., the publisher's grandson, witnessed Sinatra's arrival and the meeting, which took place over tea at Marion Davies' home. "He drove up by himself — no limousines, no bodyguards, no hangers-on," John Hearst would later recall. "He was very contrite."[30]

Assured of Sinatra's patriotism and anti-Communism, Hearst accepted the singer's profuse apologies, not only lifting the ban on coverage in the Hearst papers but also ordering his more strident columnists, like Mortimer and Pegler, to tone down their rhetoric.[31] Sinatra could once again be mentioned in Louella Parsons' gossip column — clearly, a mixed blessing.

* * *

In his 1997 Sinatra biography, author Donald Clarke noted: "After August 1946 Frank Sinatra did not have a record in the top five of the *Billboard* pop charts until 1954; in 1952 and 1953, he had no hits at all."[32] And yet the man was turning out some of his more memorable recordings. In 1947, Sinatra's most prolific year in a recording studio (68 sides recorded), he produced such enduring classics as "Stella by Starlight," "Almost Like Being in Love," "The Nearness of You," "One for My Baby," "All of Me," "Laura," "Fools Rush In," "It Never Entered My Mind," "Body and Soul," "I'm Glad There Is You," and "Autumn in New York."[33] If not at the top of the charts, Sinatra's records were still selling; nevertheless, Old Gold cigarettes canceled Sinatra's radio show, *Songs by Sinatra*, in April 1947,[34] most likely in response to the spate of bad publicity generated by his association with the mob gathering in Havana and the Lee Mortimer incident. The singer actually gained, monetarily, when *Your Hit Parade*, a popular radio show sponsored by Lucky Strike cigarettes, later picked up the now-available Sinatra as its star attraction;[35] the only trouble was, he was singing other people's hits every week, not his own.

Sinatra's movie career had peaked with the huge box-office success of *Anchors Aweigh* in 1945, but began taking on water following the 1947 release of *It Happened in Brooklyn*, panned as it was by most critics It did not help that Sinatra began filming two of his biggest cinematic stinkers in that same year: *The Kissing Bandit*, an improbable *Zorro*-like musical comedy for MGM, and *The Miracle of the Bells*, an RKO picture in which Sinatra played, of all things, a priest.

As to the former picture, released in late 1948 after the studio's frantic but unsuccessful attempts to fix it, Sinatra himself summed up its place in his career. His words came on the occasion of the birth of his first grandchild, Nancy's daughter Angela Jennifer (A.J.) Lambert, in May 1974. "All I ask is that Nancy never let the child grow up and see *The Kissing Bandit*," Sinatra said, only half in jest. "I've been trying to change my name ever since. As a matter of fact, the picture was so bad that on leaving the theater, I made a citizen's arrest of the cashier."[36] Tom Santopietro, in his first-rate chronicle of Sinatra's movie career, called *The Kissing Bandit* a "Technicolor farce wherein Frank plays a bumbling Hispanic would-be bandit in 1840s California." Actor Sinatra "speaks with a noticeably thick New Jersey accent," Santopietro wrote, adding that "he has absolutely no feel for the material" and "looks trapped, desperate for a way out."[37]

The Miracle of the Bells can best be described as a George Evans attempt to offset the image of Frank Sinatra as a mob associate and a cheating husband.[38] Bing Crosby, although untouched by any Mafia link, was at the very least a triple-A womanizer, if not in Sinatra's league. But he still retained the public's esteem, thanks, in large measure, to his sterling portrayal of Father Chuck O'Malley in *Going My Way* (1944) and *The Bells of St. Mary's* (1945). So, why not an ecclesiastical boost for Frank Sinatra? For one thing, the story line of Sinatra's picture can't compare with the wartime appeal of Crosby's two "Dial 'O' for O'Malley" blockbusters. In *The Miracle of the Bells*, a young actress dies from an unspecified disease after making just one film and is brought back to her coal-mining hometown in Pennsylvania for burial. As she lies in repose before the church altar, religious statues rotate, slowly and inexplicably, to face her coffin. Father Paul (Sinatra), flashlight in hand, investigates the "miracle" in the church basement and concludes that abandoned mine shafts may have caused the earth to settle and, therefore, the statues to move. But in the end, the good father is persuaded by the actress's press agent to accept a more heavenly explanation. Aside from the screenplay, Sinatra's acting may have had a part in the movie's dismal reviews when it was released, in March 1948. *Time* magazine, for one, noted that "Sinatra plays the priest with the grace and animation of a wooden Indian."[39]

In May 1947, Sinatra returned to the site of his first triumph as an entertainer, the Capitol in New York City, where he had performed as one of the "singing and dancing fools" in the Hoboken Four, on Major Bowes' Amateur Hour radio show. Thanks to Sinatra, who was always giving black musicians and entertainers a leg up, Sammy Davis, Jr., and the Will Mastin trio appeared as part of the under bill. Theater management wanted a more established act in that spot, but Sinatra insisted on using Davis' group and paying them more than they had ever before earned in the business — $1,250 a week.

Sinatra played another important venue that summer — Corpus Christi Church in Hasbrouck Heights, New Jersey. It was a command performance, one might say. The singer took time from his otherwise busy schedule to remember an old friend's help, early in his career. He sang at the wedding of Mafia boss Willie Moretti's daughter. Moretti, who employed Nancy Barbato Sinatra's cousin as one of his *capos*, likely took the occasion of his daughter's wedding to remind Sinatra of his marital responsibilities. Back home at Toluca Lake toward the end of that summer and into early fall, the Sinatras enjoyed some semblance of a stable home life. Nancy got pregnant once again, and this time, perhaps feeling more hopeful about her future with Frank, she would carry the baby to term. Unfortunately, her hopes in that regard would follow a familiar rocky path.

* * *

After Sinatra "went Hollywood," his press agent bios began referring to Hasbrouck Heights, New Jersey, an upscale Bergen County suburb of New York City, as his hometown. Hoboken, 12 miles to the south of Hasbrouck Heights, in seamy, corrupt Hudson County, apparently was no longer good enough. Indeed, Sinatra would maintain a love-hate relationship with his true hometown for most of his life. The reasons vary. He certainly was no slum kid — he grew up under comfortable financial circumstances and, his emotional wants notwithstanding, never wanted for material things. Still, his childhood memories had to have been painful in certain ways. Embarrassed by his mother's abortion business (as a teenager, he'd been barred from singing at a church dance because of Dolly's reputation) and lacking a strong male figure to emulate (thanks to Marty's unwillingness to challenge his wife on any issue), Frankie got expelled from high school at 15 and never held down a non-singing job for more than a week or two thereafter. He had no direction. After he started singing, he looked to the city across the river as his ticket out of the grimy, joyless place he grew up in. When his father threw him out of the house, at 17 or 18, because of his idleness, New York City is where Sinatra went, lasting only a week or so on his own before returning to the same old routine at home.

And yet, after Frank became a professional of sorts and went on the road with one of Major Bowes' vaudeville groups, he quit mid-tour, homesick for familiar surroundings. Perhaps it was innate — an Italian or Irish or Jewish or German immigrant thing luring one back to old neighborhoods, like the impulse that drives salmon to return to the specific streamlet of their hatching to spawn. Later in life, during a moment of reflection, Sinatra expressed the feeling this way: "When I was there [in Hoboken], I just wanted to get out. It took me a long time to realize how much of it I took with me."[40]

Even as her son tried to distance himself from his roots, Dolly Sinatra remained a force in Hoboken politics and life. In May 1947, she helped engineer the defeat of Mayor Bernard McFeely, a 16-year incumbent whom she had previously supported, and was instrumental in electing local businessman Fred M. DeSapio as the first Italian-American mayor in Hoboken history.[41] Perhaps in gratitude for Dolly's support in the election or, just as likely, in an effort to give his declining city a boost, Mayor DeSapio decided it was time for Hoboken to host a month-long celebration, the highlight of which would be a special day honoring its most famous native son. He decreed that October 30, 1947, would be "Sinatra Day" in Hoboken — surely a welcome respite from negative publicity Sinatra had been receiving.[42]

It was already a busy month for Sinatra, who spent October 19, 22, 24, 26, 29, and 31 in a Columbia recording studio in New York City, turning out one Axel Stordahl-arranged standard after another.[43] But he took Thursday, October 30, off and joined his mother, father, and Nancy on the steps of City Hall at 7 p.m. to accept a large wooden "key to the city" from Mayor DeSapio. Its inscription read: "To Frank Sinatra, from the Hearts of the Citizens of the City of Hoboken, New Jersey, 'Sinatra Day,' October 30, 1947."[44] A throng witnessed the event — some estimates put the crowd at 20,000 — and lined the thoroughfare as Frank took a triumphal ride up Washington Street, Hoboken's main drag, in the open cab of a firetruck driven by his father, still a member of the city's fire department. The weather did not cooperate, and Frank had to abandon the procession after 10 blocks, scurrying into a following limo to avoid the soaking rain. A planned outdoor ceremony and other festivities were hastily canceled, to the disappointment of many. Sinatra, overdue at a benefit in Madison Square Garden, rushed off.[45]

A few detractors have claimed that some of the good citizens of Hoboken were less than happy to see their illustrious compatriot on this occasion; indeed, there were stories of garbage being thrown at Frank as he rode up Washington Street and verbal insults being hurled his way. As a result, it has been alleged, Sinatra vowed never again to appear in public in the city of his birth.[46] Those accounts are undoubtedly wrong. Given the extensive press coverage of the Sinatra Day event, reports of such unruly behavior surely would have made it into contemporary newspaper accounts, but nothing of that nature appeared.[47] There *was* an incident that caused Sinatra to stay away from Hoboken for three decades, but Sinatra Day wasn't the occasion that precipitated the estrangement. That episode would come five years later.

* * *

Sinatra made two appearances at the Capitol Theatre in 1947, the second one running from November 16 through December 3, with the singer performing as many as eight shows a day. It was during one of those two Capitol engagements that old friend Lana Turner surfaced. In her autobiography, Turner asserts that she saw Frank a few times for drinks and dinner while he was appearing at the Capitol, but insisted that there was no romantic side to their meetings, despite what the gossip columnists might have written.[48] She had just finished shooting *Homecoming,* a romantic drama with Clark Gable, which would become one of MGM's highest-grossing pictures of 1948. Given Lana Turner's poor track record for veracity on the subject of her sexual relationship with Frank Sinatra, it's hard to imagine her and Sinatra abstaining, especially with Nancy 3,000 miles away. It wasn't in either of their natures.

* * *

An incident occurred in 1948 that, if true, had to have been one of the most reckless acts of Frank Sinatra's life. If true, it would also qualify as one of the most courageous. Nancy Sinatra first reported on the matter in her 1995 biography of her father. Her initial source was obviously Frank himself, but afterwards, two other Sinatra biographers, as well as a central figure in the plot, all independently confirmed and expanded on Nancy Sinatra's account.

J. Parnell Thomas, chairman of the House Un-American Activities Committee, once famously called Frank Sinatra "a sort of Mrs. Roosevelt in pants."[49] It was the ultra-conservative Thomas' attempt to sully the singer by likening him to former First Lady Eleanor Roosevelt, who, during her husband's time in office and even more so after his death, was this country's greatest champion of worldwide human rights. Sinatra probably considered the congressman's intended insult as a compliment, for he, too, at least on a macro scale, was a champion of human rights. And among those rights Sinatra supported most fervently were the rights of American Jews to live their lives free from discrimination and the rights of Jews everywhere, after the Holocaust, to have a homeland in which they could feel safe.

When news of the Nazi extermination camps broke during the war, Frank had hundreds of medals made, each bearing the image of St. Christopher on one side and the Star of David on the other. He then handed them out to servicemen, friends, policemen, and others until the supply was exhausted. The singer, throughout his career, was quick to accept requests to perform at benefits for Jewish causes. Later in life, when he learned that the most exclusive country club in Palm Springs excluded Jews, he became one of the few Gentiles to join the Jewish country club instead. Sinatra wasn't perfect — in a fit of anger, he might use an epithet that denigrated any number of minorities, ethnic or religious, but in his heart he did not have the slightest prejudice or bias. With those traits of character in mind, then, the story that Nancy Sinatra and the others related is entirely plausible.

In March 1948, Teddy Kollek, who would become the mayor of Jerusalem in 1965 and serve in that capacity until 1993, was a Haganah operative, working undercover in New York City on behalf of the newly created nation-state of Israel. The Haganah was Zionism's core of stealth fighters and intelligence gatherers, a sort of combined Central Intelligence Agency and Seal Team 6. At the time, Kollek's main purpose was to facilitate arms shipments to Israel so that fighters there could defend themselves against neighboring Arab countries, upset over the United Nations' creation of a Jewish homeland and vowing to crush the nascent state.

The United States had been the first country to recognize Israel, but that was as far as its support extended. In fact, our country placed an embargo on shipments of military supplies to Israel, complicating the Israelis' ability to defend their new nation. Kollek knew that he and his fellow Haganah members were being watched by the FBI, even as a ship's captain waited in New York harbor to receive cash funds — a reported $1 million — to buy arms in Mexico and then get those arms directly to Israel. Their problem was simple: how to deliver the money to the ship's captain without the FBI intercepting it.

The New York headquarters of the Haganah operatives were in a small hotel above the Copacabana nightclub, at 10 East 60th Street. As Kollek remembered, he and his agents frequented the Copa and became friends with Sinatra when he appeared there. As to that aspect of the story, Kollek was mistaken; except for a one-nighter to help out comedian Phil Silvers in September 1946, Sinatra didn't personally perform at the Copacabana until March 1950. What is more likely is that Kollek ran into Sinatra at the Copa in late March 1948 (records confirm Sinatra being in New York at that time) while Sinatra was there to watch another entertainer perform, something he often did when not engaged himself. Desperate to get the money to the ship's captain and knowing Sinatra's affinity for the Jewish cause, Kollek took a chance.

"I went downstairs [from the hotel] to the bar and Sinatra came over, and we were talking," Kollek later said. "I don't know what came over me, but I told him what I was doing in the United States and what my dilemma was. And in the early hours of the following morning I walked out the front door of the building with a satchel, and the Feds followed me. Out the back door went Frank Sinatra, carrying a paper bag filled with cash. He went down to the pier, handed it over, and watched the ship sail."[50]

Sinatra's mission remained secret for many years, but there would come a time when Kollek and other Israeli leaders would make known their debt to the singer — not officially, but in the way that they honored the man every time he visited their country.

It is unclear if Sinatra ever considered the risk he was assuming when he agreed to help Kollek. He had a history of acting on impulse, which got him into more than his fair share of scrapes. FBI Director J. Edgar Hoover was not an admirer of Sinatra's — in fact, he had an open file on the singer and would have reveled in a chance to connect him to illegal activity. Catching Sinatra in the act of aiding and abetting a foreign government to subvert the laws of the United States would have been quite a coup for Hoover, who wouldn't have hesitated to make an example of the singer. Fortunately for all concerned, that did not happen. This service Sinatra did for the State of Israel, in a way that did not harm his own country, was probably a source of great pride for him. Wisely, he kept it to himself until much later in life, when his cloak-and-dagger escapade could be celebrated instead of condemned.

* * *

At the end of 1947, James Petrillo, head of the American Federation of Musicians, had called for a nationwide strike against the record companies. The members of this union made up almost the entire pool of musicians used in studio recording sessions, and, as records featuring live concert and nightclub performances had not yet become a viable option, the strike sent the recording industry into a tailspin. It would last almost all of 1948. A few artists would try to record *a cappella*, with vocal groups backing up their own voices, as Sinatra had done in 1943 during a similar strike. Most would just wait out the strike.[51] The year proved disastrous for Sinatra's own production. He would record just 10 sides, using pre-recorded music or vocal groups as accompaniment while the strike endured. None of these records achieved commercial or critical success.[52]

Frank did get rave reviews for his performance as a father in 1948. After being absent for the births of his first two children — Nancy Jr. and Frankie — he finally was there for Nancy Sr. when she needed him most. The Sinatras were entertaining guests at their Toluca Lake home on the night of June 19 when Nancy, nine months pregnant, excused herself and went upstairs to their bedroom to lie down. Frank continued to play charades with the guests, checking on Nancy every once in a while. A little after 2 a.m., she told Frank it was time. He led her to the car and rushed to Cedars of Lebanon Hospital in Los Angeles. Despite Nancy's labor pains, the couple was experiencing for the first time one of the matchless joys of parenthood: the arrival of a baby. Nancy would later recall that Frank "had a good time" as he ran red lights getting her to the hospital.[53] Christina "Tina" Sinatra was born shortly thereafter, on Father's Day, Sunday, June 20. After seeing to Nancy and the baby, Frank returned to Toluca Lake, where their guests were still waiting for the news, which Frank delivered in style by acting out a charade announcing the birth.

Later that summer, Sinatra moved his growing family to a big new house on three acres, at 320 North Carolwood Drive in Holmby Hills.

Among their neighbors in this exclusive section of Los Angeles were Walt
Disney, the Humphrey Bogarts, and Loretta Young. It would be the last
home the Sinatras occupied as a cohesive family unit. The $250,000
expense for the new estate, added to the $150,000 Sinatra spent for a place
in Palm Springs the year before, put a strain on the singer's resources, at a
time when he was being dunned for back taxes by the IRS. Gossip columnist Sheila Graham estimated that Sinatra had made $11 million since
coming out as a solo act (more than $100 million in today's dollars); yet, he
was spending at a rate that left him broke. His profligacy in 1947 and 1948
would come back to haunt him two years later, when the remnants of his
career took a nosedive . . . into the Ava Gardner abyss.

8

"Jesus, he was like a god in those days, if gods can be sexy."

The torrid love affair between Frank Sinatra and Ava Gardner began with a bang — not the kind of bang you might imagine, but one involving guns, shots fired, cops rushing to the scene, and a night spent in police custody. They had danced with one another before this, when Ava and eccentric millionaire Howard Hughes ran into Frank and Lana Turner at a club in 1946. But that was all that happened — a few dances with the other guy's date and, perhaps, a stirring of attraction. And they may have had dinner together once before, just the two of them, but that was all that happened — dinner, a few tender moments, and, afterward, soft, tentative probing by two lonely souls.

The setting for the catalyst that would turn playful flirtation into passionate, lifelong love was Palm Springs, California, sometime during the spring or summer of 1949.[1] Twenty-six-year-old Gardner, with two Hollywood marriages already behind her, would describe her spur-of-the-moment date with the still-married 33-year-old Sinatra as "wonderful," all the more astounding for the fact that, aside from a little drunken groping, once again there had been no sex.[2] Ava and her sister Beatrice — or "Bappie," as she was called — were there in the desert resort on holiday from Ava's duties as a contract player for Metro-Goldwyn-Mayer. Bappie, divorced and older by two decades, had been Ava's almost constant companion and chaperone ever since the newly signed 18-year-old starlet had traveled cross-country in August 1941 from her native Grabtown, North Carolina, to the exciting but scary new world of Hollywood. Mickey Rooney, MGM's reigning superstar (and *superstud*) at the time, latched on to the virginal Gardner from the moment he set eyes on her, showering her with attention and claiming her for his own lustful ambitions.

Though flattered, Ava resisted the priapic Andy Hardy's advances. The more she refused to have sex with him outside of marriage, the more he wanted the woman that many considered the most beautiful addition to the Tinseltown firmament in years. And so, Rooney proposed marriage, repeatedly, meeting resistance from the doubtful Gardner each time. By Rooney's own count, he proposed 25 times in the few months they'd known each other before Ava finally agreed to marry him.[3] On January 10, 1942, Ava Gardner became the first of Mickey Rooney's eight wives. Upon meeting Ava on that happy occasion, Rooney's mother, with full knowledge of her son's chief interest in life, remarked to the new bride, "Well, I guess he ain't been in your pants yet."[4]

The Gardner-Rooney marriage would be short-lived, but it was during the marriage, in 1942, that Ava met Frank Sinatra for the first time. She and Mickey were having dinner — the location has been variously reported by Gardner as a Sunset Strip nightclub[5] and the MGM studio commissary[6] — when Sinatra stopped by their table to say hello. (Sinatra was still with Dorsey at the time and not yet signed by MGM, so the nightclub meeting locale seems more likely.) However brief the encounter, Ava Gardner was smitten, although it would take years for anything further to develop.

"Jesus, he was like a god in those days, if gods can be sexy," Gardner said of the Sinatra she met that day. "A cocky god, he reeked of sex — he said something banal, like: 'If I had seen you first, honey, I'd have married you myself.'"[7]

In between that first meeting of the future lovers and the 1949 *shoot-'em-up* escapade outside Palm Springs, Gardner had also married bandleader Artie Shaw, on October 17, 1945, becoming the fifth of *his* eight wives. Shaw, music genius that he was, treated Gardner like an insensate object created solely for his own pleasure. Ava was already insecure about her intellectual shortcomings, but her second husband, lacking the sweetness that Mickey Rooney had always exhibited, made her feel even more inadequate in that regard. Shaw's friend, screenwriter and novelist Budd Schulberg, put it bluntly.

"The trouble with Artie, he really was a male chauvinist," Schulberg said. "The only sort of thing he could think to say about [Ava] was what a beautiful ass she had. He would praise her physically but never showed much interest in her as a person, treated her like a dumbbell."[8] Despite the mental abuse Shaw heaped upon Ava during their brief marriage (he divorced her in 1946), he would maintain a Svengali-like hold over her for years to come.

Gardner's depression over the breakup of her marriage to Shaw probably hastened her descent into alcoholism and promiscuity. She took up with Howard Hughes, until he got physical with her and she responded in kind.[9] Brief affairs with actors David Niven, Kirk Douglas, Howard Duff, Robert Taylor, Robert Walker, and Robert Mitchum followed.[10] But it was the drinking that threatened to destroy her. As Gardner biographer Lee Server put it, "Everyone drank then, and many drank too much, but [Ava] had a fierce capacity even by the high standards of 1940s America. She had never stopped hating the taste [of alcohol] . . . but through the years in Hollywood she had come to crave the effects."[11]

On that fateful night in 1949, Ava and Bappie were attending a party at the Palm Springs home of producer Darryl F. Zanuck when Ava saw Frank Sinatra across the room, "grinning [at her] like an excited young boy."[12] Her thoughts went back to their past encounters and to the "sexy god" image she had formed of the singer, seven years before. He was still tremendously attractive, and his reputation as a womanizer was well known. Ava and Frank were both drinking heavily and becoming more flirtatious as the evening wore on. Finally, they took off together, leaving Bappie to find her way back to the vacation home she and Ava were renting. Ava managed to filch a bottle of liquor from Zanuck's bar before she and Frank climbed into his Cadillac convertible and drove into the night, passing the bottle back and forth amid raucous laughter.

After a while, the highly intoxicated couple — intoxicated with booze *and* with each other — came to the desert town of Indio, California, which appeared to be shut down for the night. Frank pulled over and reached into his glove compartment. He removed first one handgun, passing it to Ava, then another for himself. Both were fully loaded. Attempting to demonstrate his prowess with the weapon, Frank took aim at a traffic light, fired, and hit it squarely, getting a rise from Ava, who joined in the fun. As they slowly drove through the town, they shot out street lamps and storefront windows along the main drag. One of the happy-go-lucky pair managed to graze an unfortunate passer-by with a misdirected shot. Police soon arrived at the scene of the commotion and took the two miscreants into custody. "We were both cockeyed," Gardner would later admit. "We shot out street lights, store windows."[13]

At 3 a.m., Sinatra placed a call from Indio police headquarters to Jack Keller, the West Coast assistant to publicist George Evans, awakening him from a sound sleep. Keller picked up the telephone in his Los Angeles home and heard his client's voice. "Jack," Sinatra said, "we're in trouble."[17]

After listening to Sinatra relate the story of what had to have been the most idiotic, reckless stunt ever pulled by a client, Keller sprang into action. He called a hotel manager he knew and convinced the man to empty his hotel's safe of cash (around $30,000) and to lend it to him short-term, until the banks opened. Keller then chartered a plane to take him to Indio, landing as close as he could to the small town. Upon arrival at the police station, he spoke privately with Sinatra and Gardner, chastising them for their incredibly irresponsible behavior. If the errant bullet that grazed the passer-by had veered an inch or two from its actual trajectory, killing the man instead of slightly wounding him, both Sinatra's and Gardner's careers would have been finished. Keller had a reputation for taking no guff from his clients, some of whom were among the biggest names in show business (the comedy team of Dean Martin and Jerry Lewis, for example[15]). On this night, his anger palpable, the press agent held nothing back. But first, he went about saving Frank Sinatra's hide.

The two arresting officers each got $2,000, and the police chief, on hand to personally supervise the disposition of a case involving his town's two most illustrious jailbirds, received $5,000. Keller went to the local hospital, where he paid out $10,000 on the spot to the injured bystander, who didn't know at the time who had fired the shot that creased his belly — a good thing for Keller, who otherwise might not have had enough cash to buy the man's silence. Keller, shelling out another $1,000, had the hospital records destroyed. Each shopkeeper who lost a plate-glass window got $1,000, and the town itself got $2,000 to replace street lamps and a traffic light.[16] After the beleaguered press agent loaded Sinatra and Gardner into the chartered plane for the short flight back to Los Angeles, he took Sinatra aside and advised him to stop seeing Gardner and to go home to his wife and three children.

Over the ensuing days, Sinatra stewed over Keller's effrontery in telling him how to lead his life. He and George Evans, on the East Coast, went back and forth over the phone — Sinatra complaining about Keller, and Evans defending his associate. Finally, egged on by Ava, their affair now consummated and at full throttle, Sinatra demanded that Evans fire Keller, or else. Evans refused, and Sinatra thereupon fired Evans, his press agent for the last seven years — the man who had expertly guided Sinatra's meteoric rise as a solo act, getting him out of one jam after another and holding his hand during what seemed like an endless roller-coaster ride of emotions. Evans would be dead within three months, of a heart attack that his family believed was brought on by the stress of his association with Frank Sinatra and by the breach that finally ended that association.

"My father kind of looked on Frank as a sort of son and a creation of his at the same time," Phil Evans, George's eldest son, recalled years later. "He was a hero-builder and in a sense a worshipper as well. He didn't like to admit that anything would tarnish. He covered up a lot . . . but the drain on him during those years left some of us in the family with a sour taste. . . . the price was very great in terms of stress, anxiety and pressure."[17]

Sinatra canceled a nightclub engagement as soon as he heard the news and flew to New York for the funeral. Miserable over the premature death of the 48-year-old Evans — and made even more disconsolate by the thought that he may have been the cause — Sinatra immediately arranged for the widow to be paid $14,000, money he still owed to his former press agent after the firing but had been withholding, and for young Phil Evans to be put on his payroll. Guilt was then, and always would be, an important motivator in Sinatra's life.

* * *

Metro-Goldwyn-Mayer celebrated its silver anniversary in January 1949 by assembling all of its illustrious players — 57 in all, including Lassie — for an imposing group photograph. Ava Gardner, one of MGM's most promising young stars, drove alone to the historic event. Along the way, she encountered Frank Sinatra in a strange but exciting moment, which she described in her 1990 memoir.

"As I drove to the studio, a car sped past me, swung in front, and slowed down so much I had to pass it myself," Gardner wrote. "The car overtook me again and repeated the process. Having done this about three times, the car finally pulled alongside me, the grinning driver raised his hat and sped away to that same photo session. That was Frank. He could even flirt in a car."[18]

At the MGM soundstage where the group photo was to be taken, Ava saw Frank again, of course, and one can presume that the two exchanged glances, if nothing else. But there would not have been any opportunity to talk — that would come later.

Frank was still acting the part of a happily married father of three — publicly, at least — when he engaged in his "flirtation by auto" with Ava. But no matter how often George Evans cranked out warm and fuzzy press releases and family portraits of a smiling Frank huddled around Nancy Sr. and the three little Sinatras, each one cuter than the next, nothing was going to curtail his client's womanizing. For the time being, at least, Frank was being discreet about it.

Ava was no saint when it came to sexual liaisons.[19] She was intrigued by Sinatra's apparent interest, but there was still the MGM morals clause to worry about. Louis B. Mayer had confronted Lana Turner with the clause in 1946, in an attempt to break up the simultaneous affairs she was then carrying on with Sinatra and actor Tyrone Power, both married. Ava was conscious of the risk she ran if she took up with Sinatra, no matter how attracted to him she might feel. Turner had been called on the carpet for dating married men, and Gardner, at that point in her career, was no Lana Turner in box-office appeal.

The language in the clause was so subjective that Mayer could give it whatever interpretation he chose: "The artist agrees to conduct himself with due regard to public conventions and morals and agrees that he will not do or commit any act or thing that will degrade him in society, or bring him into public hatred, contempt, scorn, or ridicule, that will tend to shock, insult, or offend the community or ridicule public morals or decency, or prejudice the producer (MGM) or the motion picture industry in general."[20] Pronouns used in legal documents in those days didn't bother to acknowledge the feminine gender — the masculine pronoun in the contract applied equally to both males and females, even if the application of those words didn't. In the movie business, it was the female star who was most often chastised for deviating from "public conventions and morals," etc. etc., in contravention of *his* obligation to conduct *himself* appropriately.

It wasn't surprising, then, that it was Frank who made the first move, not too long after the MGM group photo. The two had run into each other a few times before he finally asked her out for "drinks and dinner."

"I looked at him," Gardner wrote, describing her reaction. "I damn well knew he was married, though the gossip columns always had him leaving Nancy for good, and married men were definitely not high on my hit parade. But he was handsome, with his thin, boyish face, the bright blue eyes, and this incredible grin. And he was so enthusiastic and invigorated, clearly pleased with life in general, himself in particular, and, at that moment, *me*."[21]

They went out that night and, afterward, he took her to a friend's apartment, apparently prearranged, to be alone. They kissed, deeply, and were about to take the next step when Ava pulled back. Despite the heavy drinking both had engaged in, something didn't feel right to her. Her attraction to Frank hadn't diminished — she just felt, for whatever reason, that the time and place were wrong.[22] And to Sinatra's credit, he held his temper in check and didn't object to her leaving. They wouldn't see each other for a while, until that night in the desert.

* * *

Despite Frank Sinatra's "enthusiastic and invigorated" demeanor when he approached Ava Gardner in early 1949, he must have realized that his career was in a downturn. His only two picture releases in 1948 — *The Miracle of the Bells* and *The Kissing Bandit* — had bombed, both with critics and at the box office. More important, he was no longer the nation's top male vocalist, the aspect of his career that mattered most to him and that was his bread and butter.[23] A *Billboard* poll at the end of 1948 ranked him fifth, after Al Jolson (a 1920s singer, often in blackface, who was seeing a revival of his earlier popularity), Bing Crosby, Perry Como, and Billy Eckstine.[24] Sinatra's record production would pick up in 1949, but not one of the 25 sides he made that year would enhance his legacy. At one Hollywood session on February 28, 1949, he recorded two popular songs, both from the hit Broadway musical *South Pacific*. *Down-Beat* described Frank's recording of "Some Enchanted Evening" as being "without intimacy," perhaps the unkindest cut anyone could inflict on the man many considered the *master* of vocal intimacy. Frank's rendition of "Bali Ha'i," according to that same magazine, "very seldom came to life."[25]

Sinatra's long affiliation with *Your Hit Parade* ended in May 1949, partly as a result of his exasperation at having to sing the type of songs that were then winning the public's favor. The show's sponsor, Lucky Strike, re-signed him in September for a show with a different format — a 15-minute, five-times-a-week show called *Light Up Time*. It was more work than the once-a-week *Your Hit Parade*, but Sinatra needed the money *and* the public's attention. Already in 1949, Billy Eckstine was topping Sinatra in the annual *Metronome* poll.[26]

In an effort to resurrect Sinatra's fading box-office appeal and recapture the magic of 1945's *Anchors Aweigh*, MGM teamed him up again with Gene Kelly for two new pictures, both filmed in 1948.

Take Me Out to the Ball Game, which premiered on March 10, 1949, had Sinatra and Kelly starring as two professional players in the early days of baseball who also performed as song-and-dance men on the vaudeville stage during off-season. "Freed from the constraints of roles as priest and kissing bandits," Tom Santopietro wrote, "real-life sports fan Sinatra seems emotionally and physically liberated by the sheer physicality of the role."[27] The movie traded on the familiar theme of Sinatra as country bumpkin, helped along in his relationships with the opposite sex by a worldlier Kelly. It opened to mixed reviews: *Hollywood Reporter* said that "Sinatra sings and gags his way through a most pleasant role"; but *Time* magazine called the picture "a lazy, Technicolored cine-musical."[28]

On the Town debuted in December 1949 and was, by far, the more successful movie. It put Sinatra and Kelly back in sailor suits and turned them loose on shore leave in New York City (along with accomplished comedic actor and *Ball Game* co-star Jules Munshin) in a song-and-dance romp based on the hit Broadway musical of the same name. (It would be Sinatra's last dancing role.) The film's opening rendition of "New York, New York" is one of the most enduring moments in the history of Hollywood musicals. The movie also had the distinction of being the first musical with all of its production numbers filmed outdoors on location.[29] Sinatra's earlier movie, *It Happened in Brooklyn*, did shoot his Brooklyn Bridge sequence on the bridge itself, but that was just one scene. *On the Town* went to town, so to speak, with its New York City locales.

The uptick that this latest movie gave to Sinatra's career wouldn't last; in fact, four months after its release, MGM terminated Sinatra's contract — the culmination of a number of things. During the film's production in late 1948, Sinatra made a wisecrack that offended Louis B. Mayer. Mayer had been seen around the studio back lot nursing an injury, which he attributed to his having fallen off a horse. Sinatra put forth a different version. "He didn't fall off a horse," Frank was heard to say, "he fell off Ginny Simms."[30] Simms, an actress, was Mayer's mistress at the time, and Mayer, the arbiter of Hollywood's toughest morals clause, didn't take kindly to this joke at the expense of his own morals, especially from a star whose glitter was rapidly diminishing. He called Sinatra into his office and confronted him.

"So," Mayer said, "I hear you've been making jokes about my lady friend." Very seldom would Sinatra's bravado withstand a challenge from someone more powerful than he, and this was not one of those times. "Yeah, I wish I could take that back," Sinatra said. "I'm so sorry. I wish I'd never said anything so stupid."[31]

After production on the movie wrapped, another flap developed between Sinatra and the studio. Among musicians and actors, especially temperamental ones like Frank Sinatra at this stage of his career, billing was everything.[32] Where would his or her name appear in the movie's credits or on a theater marquee or in ads or handbills for a show? Would one's name appear above the movie title, the preferred spot? Failing that, would he or she come first in the listing of the starring cast? Placement of the actor's name was considered a status symbol, in a town where status meant everything. With *Take Me Out to the Ball Game*, Frank Sinatra got top billing over Gene Kelly, his friend since the days of *Anchors Aweigh* but a rival nonetheless. *Ball Game* had received a less than spectacular reception when it premiered in March 1949, and that fact, along with the other question marks then surrounding Sinatra's career, led Mayer and his studio executives to reverse billing for *On the Town* and to put Kelly's name over Sinatra's.[33] Frank was fuming over that decision, but there was an even more substantive problem.

Frank Sinatra and Ava Gardner, throwing all caution to the wind, were now being seen in public, linked as a couple. On December 8, while in New York City together, they went to a performance of *Gentlemen Prefer Blondes*, a new Broadway musical. They were with other friends and probably thought they could blur the appearance of who was with whom, and might have got away with it, except for the fact that gossip columnists also caught them going in and out of Hampshire House, a luxury hotel where Sinatra's pal Manie Sacks maintained a suite of rooms. It didn't help that on December 12, Frank's 34th birthday, they were also seen together at the Copacabana, where Frank's friends threw a party for him. Nancy Sinatra soon read about the whole affair, but said nothing . . . not yet, anyway. It would take one more display of her husband's extreme indifference to her feelings to blow the lid off things. That came right after George Evans' funeral in New York, on January 27, 1950.

The next day, Frank flew to Houston, directly from New York, for an engagement at the Shamrock Hotel, the newest venue in Texas. It was a big deal — not only was Sinatra opening the hotel, but it would be his first nightclub appearance in more than four years. Already outed in gossip columns, Ava Gardner went to Houston to lend her support to the man she now considered her lover. She had actually asked permission of the studio to join Sinatra in Houston, but Mayer refused. She went anyway.[34]

During the Shamrock engagement, the mayor of Houston invited Frank and Ava to dinner at the finest Italian restaurant in that city. A *Hous-*

ton Post photographer showed up halfway through the meal, perhaps invited by the mayor or restaurant owner, each of whom would have welcomed the publicity. Sinatra exploded when he saw the photographer, lunged for the camera, and created a scene. The exposure of him and Ava together was only magnified by the outburst, appearing in papers all over the country, including the *Los Angeles Times*.[35]

With George Evans no longer around to moderate Frank Sinatra's behavior and to act as not only a buffer with the press but also a reassuring presence for Nancy Sinatra, the marriage finally succumbed to the inevitable. Sinatra sent two of his go-fers to the Holmby Hills house to pick up his clothes and things, and Nancy had the locks changed. On February 14, 1950, Valentine's Day, she announced that she and Frank had separated. There was not yet any talk of a divorce.[36]

The news of the separation wasn't lost on Willie Moretti. Like most mob bosses of his era, Moretti praised the sanctity of marriage while keeping mistresses on the side, there when you needed them but otherwise out of sight. Using his alias, Moretti sent his friend Frank a telegram: "I am very much surprised what I have been reading in the newspapers between you and your darling wife. Remember you have a decent wife and children. You should be very happy. Regards to all, Willie Moore."[37]

Ava had to face the music with Louis B. Mayer. Called to his office, she expected the worse, but in the end, all she got was a tongue-lashing. "You were denied permission to leave Los Angeles," Mayer said, reminding her of their conversation before she went to Houston, "because I knew what was going on. Have you read the papers? Do you know what Hedda and Louella are saying about you? Have you read your fan mail? They're calling you Jezebel and a bitch. A home wrecker."[38]

Gardner was somewhat cavalier about the hubbub she and Frank were causing in the press. "I didn't understand then and, frankly, don't understand now," she said years later in her memoir, "why there should be this prurient mass hysteria about a male and female climbing into bed and doing what comes naturally." But it wasn't the newspaper coverage that would put a strain on their relationship, Ava claimed. In what may have been the biggest understatement on that subject, she said: "Neither one of us had exactly what you could call a tranquil temperament. Both Frank and I were high-strung people, possessive and jealous and liable to explode fast."[39]

Now that the "high-strung," "possessive and jealous" Sinatra and Gardner were together as a couple, for the entire world to see, the *explosions* would commence almost immediately, the first of which involved, once again, a gun.

9

"He opened his mouth to sing and nothing came out. Not a sound."

As the premier nightspot in New York City, the Copacabana had been packing club-goers in for 10 years before Frank Sinatra made his debut there, in March 1950. Jules Podell and Jack Entratter ran the establishment on behalf of the owner of record, Monte Prosser; but "the main money and muscle behind the scenes" was Frank Costello,[1] heir to Lucky Luciano and head of New York's most influential crime family. Right after Sinatra broke records at the Paramount in early 1943, his agent tried to book him into the Copa, but Jules Podell turned thumbs down on the brash young singer and his swooning bobby-soxers, disparaging them as hardly in the same class as the Copa's elegant patrons. Sinatra then demonstrated his appeal with sophisticated adult audiences, too, wowing them at the Riobamba, a rival New York nightclub owned by gangster Louis "Lepke" Buchalter. Frank Costello was one of Sinatra's biggest Mafia benefactors, along with Willie Moretti and Angelo "Gyp" DeCarlo — all the more reason to wonder why Sinatra hadn't made a Copa appearance before this.[2]

In any event, the scheduled eight-week engagement at the Copa promised to be a pivotal moment for Sinatra, a chance to breathe new life into his lagging career, and the normally self-confident singer was a nervous wreck. It would be his first appearance, other than a one-night benefit in Los Angeles, since the breakup of his marriage six weeks earlier; it would also represent Sinatra's much anticipated return to a nightclub stage, after an absence of five years. In fact, his last club engagement had been at the Riobamba in 1945. Since moving to California in 1944, Frank had been concentrating on acting in the movies, making records, and crossing female stars off the list on his dressing room door.

Even as Frank Sinatra's career seemed on the skids, Ava Gardner's was in its ascendancy. She had already appeared in 16 pictures since arriving in Hollywood in 1941, including standout performances in *The Killers* (1946), co-starring Burt Lancaster, *The Hucksters* (1947), co-starring Clark Gable, and *One Touch of Venus* (1948), co-starring Robert Walker. Meatier roles would follow, but in early 1950, she was slated to begin work in Europe on *Pandora and the Flying Dutchman*, co-starring James Mason. It gave her a perfect opportunity to stop off in New York City in March, on her way to London, and give moral support to Frank, who needed all the support he could get.

Sinatra had arrived early to begin rehearsals before the March 28 Copa opening. He rented a two-bedroom luxury suite at the Hampshire House (one bedroom, ostensibly, for Ava and her sister Bappie, and one bedroom for himself). He and Ava had stayed in Manie Sacks' suite at the same hotel a few months earlier. The hotel was supposed to be quiet and discreet, a place to avoid the prying eyes of the press, but that hadn't held true the previous December and it didn't hold true in March. New York's *Journal-American*, a Hearst paper, ran a story about Frank and Ava cohabitating there, with the headline "Stars Staying at Same Hotel."[3] Columnist Earl Wilson asked Ava for an interview to give her a chance to explain her and Frank being together, but she declined and issued a statement instead.

"The main reason I am in New York is because I am on my way to make a picture," Gardner said in her statement, which she showed to Sinatra before its release. "The main reason Frankie is here is because he is scheduled to open at the Copacabana. Inasmuch as Frank is officially separated from his wife, I believe I have a right to be seen with him."[4] The statement made no mention of public sightings of the couple in December and January, *before* the separation. Sinatra added his postscript to Gardner's press release: "The fact that I have had a few dates with her means nothing. Why shouldn't I have dates? I'm separated from my wife. I don't intend to sit home alone."[5] George Evans must have been spinning in his grave at the thought of the hole his former client was digging for himself. Rubbing the press's nose into the mess of a scandal is never a good strategy. It only encourages more coverage.

Jimmy Silvani, a cousin to Sinatra bodyguard Al Silvani, was part of the entourage backstage on opening night. Years later, he described an almost pathetic Frank Sinatra on that evening, far removed from the tough-guy image the singer had always so assiduously promoted.

"Sinatra practically collapsed before that first show at the Copa," Silvani said. "He kept saying, 'My career is over. I'm fucking washed up, and now I have to go out there and face those people – the same goddamn people who aren't buying my records, who aren't seeing my movies.' He was taking a lot of pills at this time, pills to get up, pills to relax, pills to go to sleep."[6] New York socialite Mary LaSalle-Thomas, a friend of Ava's, also commented on Frank's pill-popping. "He was on so many different prescriptions at that time," she said, "for his throat, for his back, for his head, to sleep — *especially* to sleep — he was practically an addict."[7]

If Sinatra's nerves were shot, perhaps the pills had something to do with it, but he was also suffering a crisis of confidence — something he'd never had to deal with before, no matter what the career challenge. It didn't help that 9-year-old Nancy Jr. was calling practically every night to tearfully ask Daddy to come home. Her pleas were likely coached by Nancy Sr., but who could blame her? She still entertained the hope that Frank would return to her, encouraged in that thought, no doubt, by the $10,000 mink coat he'd sent just two days before, for her birthday.[8] She should have understood her husband by then, his motivation by guilt in practically all things, including expensive gifts. Nancy had sent him a telegram that day ("Best of luck on your opening night, Love, Nancy"), which only added to his stress.[9]

Sinatra was sitting in front of his dressing room mirror just before going on, according to Jimmy Silvani, "staring at himself, mumbling, 'You can do this, Frank. You can do this, pal. Just go out there and do this.'" That's when Ava walked in, dressed to the nines. She went over to stand right behind

Frank and stared at the mirror image of them both. "Francis Albert Sinatra," she declared for all to hear, "you are the greatest goddamned entertainer who ever walked the face of this earth. I believe in you, I love you. And I salute you." She lifted a champagne glass to their image in the mirror and then said, "Now I want you to get on out there, Francis, and prove me right."[10]

Frank rose and embraced her, buoyed by her words and gesture. And then he went "out there," only to experience one of his toughest nights in show business. The reception should have been better. Many of his mobster friends were there at the ringside tables they always commanded, including Frank Costello, Willie Moretti, and Joe Fischetti. Dolly and Marty Sinatra were there, joined by Sinatra stalwarts Phil Silvers, Manie Sacks, and Sammy Cahn.[11]

The show didn't start well: Sinatra unthinkingly chose "Nancy (With the Laughing Face)" as his opening number, a song written for daughter Nancy by Phil Silvers, but some in the crowd sniggered anyway, glancing toward the very conspicuous Ava and knowing all about Frank leaving Nancy for her. Later that night, Ava was furious. "Did you have to sing that fucking song?" she demanded. "It made me feel like a real fool."

"It's been a good luck song for years," Frank pleaded. "I sing it in almost every big show. It doesn't mean anything." Ava wasn't mollified: "Well, don't expect me to sit out there every night and get laughed at," she responded. "Either the song goes or I go."[12]

Not surprisingly, the song went, not Ava.

Frank's magical hold on an intimate nightclub audience, so apparent at his Riobamba engagement five years earlier, was gone. When one table wouldn't quiet down during a number, he finished the song, then asked, "Am I speaking too loud for you ladies?" After a few more songs failed to gain the audience's full attention, he was forced into making a general plea: "This is my opening night. C'mon, give me a break." Ava was incensed. "Those bastards," she later complained. "They wouldn't cut him a break. He was trying so hard. Fucking New Yorkers. They're a tough crowd."[13]

Frank's friends raved about his performance, but newspaper critics were less enthusiastic. The *Herald Tribune*'s review was typical: "Whether temporarily or otherwise, the music that used to hypnotize the bobby-soxers . . .

is gone from the throat. Vocally, there isn't the same old black magic there used to be . . . ." *Variety,* the show business chronicle, was slightly more temperate: "Today he may have less voice than ever before, but he has a compensating quality that considerably makes up for his vocal void. That would be salesmanship."[14] Ava returned to the hotel suite one afternoon after shopping, only to hear Frank shouting into the telephone, apparently at someone who had authored a particularly nasty review. "You wouldn't know a good performance if it bit you in the ass," Sinatra screamed. "Why do you have to get so goddamn personal, anyway? I can take the criticism, but you ruin it by getting so personal."[15]

Ava stuck it out in the Copa showroom for 10 nights, enduring disrespectful audiences and unwanted familiarity from Sinatra's gangster friends, whom she not-so-secretly detested. She spent the 11th night, or part of it, with ex-husband Artie Shaw, who was then living in New York City.[16]

There are several versions of what happened next, all with a familiar starting point — Frank and Ava quarrelling. Ava's version had them in a restaurant, with Frank making eyes at another woman during dinner and the temperamental actress storming out. She returned to the Hampshire House and phoned Shaw before going over to his apartment, looking not for a romantic tryst (he was living with a girlfriend) but for a friendly shoulder to cry on. Shaw told her to come right over, which she did. But back at the hotel suite, she'd left her phone book open to Shaw's page, and that's how Frank was able to follow her there.[17] In Shaw's account, he invited both Ava and Frank to a party at his apartment, but only Ava showed up.

Sinatra was intensely jealous of Gardner's former husband and the influence he still had on her. Shortly after Ava arrived at Shaw's place, Frank showed up, with Hank Sanicola in tow.[18] Frank didn't go any place where his physical well-being might be in jeopardy without at least one of his burly employees accompanying him. Shaw was polite and offered Sinatra a drink, but Frank, after seeing for himself that there was nothing sexual going on, with Shaw's girlfriend present, turned and left without a word.

Ava went back to their hotel 20 minutes later. Frank was already in his room, with the door closed, so she sat for a while, by herself, in the suite's living room. Then the phone rang.

"It was Frank [calling from his room], and I'll never forget his voice,"

Gardner wrote in her 1990 memoir. "He said, 'I can't stand it any longer. I'm going to kill myself — now!'" Ava heard a tremendous explosion in her ear. Their escapade in the desert the year before had taught her the sound of a gunshot. She threw down the phone and ran to Frank's room. "I didn't know what I expected to find — a body?" she said. "And there was a body lying on the bed. Oh God, was he dead? I threw myself on it saying, 'Frank, Frank . . .' And the face, with a rather pale little smile, turned toward me, and the voice said, 'Oh, hello.'" [19] Feigning suicide, Sinatra had fired a shot through his pillow and into the mattress.

"I remember my feelings very well," Gardner said. "They were not of anger or frustration, they were of overwhelming relief. He was alive, thank God, he was alive. I held him tightly to me." [20] She didn't ask him any questions, knowing what had motivated him — the jealousy, the childish attempt to get her attention. Behavior that would become all too familiar.

The phone rang in their suite — it was the hotel desk clerk, asking about shots other guests had heard and wondering if Mr. Sinatra had heard them, too. (Several witnesses reported hearing two shots.) Their answer was no, of course, but now Frank and Ava had to get rid of the gun, pillow, and mattress, in case people showed up to investigate and their denials were not believed. Bappie took the gun and hid it under a pillow in her own room. Hank Sanicola, a floor below, was called; he came to their room immediately and dragged the telltale pillow and mattress down a back stairway to his own room, just moments before two policemen arrived. [21]

According to Gardner, who wrote the only firsthand account of the incident, the officers were invited in and Frank spoke to them; then they left, accepting Sinatra's assurances that nothing had happened in his suite. As any trained law enforcement officer knows, when a gun is fired in an enclosed space, like a hotel room, or even a hotel suite, the gunpowder smell will linger for hours and also engulf the shooter. The cops had to have realized that the shot or shots came from Sinatra's hotel suite. No one appeared to be hurt, so they let the matter slide.

There were no further eruptions between Frank and Ava — at least none that made the papers. Within a day or two, Ava left for England to begin filming *Pandora*. She had already received numerous reminders from Louis B. Mayer that she was late in reporting to the set.

In a rare moment of self-reflection, Sinatra later confided to Hank Sanicola that his obsession with Ava Gardner was getting the best of him. "I
think I'm slipping," Frank said. "Man, this dame has gotten to me so much,
I'm out of control. How could I have done that? What the hell was I thinking?"[22]

The Hampshire House incident would be just the first of four faked suicide attempts by Frank Sinatra, or bungled real attempts, before the
Sinatra-Gardner affair played out its final scenes.

* * *

During the first few months of 1950, Frank Sinatra endured what might
today be termed a "perfect storm" — a series of distressing events that threatened not only his career but also his mental and physical well-being.[23] In
fact, those and subsequent events brought the cocky singer to his knees for
most of 1950, 1951, and 1952, a period he once referred to as his own personal "Dark Ages."[24] To borrow from one of Sinatra's signature songs — a
crowd pleaser he would later call his "national anthem" — *the record shows
he took the blows*, but the "My Way" swagger we associate with Frank Sinatra was nowhere to be found.[25]

Publicist George Evans had been fired by Sinatra late in 1949, so his
sudden death in January 1950 had nothing, technically, to do with the
singer's career. Still, Sinatra blamed himself for the 48-year-old's heart
attack. The separation from Nancy and the children, made "official" by
Nancy's phone call to Hedda Hopper on February 14,[26] added to Frank's
guilt feelings, even if the seriousness of his affair with Ava Gardner, and the
openness with which they carried it on, precluded any other outcome.
Nancy's usual tolerance for her husband's dalliances had reached its breaking point.

While these first two setbacks may seem more personal than professional, in 1950s America the two realms were treated as one, especially by
gossip columnists Louella Parsons and Hedda Hopper, both with reader-
ships in the tens of millions. As to Sinatra's blatant in-your-face womanizing,
beginning in 1946 with Marilyn Maxwell and Lana Turner, George Evans
had always been on hand to tamp down the resulting fallout. Now, with
Ava, Evans wasn't around to spin the tabloid press's coverage. Gardner took

the brunt, as the "other woman" usually does, but Sinatra's record sales were suffering, too. Unfortunately, the man most responsible for Sinatra's success as a recording artist, besides the singer himself, picked this moment to leave Columbia Records.

Manie Sacks was Frank Sinatra's most trusted mentor, in addition to being one of his dearest friends — Frank had asked him to be godfather to his only son, Frank Jr., in 1944. It was Manie who had helped engineer the deal that eventually freed Sinatra from Tommy Dorsey's onerous claim on future earnings. In the same issue in which George Evans' obituary appeared, *Variety* announced that Sacks was moving to RCA Victor Records, for a lot more money than he had been earning at Columbia. Though not generally known at the time, Manie had tried to take Sinatra along with him, but RCA Victor nixed that idea. Executives there correctly saw Manie's once-great protégé as too big a risk to their bottom line. They didn't have to look further than Frank's declining record sales or to the fall in his popularity ratings in *DownBeat* and *Metronome* magazines. Frank didn't begrudge Sacks this opportunity to make a better living; they would remain friends until Sacks' death, in February 1958.[27] The real blow came in the form of Manie's replacement. Mitch Miller was named Columbia's new A & R man — head of artists and repertoire and, therefore, arbiter over the pop-singles end of the business.[28]

Miller and Sinatra, both music geniuses in their own right, would prove to be a disaster together, as inimical to a smooth working relationship as the proverbial oil and water. Their personalities didn't mix — both were A-types who wanted to control every aspect of a recording session. Neither did their tastes in music coincide. Ironically, Miller's view of popular music more closely matched the record-buying public's preferences in the early 1950s, not Sinatra's. While still at Mercury Records, before moving to Columbia, it was Miller who guided singer Frankie Laine through his recording of the frenetically paced, whip-cracking "Mule Train," which became one of the biggest hits of 1949. Laine and Vic Damone would both move from Mercury to Columbia with Miller, so great was their respect for his commercial judgment, which, at times, ran to the gimmicky.[29]

Sinatra resisted Miller's attempts to move him from a mostly ballads repertoire to one with a greater mix of up-tempo songs, the type of records that were then selling. (As Columbia's hottest recording artist in the 1940s, Sinatra had in his contract the final say on all song choices.) On one occasion, early in their relationship, Miller went to the trouble of arranging the music for two new songs he wanted Sinatra to record. He hired musicians and brought Sinatra to a New York studio to hear the songs, thinking they might be hits. Sinatra listened, then said, "I won't do any of this crap," before walking out of the studio.[30] Miller called in a new singer he had recently discovered, a fellow named Al Cernick, to make the recordings instead of Sinatra. Both sides — "The Roving Kind" and "My Heart Cries for You" — became big sellers for the newcomer, who by then had changed his name to Guy Mitchell, the last name in honor of Mitch Miller.[31]

Sinatra relented at times and tried to do it Miller's way, turning out a number of rhythm-based sides in 1950, like "American Beauty Rose," "When You're Smiling," "It's Only a Paper Moon," "My Blue Heaven," and "Should I?"[32] — all good tunes, but none of them hits, which only rankled Sinatra more. In one ego-clashing session, Sinatra told Miller to get out of the recording studio. When Miller did not comply, Sinatra ordered Hank Sanicola to bodily remove him. But other Columbia artists, like Rosemary Clooney, were taking Miller's advice, sometimes grudgingly, and making hit records — Clooney, with "Come On-a My House" (a song she hated but recorded under duress) and "Mambo Italiano."[33]

With his records not selling and Columbia refusing to advance him more money (he was already into them for $200,000 that he'd borrowed to pay back taxes), Sinatra was experiencing financial pressure — not for the first time, because his reckless spending often left him in that condition. Now, it was becoming acute. Nancy had been awarded $2,750 a month in separate maintenance and some cash (later, she would get more), plus the Holmby Hills house and one of the Cadillacs, even as Frank was doing little to economize. Instead, he began working harder. While still performing at the Copacabana in April 1950, as part of his original eight-week engagement, he took on the added burden of daytime performances at the Capitol Theatre, all while keeping up his five-times-a-week radio gig for *Light Up Time.* The strain on his voice was becoming evident to everyone. "It was pathetic," a Columbia recording engineer remarked. "Sinatra would open his mouth and nothing would come out but a croak."[34]

April was a busy month for Frank in Columbia's New York recording studio — he recorded eight sides in three separate sessions, the last on April 24 — in addition to his other commitments. Mitch Miller couldn't help but notice Sinatra's faltering voice during the April sessions. They were costing Columbia money; all the retakes increased studio rental fees and meant overtime for the musicians and technicians.

"Listen, Sinatra had a marvelous voice, but it was very fragile," Miller recalled years later. "There were certain guys . . . who could stay up all night and drink and sing the next day . . . . But if Frank didn't get enough sleep, or if he drank a lot the night before, it would show up. And Frank was a guy — call it ego or what you want — he liked to suffer out loud, to be dramatic. There were plenty of people, big entertainers, who had a wild life or had big problems, but they kept it quiet. Frank had to do his suffering in public, so everyone could see it. And this was a time he was having trouble with Ava, she was in Spain, and it showed in his work. He would come in to record, and he couldn't get through a number without his voice cracking."[35]

Another Columbia recording engineer in 1950 put Sinatra's vocal problem more succinctly: "He couldn't sing anymore, plain and simple. The songs were there; the voice was not."[36]

George Evans, during his seven-year association with Sinatra, was often called upon to play the role of nursemaid rather than publicist. In a rare disparaging comment about his most famous client, Evans once remarked on Frank's inability to handle "emotional tension." It "absolutely destroyed him," Evans said. "You could always tell when he was troubled. He came down with a bad throat. Germs were never the cause, unless they were guilt germs."[37]

On April 27, 1950, MGM announced that it was dropping Frank Sinatra's contract, a year earlier than its stated termination date. Frank had to have seen it coming, after a string of failed pictures, excepting *On the Town*, and after his run-in with Louis B. Mayer. Indeed, Music Corporation of America, his agent, and MGM had been in negotiations regarding the break-up. The studio let him down gently, wording its press release to make it seem that the decision was a joint one, to give Sinatra a wider range of acting options. But in truth, he was being fired, and he knew it. "As a freelance artist," the statement read, "[Frank Sinatra] is now free to accept unlimited, important personal appearances, radio, and television offers that have been made to him." It was all nonsense, of course. No one was beating down Sinatra's door with any offers. Within two years, MCA and Columbia Records would drop him, too.

Ava Gardner, working in Spain on her picture, was getting impatient. Frank had sworn that he would marry her as soon as Nancy gave him a divorce, but Nancy wasn't budging. Her attorney, issuing a statement on her behalf, said that "Mrs. Sinatra has no plans for divorce. The separate maintenance is just her way of making Frank save his money. She'll put it all away as a nest egg. Then, when nobody else wants him, she'll take him back, and they'll have something to live on."[38] Ava couldn't have been happy reading words like this, the equivalent of flashing a red cape in front of an angry bull. Indeed, while filming *Pandora* in Spain, Gardner discovered she had a taste for bullfighting . . . and for bullfighters. She soon took up with one of her co-stars, Mario Cabré, a "toreador-turned-actor" who proved to be a not-so-discreet lover. Gardner would claim that she had just one night of intimacy with the Spaniard,[39] who spoke no English, but most observers on the scene thought differently.[40] Cabré began proclaiming his love for the American film star, and the press in the United States soon picked up on this juicy new development. Frank was on the phone with Ava whenever he could get an overseas connection and track her down in Spain. She denied an affair with the bullfighter, but Frank's jealous nature would not let it rest. The rumors ate at him, until, at last, his most precious possession — his voice — failed him entirely.

The bottom fell out on May 3, 1950, during the 2:30 a.m. show at the Copacabana.[41] The stress of work, MGM's cancellation of his contract, and Nancy's financial pressure all pushed Frank to the breaking point. If that were not enough, Ava's transgressions, real or not, weighed heavily on him. Skitch Henderson, Sinatra's conductor at the time, described what happened that night.

"It was tragic and terrifying," Henderson later recalled. "He opened his mouth to sing after the band introduction and nothing came out. Not a sound. I thought for a moment that the unexpected pantomime was a joke. But then he caught my eye. I guess the color drained out of my face as I saw the panic in his. It became so quiet — so intensely quiet in the club — they were like watching a man walk off a cliff. His face chalk-white, Frank gasped something that sounded like 'Good Night' into the mike and raced off the stage, leaving the audience stunned."[42]

According to another source, Sinatra began singing "Bali Ha'i" but one of the high notes was too much for him. A doctor diagnosed the problem as "submucosal hemorrhage" and ordered Sinatra to observe 10 days of complete silence.[43] The Copa hastily called Billy Eckstine to fill in for Sinatra, who took off to South Florida for a rest, at the home of Mafia pal Joe Fischetti. Nancy repeatedly called him in Florida, but he refused to take her calls.

On May 12, Sinatra left Miami for Spain, with friend and songwriter Jimmy Van Heusen along for company. He'd been booked to play the Chez Paree in Chicago, but blew off the engagement without repercussion — Fischetti and the Chicago mob ran the joint and understood his predicament. Looking relaxed, Frank joked with reporters before boarding his flight. Ava had requested he bring her Wrigley's Spearmint gum and Coca-Cola — two of her favorite things that she couldn't get in Spain. Frank had another surprise for her, "a $10,000 diamond-and-emerald necklace."[44] Given his financial circumstances, he had to have obtained that spectacular piece of jewelry with Fischetti's help, legitimate or otherwise.[45] The gesture would be wasted on Ava, as would Frank's visit.

※　※　※

"So what is it with you and this fucking greaseball?" Frank asked of Ava, soon after getting off the plane in Barcelona.

"Who? You mean Mario?"

"Is that what you call him?"

"Nothing."

"It's in all the papers, sweetheart."

"Frank, you of all people know better than to believe what you read in those things . . . . We're making a movie together, that's all."[46]

※　※　※

Sinatra's trip resolved nothing and may have even made matters worse between him and Gardner. Part of it was the Cabré thing, but they didn't need the Spanish interloper as an excuse to fight. One serious concern was Frank's continuing reliance on pills. He and Ava chartered a boat for a relaxing afternoon of fishing in the Mediterranean, but Ava became so agitated by Frank's apparent addiction that she threw his pill bottles overboard. Sinatra jumped into the sea after them.[47] When Frank left Spain, earlier than he had planned, Ava's words were still reverberating in his head. "I simply can't do it anymore," she had said. "I just want you to leave me alone. Go home and get a divorce. And if you can't, then fuck you, Francis. Fuck you, you hear me?"[48]

In Paris for a brief layover before returning home, Sinatra told Van Heusen, "I'm willing to leave my wife and kids for this dame, and she treats me like *this*? Nancy won't give me a divorce, man. She's Catholic. She's Italian. What can I do?" Later, after they were back in the States, Sinatra appeared to have reached a decision — he was through with Ava. Van Heusen, sensing that Frank meant business, readily agreed. "Move on, Frank," the songwriter told his patron and buddy. "No dame is worth what she is putting you through."[49]

Before too long, Ava Gardner would be the least of Frank Sinatra's troubles.

10

*"Frank, as an artist,
you are incomparable.
Nobody can touch you.
But where you're a failure
is as a human being."*

Frank Sinatra had endured a pounding in that first half of 1950 — losing George Evans and then seeing Manie Sacks defect to RCA Victor; Nancy locking him out of the house on Valentine's Day; getting fired by MGM's Louis B. Mayer in April; suffering for five weeks at the Copacabana, through poor reviews, disrespectful audiences, and, on May 3, a complete breakdown of his voice; and losing Ava, apparently, as a result of the disastrous trip to Spain, where he'd let jealousy, his depression, and addiction to prescription drugs get the best of him.

Coming back to the States in a funk, he caught a flight to the West Coast, laden with gifts for Nancy and the kids. Trinkets, really, which was all he could afford — nothing on the order of the fur coat he'd given his wife for her birthday a few months earlier. His reception at the Holmby Hills house was as cool as it had been elsewhere, not helped by his wishing

Nancy a belated happy Mother's Day. Nancy Jr. was the exception, running to him and leaping into his outstretched arms. Her joy at Daddy's homecoming — bolstered, no doubt, by a near-10-year-old's hope that it might be permanent — had to have distressed Frank even more. Six-year-old Frankie stood, emotionless, by his mother's side. Tina, almost 2, grabbed her mother's leg, unsure of who the man at the door was. Frank reached down and took her up in his other arm, hugging both girls. Nancy Sr. just stared, showing no warmth or affection.[1] Those feelings had been wrung out of her, at least to the extent that she could show them in Frank's presence. Years later, Nancy Jr. would describe what her mother was going through at the time.

"She was deeply in love and terribly hurt," Nancy Sinatra wrote in 1995. "I would hear her crying quietly at night while I was going to sleep. She would never show it in front of us, never, but my room was next to hers and I would tiptoe out and I'd listen at the door and she'd be crying. Sometimes I would go to her and just put my arms around her. And sometimes I would just go away, thinking, 'Mind your own business. Daddy's just on the road again,' and cry myself to sleep."[2]

Then, suddenly, at the end of May, there was a glimmer of hope — Bob Hope. When no one else was willing to take a chance on Frank Sinatra, Bob Hope gave him a job. Frank's agent, Music Corporation of America, was losing interest in him as a client and hadn't been pushing much on his behalf. So it was left to Frank's attorney, Henry Jaffe, to arrange this one-time guest appearance on Hope's Saturday-night television show for NBC, called the *Star Spangled Revue*. Sinatra was excited about it — not only would it be his first time on television, it might also represent a new beginning.

Bob Hope was having trouble adjusting to the new medium, but with his radio audiences deserting him for television, he had no choice but to persevere. His show had a cobbled together variety format, reminiscent of the comedian's vaudeville days and held together by his personal appeal, which remained strong. On May 27, 1950, the night Sinatra appeared as a guest, actress Beatrice Lillie and singer Peggy Lee were also on. Lee had been on the bill with him at the Paramount when Frank made his solo debut, so it was like old home week, in a sense. Frank played along in a couple of comedy skits with Bob and the others, including one in which he became Bing Crosby. His high point, though, was a rendition of "Come Rain or Come Shine," proving to one and all that his voice was back, baby.

As one writer commented, "He nailed [the song] with a suggestion of cockiness that was in equal parts annoying and appealing. His absolute composure, performing live in front of an audience whose size he couldn't even begin to guess at, made it instantly obvious that he would have no problem climbing back to the top."[3] But as to his overall debut, *Variety* was less enthusiastic. "If TV is his oyster," the entertainment industry paper noted, "Sinatra hasn't broken out of his shell."[4] *Variety* would prove to be the more prescient observer.

Still, Frank's resurrected voice gave Henry Jaffe the ammunition he needed to open negotiations with CBS on what he hoped would be a dramatic turnaround in his client's fortunes. In the meantime, Frank returned to the recording studio in late June with Mitch Miller and cut two sides. The A-side, "Goodnight Irene," turned out to be his best-selling record in three years,[5] although it did not chart high enough to be considered a hit. When Jaffe told him what he'd been able to get out of CBS Chairman William Paley, Frank was ecstatic. Come October, he would be hosting his own weekly variety television program, *The Frank Sinatra Show*, on that network, as well as a weekly show on CBS Radio — *Meet Frank Sinatra*. The package deal was for three years, at $250,000 per year,[6] or almost $2.5 million in today's dollars. For a guy who'd been forced to borrow money for back taxes and who was effectively broke, thanks to his own lifestyle and support obligations to Nancy, this was a godsend.[7]

Ava was in London, finishing up filming for *Pandora and the Flying Dutchman*. They'd reconciled after the Spain fiasco, and, fortuitously, Frank got a booking to play a two-week engagement at the London Palladium, a venue on a par with New York's Paramount Theatre. He boarded an overseas flight on July 5 in a frame of mind he hadn't experienced in years — one of optimism, even happiness, or as close to happiness as his demons would allow.

Determined to succeed in what he had to have viewed as a new lease on life for his career, Frank threw himself into rehearsals for his July 10 opening night, buoyed by the reception he was receiving from the British public. He and Ava were mobbed wherever they went, even before he appeared on stage, but this time, Frank was enjoying the attention, willingly signing autographs and responding to the press with good humor, not rancor. It was like the bobby-soxer phenomenon all over again. Britain had been engulfed in war while Frank was enjoying his early success in the States. Now it seemed like English women wanted to make up for what they had been denied back in the early 1940s.

This was the Frank Sinatra that Ava had fallen in love with, and she responded to him in a way that fed his ego, making him stronger still. As biographer James Kaplan put it, Frank had "gotten his mojo back. He was a cock of the walk again, and she liked him that way."[8] And when he stepped onto the stage at the Palladium and began to sing to the standing-room-only crowd, "Frank knocked them dead."[9]

Sinatra's hard work in rehearsals — full day sessions, every day — in preparation for the engagement had paid off. Ava was in attendance for every performance, and Frank sang each song as if he were singing to her alone.[10] The reviews were the best he had received in five years, reflective, perhaps, of not only the grand performance but also the respectful way he treated the British press.

"I watched mass hysteria," one critic wrote. "Was it wonderful? Decidedly so, for this man Sinatra is a superb performer and a great artiste. He had his audience spellbound." Another reviewer was even more effusive, if that was possible: "Bless me, he's GOOD! He is as satisfying a one-man performance as the Palladium has ever seen."[11]

When Frank left London after this triumph, to fulfill a recording date in New York on August 2 and an Atlantic City gig later that month, Ava stayed over to finish shooting scenes for *Pandora*. They'd had a few squabbles in London, but neither of them expected their relationship to be without the occasional flare-up. As his plane touched down back in the States, Sinatra was "sitting on a rainbow" and probably thinking in an upbeat tempo, "What a world . . . what a life . . . I'm in love." It was as though the words of his "I've Got the World on a String," a hit for Capitol Records a few years into the future, were now suddenly defining his life

— a life not even four months removed from the moment that a shot was fired into a pillow and mattress at the Hampshire House hotel.

* * *

Sinatra and Gardner were back together in New York in September 1950, staying at the Hampshire House, ironically, but in Manie Sacks' suite, which Frank had borrowed once again from his friend and former mentor at Columbia Records. The debut of Frank's new CBS television show was set for early October, so he was busy getting ready. Ava was to depart for California in November to begin filming what would become one of her most successful movie roles, that of black-passing-for-white singer Julie LaVerne in the MGM remake of *Show Boat*, the acclaimed Jerome Kern-Oscar Hammerstein II musical.[12] Second only to actress Esther Williams in the number of fan requests for her photo (3,000 per week),[13] Ava Gardner was fast becoming money in the bank for MGM.

On September 27, 1950, the couple took in the Ezzard Charles-Joe Louis Heavyweight Championship fight at Yankee Stadium. Former champ Joe Louis, to whom Sinatra would give significant financial support in his later years,[14] hadn't fought for more than two years (he came out of retirement because he was broke and owed a substantial amount in back taxes — a common celebrity problem, it seemed) and was out-boxed by the lighter (35 pounds) and quicker Charles, the reigning champion; Charles won a 15-round unanimous decision.

Frank would suffer a technical knockout the next day — in the arena of public opinion, at least — when Nancy Barbato Sinatra appeared before Judge Orlando Rhodes in a courtroom in Santa Monica, California, to tearfully make her case for separate maintenance and support from her estranged husband. Frank did not contest the action. Clearly, their lawyers had hammered out a settlement, and all that remained was for Nancy to put a sufficient factual basis on the record, so that the judge could finalize the arrangement.

"On numerous occasions, he would go to Palm Springs for weekends without me," Nancy told the judge. "He also stayed several days at a time. This happened many times. When we had guests, he would go off by himself and not feel like talking. This made me terribly nervous and upset."[15]

This public testimony by Nancy, excerpts of which appeared in the *Los Angeles Times* the next day, was almost certainly scripted by the respective attorneys to allow Nancy to get the agreed upon financial support without unduly damaging Frank's career. (She had to establish a factual basis for the separation, but that's a low hurdle in most uncontested matters.) Frank would take a hit, but not the lambasting he could have received if Nancy had fully vented her heartache. An approach in that vein would have affected his livelihood, which, in turn, would damage the interests of Nancy and the children.

Accordingly, there were no accusations of marital infidelity, no mention of Ava or Lana or Marilyn or any of the *other* other women who had plagued the 11½-year marriage. Nancy was awarded one-third of Frank's gross earnings up to $150,000, and 10 percent of the next $150,000. She also got the Holmby Hills house and its furnishings, shares of stock in the Sinatra Music Corporation, and a 1950 Cadillac. Frank got Twin Palms (his Palm Springs hideaway), a 1949 Cadillac, and other incidentals. There was no cash to speak of — Frank had been too big a spender for any fattening of bank accounts.

Nancy made it clear in court that she was requesting a financial arrangement, not a divorce. "It doesn't look now that they will get a divorce," her attorney said afterward.[16] Nevertheless, Ava was happy about the settlement; it was the first step in what would eventually become a divorce — that was her calculation, anyway. "All I want is for Nancy to come to her senses and live her life so that I can live mine," Ava told a friend. "Is that selfish? No, I don't think it is. I just don't. Can't she go on with her life, for Christ's sake?"[17]

While not being mentioned in court as a "correspondent," Ava still took the brunt of the adverse press coverage when, in reporting the proceeding, the *Los Angeles Times* ran tandem photos — one showing the demurely dressed Nancy as she left the courtroom, the other showing Frank and a not-so-demurely-dressed Ava at the Joe Louis-Ezzard Charles prizefight. Unbothered by it all, Ava flew to California to begin shooting *Show Boat*, happy at the prospect of the meaty role she would play and a chance to demonstrate her singing talent. Her character, Julie LaVerne, had two of the highly regarded solos in the movie: "Bill" and "Can't Help Lovin' Dat Man."[18]

* * *

The Frank Sinatra Show, in its 9 to 10 p.m. Saturday-night time slot, was up against the stiffest competition on television — Sid Caesar and Imogene Coca in their blockbuster comedy hit, *Your Show of Shows* — but there was an even more serious threat to the show's success — namely, Frank Sinatra. The first broadcast, on October 7, 1950, was a disaster. Network executives wasted no time in hand-wringing and immediately brought in a new producer, Irving Mansfield, to try to fix things.

"After Frank's first television show bombed," Mansfield said, "I was called in to produce, and I lived in hell for the next eight weeks. He was impossible to work with — absolutely impossible. A real spoiled brat. He was with Ava then, and the two of them were living in Manie Sachs's [sic] suite at the Hampshire House, and every day her life was a hell on earth because he was always accusing her of running out in the afternoon to sleep with Artie Shaw. Whenever he couldn't get her on the phone, he'd start screaming on the set that she was having an affair with Artie. 'I know she's with that goddamn Artie Shaw,' he'd yell. 'I know she's with that bastard. I'll kill her. I'll kill her. I'll kill her.' He was crazy on the subject."[19]

Part of the problem was getting through the protective shield that Sinatra always kept around himself. Mansfield was rarely able to communicate directly with the star of the show he was producing — not a workable scenario, by anyone's estimate.

"He was constantly surrounded by his entourage," Mansfield said. "Ben Barton, Hank Sanicola, some gorilla named Al Silvani, and a bunch of other hangers-on — and they shook and shivered every time he yelled. They talked in hushed tones and stood around him like goons protecting a gangster. I couldn't get near him."[20]

In a recording studio, Sinatra's work ethic was beyond reproach. He expected and settled for nothing less than excellence, from himself and from everybody else involved in the recording session — musicians, engineers, technicians. He couldn't read music, but he knew every note that would be played, knew it cold. "If a flute player in the back row hits a bad note," he once remarked, "baby, I know it."[21] It was no idle boast. But on the set of a movie, or even his own television show, Sinatra was a different animal. It is hard to understand this phenomenon — the obsession with perfection as to the singing/recording aspect of his career, juxtaposed with an almost sloppy approach to acting in a movie or performing on television, both important pillars of his career. Recognizing several superb motion picture performances by Sinatra, writer Pete Hamill, who knew the singer well, commented on that very same dichotomy.

"He also made some junk," Hamill said. "But he simply didn't take acting seriously enough to become a great actor. Too often, he settled for the first, most superficial take, avoiding the effort that would force him to stretch his talent, acting as if he were double-parked. Too often, in too many movies," Hamill continued, "he cheated the audience and he cheated himself. He never cheated in the music."[22] Irving Mansfield noted the same attitude on the set of *The Frank Sinatra Show*, although there was a more pronounced nastiness to it.

"Frank was always late, sometimes two and three hours late; he hated to rehearse and refused to discuss the weekly format," Mansfield said. "Usually, he ignored the guests entirely. Once he wanted to book Jackie Gleason, who was very hot at the time, but Frank would not rehearse. Even though he and Jackie were pals, Jackie refused to go on the air without a rehearsal, and we ended up having to pay him $7,500 plus expenses for being the guest star who did not do Frank's show. Another time," Mansfield continued, "I came to work and was told by the goons that Brian Aherne was the guest star for the following week. 'Frank wants to class up the show,' they said. What could I do. Aherne was a B actor with a mustache and no flair for television. He was a disaster and Frank was furious afterwards. 'Why'd you put that bum on my show?' he screamed. 'It wasn't my idea,' I said. 'It was yours.' He refused to talk to me again for days."[23]

Mansfield stuck it out for eight weeks, then abruptly departed on his own terms. "Frank, as an artist, you are incomparable," he told the singer. "Nobody can touch you. But where you're a failure is as a human being."[24]

* * *

Before long, unsubstantiated rumors started filtering back to Frank that Ava was having an affair with her co-star in the picture — the handsome actor/singer Howard Keel. And, as often happened when Frank suspected Ava of cheating on him, he took liberties himself, in retaliation. Singer Rosemary Clooney told of an incident in New York around this time, when Frank was alone in the city. The tale gains credence from the fact that Clooney's own sister, Betty, was the woman involved. Frank launched a heavy charm offensive one evening as the two sisters sat sipping their drinks in a nightclub. He not only made eyes at Betty, he actually went to the microphone and sang a spontaneous rendition of "I'll Never Smile Again" directed quite plainly to her alone. Rosemary warned her sister about Sinatra; he was "crazy about Ava," she said. But Betty paid her no mind. "When we left the club," Clooney recalled, "we all got into a taxi. Then they dropped me off."[25]

Although Gardner's dressing room on the set of *Show Boat* was a hangout for her, Keel, and some of the other actors (liquor wasn't allowed on set, but Ava kept a stash in her dressing room), there's no hard evidence that she was having an affair with Keel. She did make a try with actor Robert Stack, however.

Stack was seated in a restaurant with a friend and discussing a film he'd just completed, in which he played a bullfighter. Ava, at the next table, overheard that aspect of the conversation and wangled an invitation to join Stack and his companion. She already knew a lot about bullfighters, thanks to her affair with Mario Cabré while filming *Pandora and the Flying Dutchman* in Spain. "How did it feel to face an animal that wants to kill you?" she asked Stack. Later, back at Ava's place, the talk turned to another of Ava's favorite subjects.[26] How did Stack feel about "shared sex," she wanted to know. She went on to explain that she was friendly with another couple, whom she could call to come over right then and there, to join them. Stack suddenly developed a stomach virus and beat a hasty retreat from the premises.[27]

* * *

In 1950 and 1951, thanks to the new-age wonder of television, the most recognizable political figure in the United States, other than President Harry S. Truman, was Senator Estes Kefauver, Democrat from Tennessee. Kefauver was then heading up a special Senate committee investigating organized crime and its influence on interstate commerce.[28] In addition to operating in Washington, D.C., the committee went on the road, with stopovers in major U.S. cities — 14 in all, including New York City, Chicago, Detroit, and New Orleans. After the committee's hearings hit the airwaves coast to coast, Americans became riveted to their flickering 7-inch sets, awakening for the first time to the reality of the vast underworld around them. Crime figures big and small, as well as other "civilian" witnesses having some connection to those mobsters, like former New York Mayor William O'Dwyer, were subpoenaed to testify at the public sessions. Among the headliners were Tony "Joe Batters" Accardo; Los Angeles-based mob boss (and self-proclaimed Sinatra friend) Mickey Cohen; Sinatra benefactors Frank Costello, Willie Moretti, and Longy Zwillman; Meyer Lansky; and Virginia Hill, former girlfriend to Benjamin "Bugsy" Siegel, who was "hit" on syndicate orders in 1947.[29]

Most of the witnesses "took the Fifth" — that is, they invoked their Fifth Amendment protection against self-incrimination. A few, like Willie Moretti, opened up a bit too much before the committee. Although Moretti said nothing of evidentiary value, his "colleagues" were nervous that he might do so in the future . . . and they took steps to make sure that didn't happen. Moretti was murdered gangland-style in a New Jersey restaurant in October 1951. Committee Chairman Kefauver also introduced Americans to a word that most had been unfamiliar with: *Mafia*.

"The Mafia is a shadowy international organization that lurks behind much of America's organized criminal activity," Kefauver said. "It is an organization about which none of its members, on fear of death, will talk. In fact, some of the witnesses called before us, who we had good reason to believe could tell us about the Mafia, sought to dismiss it as a sort of fairy tale or legend that children hear in Sicily, where the Mafia originated. The Mafia, however, is no fairy tale. It is ominously real, and it has scarred the face of America with almost every conceivable type of criminal violence. Including murder, traffic in narcotics, smuggling, extortion, white slavery, kidnapping, and labor racketeering."[30]

On March 1, 1951, in New York City, Frank Sinatra would audition for a role he desperately wanted to avoid playing: witness for the Kefauver committee.

11

"You're not going to put me on television and ruin me just because I know a lot of people, are you?"

Frank Sinatra had been finessing his connections to organized crime figures for four straight years, ever since the story of his Havana sojourn, spent mostly in the company of Lucky Luciano and a dozen other Mafia big shots, broke in Scripps-Howard newspapers across the country in early 1947. Reporter Robert Ruark filed the series of articles, based on his own sightings of Sinatra and on tips he'd received from reliable sources.[1] Sinatra tried to explain his being seen in Havana with Luciano and the others by making exculpatory statements to Hedda Hopper and others, but he couldn't keep his stories straight, giving first one version, then another. The lies served their purpose, however, and Frank was able to ride out the storm. His life and career in early 1951 were in freefall, but there were plenty of *other* reasons that was happening — problems with his voice, MGM canceling his film contract, plummeting records sales, Nancy's obstinacy on the question of divorce, and Ava's disconcerting way of arousing incomparable pleasure one day and inflicting intolerable pain the next.

Everyone, from publicists to the stars themselves, shaded the truth in their dealings with Hollywood gossip columnists. It was all part of the game, expected even. But lying to a federal officer under oath? That was a horse of a different color, and the prospect of being hauled before the Kefauver committee to testify about his friends in the Mafia — on live television, reaching tens of millions of Americans — had Frank Sinatra scared half to death.

Joseph Nellis was an associate counsel to the committee, having been recruited for that post in late 1949 by Senator Estes Kefauver, a friend of Nellis' father. Nellis would rise to become an important figure in Democratic politics, including a stint as legal adviser to presidential candidates Adlai Stevenson and Hubert Humphrey, but when he got the call from Kefauver, he was a 32-year-old lawyer in private practice.[2] Months later, he would be questioning Frank Costello on behalf of the committee — Costello, head of one of New York's Five Families. It was a seemingly daunting task, but you knew where you stood with actual Mafiosi — they took the Fifth on every question. A tougher challenge lay ahead. In early 1951, Nellis was assigned by Kefauver himself to the task of interrogating Frank Sinatra, a man who couldn't take the Fifth and who probably couldn't afford to be 100 percent truthful — his career would have suffered in either instance. At a committee meeting, Kefauver handed Nellis a manila envelope containing eight enlarged photographs and asked him to set up a meeting with Sinatra.

"I almost fell off my chair," Nellis later explained, describing his reaction to the photos." I opened the envelope and saw a picture of Sinatra with his arm around Lucky Luciano on the balcony of the Hotel Nacional in Havana; another picture showed Sinatra and Luciano sitting at a nightclub in the Nacional with lots of bottles having a hell of a time with some good-looking girls. One picture showed Frank getting off a plane carrying a suitcase, and then there were a couple of pictures of him with the Fischetti brothers, Lucky Luciano, and Nate Gross, a Chicago reporter who knew all the mobsters."[3]

Kefauver was particularly interested in learning more about Sinatra's connection to Luciano, who was heavily involved in multinational drug trafficking, even while still barred from entering the United States. And so, Joe

Nellis got in touch with Sinatra's lawyer — probably one of the Jaffe brothers, Saul or Henry — to discuss how and when Sinatra would appear before the committee. Whichever Jaffe got the call, he had to have known that this was the major leagues, *the Show*, and that a pinch-hitter with special skills was needed. And he got the absolutely best lawyer for the job.

Sol Gelb had been one of Thomas Dewey's assistants when Dewey prosecuted Lucky Luciano, among others, and convicted the Mafia chief of running a prostitution racket in New York. He was also a crime buster in Manhattan District Attorney Frank Hogan's office when Louis "Lepke" Buchalter was convicted of murder, later to be executed for the crime. After entering private practice, Gelb successfully defended Teamster boss Jimmy Hoffa (he got a hung jury, which is a win in any defense attorney's book). Most important, "Gelb was a tough lawyer who knew organized crime inside and out, and he had no fear of Kefauver."[4]

Discussions between Sol Gelb and Joseph Nellis about the manner in which Sinatra would be questioned — in public and on television, or at a private deposition — were ongoing during the month of February 1951. Gelb, being an excellent attorney, would have kept his client informed about those discussions. Frank was in New York City anyway, staying at Manie Sacks' apartment in the Hampshire House while doing his Saturday-night television show for CBS, and not much else. He'd had an unremarkable recording session at Columbia's New York studio on January 16 and did a guest appearance on Milton Berle's *Texaco Star Theater* that same date. Two more recording sessions were scheduled, on March 2 and 27, so he wasn't going anywhere while he waited for his attorney to work things out with Nellis.[5] And the waiting was getting to him.

Singer Eddie Fisher, the latest heartthrob for the younger set (just as Sinatra had been a decade earlier), was performing at the Paramount Theatre in February. One night, walking past the Paramount in Times Square, Sinatra noticed the crowds of excited people waiting to get into the theater, another stark reminder of the depths to which his own career had sunk. That experience, along with the pressure of a likely appearance before the Kefauver committee and the continuing turmoil over Ava, who was back in California filming *Show Boat*, pushed him over the edge. When he got back to Manie's apartment, Frank went to the kitchen and turned on the gas oven without lighting it. Fortunately, Manie returned home a short time later and smelled the odor. He rushed to the kitchen and found Sinatra, sobbing on the floor.[6] Given Frank's state of mind, this suicide attempt may have been real, no matter how ineptly it was carried out. There's no report of any medical attention being summoned, so it was probably just left to Manie, and whatever friends he may have called on for help, to roust Frank out of this black mood and put him back on his feet, literally and figuratively. It wasn't long before he got a bit of good news. He was not going to become Senator Kefauver's latest television star, at least not yet.

Thanks to his attorney's clout, Frank Sinatra caught a break. Gelb was able to successfully argue his client's vulnerability. If Sinatra were forced to testify in public, his career would be ruined, Gelb told Nellis, and that would be an unfair burden to place on any man, just because he knew a few people of unsavory reputation. The defense attorney won his client a reprieve — perhaps temporary, but still a stay of execution — by getting Nellis to agree to a compromise. Sinatra would give his testimony under oath, but it would be given in private, at a safe time and location away from the prying eyes of the press. If word got out that the Kefauver committee was even interested in talking to Sinatra, that alone would probably be enough to spell ruin for him. And so, on March 1, 1951, at 4 a.m., Frank Sinatra and Sol Gelb surreptitiously entered one of New York's landmark buildings, Rockefeller Center, and rode the elevator to a top floor. Waiting to escort them to a private law office were Joseph Nellis and a court stenographer, on hand to record the singer's testimony, word for word.

Sinatra acted "like a lost kitten, drawn, frightened to death," Nellis recollected years later. "He kept shooting his cuffs, straightening his tie. He knew that I was going to ask him about Willie Moretti and Lucky Luciano, but he didn't know about all the photographs I had."[7]

Nellis showed Sinatra the photos of him in Havana, consorting (and cavorting) with Luciano and the others, *before* he began questioning the singer about that trip to Cuba,[8] thereby cutting Sinatra another break. A more experienced government attorney, in this situation, might have kept from Sinatra the fact that he had the photos in his possession, allowing Sinatra to spin whatever web of lies he cared to invent, under oath and on the record. Exposing the singer's lies and evasions by producing the photos *later in the interview* would have turned Sinatra (and, maybe, Gelb) into an even more quivering mass of soft putty, giving Nellis a great advantage. But armed with knowledge that the photos existed and were right there on the table before him, Sinatra had to tread carefully. He couldn't continue with the stories he had invented soon after the 1947 Havana trip, at least not plausibly. And he also couldn't admit having any participation in criminal activity. Not matter what, he had to deny that possibility to the bitter end.

The photo of Sinatra leaving the plane in Havana showed him carrying a sizable piece of luggage (when carry-ons were not part of the air-travel culture) and being flanked by Joe and Rocco Fischetti, as though they were running interference for him. Joe and Rocco, along with another brother, Charles, were part of the Chicago mob hierarchy (Tony "Joe Batters" Accardo was the big boss at the time). Nellis probed Sinatra about his relationship with the Fischetti brothers. He asked how Sinatra had met the Fischettis, and Sinatra replied that his first meeting, with Joe, had occurred in Chicago, while he was performing in that city.

"He [Joe] had a little speedboat on the lake," Sinatra said, "and one afternoon he took me for a ride." One thing led to another, according to Sinatra — "Having dinner with him, going to the theater" — and Joe then introduced him to Rocco and Charles. After that, there were just casual encounters with the three brothers.[9] Sinatra omitted any mention of his recuperative stay-over at the Miami home of Joe Fischetti in early May 1950, after this voice had given out at the Copacabana, or of the fact that the Fischettis were secret owners of the Chez Paree in Chicago, where Sinatra had performed. In fact, he had been booked to perform there starting May 14, 1950, but canceled that engagement, surely with Joe Fischetti's okay, to go see Ava in Spain. Nellis asked if Sinatra ever had "any business dealings with any of the Fischettis." Sinatra's curious reply? "Not an ounce."[10] Nellis persisted in his questioning on this subject as Sinatra piled one coincidence upon another in trying to explain how he happened to arrive in Havana on the same plane from Miami with Joe and Rocco Fischetti.

> Q. Where were you staying in Miami when you met
> them?

A. I had a little cottage.

Q. How did you happen to bump into the Fischettis?

A. I went to either the Beachcomber or one of the clubs downtown in the entertainment center, and I saw Joe, and then later that evening I met Rocco. He came in with some friends, and I said hello and met his friends, and that was it.[11]

On that same night he ran into Rocco and his friends, Sinatra told Nellis, "I said to Joe, it is too cold. I think I am going to get out of here and go where it is warm. I said I think I will go down to Havana, and if I went down I would stay a couple of days because I promised my wife I would meet my wife in Mexico around February 14. It was St. Valentine's Day; that comes back to my mind. Then that is when [Joe] told me they had also contemplated going to Cuba. I think the next day he called me on the phone and wanted to know when I was going down to Cuba. Apparently, at that time I probably did say what morning I was going, either the following morning or the morning after he called me, and when I got out to the airport, they were checking the baggage through; that is when I saw them on the plane."[12]

Sinatra was clearly freelancing here, far afield of any pre-interview instructions that Sol Gelb may have given him about making his answers short, succinct, and responsive to the question. As any experienced prosecutor knows, a witness who goes on and on, as Sinatra was doing, is probably lying.[13] Nellis was incredulous over the rambling response Sinatra had given and the illogic of the events happening so neatly as to fit into an innocent set of coincidences. He pressed on with the inquiry.

Q. And you had given him your phone number where you were staying?

A. Yes, he asked me for the phone number, and I gave it to him.

Q. Now, you rode over together on the same plane?

A. Yes.

Q. When you got off the plane, you got off with them together?

A. No, actually I didn't know. As a matter of fact, I sus-
pect, now that we discuss it, that when the plane
landed, they may have seen the guys with the cameras.
They may have seen somebody with a camera because
why should they fall behind. I found myself alone.
[Sinatra was forgetting what he had just viewed in one
of the photos. Rocco was a few steps behind him, but
Joe was right at his shoulder.]

Q. Were you carrying any baggage off the plane?

A. Yes.

Q. What was it?

A. A tan piece of hand luggage, a briefcase like. [That
was the description Frank had floated four years earlier, but the "piece of hand luggage" Sinatra was
carrying from the plane was clearly much larger than
a briefcase.][14]

Five months after this interview, Hearst columnist Lee Mortimer, citing
sources in the U.S. Bureau of Narcotics, would allege in a magazine piece
that Sinatra was carrying in this hand luggage $2 million in cash for Lucky
Luciano. According to Mortimer, the Feds knew that Luciano was in
Havana — his lifestyle there hardly allowed for keeping his presence a
secret — but they hesitated in demanding that Cuban dictator Batista evict
him from the country. They had Luciano's phone tapped and were collecting intelligence. On the night before Sinatra left Miami for Havana, he and
Joe Fischetti went to the Colonial Inn in Hallandale, Florida, just to the
north of Miami. The place was, in reality, an illegal gambling casino owned
by Meyer Lansky and Joe Adonis, and it generated enormous amounts of
cash. An ingenious way to get a share of that cash out of the United States
and into the hands of Mafia legend Luciano was to recruit celebrities, like
Sinatra, to carry it into Cuba. Because of their fame and stature, these
celebrities were unlikely to be stopped or inspected by Cuban authorities,
whereas known criminals invited such scrutiny.[15] "The same week Sinatra
and the flying Fischettis visited 'Lucky' in Cuba," Mortimer wrote, "the
Feds reported that two million dollars had been delivered to Luciano by

Rocco Fischetti, transported *'in the hand luggage of an entertainer.'*[16] [Emphasis supplied.]

Nellis had the same or similar information, from the same source as Mortimer. According to intelligence that the U.S. Bureau of Narcotics provided to the Kefauver committee's staff investigators, "Frank Sinatra was suspected of delivering money to Luciano" in Havana,[17] which explains Nellis' continuing interest in the bag or any other package that Sinatra might have carried from the plane.

> Q. Could you have had a paper-wrapped bundle?
> A. No, I don't remember actually, but I don't think so. I think I had a topcoat and a bag.
> Q. What was in the bag?
> A. Sketching materials, crayons, shaving equipment, general toiletries.
> Q. Do you habitually carry that bag?
> A. All the time, constantly. I am now. I also use it for papers.
> Q. How large a bag is it?
> A. It is about the size of a briefcase with a handle on it. Instead of carrying under your arms, like a little overnight bag.
> Q. Did either of the Fischettis give you anything to carry into Cuba?
> A. No, sir.
> Q. Did anybody else give you anything to carry into Cuba?
> A. No, sir.[18]

Sinatra went on to explain how, after checking into his hotel, he and Nate Gross, a reporter he knew from Chicago's *Herald American*, went out on the town for some fun, and . . . funny thing, they kept running into Lucky Luciano wherever they went. Sinatra told Nellis he wasn't certain who Luciano was.

"I remarked to Nate, I said that name is familiar," Sinatra said, presumably with a straight face. He then elaborated further. "Yes, [Gross] said, that's the guy you think it is. He started to tell me something of the history of the man. I was a boy and remember when his trial was on and remember reading about it . . . ."[19] Luciano was convicted on June 7, 1936. Sinatra was 20 at the time and had already appeared on Major Bowes' Amateur Hour as part of the Hoboken Four. Within a couple of years, he would be doing a private audition for Frank Costello, Luciano's successor as head of the family, and Willie Moretti.

> Q. There has been stated certain information that you took a sum of money well in excess of $100,000 into Cuba.
> A. That is not true.
> Q. Did you give any money to Lucky Luciano?
> A. No, sir.
> Q. Did you ever learn what business they were in?
> A. No. Actually not.[20]

Seeing he was getting nowhere, Nellis abandoned the money-courier tack and pressed forward on Sinatra's association with gangsters generally.

> Q. Where did you get started in the entertainment business?
> A. In a small club in Hoboken. I must have been around seventeen.
> Q. What's your attraction to all these underworld characters?
> A. I don't have any attraction for them. Some of them were kind to me when I started out, and I have sort of casually seen them or spoken to them at different places, in nightclubs where I worked, or out in Vegas or California.
> Q. Do you know Frank Costello?
> A. Just to say hello. I've seen him at the Copa and at the Madison, and once we had a drink at the Drake,

where I stay when I am in New York.

Q. What about Joe Doto? [Doto was known as 'Joe Adonis,' because of his preoccupation with his physical appearance.]

A. I've met him. He's the one they call 'Adonis,' right?

Q. Right. How well do you know him?

A. No business. Just 'hello' and 'goodbye.'

Q. Well, what about the Jersey guys you met when you first got started?

A. Let me tell you something, those guys were okay. They never bothered me or anyone else as far as I know. You're not going to put me on television and ruin me just because I know a lot of people, are you? [At one point, Sinatra asserted that the 'Jersey guys' were simply 'people that his mother knew, that his family knew.'[21]]

Q. Nobody wants to ruin you, Mr. Sinatra. I assure you, I would not be here at five in the morning at your lawyer's request so that no newsmen could find out we're talking to you if we intended to make some kind of public spectacle of any appearance before the committee.

A. Well, look. How in hell is it going to help your investigation to put me on television just because I know some of these guys?

Q. That will be up to Senator Kefauver and the committee. Right now, if you're not too tired, I want to continue so we can see if there is any basis for calling you in public session.[22]

Despite his nervousness, Sinatra actually handled this part of the inquiry well. He lied, of course, about the extent of his familiarity with Luciano and the others, but he had no choice in that regard if he hoped to escape being called before the committee in a public, televised session. He soft-soaped his association with the Mafia figures, even to the extent of calling them "okay." They "never bothered" him "or anyone else as far as" he knew. Some of them were even "good people, who supported the Church," in Sinatra's words.[23]

> Q. Let's get back to what I was asking you about. And I will ask you specifically. Have you ever, at any time, been associated in business with Moretti, Zwillman ...
>
> A. Who?
>
> Q. Abner Zwillman of Newark. They call him 'Longy.' Or [Jerry] Catena, [Meyer] Lansky, or [Bugsy] Siegel?
>
> A. Well, Moore, I mean Moretti, made some band dates for me when I first got started, but I have never had any business dealings with any of those men.
>
> Q. But you knew Luciano, the Fischettis, and all of those I have named?
>
> A. Just like I said, just in that way."
>
> Q. What is your attraction to these people? [Nellis was repeating himself, perhaps an indication of retreat or fatigue.]
>
> A. Well, hell, you go into show business, you meet a lot of people. And you don't know who they are or what they do.
>
> Q. Do you want me to believe that you don't know the people we have been talking about are hoodlums and gangsters who have committed many crimes and are probably members of a secret criminal club?
>
> A. No, of course not. I heard about the Mafia.
>
> Q. Well, what did you hear about it?
>
> A. That's it's some kind of shakedown operation. I don't know.[24]

Sol Gelb had to have been completely satisfied about the way his client had performed under the circumstances — that is, being confronted at the start of the interview with eight incriminating photos. Indeed, despite a shaky start and some body language that telegraphed his nervousness (body language is *not* noted in the transcript of an interview), Sinatra had made no damaging admissions and had papered over his obviously friendly associations with these wise guys, in a polite but firm way.

Nellis handed Sinatra a subpoena when they were finished, two hours after the meeting started, but it was really an empty gesture, an attempt to snatch some psychological victory, by keeping Sinatra on edge, after the singer had so effectively insulated himself from any prosecutable, or exploitable, connection to Luciano, Costello, Moretti, and the others. As they left the building, Gelb told Sinatra not to worry, despite the subpoena. The attorney had been strangely complacent during the whole meeting, not injecting himself very often into the fray and allowing Sinatra to carry his own water. It was a good strategy, because it worked. When Nellis met with Senator Kefauver later that same day, he told his boss that he thought Sinatra had frequently lied during the session, but still recommended that Sinatra not be called before the committee in public session.

"He's not going to admit any complicity concerning Luciano or the Fischettis in terms of being a bagman or courier for them or anybody else," Nellis opined. "If we take him into public session, his career will really be jolted — possibly beyond repair. He may even balk at the TV cameras and raise a lot of hell without saying anything."[25]

Senator Estes Kefauver had political ambitions of his own. He would run for the Democratic nomination for president in 1952 and again in 1956, and was already thinking about how his committee hearings might enhance those efforts. Sinatra had been a stalwart of the Democratic Party since 1944, when he came out for FDR so strongly, at fundraising events and get-out-the-vote rallies. Additionally, Sinatra was still appreciated by a large segment of the American public, despite his recent career downturn. Why risk turning off so many potential voters by calling Sinatra in for a public lambasting, when nothing concrete would likely result from the spectacle? And, given the press interest in Sinatra, it would certainly be a spectacle.

Kefauver wisely accepted Joe Nellis' recommendation. Sinatra was home free, at least with regard to this particular battle with a government inquiry. In years to come, he would be questioned in other state and federal probes, at times publicly, about the same subject — his ties to some of the most brutal men in America. But he had been blooded in this early-morning session on March 1, 1951, and met the challenge. He would be embarrassed at times in the future, when called upon to testify, but he would never be prosecuted, for lying or anything else.

That night, Sinatra's cronies threw a celebratory shindig for him at Toots Shor's place. The wisecracks flew like staccato bursts from a tommy gun, mostly at the expense of Estes Kefauver. Sinatra was emboldened, and he took that newfound bravado with him to the recording studio the next night, where he recorded Axel Stordahl arrangements of two of Rodgers and Hammerstein's most beautiful songs: "We Kiss in a Shadow" and "Hello Young Lovers," both from *The King and I*.[26] The voice needed coddling along the way, with soothing tea to calm the throat — 22 takes were required before "Hello Young Lovers" met everyone's satisfaction[27] — but both songs became instant favorites of Sinatra fans everywhere. Three-and-a-half weeks later, Sinatra was back in the recording studio for an even more dramatic session.

On March 27, 1951, Sinatra recorded three songs, but one stands out.[28] As one biographer put it, "It has always been taken for granted that he put all his grief over Ava Gardner into his performance, and it became one of his all-time classics."[29] Another said of this singular record, "His emotion is so naked that we are at once embarrassed and compelled: we literally feel for him."[30] Legend has it that Sinatra completed the song in one take and then, without a word to anyone but with a distressed look on his face, grabbed his hat and coat and walked out of the studio.[31]

The song? "I'm a Fool to Want You," its words still haunting, even today, to any lover of Sinatra's ballads.

12

"I am now convinced that a divorce is the only way for my happiness, as well as Frank's."

From the moment she stepped off a train at Union Station in Los Angeles on August 23, 1941, with a seven-year, $50-per-week Metro-Goldwyn-Mayer studio contract in hand,[1] Ava Gardner was, by anyone's standards, one of the most beautiful new stars in Hollywood. She had been raised dirt-poor in North Carolina, and the idea that she would become an actress seemed far-fetched. The first inkling of such a notion may have come two years earlier, while Ava was visiting her married sister Bappie in New York City. As a special treat, Bappie took her then-16-year-old sister to a dress-up nightclub. Actor Henry Fonda was there at a nearby table, and Ava was coaxed into asking him for an autograph.

Fonda, whose greatest films still lay in the future, graciously obliged his young fan, and then told her something she'd remember for the rest of her life.

"Oh, you're a lovely little girl," Fonda said. "You should go to Hollywood."[2]

After turning 18, Ava lived with Bappie and her photographer husband, who took headshots of his young sister-in-law and displayed them in his shop window to attract portrait business. Someone at a talent agency, a passer-by, saw Ava's picture, and she was invited to a film studio in New York for a screen test. Liking what he saw, the agent shipped the film off to MGM in Hollywood, minus the audio — Ava's thick Southern accent, a correctible flaw, might have been off-putting to the studio. The video portion of the screen test certainly wasn't.[3]

"Tell New York to ship her out," studio executive George Sidney was reported to have said after viewing the test (he'd later direct Gardner in *Show Boat*), "she's a good piece of merchandise."[4]

Ava Gardner was also a good piece of something else, once she was broken in by Mickey Rooney, Howard Hughes, and Artie Shaw. Before, during, and after becoming romantically involved with Frank Sinatra in 1949, she would be linked sexually to men of all descriptions — a rich eccentric like Howard Hughes (today he would be a billionaire; back then he was just a multimillionaire); Hollywood stars like her; at least one movie director; a great white hunter in Africa; a couple of Spanish bullfighters; even a props man on a movie set. For all we know, considering Ava Gardner's reputation, there might've been one or two sweaty washing-machine repairmen in the mix. She was not choosy, about the men she bedded or those she married. Her three husbands (Mickey Rooney, Artie Shaw, and Frank Sinatra) had 20 wives among them.[5] One commentator, knowledgeable about that era, characterized Ava as being "as close to a nymphomaniac as a Hollywood star could be . . . without losing her contract."[6]

Ava Gardner's physical beauty doesn't explain Frank Sinatra's obsession with her — an obsession so destructive that you have to wonder at times about the man's rationality. Sinatra's sexual conquests — again, before, during, and after his relationship with Gardner — were even more prodigious than hers and, naming just *two dozen* of the most extraordinary, included Marilyn Maxwell, Lana Turner, Marilyn Monroe, Natalie Wood, Lauren Bacall, Angie Dickinson, Kim Novak, Dinah Shore, Marlene Dietrich, Judy Garland, Elizabeth Taylor, Peggy Lee, Juliet Prowse, Dorothy Provine, Jacqueline Kennedy Onassis, Jackie's sister Princess Lee Radziwill, Grace Kelly, Lady Adele Beatty, Mia Farrow, Joi Lansing, Jill St. John, Lee Remick, Peggy Lipton, and Gloria Vanderbilt. There were many others, like

Alora Gooding and Jeanne Carmen and Abbey Lincoln — not as famous, but just as (or almost as) beautiful.[7] And, probably, hundreds of A-list prostitutes —a favorite sexual outlet of Sinatra's, often facilitated by his friend, composer Jimmy Van Heusen, and offering as it did a "love 'em and leave 'em," entanglement-free release.

George Jacobs, Sinatra's personal valet for 15 years (1953-1968) and therefore in a position to know about this aspect of his boss's life, offered an overall assessment in his 2003 memoir: "No man has ever slept with so many famous women."[8]

What was it, sexually, that Gardner could offer Sinatra that was so different from what all these other women offered? Did she have some special way of going about it? *Kama Sutra* aside, there are only so many ways that a woman can give a man pleasure, and, Hollywood morals being what they were, most of the women on Sinatra's list — the one given here in this chapter or the one on the back of his dressing room door at MGM studios — were probably as adept in that department as Ava Gardner. She had held no special allure for former husband Artie Shaw; the clarinetist and bandleader dumped her after one year.

Was it an attraction of like personalities that pulled Sinatra and Gardner together? They were both among the most hot-tempered, jealous, and short-fused people in the entertainment business. Both had a propensity to throw things when angry, out windows or at other people. There was no such thing as a slow boil when it came to those two; they erupted. Or was it a matter of opposites attracting? Frank was guilt-ridden his whole life — initially by the experience of living under the same roof as Dolly, then mostly over his abandonment of Nancy and the kids, but with an assortment of other *mea culpas* tossed in. Ava, like Dolly, never felt guilty about anything. Whatever pleasure Ava provided to Frank, she also gave him an extraordinary amount of pain. While on their honeymoon in Havana, in late 1951, she phoned Lucille Wellman, a friend. "We've already had fifteen fights," she told Wellman, "and that's just today. He's under a lot of pressure. I'm just not the patient, understanding type."[9]

Skitch Henderson, Sinatra's conductor for nightclub appearances, had his own take on the power Ava had over Frank. It was an opinion he kept to himself, until long after the principal actors in this drama were gone.

"She was like a Svengali to him," Henderson said. "She was an enigma. A mysterious presence. You didn't quite know how she had done it to him, and I'm not sure I wanted to know. She was ruthless with him. And it used to affect his mood a great deal. It could be horrible to be with him then. Her acid tongue and her ability to just put you away. If ever I knew a tiger, or a panther . . . I'm trying to think of an animal that would describe her . . . To be honest — I never let anyone on to this — but I did what I could to stay out of her way. I was scared to death of her."[10]

Shirley MacLaine saw something not many others did. In her 1995 memoir, published while Sinatra was still alive (in contrast to other commentators, who waited until Ol' Blue Eyes was in the grave before letting loose), she wrote of this particular aspect of Sinatra's life. "Ava satisfied an insatiable need of Frank's to be bullied by a strong mother-figure," MacLaine said. "As I watched his obsession with Ava's unpredictable behavior, I could see the similarity between her and Dolly."[11]

In 1988, two years after suffering a stroke, Ava Gardner reached out to Peter Evans, a well-known British writer (Ava had been living in London for some time and considered it her home). She wanted Evans' help in writing a book about her life. Bantam Books would publish what purported to be Ava's autobiography in 1990, after Gardner's death on January 25 of that year. It was most likely ghostwritten, and Ava would have seen all or part of the manuscript beforehand. So she knew what to expect from the Bantam Book version of her life and, evidently, wasn't satisfied with that version.

After taking her call late one night in January 1988 and hearing her proposal, Evans responded in the affirmative, but with one reservation.

"Sounds great, Ava," Evans said. "Does Frank approve? I don't want to upset Frank."[12]

Evans and Sinatra had had a run-in some years earlier, and knowing that the former lovers remained friends more than 30 years after their divorce, the writer was being prudent. With Sinatra, as everyone knew, an abundance of caution was always the right policy. Ava paused a moment, then replied to the question, as only Ava Gardner could.

"Fuck Frank. Are you interested or not, honey?"[13]

Evans agreed to be Ava's new ghostwriter, but before beginning the process, he reached out to people in the entertainment business who had known Gardner and might be able to give him insight into what made her tick. One of those he called was Peter Viertel, then living on the Spanish Costa del Sol with his second wife, actress Deborah Kerr. Viertel had been a friend of Artie Shaw's and knew Gardner ever since her marriage to Shaw. He also wrote the screenplay for *The Sun Also Rises*, a 1957 film based on Ernest Hemingway's novel of the same name, in which Gardner starred.

"Don't even think about it," Viertel warned Evans, "if you value your sanity; she was a ballbreaker then [in 1946] and she'll still be a ballbreaker. But she's also beautiful and smart, and you're going to go ahead with her book whatever I say."[14]

Viertel was right — Evans did go ahead with the book. But he also valued Viertel as a source and later sat down with him over lunch for a more extensive interview. Viertel was a product of Hollywood, having been raised in the movie capital, and he knew many of the stars of the 1930s and '40s. The two friends chatted and shared anecdotes before getting down to Gardner, the reason for their meeting.

"Let me tell you something: Nobody handles Ava Gardner," Viertel said. "Artie Shaw was a smart guy, a regular polymath — as well as a male chauvinist shit of the first order — and he couldn't handle her, and neither could Luis Miguel Dominguín, one of the bravest bullfighters in Spain."

"What about Sinatra?" Evans asked.

"Sinatra, the poor bastard, never stood a chance," Viertel said, shaking his head, "and he loved her probably most of all. He was too possessive of her; that was the problem, or one of the problems — no one is ever going to possess Ava."[15]

* * *

In April 1951, MGM executives were crowing about the good reception *Show Boat* was receiving in test screenings, even before its formal premiere, set for later that year. Among the things viewers liked best was Ava Gardner's performance. As a reward, the studio granted Ava time off, along with the promise of a big salary increase at contract renewal time. Flush with that good news, she joined Frank back in New York City, where he was still struggling with his television show for CBS. Ava visited the set to observe and was unimpressed with the production. "I got a nervous breakdown just watching," she later recalled.[16]

On April 25, Sinatra began a two-week engagement at the Paramount, the scene of his stunning debut as a solo act on December 30, 1942, and of the Columbus Day riot his fans caused in October 1944, when thousands couldn't get into the 3,600-seat theater to see any of his shows. In April and early May of 1951, however, the "Voice that Thrilled Millions" was playing to sparse audiences. Joe Bushkin and his orchestra were backing up the singer at the Paramount. Bushkin also appeared as a guest on *The Frank Sinatra Show*.[17]

"This was a tough period for Frank," remembered Bushkin, a Dorsey-band alumnus and Sinatra pal. "He was not drawing. Some shows, like the supper show, the theater would be half-empty."[18]

Sinatra complained to Bushkin about the financial burden his payments to Nancy were causing. "I have no idea," Sinatra told his old buddy, "how the hell I'm gonna come up with the money I need to get semi-even with all this."[19] Bushkin was only *semi*-impressed with this tale of financial woe.

"Well, he was making some good money," Bushkin said, "but he was very good about spending it, you know. And this was a time when he was really in love with Ava. But she could be rough on him. She was very independent, and she didn't tolerate any nonsense from a man that she was with, you know? And if there was something that he said, she would kind of blow up, you know? Like all of a sudden, she's yelling, 'Who the fuck do you think you are?' That kinda thing. She was always the bandleader in that duo. That's a way of putting it: She was the bandleader."[20]

Despite the poor attendance at his Paramount engagement, which ended on May 8, Sinatra's voice was regaining some of its former strength, after the Copacabana breakdown in the spring of 1950. His recording of "I'm a Fool to Want You" on March 27, 1951, had shown it. In fact, an argument could be made that there was an added quality to his voice now, one not present in the boy singer of the 1940s. At the halfway point in the 20th century, however, America's taste in music was on a different tack, as Sinatra himself learned by virtue of his declining record sales. It may have been brought home earlier, when, as the lead singer on *Your Hit Parade*, he'd been required to sing one particular week's No. 1 hit — "The Woody Woodpecker Song," a mindless tune based on a cartoon character.[21] It would top the charts for six weeks. The records that were selling were novelty songs, about "that doggie in the window" and about a rolling, whip-cracking "mule train" and about doing "The Hucklebuck" — gimmicky records, just what Mitch Miller at Columbia Records specialized in. And it was Miller who brought to Sinatra a song that would forever be associated with his embarrassing decline in popular appeal at that point in his career.[22]

Dagmar, a West Virginia-born actress whose main claim to fame was her bountiful bosom, was on the bill with Sinatra at the Paramount. (During the show, Sinatra would warn the audience not to sit in the front row of the theater, lest they be smothered when she took a bow.) Miller's new song for Sinatra — they would record it at a May 10 session in New York — was "Mama Will Bark," a stupid and confusing ditty in which a girl fends off her boyfriend's amorous advances, fearing that her dog would wake up her mother, or something to that effect. Dagmar supplied the reluctant-girl part, and Frank sang the male lead (he refused to bark, however — a stand-in provided that sound effect).[23] For the rest of his life, Sinatra would blame Mitch Miller for pressuring him into recording that terrible song, but the truth is, Sinatra made the decision. His contract with Columbia Records gave him the final say on all material, so he could have vetoed anything Miller put in front of him. He didn't, because he desperately wanted a hit. The added tragedy of "Mama Will Bark" is that it was released (in June 1951) as the B-side to a truly great recording, "I'm a Fool to Want You."

* * *

The biggest source of Ava's frustration — and, therefore, of Frank's torment — during the first two years of their relationship was Nancy Sinatra's refusal to give Frank a divorce. Claiming to be a devout Catholic, despite the abortion she underwent in 1947, Nancy remained resolute. At the court proceeding in September 1950, at which she was awarded a sizable support and maintenance package, she had expressed a forlorn hope that Frank would return to her some day. Rankled by Frank's passivity on the issue, Ava made him pay dearly for her continued status as a "Jezebel" and "home wrecker," instead of the status she aspired to — Mrs. Frank Sinatra.

But Nancy was overplaying her hand. Even Hedda Hopper, a champion of the wronged wife among Hollywood gossip columnists, had begun to turn against her in this two-year imbroglio. As divorce discussions dragged on, Hopper urged Nancy, in print, "to think of the children and let him go."[24] Then, on May 29, 1951, after Frank begged her, in person, for his freedom, Nancy announced to the press that she would agree to a divorce. "This is what Frank wants," Nancy told reporters, "and I've said yes. I have told the attorneys to work out the details."[25] Later, in that era's celebrity tradition of airing dirty laundry in public, Nancy called Louella Parsons to put a fine point on things.

"I don't think a woman can be blamed for trying to hold her home together, especially when there are children," Nancy told Parsons. "I held out a long time because I love Frank and I thought he would come back. But, when I saw that there was absolutely no chance, and that he really wanted to marry someone else, I had my lawyer get in touch with his lawyer. I am now convinced that a divorce is the only way for my happiness, as well as Frank's."[26]

The news brought a respite to Sinatra on two fronts, the stormy relationship with Ava as well as his declining career prospects. With this thorn removed from the paw of the panther — or whatever ferocious animal Skitch Henderson settled on to describe Ava Gardner — there was peace in the valley, for a while. And, as was often the case with Sinatra, his professional life prospered when his personal life was not in turmoil. He had a successful one-week gig in early June at New York's Latin Quarter, a smaller venue than the Copacabana, but a prestigious one nonetheless. On June 9, 1951, his CBS television program aired its final show of the season. It was a rocky first season, but he would be coming back in the fall.

One thing Sinatra was particularly excited about was a picture deal he'd just accepted. Since being dropped by MGM a year earlier, Sinatra was *persona non grata* in Hollywood; no movie studio had shown the slightest interest, until now. Universal International signed him to play the lead in *Meet Danny Wilson*, a film that might have been written with Frank Sinatra in mind — the similarities between its title character and Sinatra were so flat-out striking.[27] Frank's co-star would be actress Shelley Winters. Biographer Tom Santopietro explained the significance of this picture. "What makes *Meet Danny Wilson* so interesting to view," Santopietro wrote, ". . .

are two factors: (1) for the first time, the 'real' and 'reel' Frank Sinatras intersect, and (2) the film represents the first comprehensive and decisive proof that Frank Sinatra had the makings of a dramatic actor."[28]

Sinatra, as Danny Wilson, plays a down-on-his-luck singer who rises to sudden stardom. Several scenes in the picture are reminiscent of real-life episodes in Sinatra's life — a mob manager who takes 50 percent of the singer's earnings as his cut (channeling the deal with Tommy Dorsey); attending a prize fight with a beautiful girl on his arm (as Frank often did, with Ava and others); the sex-charged electricity in the room when he sang (always present when Sinatra was at his best); and an SRO appearance at the Paramount Theatre, complete with screaming fans (but no bobby-soxers). The film also gave Sinatra outstanding songs, all of which he sang to perfection: "Lonesome Man Blues," "She's Funny That Way," "That Old Black Magic," "When You're Smiling," and "How Deep Is the Ocean."[29]

One sour note occurred during the July 1951 filming. Sinatra and Winters did not get along — their personalities clashed repeatedly. She was put off by his brusque manner and lax work ethic on the set and intimidated by his superior voice when they were called upon to sing a duet. He thought of her as a loud-mouthed broad and, in front of others, used words like "bowlegged bitch of a Brooklyn blonde" to describe her. She countered with "skinny, no-talent, stupid Hoboken bastard."[30]

The feuding came to a head just days before the shooting was to wrap. In one scene, Sinatra was supposed to say to Winters and her love-interest in the film, "I'll go have a cup of coffee and leave you two lovebirds alone." Instead, he said, "I'll go have a cup of Jack Daniel's or I'm going to pull that blond broad's hair out by its black roots." Winters exploded and walked off the set. She stayed away for three days, only returning to finish the picture after getting a tearful call from Nancy Sinatra, whom Winters considered a friend. Nancy said that Frank wouldn't get paid the $25,000 he was contracted to receive until the picture was done and that she and the children desperately needed the money.[31]

Sinatra had been in a foul mood to begin with. *Show Boat* was released in July, amid tumultuous praise for Ava Gardner. Frank didn't begrudge her that, but Ava's success placed his failures in stark contrast, especially when he had to accompany her to the Hollywood premiere. They skipped the after parties, so intent was he on avoiding more press scrutiny. Another blow was struck in July: CBS pulled the plug on his weekly radio show, after just nine months.

But all was not doom and gloom. That summer, Paul "Skinny" D'Amato, titular owner of Atlantic City's 500 Club (called "The Five" by insiders), invited his friend Sinatra to appear for 10 days at the hottest venue on the Jersey Shore.[32] D'Amato, tagged "Mr. Atlantic City" for his philanthropic and other civic activities in that fading New Jersey resort, was the frontman for Philadelphia Mafia boss Angelo Bruno.[33] He was also a close friend of up-and-coming Chicago mobster Sam "Momo" Giancana, whom he would introduce to Sinatra at The Five in 1953.

Frank had never run from his Italian heritage — he reveled in it, a fact that endeared him to New Jersey's Italians. Whenever the singer appeared in that state — at whatever stage of his career, the heights or the pits — his fellow New Jerseyans came out in force to support him, as they did in 1951. D'Amato needed a dozen extra cops to manage the crowds. Those who were lucky enough to get inside the club reacted madly to every song and gesture by Sinatra. Elsewhere, Frank Sinatra was a pariah; here, at The Five, he was the conquering hero, returned home.[34]

"It was like you were seeing the Messiah come to town," a waitress at a nearby restaurant remarked. "That's how he was to the Italians. They went crazy."[35]

In August, Frank and Ava took a brief vacation in Acapulco. Upon their return to California, they announced their engagement, before Frank hurried off to fulfill a two-week engagement at a casino-hotel in Reno, Nevada, while sporting a pencil-thin mustache for the first time in his life. The look did not suit him ("pimp-like," Pete Hamill called it) and would soon disappear, at just about the same time the newfound bliss in the Sinatra-Gardner affair would.

They were staying at Lake Tahoe for the Labor Day weekend, with Hank Sanicola and his wife. An argument ensued, once again over some petty jealousy or perceived slight. Ava left in a huff and drove back home to Los Angeles. Shortly after arriving, she got a frantic call from Sanicola.

"Oh, my God, Ava. Hurry back!" Sanicola implored. "Frank's taken an overdose!"[36]

Gardner flew back to Tahoe and rushed to the house Sinatra had rented. Frank was okay — he'd taken too many phenobarbital pills, but not enough to warrant his stomach being pumped. He was sitting up when Ava walked into the bedroom and gave her a wan smile. "I thought you'd gone," he said.

"I could have killed him, but instead I forgave him in about 25 seconds," Ava wrote in her 1990 memoir. "We had no time for these nerve-destroying incidents. I know now that Frank's mock suicide dramas — his desperate love signals to get me back to his side — were, at root, cries for help. He was down, way down."[37] Gardner put it more bluntly, years later, when she talked to Peter Evans about her life with Sinatra. "Frank was flat broke when we tied the knot," she said. "The poor darling was on his ass. His voice had gone. His records weren't selling. His movie contract had been dropped. His confidence was shot."[38]

There was one source of support that Frank Sinatra could always count on when he was down: his friends in the mob. Paul "Skinny" D'Amato had given him a strong payday, when he performed for 10 days to a packed showroom every night. They had to add an extra show on several of those evenings, just to accommodate fans waiting outside for a chance to hear their Frankie sing. In early September, Sinatra performed for the first time in Las Vegas, the city he would dominate in later years, based on his unmatched power to draw high rollers to the casinos.[39] Moe Dalitz, who ran the Desert Inn for the Detroit and Cleveland mobs,[40] booked Sinatra into his main showroom. He and Sinatra had been friends ever since their first encounter in Havana in 1947, during the Lucky Luciano mob summit.

Las Vegas was designated a wide-open city by the syndicate, with each hotel-owning cartel of mobsters respecting the turf of other gangs. "Live and let live" was the policy, with plenty of skim for everyone. Meyer Lansky, Joe Adonis, Frank Costello, Longy Zwillman, and Doc Stacher owned the controlling interest in the Sands Hotel and Casino, which opened its doors in 1952. Sinatra was permitted to buy a 2 percent share of the Sands shortly after it opened, with the understanding that he would make it his exclusive venue when performing in Las Vegas and that he would persuade his entertainer friends to perform there as well. Later, as his star rose, he acquired an additional 7 percent, bringing his total share to 9 percent.[41]

The Riviera and Sahara, when they opened, were controlled by Tony "Joe Batters" Accardo, Sam Giancana, and the Fischetti brothers, all leaders in the Chicago mob. New England mob boss Raymond Patriarca controlled the Dunes Hotel and Casino. A few years into the Las Vegas boom, Caesar's Palace became the biggest moneymaker, and Accardo, Giancana, Patriarca, Jerry Catena (a Genovese family underboss), and Vincent "Jimmy Blue Eyes" Alo all had a piece. Jimmy Hoffa got them Teamster Union pension funds to finance the deal.[42]

Sinatra used his Reno and Las Vegas engagements over the summer and early fall of 1951 to establish a six-week residency in Nevada, the minimum requirement for a quickie divorce in what was then the divorce capital of the United States. Although Nancy got an interlocutory divorce decree in California on October 30, 1951, it would not become final, legally, for one year. Not content to wait any longer, and not willing to suffer Ava's wrath if that were to happen, Frank got his own Nevada divorce.

He and Ava were now free to marry. They flew back to New York, then traveled to Philadelphia to obtain a marriage license. Hoping to avoid the New York press, it was their plan to get married there, at the home of Lester Sacks, Manie's brother. But the marriage almost didn't happen, because of Ava's old pursuer, Howard Hughes. The bombshell came in the form of a letter, which, Ava suspected, Hughes had instigated.

"Apparently it had been given to the head bellman, and as it was handwritten and addressed personally to me," Ava recalled, "it was brought directly to my room. I opened it, I read it through, and I could hardly go on breathing. It was from a woman who admitted she was a whore and claimed she had been having an affair with Frank. It was filthy. It gave details that I found convincing, and I felt sick to my stomach."[43]

Ava rushed to her bedroom and locked the door, telling Bappie to announce to the gathered friends that the wedding was off. "Now the bedlam began," Ava said. "Frank was going crazy." Finally, she let herself be convinced to go through with the nuptials, but the experience left an indelible mark on the marriage, as if it needed any more impediments to its success.

The entourage traveled to Philadelphia on November 7, 1951, and Francis Albert Sinatra married the love of his life, Ava Lavinia Gardner, amid popping champagne corks and the good wishes of their closest friends and family. Dolly and Marty Sinatra were there, of course, as was Bappie. Manie Sacks gave away the bride. Hank Sanicola and Ben Barton, Frank's partners in a music company, were there, along with pianist/arranger Dick Jones and Axel Stordahl, Frank's primary arranger during the early Columbia years, the good years. The press had not been fooled, however, and Frank had his usual run-in with them outside Lester Sacks' home. But he and Ava managed to slip away to the airport, where a private Beechcraft was waiting to whisk them to Miami, the first stop on their honeymoon. The next day, they flew to Havana, hoping to avoid any further blowups with members of the Fourth Estate.[44]

Later, back in the States, it wouldn't take long for the battles to resume, fueled by the same old jealousies, but also by the growing disparity between Ava's successful movie career and Frank's dismal prospects in just about every aspect of his professional life. Gardner landed a role in Twentieth Century Fox's *The Snows of Kilimanjaro,* co-starring Gregory Peck; she was on loan to Fox from MGM. At Frank's insistence, she agreed to do the picture, but only if the studio compressed her scenes into 10 days of shooting, so as not to cause her to be away from Frank for long.[45]

Meet Danny Wilson had premiered in San Francisco on February 8, 1952, and did poorly with reviewers and audiences alike.[46] Hoping to give the film a boost, Sinatra persuaded Robert Weitman, his old friend at the Paramount Theatre, to feature *Meet Danny Wilson* on the same program in which he would be appearing live, March 26-April 8. Weitman reluctantly agreed to run the picture. Both the movie and Sinatra's live show were "a box-office disaster." During the Paramount engagement, on April 1, 1952, CBS announced that it was canceling *The Frank Sinatra Show* due to poor ratings (in its new time slot, the show had been pitted against "Mr. Television" himself, Milton Berle). *The World Telegram and Sun* had a succinct way of describing Sinatra's circumstances in the spring of 1952: "Gone on Frankie in '42; Gone in '52."[47]

Ava was in New York with Frank for the Paramount engagement, but her presence did little to help his morale. While in New York, Ava and Frank went to the Copacabana one night to see a new singing sensation, Johnnie Ray, then making his debut at the famed club. Ray was Mitch

Miller's latest discovery at Columbia Records and was riding the top of the charts with his hit "Cry," a schmaltzy bit right smack in Miller's wheelhouse. Sinatra detested the performer and the performance (he thought Ray had made a pass at Ava backstage at the Paramount when Ray had dropped by) but kept his feelings to himself, for the most part, when a reporter asked him for his impression. The contrast to Sinatra's recent nightclub and concert appearances was stark — the Copa was packed for Johnnie Ray's show.

Frank and Ava headed back to California, but on April 22, they left for Hawaii. He was booked for a series of concerts there and asked Ava to go along. One of the dates was in a tent, of all places, at the Kauai County Fair. A leaky tent, in fact. It poured during Frank's performance. He was meticulously turned out in his black tuxedo, as usual, and carried on for the few hundred folks who braved the weather to see him, despite water dripping on him. It had to have been a humiliating experience for Sinatra and was an indication of how badly he needed a payday. After the performance, he expressed his feelings to Ava, within earshot of a reporter, unfortunately.[48]

"I'm really washed up," Frank said. "I oughta just face it. The public is finished with me. I had my day in the sun."[49]

Ava wouldn't stand for that kind of talk. She tried to dispel Frank's black mood. "Over my dead body," she said. "No one with your talent is ever washed up. This is just a bad time. Trust me."[50]

With a saucy look, she added something that brought a smile to Frank's lips.

"Rub my ass," she quipped. "It'll give you good luck."[51]

Frank did as Ava suggested.

"You know I love you, don't you," he said.

"Of course you do," she said.[52]

The good luck would come in time, thanks in no small measure not only to Ava Gardner's magnificent derrière but also to her intercession, at a crucial moment in Frank's career, with Harry Cohn, the powerful head of Columbia Pictures. Cohn ultimately controlled every aspect of his studio's operations, including the choice of actors for important roles. He had recently purchased film rights to a 1951 novel by first-time author

James Jones. The book detailed the seamy side of Army life at Schofield Barracks in pre-war Hawaii and would go on to win the National Book Award for Fiction in 1952. It would also be the spark for the most amazing turnaround in entertainment history.

13

"I knew Maggio. I went to school with him in Hoboken. I was beaten up with him. I might have been Maggio."

Frank Sinatra, the brash Hoboken kid who planted his flag at the pinnacle of show business success in the 1940s, turned into "Mr. Ava Gardner"[1] in the early 1950s — that's how low he had sunk, in his own mind and in the public's perception of him. That perception was enhanced by a special provision Ava had inserted into her new Metro-Goldwyn-Mayer contract in 1952. She had clout in the negotiations because of the smashing box-office results for *Show Boat*, which became the third-highest-grossing picture of 1951. Not only could MGM count on Gardner to carry any film she was associated with; the studio could also farm her out to other production companies for much higher fees than before. MGM willingly increased its per-film payment to Gardner from $90,000 to $130,000, thereby catapulting her into the upper reaches of Hollywood salaries. Studio executives also agreed, reluctantly, to a contract requirement that Gardner insisted upon — one that became known as "the Frank Sinatra Clause."[2]

This was not something Ava would have done on her own; it's obvious that she and Frank discussed the matter beforehand. The clause required the studio, during the 10-year term of the new contract, to co-star both Ava and Frank together in at least one motion picture. Once again, it was Sinatra trying to jump-start his movie career any way he could, even to the extent of riding his wife's coattails. MGM so watered down the clause with legalese that it would, in the end, be no guarantee at all. And the studio never made good on it. All it achieved was Frank's further humiliation.[3] But there was more to come.

In May 1952, Ava suffered a miscarriage, triggered by a drunken brawl with Frank. She may not have realized she was pregnant — in any event, she hadn't shared that information with her husband. Frank was appearing at the Cocoanut Grove in Los Angeles. Ava attended opening night, but many of their friends deliberately stayed away during Sinatra's run, so as not to be subjected to the cringe factor of another sub-par performance.[4] Back at home after one night's late show and fueled by alcohol and Frank's continuing despair, the two went at it again, but with a difference. Frank slapped her, something he had never done before. She fell over a table, went down to the floor, and started to bleed. Frantic and immediately remorseful, Frank called for an ambulance, and Ava was rushed to Cedars of Lebanon hospital.[5]

The incident never made the papers, but was revealed for the first time in Lee Server's biography of Gardner. Actor Roddy McDowall, a close Gardner friend, confirmed the details years later, based on a conversation he'd had with Ava. She was treated at the hospital just before dawn on May 24 by Dr. Leon Krohn, a gynecologist and friend of Frank's,[6] which may explain how it was kept quiet. Frank was with her afterward, helping her to recuperate, but he kept a recording date right in Hollywood on June 3.

It was his next-to-last session for the Columbia label. Within weeks, Columbia would announce that, because of poor sales, it was dropping its former recording star when his contract expired at the end of the year. At this penultimate session, Frank recorded five sides, including a memorable rendition of "The Birth of the Blues"; the other recordings, including the awful "Bim Bam Baby," were mostly paeans to the Mitch Miller influence.[7] Frank's booking agent, Music Corporation of America, also cut him loose at about the same time, but did so in a nasty, almost retaliatory way. Frank was no longer a profitable client and, according to MCA, owed the agency back commissions, which he wouldn't, or couldn't, pay. MCA bought full-page ads in the two most influential entertainment media — *Variety* and the *Hollywood Reporter* — to announce its parting with Sinatra.

Columbia and MCA had been the twin pillars of Frank's early solo career, having combined forces in 1943 to get him out from under Dorsey's onerous deal involving his future earnings. Losing them both like this had to have been a bitter pill. By June 7, Ava and Frank's seven-month anniversary, Ava was better and Frank was off to Chicago for a nightclub engagement. Given the financial straitjacket he was in, he couldn't pass it up. Besides, it was a Mafia favor he couldn't refuse.

Later in Sinatra's career, Chicago became one of his favorite cities in which to perform. It was the setting for his 1964 production of *Robin and the 7 Hoods*, a 1930s mob spoof featuring Rat Packers Frank, Dean, and Sammy, along with Bing Crosby. (Peter Lawford and Joey Bishop had been banished from Sinatra's inner circle at that point.) Sammy Cahn and Jimmy Van Heusen wrote a lively score for the movie, including the Academy Award-nominated song "My Kind of Town (Chicago Is)." The song became a showstopper in Sinatra's concert and nightclub performances from then on, especially in the Windy City. But in June 1952, Chicago was, for Sinatra, anything *but* his kind of town. Frank was booked into the Chez Paree, his pal Joe Fischetti's place, but the engagement failed to raise his spirits, for good reason. At some shows, he played to an audience of just 150 paying customers, in a room that seated 1,200. It seemed like Sinatra couldn't catch a break, no matter how hard he tried.

Frank's press agents, with the help of Ava and Manie Sacks, persuaded him to make peace with the press — the constant barrage of negative publicity was killing him. Unfortunately, their proposed solution to the problem violated Sinatra's career-long insistence on privacy regarding his personal life and caused lasting damage to his image, especially in Hoboken among the people who knew him growing up. Frank agreed to have his publicists write a two-part series for *American Weekly*, the Sunday supplement folded into every Hearst newspaper in the country and reaching tens of millions of readers. The articles, published in July 1952, carried a Frank Sinatra byline.[8] In other words, he would appear to be telling his own story — a concocted story, as it turned out — and, in effect, asking for understanding and forgiveness.

The lyrics for "My Way" — Sinatra's most requested song in later years, one he often referred to as "the anthem" — portray a man with the strength "to say the things he truly feels, and not the words of one who kneels."[9] In the *American Weekly* pieces, titled "Frankly Speaking," Sinatra not only kneeled, he groveled.

"The press generally has been wonderful to me," Sinatra's ghostwriter wrote, "and I know that without their help I never could have become famous or earned more money than I ever believed existed when I was a slum kid in Hoboken. My only excuse for being abrupt and curt . . . is that I was nervous and distraught from the events of the past year."[10]

The articles fabricated a "slum" upbringing, interspersed with "race wars" and "vicious gang fights," all to curry favor with the media and public. He was claiming *victimhood*, so that his press adversaries would take it easy on him. His parents, Sinatra said, were so poor they "needed whatever money" he "could bring into the house." And so, young Frankie was forced into "hooking candy from the corner store, then little things from the five-and-dime, then change from cash registers, and finally, we were up to stealing bicycles."[11] Dolly, who had managed the Sinatra family's rise in Hoboken so assiduously that Frank never wanted for anything, had to have been livid when she (and her friends) read this blather.

"Slacksey O'Brien," as Hoboken folks knew, had had his own charge account at a local department store. His mother bought him a shiny new bike and, later, when he was 15, a used Chrysler convertible to tool around in. The family took vacations to the shore and the mountains, and Frank always had enough pocket money to treat friends to a movie or ice cream soda. After reading the articles, Dolly commented to one reporter, "I didn't know any of those things he said he did. I brought him up right."[12] We don't know how she expressed her displeasure in private, but can presume she used more colorful language.

As to his Mafia connections, Sinatra acknowledged knowing some disreputable characters, but once again chalked it up to the unavoidable consequence of being a saloon singer. They owned the clubs he performed in. Sinatra was contrite regarding his 12-year marriage to Nancy, but said it

Portrait of Frank Sinatra, Liederkranz Hall, New York, N.Y., circa 1947.

Portrait of Frank Sinatra, Liederkranz Hall, New York, N.Y., circa 1947.

Frank Sinatra and Ava Gardner on their wedding day, November 7, 1951. Frank considered Ava the love of his life, but it was a tempestuous relationship, start to finish. They separated in October 1953 and divorced in 1957, but Frank took on a protective role regarding Ava Gardner for the rest of her life. She died in January 1990.

SOURCE: BETTMANN/CORBIS

Lana Turner, in October 1941, inspecting the ankle-flattering bracelet design embroidered on dressy, fine point lisle cotton mesh hose. Nylon was being used for parachutes and other war-related purposes at the time. In her memoir, Turner would claim that she and Frank Sinatra did not have a romantic relationship, but the consensus of opinion says otherwise. Their affair began in the mid-1940s.

SOURCE: LIBRARY OF CONGRESS

Mug shot of Willie Moretti, underboss to Frank Costello and in charge of gambling and other illegal activity in northern New Jersey. He lived in Hasbrouck Heights, New Jersey, from the early 1930s. The young Sinatra family (Frank, Nancy, and Nancy Jr.) moved into a house around the corner from Moretti in 1942 and would remain his neighbor through 1944. Moretti ran the illegal casino in the Riviera nightclub in Fort Lee and had a behind-the-scenes interest in the Rustic Cabin, where Frank got his first important singing job in 1938.

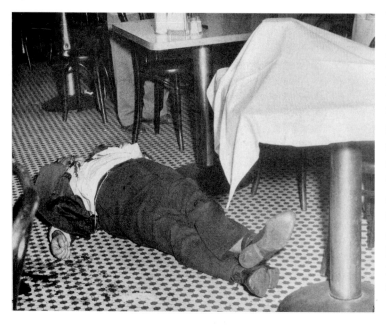

Willie Moretti lies dead on the floor of Joe's Elbow Room, a Cliffside Park, New Jersey, restaurant, gunned down in a gangland assassination on October 4, 1951, after Moretti got too friendly during testimony before the Kefauver Committee.

Mafia boss Frank Costello is shown seated behind a microphone while testifying, in 1951, before the Senate's Kefauver Committee investigating organized crime. Costello survived an assassination attempt in 1957 and went into retirement. Author Mario Puzo supposedly modeled the Don Vito Corleone title character in his best-selling novel, The Godfather, largely on Costello, who gave Frank Sinatra assists early in his career. *World Telegram & Sun,* photo by Al Aumuller

Mug shot of Carlo Gambino, another Five Families mob boss and fan of Frank Sinatra.

Regional editors, index, and the complete weather report appear on Page 2.

EAST **The Record** BERGEN

Friend of the People It Serves

Vol. 68 — No. 158   60 PAGES — Four Sections   MONDAY, DECEMBER 9, 1963   7 ☆

Kidnappers Grab Younger Sinatra

Frank Jr. Seized Before Show By Armed Pair

Stateline, Nev. (UPI) — Frank Sinatra Jr., 19, was kidnapped at gunpoint from this Lake Tahoe gambling center last night, and police in two States issued an all-points bulletin for two young prison refugees suspected of the abduction.

A driving snowstorm at this 6,225-foot high resort in the Sierra Nevada hampered efforts by F. B. I. agents and California and Nevada sheriff's deputies to find the son of the famous entertainer.

Roadblocks were set up on three roads leading from the area. But 11 hours after the kidnapping, Sinatra and his abductors were still missing.

The young singer was forced from his motel room shortly before he was to perform at a plush gambling casino (Harrah's) at 10 o'clock last night.

CALLED DANGEROUS

With Sinatra was John Foss, a member of the band with whom the young singer was appearing. The gunmen bound and gagged Foss and as they left with Sinatra, one warned "Don't move for 10 minutes or you want to see the kid again."

The abductors were armed with a sawed-off shotgun and a .45-caliber pistol.

Nested in the all-points bulletin the were Joseph J. Sorce, 23, and Thomas Keating, 21, both from Los Angeles County. They already face kidnapping charges rising from their escape October 30 from the Chino Institution, Tracy, Calif. State Prison, when they forced a 16-year-old boy to drive them to freedom. They are suspected of robbing two Southern California banks after their escape and were described as extremely dangerous.

Sinatra's father arrived at Reno early today from Palm Springs, Calif., after being notified of the abduction. He was held incommunicado at a Reno hotel.

The youth's mother, Nancy Sinatra, Sinatra's first wife, was keeping her phone line open at her Hollywood home in case the abductors made a ransom demand.

Stateline straddles the boundary. (Continued Page 12, Column 4)

LONG ORDEAL IN FORT LEE

Distraught Sinatras Await Word

By DAVID SCHMERLER
(Staff Writer)

Fort Lee — The anxious hours of early morning went slowly by the the last Mrs. Nancy Sinatra was one of those

FLIES TO KIDNAP SCENE: Frank Sinatra steps from a private plane, his concern for Frank Jr. etched into his face, as he was kidnapped from a motel last night. (U. P. I. Telephoto.)

Johnson Gets Record Guard

But N. Y. Police Admit That Determined Assassin Could Have Killed Him

New York (UPI) — The police admitted today that a determined assassin could have killed President Johnson in spite of the record 2,000-men security guard laid on for the three-hour visit to New York City.

"If some one had wanted to put down manned by security can the President, he could have done it," said a veteran plainclothes policeman assigned to yesterday's protective forces. "There is no way to stop a determined assassin."

The officer conceded, however, that it would have been difficult for a sniper armed with a high-powered rifle to have hit the President.

A phalanx of 20 motorcycle policemen surrounded the limousine about," the detective said. "Some one could have tossed a hand grenade under the car. There is just too much to watch.

The elaborate security arrangements for the Presidential trip started last week when it was announced that Johnson would go to New York to attend the funeral of Herbert (Continued Page 12)

BOLIVIA MINERS RADIO THREATS IN ULTIMATUM

Union Is Still Holding Foreign Hostages; Four Americans

TROOPS CALLED UP

Government Says No To Bid To Release Red Leaders

La Paz, Bolivia ☆ — Communist-led tin miners holding four Americans among 21 hostages today gave the Government 24 hours to free two arrested Communists or suffer consequences. The ultimatum raised fears for the hostages' safety.

The Federation of Mine Workers sent their word to the Government by way of radio transmissions from their stronghold more than 130 miles south of this capital.

The miners, led by leftist vice-president Juan Lechin, defied a Government troop buildup and an offer from President Johnson of full United States assistance to the Government to win freedom for the hostages, held since Friday night.

The miners' broadcast said the Union wanted the release of the two Communist Union heads arrested by the Government during the day on Friday.

The leaders, Irineo Pimentel and Federico Escobar, were arrested on a court order in connection with union agitation against a Government crackdown on the Union's power in the operation of the mines. Bolivia's main source of income.

The broadcast said the Union was giving the Government the ultimatum to resolve the problem of detained Union leaders or suffer consequences.

But, investigators said, if the giant plane began to (Continued Page 12, Column 4)

REDS READY 7-YEAR TO HIKE CHEMICAL Y

BEYOND HELP: Firemen stand by helplessly on the rim of a giant crater bearing the 707 jetliner near Elkton, Md. (U. P. I. Telephoto.)

81 Die As Jet Plunges In Flames In Maryland

Witnesses Say Pan American Craft Was Struck By Lightning En Route To Philadelphia

Elkton, Md. (UPI) — A Pan American World Airways jetliner en-route from Puerto Rico to Philadelphia crashed in flames last night, apparently during a thunderstorm, killing all 81 persons aboard.

About two dozen policemen at the scene of the crash said the plane was struck by lightning.

It was at this precise moment last night that the plane's pilot radioed the Philadelphia control tower he was in a holding pattern before the three other Americans were in flames.

Plane Victim's Wife Hopeful He's Alive

Paramus Woman Still Can't Believe Mate Died In Jetliner Crash

By NANCY FAYE
(Staff Writer)

Paramus — The sobbing wife demanded that a last desperate phone call be placed to her husband last night in Puerto Rico confirming that the 36-day-old infant daughter of Mr. and Mrs. Leo Davila of Philadelphia, one

TWO MEN DIE IN CAR CRASH

Trapped In Wreckage Of Burning Auto

East Rutherford — Two men, one a 40-year-old smoke driver and his 16-year-old passenger, were burned to death Saturday night when their car hit

N. J. Legislature Back In Session

By JAMES P. LEAHY

Frank Sinatra with his mother and son at his father's funeral in Fort Lee, New Jersey, on January 28, 1969. Mild-mannered and soft-spoken, Marty Sinatra had deferred to wife Dolly in almost every respect while Frank was growing up — something that may have caused Frank to lose respect for his father. They became closer in later years, and Frank was truly devastated by his father's death.

Frank and wife Mia Farrow on a July 27, 1967, visit to his parents in Fort Lee, New Jersey. The 30-year age difference did not bode well for the marriage, which lasted little more than two years. Frank and Mia remained on good terms in later years.

President Richard M. Nixon, whom Sinatra supported in the 1972 presidential election, invited Frank to an April 17, 1973, dinner at the White House honoring Italian Prime Minister Giulio Andreotti (pictured far left). Frank (at center with the First Couple to his left) sang for 40 minutes to an enthralled audience. It was the first time Sinatra had sung in public in almost two years. He'd retired suddenly in 1971, while still relatively young (55) and in fine voice, shocking the entertainment world.

Frank Sinatra, shown filming a scene from *Contract on Cherry Street*, on June 22, 1977, in Korvette's department store, Paramus, New Jersey. Frank's mother had died approximately five months earlier in a plane crash, and at the time this movie was being filmed, the Hoboken Public Library, 18 miles from Paramus, was dedicating part of its facility for a Sinatra collection, which included a painting of Frank and Dolly. The library and Hoboken mayor invited Frank to attend the ceremony. When he failed to show for the event, the headline in the *New York Daily News* the next day read "No Homecoming for Ol' Blue Eyes; Hoboken Heartbroken He Stands 'Em Up."

Sinatra, in another scene for the same picture, *Contract on Cherry Street*. It was his first made-for-TV movie and received poor reviews. Sinatra was 61 at the time.

Frank Sinatra and Liza Minnelli, in concert at the Brendan Byrne Arena in East
Rutherford, New Jersey, on December 12, 1990 — Sinatra's 75th birthday.

Sinatra performs a solo during his December 12, 1990, "birthday concert." He was in decline as a performer by this time, as his memory began to fade.

was flawed at its inception: In his youthful exuberance, he had been unable to distinguish between friendship and love. He glossed over his infidelities, insisting that he and Ava had not begun their relationship until after he and Nancy were officially separated.[13] It was a tissue of lies, topped off by this embarrassing sign-off: "Well, there it is. That's my side of the story, and I must say I feel better for having gotten it off my chest. I know that I never meaningly hurt anyone, and for any wrongs I may have done through emotional acts or spur-of-the-moment decisions, I humbly apologize."[14]

Forty years later, Sinatra acknowledged to his daughter Nancy that the information in the *American Weekly* pieces was bogus. "It's C-R-A-P." he told her. "They made it all up."[15]

It is hard to imagine a more abject, demeaning recital of one's past sins. Ava was among the instigators of the article idea, but her opinion of Frank could only have been diminished after reading the end product. It clearly affected her attitude toward him, as evidenced by her subsequent behavior. She was assigned by MGM that summer to do a Western with Robert Taylor, Anthony Quinn, and her co-star from *Show Boat*, Howard Keel. *Ride, Vaquero!* was directed by John Farrow, father of Mia Farrow, then a gangly 9-year-old. The cast and crew moved to Kenab, Utah, for a month, where the outdoor scenes were to be shot. The scenery was gorgeous, but the area desolate. "It was the asshole of creation," Howard Keel recalled. "Beautiful territory, but . . . there was nothing there and nothing to do there. Nothing."[16]

Ava found something to do. According to Mia Farrow, Ava and John Farrow carried on an affair during the shooting of this picture.[17] The Hollywood rumor mill being in full operation, Frank had to have learned of Ava's infidelity, not the first of their relationship, but perhaps a first during their marriage. To compound things, late that summer Frank found out that Ava had been communicating again with Howard Hughes. Whether or not they were engaging in sexual relations was immaterial to Frank; his jealousy encompassed any contact whatsoever with past, current, or potential future rivals. During one drunken episode, Sinatra actually went out searching for Hughes, with a .38 revolver hidden in his jacket. Fortunately, he didn't find him. On another occasion, once again while drunk, Frank traced Ava to a Beverly Hills restaurant and barged in, only to find her having dinner with

Lana Turner and another girlfriend.[18] Frank started quarreling with Ava, perhaps following up on an earlier argument that night, but so loudly that everyone in the restaurant could hear. Ava and her friends ignored him, continuing their mealtime conversation as though he weren't there. That only infuriated Frank more. He left the place in a rage, shouting, without rhyme or reason, "Lesbians! You're a bunch of goddamned lesbians! All of you! Lesbians! Lesbians! Lesbians!"[19]

In late August, Frank, with a temporary Ava truce in effect, headed East to prepare for his much-anticipated engagement at Bill Miller's Riviera,[20] a nationally famous nightclub and illegal casino, high atop the Hudson Palisades in Fort Lee, New Jersey. He was scheduled to open there on September 5. Ava would fly in on September 10 to be with Frank for this important nightclub gig, as well as be on hand for the New York premiere of *The Snows of Kilimanjaro* on September 17.

The Riviera came into being in 1931, the same year the George Washington Bridge opened. Its original owner, Ben Marden, converted an older roadhouse, the Villa Richard, into his own club, secure in the knowledge that the new bridge, along with the big-name entertainers he planned on booking, would attract an abundance of new customers from New York City, now just a 10-minute drive away. The club burned down on Thanksgiving night, 1936, only to reopen in more spectacular fashion six months later, in May 1937. The *new* Riviera featured an art deco design, a rotating bandstand, a retractable roof that allowed patrons to dance under the stars, a line of scantily clad showgirls that would only be duplicated two decades later on the Las Vegas Strip, and "the Marine Room," a mob-run casino. The club was dark during World War II, but reopened in 1946 under Bill Miller's ownership. (Ben Marden would go on to run an illegal casino at the Colonial Inn in Hallandale, Florida, as a front for Meyer Lansky and others.[21]) The Riviera met its demise in late 1953, when the property was condemned to make way for the Palisades Interstate Highway.[22]

Gambling was then illegal in New Jersey, but the Garden State was one of the most corrupt in the nation, and law enforcement was easily bought off. But it didn't hurt to be careful. To get to the casino, a customer had to walk down a hallway on the main floor, past the restrooms, and enter a janitor's closet; there, he or she had another step to perform — plug in a fan

— before a wall opened to reveal a carpeted stairway leading to the second-floor gambling den.[23]

Newark mob boss Longy Zwillman and Mafia *capo* Willie Moretti ran the casino on behalf of the Frank Costello crime family in New York.[24] When Moretti was bumped off in October 1951, Hoboken native Angelo "Gyp" DeCarlo took his place at the Riviera.

"Everyone knew Bill Miller's Riviera was all mobbed up," Joseph Coffey, a retired NYPD lieutenant who had commanded that department's organized crime unit, recalled. "Most nights, the mobsters held court at the ringside tables. Back then, performers couldn't get work in any of the nightclubs unless they were connected to a mob guy, and the Riviera was a mecca for the mob. Gangsters from all over the country would go to the joint. They ran it."[25]

The mobsters involved in the Riviera were all Sinatra benefactors at one time or another, so it seems strange that there's no record of him performing there before this September 1952 gig. In her 1995 biography, Nancy Sinatra gave a detailed account of all her father's nightclub appearances, throughout his career, and she makes no mention of any performance at the Riviera prior to 1952. But in fact, Frank Sinatra may very well have performed at Ben Marden's Riviera, in 1938 or 1939, at about the same time he was singing at the Rustic Cabin, just up the road from the Riviera. Irene Bruno Orifice, in a December 6, 2013, interview for the Fort Lee Museum and again in an August 21, 2015, interview with this author, spoke of an earlier Sinatra appearance, as related to her by her father, Jack Bruno, who was a captain of waiters at the club. Sinatra was known as 'the singing waiter" back then, Ms. Orifice recalled, and did not draw very well when he sang at the Riviera. The club was less than half filled, which may be the reason he wasn't invited back until much later.[26]

This earlier, heretofore unknown Riviera appearance is entirely plausible, when viewed in combination with another piece of information: the "audition" Sinatra performed for Frank Costello and Willie Moretti around this same time, in 1938 or 1939, as related by pianist Chico Scimone.[27] Clearly, that command performance was a tryout for the Riviera, in front of the two mob guys who ran the Fort Lee nightclub behind the scenes, and it supports Ms. Orifice's story. Scimone told Costello and Moretti that Sinatra sang "fine," a lukewarm endorsement that was good enough to get him into the Riviera for this one shot.

In any event, on opening night, September 5, 1952, Sinatra was welcomed by a big Riviera audience and received good, if not excellent, reviews. *Variety* praised his "self-assurance" and "knowing way with a crowd, whatever the misadventures of his personal life and career."[28]

As promised, Ava arrived on September 10, and together they drove to Hoboken so that Frank could fulfill a promise he'd made to his father. The Hoboken Fire Department was holding a dinner at the Union Club, the place where Frank had gotten, with Dolly's help, his first full-time singing job as a solo act. Marty wanted Frank to sing a few numbers for his friends in the department, as well as for the other guests at the dinner — something he'd have time to do and still make it back to the Riviera, just 14 miles away, for his first show that night. Kitty Kelley interviewed Tony Macagnano, a childhood friend of Sinatra's, who was there at the Union Club the night of Sinatra's appearance.

"He came with Ava in a limousine," Macagnano recalled, "and his mom made sure there were cops with billy clubs to help him get through the crowd." Macagnano approached Sinatra and asked if he'd be willing to visit a mutual friend of theirs, sick in hospital, but Sinatra had a show to make at the Riviera and couldn't do it. And he had Ava along with him, someone he knew would not be approving of an old-home-boy detour. Frank couldn't stay for the dinner, of course, but he did go onto the stage and began to sing. When he "hit some clinkers," Macagnano said, "people booed him and threw fruit and stuff, kidding around." Sinatra blanched at the insult and hurried offstage and out the back door of the club. As he was leaving, he told a policeman friend, "Tony, I'll never come back and do another thing for the people of Hoboken as long as I live."[29] He would keep that vow for the next 32 years.

On Wednesday, September 17, Frank and Ava attended the premiere of *The Snows of Kilimanjaro*, and, understandably, she was the center of attention. Thousands of people crowded the entrance to the Rivoli Theatre to get a glimpse of her and, if possible, a ticket to see the movie. Afterward, Ava went back to the Hampton House, and Frank headed to Columbia's New York recording studio for his last session with that label. Percy Faith arranged the music and led the studio orchestra for the one side they were scheduled to cut. Mitch Miller was there to preside over what had to have been a humiliating end to Sinatra's association with Columbia, but Sinatra rose to the occasion and recorded one of his most haunting ballads ever, in a career filled with haunting ballads — Cy Coleman's "Why Try to Change Me Now."[30]

When Frank got back to the hotel after the session, Ava was in a pissy mood, and he tried to avoid letting her goad him into a full-throated fight. He was too exhausted, physically and emotionally, to get in the ring with her, and he had a show to do the next evening. Despite their bickering, Ava was at the Riviera on Thursday night, September 18, to support her man. Unfortunately for Frank, there was another supportive celebrity present that night, a blast from the past in the person of Marilyn Maxwell.

Frank was a little too happy to see his old flame and, in Ava's opinion, too demonstrative in gesturing to her as he sang one of his love ballads. Mrs. Frank Sinatra stormed out of the place and back to the Hampton House. She quickly packed, removed her wedding band, and left it for Frank, along with a note telling him what he could do with the ring and with himself. By the time Frank got back to the hotel, after the last show in Fort Lee, Ava was already at Idlewild Airport, ready to board an early-morning flight to Los Angeles.

Frank was booked to appear at the Chase Hotel in St. Louis, a one-week gig he couldn't pass up. En route to St. Louis, he somehow lost Ava's ring and had to have a duplicate made back in New York. If there was going to be a reconciliation with Ava, he'd better have her ring (or its exact twin) ready to put back on her finger. That prospect didn't look likely; she wouldn't even take his repeated calls. When he got back to Los Angeles, nothing had changed, and they lived apart for a couple of weeks. Frank turned to his friend, columnist Earl Wilson, to plead his case to Ava — it was the only way he could communicate with her. Wilson reported on his conversations with the warring Sinatras in his October 7 column. "We're having oral battles," Frank told Wilson, "and I'm trying to fix it all up." When Wilson called Ava to get her take, she blamed the troubles on their respective careers keeping them apart.[31]

The Earl Wilson offensive may have helped — the separation ended shortly thereafter. Back together, the couple discussed Ava's upcoming November trip to Africa, where she would begin on-location shooting for her next MGM picture — *Mogambo*, a John Ford-directed film, in which Clark Gable and Grace Kelly, fresh off a smashing success in *High Noon*, would play the other major roles. Frank had no bookings, and no prospects to speak of, so it was decided that he would accompany Ava to Africa, with a stop-off in North Carolina to visit her relatives. It's not clear if Ava was a willing participant in that agreement, or if she merely acquiesced to keep the peace. In any event, that peace was short-lived.

Gardner biographer Lee Server gave the most inspired one-sentence description of what happened next. "[T]he truce was barely a couple of days old," Server wrote, "when they had one of their biggest fights to date, one that involved a brawl, two love goddesses, police, rumors of sex orgies, and the inappropriate use of a douche bag."[32]

The contretemps started innocently enough. Sinatra ran into old flame Lana Turner, who told him she was planning to take a week off in Palm Springs. Frank offered her the use of his home there, and she accepted.[33] Shortly thereafter, on October 18, Frank and Ava were out to dinner when an argument ensued over some trivial matter — all that was usually needed to spark their fights. They returned to their Pacific Palisades home, both of them drunk, and continued the argument, during which Frank walked in on Ava as she was taking a bath. She screamed at him to get out, and Frank was taken aback,[34] as if to say, "You're my wife, for Christ's sake, what is it that I haven't seen." Frank left the bathroom, but not before shouting, "I'm leaving, and if you want to know where I am, I'm in Palm Springs fucking Lana Turner."[35]

Ava grew suspicious and phoned Bappie, asking her sister to accompany her to Twin Palms, Frank's house in Palm Springs, no doubt hoping to catch Frank with Lana in the act. When the sisters arrived, they found Lana, but no Frank. Turner was there with her agent, Ben Cole, sitting in the kitchen and about to have a very late supper. Bappie and Ava decided to join them, with the intention of staying the night — there was plenty of room in the house, and Turner and Cole didn't mind. As they were all having a drink, Frank arrived on the scene (he had made a stop at Jimmy Van Heusen's house in Palm Springs). He ordered Ava into a bedroom, and a shouting match commenced, easily heard throughout the house, along with the sounds of items crashing. "I kept seeing Frank's red face and blazing eyes as he burst through the kitchen door," Lana Turner would later recall, "and I was worried what he might do to Ava."[36]

The stories about what happened next vary, but the predominant scenario involved Frank and Ava engaging in a prolonged war of words and flying objects. At one point, he ran into the bathroom, filled a douche bag hanging there with water, and returned to the porch area, where Ava was saying goodbye to Lana. Frank doused them both with the water. A neighbor called the police.

"The squad cars came roaring up the driveway," Lee Server reported, "red lights flashing, radios squawking, and several officers rushed up to the house as Sinatra was trying to evict his wife bodily and Ava was clinging to the doorway with both hands."[37] It took the arrival of the police chief to finally calm things down. "Bappie and I went off with the cops," Ava later said, "leaving Mr. Sinatra to be king of the roost."[38]

That Monday, the newspapers were agog with news of this latest Sinatra feud. "Boudoir Fight Heads Frankie and Ava to Courts," read the headline in the *Los Angeles Daily Mirror*. The *Los Angeles Times* was equally aroused: "Sinatra-Ava Boudoir Row Buzzes," it blared. The newspaper pieces were short on details, but lurid talk abounded among the Hollywood gossips, to include Frank catching Ava and Lana in bed together. One version had the two actresses locked in a lesbian embrace; another had them in a three-way with a strange man they had picked up. The salacious aspects of the episode would endure for years, to the detriment of all involved. "A lot of sick, vile rumors grew out of that incident," Lana Turner would lament, years later.[39] Ava gave a two-word quote to the papers the next day, one that needed no elaboration: "It's over."[40]

The whole affair sent Sinatra into an even deeper depression. Dorothy Kilgallen — her *Voice of Broadway* column in the Hearst chain's *New York Journal-American* was syndicated to 146 papers nationwide — filed a devastating piece, on October 24, 1952: "Frank Sinatra is frightening his friends by telephoning in a gloomy voice," Kilgallen wrote, "[and saying] 'Please see that the children are taken care of,' and then hanging up."[41] But it would take the arrival of the Earl Wilson cavalry, once again, to patch things up between Ava and Frank. Sinatra called Wilson and begged for his help in winning Ava back. Wilson's piece the next day carried the headline "Frankie Ready to Surrender; Wants Ava Back, Any Terms."[42]

When she saw Wilson's column, Ava relented and reached out for Frank, reconciling with him just in time to fulfill a commitment they had made to the Adlai Stevenson campaign. The liberal Hollywood establishment was strongly in support of the Democratic nominee, who was going up against Eisenhower and Nixon, the Republican standard bearers in that year's presidential election. A huge rally of those "Madly for Adlai" followers was planned for the Hollywood Palladium on the night of October 27, 1952, just eight days before the election. At the event, Ava went onstage to introduce Frank, amid sustained cheers from the appreciative crowd. The newspaper stories hadn't diminished the affection most Hollywood folks had for both Sinatras. Other stars had had their own beefs with the media.

"I can't do anything myself," Ava said, in a bit of false modesty, "but I can introduce a wonderful, wonderful man. I'm a great fan of his myself. Ladies and gentlemen, my husband, Frank Sinatra."[43]

Frank came out and embraced Ava, bringing the house down. He mouthed a few words on behalf of Stevenson and the Democrats, then sang "The Birth of the Blues" and "The House I Live In" for the wildly appreciative audience. Stevenson lost the election, but his political rally had healed, temporarily, Hollywood's most fragile marriage. The plans for Frank to accompany Ava to Africa for at least part of her on-location *Mogambo* shoot were back on. But before they left, both Frank and Ava started in motion a joint campaign of their own — a struggle to win Frank the movie role of a lifetime.

* * *

James Jones' first novel, *From Here to Eternity*, had so much explicit sex within its pages that two Hollywood studios turned down the film rights to the book, before Harry Cohn bought them for $82,000, over the objections of his Columbia Pictures executives. It was an astounding sum back then to pay for film rights to any novel, especially one so difficult to adapt for the silver screen. The book was over 800 pages, a problem in itself, trying to compress that length into a workable screenplay; dealing with the sex scenes was an even more challenging task. Censorship of Hollywood films, by government agencies and the Catholic Church's Legion of Decency, was at its height in mid-century. The conventional wisdom was that filmmakers would be caught in a Hobson's choice: to get past censors, they might have to defuse the sex scenes so drastically that they risked alienating an audience expecting to see the realism they had read about in the widely successful book.

As it turned out, Harry Cohn's gamble paid off big — the movie version of *From Here to Eternity*, which cost about $2.4 million to make, a not inconsiderable sum in those days, would end up grossing more that $80 million in 1953-1954,[44] which equates to almost three-quarters of a *billion* in today's dollars — quite a blockbuster. The movie would be nominated for 13 Academy Awards and go on to win the Best Picture Oscar for 1953, plus seven other Oscars. To make the great movie he envisioned, Cohn knew he needed not only a good property, like Jones' book, but also an accomplished director, a brilliant screenwriter, and a great cast of actors. Cohn ran the studio with an iron hand, and although he would often defer to his producers and directors in the choice of an actor for a part, everyone knew that final casting decisions rested with him.

Montgomery Clift was a natural choice for the lead role of Robert E. Lee Prewitt, a hard-headed soldier stationed in Hawaii, before Pearl Harbor, who took a demotion to buck private and a transfer from a cushy billet as first bugler in the Bugle Corps to become a rifleman in an infantry company at Schofield Barracks, all because another man was made top bugler in his place. The new guy was a friend of the first sergeant in that former outfit. ("Maybe it ain't sensible," Prewitt explains in the movie, "but that's the reason.") Clift already had two Academy Award nominations for Best Actor under his belt — *A Place in the Sun*, a 1951 film co-starring Elizabeth Taylor, was his most recent success — and was one of Hollywood's most sought-after method actors (along with Marlon Brando) before the casting for *Eternity* even began. In the movie, when his new company commander tries to force Prewitt — an accomplished Army boxer who quit the ring after blinding an opponent — to box on the company team, against his will, First Sergeant Milt Warden takes a liking to Prewitt's spunky demeanor and looks out for him, when he can do so without jeopardizing his own standing.

Burt Lancaster was chosen to play Sgt. Warden, another astute pick. The circus-performer-turned-actor made a brief stop on Broadway after his Army service in World War II, but caught the attention of a Hollywood agent, who landed him a starring role in *The Killers,* a 1946 film co-starring a young Ava Gardner. A series of nondescript thrillers and Westerns followed, before Lancaster gained what would become one of his most acclaimed roles. Both Clift and Lancaster would be nominated for the Best Actor Oscar for their work in *From Here to Eternity.* The same-picture competition would doom both their chances.

Joan Crawford was the first choice to play Karen Holmes, the company commander's adulterous wife. Crawford's wardrobe demands were too much for studio executives to accept, so they settled on British actress Deborah Kerr for that role. With practice, she overcame her accent and filled the role perfectly. The "kiss on the beach" scene she did with Burt Lancaster will forever remain one of the top five fully clothed (albeit in bathing suits) sex scenes in the history of Hollywood cinema. Kerr received an Academy Award nomination for Best Actress, but did not win the Oscar.

Donna Reed played dance-hall "hostess" Lorene, a name picked from a perfume ad by the madam of the New Congress Club to replace the character's real given name, Alma. The dance hall setting was a filmmaker's euphemism, of course, for a whorehouse, with Lorene/Alma becoming Prewitt's love interest. Reed would not only be nominated for Best Supporting Actress; she would win the Oscar in that category. Another casting coup for the makers of *Eternity* was the part of the heavy — Sgt. "Fatso" Judson, the sergeant in charge of the stockade. It was Ernest Borgnine's breakout role and would lead to a Best Actor Oscar two years later for his portrayal of a plain, girl-shy Italian mensch in *Marty.*

There was an outstanding supporting cast in the movie as well, but the role that would cause the most pre-production talk as to its casting was that of Private Angelo Maggio, the "terror of Gimbels basement" in civilian life and a sad sack of a soldier in Army life. He carried a chip on his shoulder and dared Fatso Judson to knock it off. Today, knowing what we know and viewing Sinatra's performance, we can imagine only one person being right for that role. But the choice wasn't so obvious in late 1952, when Harry Cohn, producer Buddy Adler, and director Fred Zinnemann were pondering it.

Frank Sinatra was a voracious reader his entire life. In 1952, he began reading and re-reading Jones' novel, concentrating on the pages with scenes involving Maggio; those particular pages soon became dog-eared from his intense laboring over them. It was a role he would do anything to get. Anything. "I was reading something I really had to do," Sinatra later recalled. "I just felt it. I just knew I could do it and couldn't get the idea out of my head. I knew I was the only actor to play Private Angelo Maggio, the tough little Italian-American G.I."[45] It became a visceral need for Sinatra, almost his own personal mantra. "I knew Maggio," he was quoted as saying. "I went to school with him in Hoboken. I was beaten up with him. I might have been Maggio."[46]

The story of how Frank Sinatra got the role of Angelo Maggio embodies the narrative of a man who wouldn't take no for an answer, a man who wouldn't stay down, no matter how many blows to body and soul he endured.

14

"You'd better come down here. You'll see something unbelievable."

Frank Sinatra was every director's worst nightmare on a movie set. Whether his career was on an upswing or not, his personal life was in constant turmoil, and he took out his frustrations on cast and crew. While filming *Young at Heart* in 1954, he ordered the producer, the husband of co-star Doris Day, and a cameraman off the set, over some minor grudge. The studio had no choice but to let the producer and the cameraman go.[1] Sinatra's spoiled-brat behavior started during the filming of *Anchors Aweigh*, in 1944, when he walked off that set over a petty grievance. He later blamed it on the woolen Navy blues he had to wear in the summer heat, yet co-star Gene Kelly wore the same uniform without complaint. Kelly was a consummate professional, but his troubles with Frank, whom he considered a friend, would continue on the sets of *Take Me Out to the Ball Game* and *On the Town*, his two later films with Sinatra, who made a fuss if asked to do a second take for any scene, something most of his acting colleagues resented.

Easygoing Jimmy Durante, Frank's co-star in *It Happened in Brooklyn*, could barely put up with his antics. Production had to shut down when Frank left the set for two days to help out Phil Silvers at the Copacabana, in September 1946. That escapade cost the studio money. On the set of *Meet Danny Wilson*, Sinatra and co-star Shelley Winters almost came to blows. Winters quit the movie for three days and only returned when her friend Nancy Sinatra begged her, so that Frank could get paid the $25,000 he had coming — money Nancy and the kids desperately needed.

Still, a studio head could be expected to put up with all that rigmarole, if his temperamental star were a box-office draw. It was business, after all. But Sinatra was not only a pain in the ass to work with; he was also a bust as a recording artist and nightclub performer, and as an actor. Metro-Goldwyn-Mayer wouldn't renew his contract in 1950, despite the success of *On the Town*, because it had no faith in his continued viability. Universal International signed him for *Meet Danny Wilson*, but when that film did poorly and when Sinatra behaved the way he did on the set, the studio dropped its option for another picture.

So when Frank picked up the phone in the fall of 1952 to call Harry Cohn, studio head at Columbia Pictures, and ask for a meeting, he had to have known that his prospects to land the Maggio role in *From Here to Eternity* were slim, to say the least. But Cohn owed him a favor, so maybe — just maybe — there was a chance.

Back in 1949, Sinatra's career hadn't yet tanked. Although record sales had fallen off, he was still drawing reasonable crowds for his live performances and was expected to do so at the Capitol in New York City, where he was booked for a four-week run. Harry Cohn called Sinatra in advance of that engagement and asked if he would intercede with the theater's management and get Columbia's latest picture, *When Miss Grant Took Richmond*, starring Lucille Ball and William Holden, on the same bill. It would mean a box-office bonanza for any movie to be paired with a Frank Sinatra live show, something Cohn apparently needed for this film. Sinatra readily agreed and, still possessing some clout, got it done for Cohn. When the singer took sick during the third week of that run, he had to cancel his performances and keep to his sick bed, in Manie Sacks' apartment at the Hampton House. Cohn heard about Frank's illness, dropped everything in Los Angeles, and flew to New York, where he stayed by Frank's side until he was better, keeping him company, chatting, doing whatever. Cohn had always reveled in his reputation as an ogre. After Frank recovered, Cohn told him, "You tell anyone about this, you son-of-a-bitch, and I'll kill you."[2]

Cohn agreed to meet Sinatra for lunch, without asking the reason. Perhaps he suspected it. After they ate, Sinatra broached the subject. "Harry," he began, "I've known you for a long time. You got something I want." Later, Sinatra related Cohn's response. "Harry said, 'You want to play God?' and I said, 'No, not that, but I want to play Maggio.' And then he looked at me funnylike and said, 'Look, Frank, that's an actor's part, a stage actor's part. You're nothing but a fucking hoofer.'" The only non-singing role Sinatra had ever attempted was as the priest in *The Miracle of the Bells*, and that picture, along with Sinatra, had bombed.[3]

"Please, Harry," Sinatra pressed, "I'll pay you if you'll let me play that role." Cohn had to have known about Sinatra's money troubles at this juncture — there were no secrets in Hollywood — so he brushed that silly offer aside. But with production costs expected to be steep (part of the movie would be shot on location in Hawaii), the thought of saving money intrigued Cohn. "What about the money?" he asked.[4]

"I get one hundred fifty thousand a film," Sinatra said.

"You *got* one hundred fifty thousand," Cohn replied. "Not anymore."

"Right," Frank said, "I used to get it, and I don't want anything near that much for Maggio."

"I'm not buying at any price," Cohn said, "but just for the record, what's yours?"

"I'll play Maggio for a thousand a week," Sinatra replied. The hook was sunk.

"Jesus, Frank, you want it that much?" Cohn exclaimed, surprised at the bargain price and giving Sinatra a ray of hope. "Well, we'll see," he said. "I have some other actors to test first."[5]

After leaving Cohn, Sinatra called the William Morris Agency, his agent after getting dropped by Music Corporation of America. Wanted to make sure they were on this from the start, he told them about his lunch with Cohn and implored them to pull out all the stops to make it happen. "I'll do it for *nothing*," he said. "For *nothing*. You've just got to get it for me."[6] Abe Lastfogel, one of Sinatra's agents at William Morris, spoke to biographer Kitty Kelley in 1983. "Frank smelled like a loser in those days," he said, "but I promised him we'd start working on Fred Zinnemann, who was also our client, and had been named to direct *From Here to Eternity*. Fred didn't want to cast Frank in the role of Maggio because he said that everyone would think that he'd bastardized the book and made it into a musical instead of portraying a stark and tragic drama. He preferred the Broadway actor Eli Wallach for the part."[7]

Leaving no stone unturned, Sinatra reached out to Buddy Adler, who he knew was producing the film. "It's an acting part, Frankie," Adler told him. "It's *me*," Sinatra insisted. "It's me."[8]

Ava joined the effort, without Frank's knowledge, by calling Harry Cohn's wife, Joan, with whom she had a friendly but not close relationship. She'd informed Frank about her connection to Joan Cohn, but he told her to stay out of it[9] — he wanted to get this part on his own, without, once again, using his wife as a crutch. Ava ignored his wishes and asked Joan Cohn to meet with her. It was urgent, she said. Joan was in bed with the flu, but invited Ava to come right over.

"That was a very brave thing for Ava to call me like that and insist on seeing me when I was ill," Joan later recalled, "but she had a mission, and nothing was going to stop her. She came to the house alone in the evening and said that Frank must never know that she had been here. We both knew how much he needed and wanted to be the boss in that marriage."[10]

Ava asked for a drink before making her pitch. "Joan," she said, "I've come to ask you a big favor. I want you to get Harry to give Frank the Maggio role in *From Here to Eternity*. He wants that part more than anything in the world, and he's got to have it, otherwise I'm afraid he'll kill himself. Please, promise me that you'll help. I'll do anything. Just give him a test. Please, Joan. Just a test."[11]

Ava's heartfelt plea stunned Joan Cohn. As the wife of a powerful studio head, she had never experienced anything like it — a woman, famous in her own right, coming to her to beg for a part for an actor husband. Still, she was moved by the scene and did promise to see what she could do. Harry had already told her about his lunch meeting with Frank. He'd also told her that he wasn't interested, that he considered Sinatra a "washed up song-and-dance man."[12]

Cohn was inundated with pleas on behalf of Frank Sinatra, he told his wife. Gossip columnists were dropping hints that the singer would be perfect for the role, Cohn said. He even got a call from his fishing buddy, Jack Entratter, asking him to consider Sinatra. Entratter, formerly a frontman at the Copacabana for Mafia boss Frank Costello, was now filling that same function for the same Mafia folks at the new Sands Hotel and Casino in Las Vegas.

"Why not consider Frank for the role," Joan asked her husband. "He's Italian and scrawny, so he'd be perfect in the scene where skinny little Maggio has to go up against that great big Sgt. 'Fatso' Judson." Harry doubted that Sinatra would stand for a screen test — it was something that established stars were rarely asked to do. "I bet he would," Joan replied, with the benefit of Ava having suggested that very thing. "I'll bet you anything you want to bet that Frank Sinatra will do a test," she said. "Just try him, Harry. A test can't hurt, and then you'll know for sure."[13]

Cohn took his wife's advice to heart and arranged, through a mutual friend, to have Ava come to his house for dinner, without Frank. As the evening progressed, Ava was in her cups before too long, but she didn't need the cover of alcohol to speak plainly, or to face down the head of Columbia Pictures. "You know who's right for that part of Maggio, don't you?" she told Cohn. "That son of a bitch husband of mine." Cohn remained silent, waiting for her to continue. "For God's sake, Harry," Ava said, "I'll give you a free picture if you'll just test him."[14] Cohn just smiled.

Sinatra was on tenterhooks for days — he had heard nothing from Cohn since their lunch meeting. Finally, he got a call. Cohn told him that he would try to arrange to screen test him for the role of Maggio, but that Frank should "call off the dogs" — that is, stop the barrage of columnists and others pestering the studio on his behalf — and let things take their course. He would be in touch.

Frank and Ava headed East — Frank with Cohn's "don't call me, we'll call you" ringing in his ears. He was beginning to despair about his chances, especially after reading that Cohn and director Zinnemann were considering stage actor Eli Wallach for the part. After a brief stopover in North Carolina to visit Ava's relatives and friends, they boarded a Stratocruiser in New York on November 7, 1952, their first anniversary. En route to Nairobi, Kenya, where Ava and he would meet up with the *Mogambo* cast and crew, they drank champagne and traded anniversary gifts. He gave her a diamond ring. She gave him a platinum watch. "It was quite an occasion for me," Gardner later recalled. "I had been married twice but never for a whole year."[15] The exchange of gifts distressed Frank even more. He was not only broke but deeply in debt, and, as a consequence, Ava would be paying for her own anniversary gift. (She didn't know it yet — the bill came later.) Frank's humiliation was almost too much to bear.

Clark Gable met them at the Nairobi airport. Aging but tanned and smiling, the veteran actor still looked every bit the handsome leading man. *Mogambo* was actually a remake of *Red Dust*, released in 1932 and starring Gable and the sultry Jean Harlow. The setting for the earlier MGM film had been a French rubber plantation in Southeast Asia, but the studio, wanting to capitalize on the recent successes of *King Solomon's Mines* and *The Snows of Kilimanjaro*, each with their rich depictions of African scenery and wildlife, gave the remake a lush setting amid the wilds of Kenya, Tanganyika, and Uganda. Two decades after *Red Dust*, MGM cast Gable in the same starring role, but added two of the screen's hottest female stars — Ava Gardner and Grace Kelly. The film would become tremendously profitable for MGM, despite the high costs of an on-location shoot in Africa. It would also bring Ava Gardner her only Academy Award nomination, for Best Actress in a Leading Role.

The undertaking was massive. Six hundred people — actors, crew, guides, hunters, support staff, and natives from several East African tribes — moved into the bush, along with the supplies necessary to sustain them, including enough liquor "to drown the Titanic." The entire entourage set up camp under the direction of their own great white hunter, Frank "Bunny" Allen, every bit the image of the hunter Stewart Granger had played in *King Solomon's Mines*.[16] Allen would end up playing a leading man role with Ava Gardner during the shoot, but later on, while Frank was back in America.[17]

Frank Sinatra was not the type who liked to rough it, even in a Hollywood-style bush camp, with most of the comforts of home. During the day, while cast members were being put through their paces by director John Ford, Frank sat by himself in camp, reading or composing the recurrent telegrams he sent off to Harry Cohn, Buddy Adler, Fred Zinnemann, and everyone else he could think of who might further his cause. He signed each missive with one word, "Maggio." The Sinatras continued their frequent battles, with only the thin walls of a canvas tent to mask them. The whole camp knew of their exchanges, but Frank and Ava were never ones to worry about who might be witness to their feuding. The camp also knew about the budding romance between Grace Kelly and Clark Gable, 30 years her senior.[18] Author Jane Ellen Wayne described the tension perfectly.

"When she wasn't working, Ava slept until the cocktail hour, but Frank had great difficulty sleeping," Wayne wrote. "Every day he hoped to hear from Columbia regarding his screen test. Had Cohn changed his mind? Would the telegram get through to MGM's jungle location? Who else was testing for the part of Maggio? The pressure mounted. He took out his frustrations on Ava, who was not bearing up well. The 120-degree temperature drained what strength she had."[19]

British actor and *Mogambo* cast member Donald Sinden described one memorable evening. "One night we'd all had dinner together like jolly chaps, and then we all retired to our tents," Sinden recalled. "A little while later a great row broke out. Frank and Ava. And you should have heard the language and the screams and shouts. What it was all about I don't know. Cursing and screaming like wild creatures." During the fight, "there were things being thrown from Ava's tent, pots and things, flying out of the tent; they were throwing them at each other! Then, suddenly silence. The argument was over, and the next thing you heard, they were in bed and the bed was creaking. And, you've never heard a bed creaking so loud!"[20]

The MGM production crew had hacked out a small landing field near the base camp, large enough for a twin-engine DC-3 to get in and out, delivering mail, supplies, and whatever else the camp needed. On Friday, November 14, the plane brought a cable for Sinatra — Columbia Pictures had decided to give him a screen test, but he had to get back to Los Angeles at his own expense. Frank was ecstatic. Ava would have to pay for his trip back to the States — something she did willingly (using her MGM expense account), not only because it meant so much to Frank, but also because she couldn't wait to be rid of him.

Following a tortuous route, as air travelers in the 1950s were sometimes required to do, Frank arrived at Idlewild Airport in New York on Monday, November 17. He was booked on a connecting flight to Los Angeles but would miss that flight, thanks to past rumors about his having been a Mafia courier. Customs officials detained him for hours, searching him and his luggage. Frank reached out to Sol Gelb, his attorney in the Kefauver committee inquiry, and explained the urgency of his predicament. All Gelb could do, however, was advise his client to be patient and cooperative. By the time customs officials satisfied themselves that he was clean, at least on this trip, the L.A. flight had departed, with no other flight scheduled until the next day, the day he was supposed to report at Columbia studios in Hollywood for the screen test. Hank Sanicola picked him up at the airport and drove him into the city, where he would stay the night. He called Buddy Adler and explained his situation; the producer told him not to worry — postponing the screen test for a day would not be a problem.

* * *

Ava hadn't been feeling well her entire time in Africa, a condition she attributed to the stifling heat and the non-stop bickering between her and Frank. Soon after Frank left for home, however, she knew there was another explanation. She was pregnant, and the realization brought her no joy, despite remarks she'd made to columnists earlier in the marriage about wanting to have a baby. The deterioration of the marriage was one factor arguing against carrying this baby to term; it wasn't clear there would still be a marriage by the time the child was born. There was also another onerous MGM clause to contend with, one that threatened to dock the pay of female stars if pregnancies resulted in lost work time. Such a clause would be considered reprehensible today, as well as illegal, but in that era, it was standard boilerplate.

The physical manifestations of early pregnancy soon brought her condition to the attention of almost the entire camp. Director John Ford counseled her to have the baby. It would devastate Frank, a Catholic, if she had an abortion, he warned. And she shouldn't worry about the picture. Ford would shoot around her, if that became necessary, scheduling her scenes to accommodate any medical needs. But Gardner had made up her mind. She was not ready to become a mother, at least not under the present circumstances of her marriage, and resolved to end the pregnancy quickly, before her husband returned to Africa.[21]

Gardner flew to London on November 23, 1952, and checked into a private clinic.[22] As a cover, the studio put out a story about its star suffering from dysentery. In her memoir, Ava wrote about the experience. "In those days, abortion was available in Britain," she recalled, "but it had to be performed for what the male sex thought were the right reasons: their reasons." A psychiatrist was called in to question her about her feelings toward the pregnancy and what its effects were on her mental health — programmed questions designed to get the right answers, so that the procedure could go forward. After some fudging of her responses, the approval was granted, and Ava got her abortion.[23] She was back on the set in Africa within a week or so, none the worse for the wear. She would not tell Frank about the abortion, at least not about this one.

* * *

Ava Gardner had been "on a mission" when she met with Joan Cohn to beg her to get Harry to test Frank for the Maggio role. On Wednesday afternoon, November 19, Frank exuded that same steely demeanor in producer Buddy Adler's office, at the Culver City headquarters of Columbia Pictures. He knew the stakes and was determined to rise to the occasion. There would be no second chance to impress.

"I was a little startled when I gave him the script of the drunk scene and he handed it back," Adler confessed, years later. " 'I don't need this,' [Sinatra] said, 'I've read it many times.' I didn't think he had a chance, anyway, so I said, 'Well, okay.' Since his was the last test of the day, I didn't intend going down on the stage." Adler sent Sinatra to the soundstage, where Fred Zinnemann waited, ready to film the screen test that this "washed up song-and-dance man" had so earnestly sought.[24]

"For the test, I played the saloon scene where Maggio shakes dice with the olives and the scene where he's found drunk outside the Royal Hawaiian Hotel," Sinatra recalled. "I was scared to death."[25]

After a while, Adler got a call from Zinnemann. "You'd better come down here," Zinnemann said. You'll see something unbelievable."[26]

The film of the screen test was already in the camera. Sinatra had nailed both scenes, needing just one take for each. When Adler arrived on the sound stage, Zinnemann told Frank to do it again. "Frank thought he was making another take — and he was terrific," Adler later said. "I thought to myself, if he's like that in the movie, it's a sure Academy Award. But we had to have Harry Cohn's okay on casting and he was out of town."[27]

Ebullient over what he knew had been a great test, Frank flew back to New York for a two-week gig at the French Casino, located in the basement of the Paramount Hotel on 46th Street. He would be getting $10,000 per week. The comedy team of Dean Martin and Jerry Lewis was then commanding $10,000 *a night*, but Sinatra wasn't in a position to be choosy. Frank was in good voice, and the engagement was a success. He flew back to Nairobi in December, gifts in hand for Ava's 30th birthday, on December 24, along with a small Christmas tree he'd put up in their tent.

The reception Frank got from Ava was lukewarm, at best. The entire cast and crew celebrated Christmas with a huge feast the studio splurged on. It also marked the end of their jungle shoot. They would pull up stakes and move the set to London in January to complete the film in studio facilities there. Frank and Ava resumed their squabbles, until the time came, in late January 1953, for Frank to return to the States for an engagement at the Latin Quarter in Boston. Ava also had an engagement that month. Right after Christmas, while Frank was still in Africa, she learned that she was pregnant, again. He was delighted by the news, but she just played along, keeping to herself her intention to also terminate this pregnancy.[28] Frank was most likely the father, but while he'd been away, she'd had sex with Bunny Allen, the hunter, and, it was rumored, with a props man who had caught her fancy one lonely night. Given her decision to have another abortion, it really didn't matter who the father was.

* * *

Despite Frank Sinatra's surprisingly good screen test, Harry Cohn preferred another man for the role. Eli Wallach had tested even better than Sinatra, in Cohn's opinion, which was shared by Fred Zinnemann and writer Daniel Taradash (whose screenplay for the film would earn him an Academy Award). A third actor, Harvey Lembeck, had also been tested. Lembeck, a comedian as well as an actor, played Sergeant Harry Shapiro in *Stalag 17*, the gritty prisoner-of-war drama starring William Holden, and would go on to small-screen success in the *Sgt. Bilko* series, starring Phil

Silvers. But he was the odd man out in the competition to become Private Angelo Maggio.

"Eli Wallach made the best test of the three of them — no doubt about it," Daniel Taradash recalled in a 1983 interview with author Kitty Kelley. "Everyone agreed. He was superb. Lembeck was not right; he tried too hard to be funny. Frank's test was good — better than expected — but it had none of the consummate acting ability of Eli Wallach."[29]

Wallach did not get the part for several reasons. He wouldn't sign a seven-year contract with the studio, something Harry Cohn was pushing for, although Cohn would probably have given in on that issue, if it weren't for Wallach's insistence on getting $20,000 for his services. Cohn offered $16,000, but despite the closeness of the two numbers, Wallach wouldn't budge. He already had an offer to do a Tennessee Williams play on Broadway — the type of acting he preferred — so it wasn't as though he'd be out of work if he didn't land the part in *From Here to Eternity*, or at least that's what he thought. But there was another problem that troubled all three men — Cohn, Zinnemann, and Taradash — as they viewed first Sinatra's test, then Wallach's, over and over again, in Cohn's basement projection room.

"One crucial difference in Frank's favor was his size," Taradash told Kelley. "Eli was a pretty muscular guy with a great physique. He did not look like a schnook. He looked like he could take two MPs with no trouble at all. Frank, on the other hand, looked so thin and woeful and so pitifully small that the audience would cry when they saw this poor little guy get beaten up."[30]

Cohn brought his wife into the discussion and ran the two tests again for her. "He's a brilliant actor, no question about it," Joan said, referring to Eli Wallach. One of the scenes in the test had a shirtless Maggio about to do battle with two military policemen. Looking at Wallach's powerful build, it seemed like a tossup as to who would come out on top — Maggio or the two MPs. That's not the way the film played out. Maggio was a loser, in that particular matchup and in life. Wallach "looks too good," Joan said. "He's not skinny and he's not pathetic and he's not Italian. Frank is just Maggio to me."[31]

Joan Cohn needn't have added that Frank Sinatra also came at a good price, something Harry Cohn had not forgotten. Sinatra had offered to do the picture for nothing, but that was out of the question; for one thing, it would make the studio look cheap. But Sinatra had also mentioned $1,000 a week, a real bargain for a name star, even a fading star like Sinatra. With the shoot expected to last eight weeks, the arithmetic was appealing to Cohn, and may well have been the deciding factor. Filming was scheduled to begin in March, on location in Hawaii, so there could be no further delay in casting the role of Maggio. All the other major parts had been finalized. Cohn sent word to Sinatra — he had the role.

On March 17, 1953, Eli Wallach opened on Broadway in Tennessee Williams' *El Camino Real*. The play closed after just 60 performances, a financial and critical bust.

* * *

There is no substantive evidence that mob pressure got Frank Sinatra the role of Angelo Maggio, although Mario Puzo's novel *The Godfather*, and the movie of the same name, launched a never-ending tide of speculation that washes over the Sinatra legend to this day. In the book and movie, Johnny Fontane, a singer down on his luck, is seeking a dramatic role that he knows will turn around his failing career, but the head of the studio making the picture has it in for him and refuses to cast him. Johnny begs help from Don Vito Corleone, his godfather, who dispatches *consigliere* Tom Hagen to Hollywood for a bit of Sicilian persuasion, in the form of a horse's head placed in the studio chief's bed. The horrified man gets the message, and Johnny Fontane gets his role in the picture.

The rumor that Puzo patterned his Fontane character on Sinatra's real-life battle to win the Maggio role is helped along by several factors, including Sinatra's past associations. Frank Costello, the primary Mafia figure on whom Puzo based the fictional godfather, was one of Sinatra's mob benefactors. Costello was also tight with Harry Cohn[32] and with a vice president in the William Morris Agency, Frank Sinatra's agent. It isn't a stretch to believe that Sinatra went to Costello for help — he went to everyone else he knew who might have influence over Harry Cohn. Costello wouldn't have said no to Sinatra. He liked him too much. But Costello putting in a good word with his friend, Harry Cohn, is not the same thing as the Mafia boss threatening the studio head with bodily harm. That aspect of the story seems far-fetched.

The mob had been infiltrating Hollywood for years. Johnny Roselli, who was connected to the Chicago mob,[33] helped Harry Cohn get the funds that allowed him to take over Columbia Pictures in the early 1930s. Roselli and Cohn were close; they wore identical ruby rings, which Roselli had made, to cement their friendship.[34] Later, Bugsy Siegel became the first, full-time Los Angeles representative of the syndicate that Lucky Luciano had originally organized. Mickey Cohen took over when Siegel met his demise in 1947. When Cohen testified before the Kefauver committee, he was asked about a phone number in his possession at the time of a search — Sinatra's number. "He's a friend of mine," Cohen replied. Although Cohen was in prison at the time that *From Here to Eternity* was being filmed, his influence over the Los Angeles mob still held sway. Both Roselli and Cohen would later brag that they had a hand in Sinatra getting the Maggio role, but again, there's no proof that either of them took any action to bring about that result. Mobsters bragging about their influence and clout is par for the course.

Mario Puzo steadfastly denied, until the day he died, that he had based his Johnny Fontane character on Frank Sinatra — he had no choice but to deny it. Sinatra would have sued him for every penny he owned and would have won the lawsuit, because there was no proof to back up that claim, if Puzo had been stupid enough to make it. A British Broadcasting Corporation program had reported that connection as fact. Sinatra sued and forced the BBC to issue a retraction.

Novelists have always used real-life situations to build their fictionalized worlds. For all we know, Cervantes based *Don Quixote* on the antics of a windmill-tilting nutcase in the neighboring province. There's a name for the genre, *roman à clef*. If Puzo's genius in creating *The Godfather* encompassed the borrowing of a story line, here and there, from Frank Costello's life or Frank Sinatra's life or anyone's life, he is not responsible for the public jumping to conclusions and mistaking fiction for fact.

Every principal involved in the story of Frank Sinatra landing the role of Angelo Maggio has denied that any mob figure exerted undue influence. Harry Cohn died in 1958, before the controversy arose, but his wife Joan said that "Frank didn't get the part that way." Abe Lastfogel, who handled Sinatra for the William Morris Agency, characterized the idea of mob threats gaining his client the role as "pure fiction." Daniel Taradash called the notion "preposterous." Fred Zinnemann said that "there was no pressure. If I hadn't wanted him, he wouldn't have done it."[35]

Frank Sinatra earned the role of Angelo Maggio with every ounce of acting ability he possessed and with every skinny, pathetic fiber of his being. He had been down for a nine-count, but then he got up and won the championship, so to speak. And he did it on heart and on skill.

15

"Ava taught him how to sing a torch song. She taught him the hard way."

While appearing at the Latin Quarter in Boston, Sinatra got the long-awaited news — the Maggio role was his. Ava was in London wrapping up the remaining interior scenes for *Mogambo*, or so he thought, and she was the only person Frank felt like celebrating with. Instinctively, he knew how instrumental she had been in convincing Harry Cohn to give him the part, despite her protestations that she had nothing to do with it, that he had done it all on his own. When a Columbia Pictures publicity man asked Sinatra how he'd managed so effective a campaign to lobby the studio, the guy was astounded to learn that Frank had had no professional guidance. "I did all that with Ava's help," Sinatra told the press agent. "She'd call Harry Cohn to lean on him, and then I'd call Louella Parsons, and later we'd both call Hedda Hopper."[1]

Frank had another nightclub engagement — in Montreal, February 6-15 — before he could begin to think about what lay ahead. For months, he had told everyone who would listen that he *was* Maggio, even to the extent of signing the telegrams he sent to Cohn, Zinnemann, and Adler that way; now he would have to prove it. Managing the task for two scenes in a screen test was an achievement, but if he didn't sustain that minor victory, relatively speaking, by delivering a superior performance in the film itself, it would all have been for nothing. He was determined to be cooperative and to make this work.

Columbia wanted him to report for rehearsals in late February. The actual filming was to begin in Hollywood on March 2, before moving to Schofield Barracks in Hawaii for the exterior scenes. Ava had specifically asked for another European film assignment. The tax laws at the time took a big chunk of her salary, but if she remained a non-resident of the United States for 18 months, she could avoid most of those taxes. Fortunately, there was a Metro-Goldwyn-Mayer property that could be filmed in England — *Knights of the Round Table*, with actor Robert Taylor as her co-star. Ava would play Guinevere to Taylor's Sir Lancelot. With Ava scheduled to begin *Knights* in England right after *Mogambo* wrapped, the likelihood was that Frank wouldn't see her for two months, a separation he knew would wreak havoc on his mental well-being, at a time when he had to be at his best.

During his Montreal appearance, he kept trying to reach Ava, without success. Finally, he found her in Rome, where, evidently, she had been exploring the seamier side of the Eternal City with Grace Kelly, a small detour on their way to London to finish their picture. On the phone, Ava sounded tired, distracted. Then, she was gone again, checked out of her Rome hotel and nowhere to be found. Worried, both about her health and about whom she might be with, Frank had Hank Sanicola go through MGM to find out when, exactly, she was supposed to begin work at its Boreham Wood Studios.[2]

As he ended his Montreal gig, Frank was able to locate Ava. She had rented an apartment at Hyde Park Gate[3] and didn't sound any better over the phone; in fact, she referred, vaguely, to a medical problem. That cinched it for Frank. Instead of flying to Los Angeles to begin rehearsals, he hopped a flight to London, arriving in time to learn that Ava had just undergone an abortion, without telling him of her intentions or giving him a chance to talk her out of it. She'd gone to a nursing home this time, to avoid the inquisition that doctors had put her through for the November abortion, which Frank still didn't know about. This new facility was also away from the city, offering a chance to escape the press's notice. She paid for the procedure herself, not wanting to alert the studio to the fact of two abortions within the span of three months. Frank had "tears in his eyes" when he visited her, according to Ava.[4] She made up a story about why she had decided to end the pregnancy, unwilling to discuss the truth with Frank — namely, that she didn't know how much longer their marriage would last and didn't know if Frank was the father.

In a day or two, Ava was well enough for them to fly to Paris for a brief vacation before both began work on their new pictures. Tensions between the two continued unabated, despite the romantic allure of the city.

Harry Cohn was getting nervous: The rest of the *From Here to Eternity* cast was in Culver City, rehearsing and, for the actors who would play soldiers in the movie, practicing military drill. Cohn sent a telegram to Sinatra in Paris, explaining why it was important for him to come back and get to work. Sinatra replied that he was practicing with the French army, so not to worry. It was tongue in cheek — he wasn't about to bite the Cohn hand that had fed him the meatiest role he'd ever received. He packed Ava off to London and started out himself on the long trip to Los Angeles. When he arrived, he was refreshed and ready to dig in.

The U.S. Army had not been portrayed in a flattering light in James Jones' novel, and Columbia Pictures had to tone down some of Jones' harsher treatment of Army life. In the book, for example, Maggio attacked two MPs physically, outside the Royal Hawaiian Hotel; the movie limited the altercation to a verbal assault, to mollify the Army's concerns about the picture fomenting disciplinary problems. Producer Buddy Adler had the responsibility of maintaining good relations with the service, whose cooperation was essential. The production was using actual Army bases and equipment.

Director Fred Zinnemann had little trouble on the set with the usually undisciplined Frank Sinatra — a pleasant state of affairs attributable, in everyone's opinion, including Sinatra's, to one man: actor Montgomery Clift. There was one rough spot near the end of the picture, when Sinatra insisted on performing a scene his way instead of under Zinnemann's direction, but they overcame their differences without a blowup on the set.

Montgomery Clift, author James Jones, and Sinatra became drinking buddies off the set, but Sinatra couldn't help but be influenced by the intensity and work ethic Clift brought to his work. Even before shooting began,

Clift embarked on a regimen that included running to build stamina and boxing (he played a fighter in the movie) with a former Golden Gloves champion and with Jones, who was himself a good amateur boxer. Sinatra saw Clift marching in close order drill and practicing how to field strip his rifle. Clift even spent time with an acting coach, trying to perfect his performance. He invited Sinatra to participate, and they worked on many of the scenes they had together. Zinnemann later commented on the "Clift-effect" in the making of *From Here to Eternity*.

"Monty was so intense about being Prewitt, he raised the level of the other actors," Zinnemann said. "He cared so much, they started caring."[5] Co-star Burt Lancaster agreed with Zinnemann's assessment. "I'd never worked with an actor with Clift's power before," Lancaster said. "I was afraid he was going to blow me right off the screen."[6]

Both Clift and Lancaster would be nominated for Academy Awards in the Best Actor in a Leading Role category, but, probably owing to the competition from two actors in the same film, neither would win that award. Sinatra, the "one-take Charlie"[7] of previous films, would have better luck. He became a perfectionist on the set, an eager learner of the acting craft he had so often disdained in the past. Author Tom Santopietro took note of the long-term effect Montgomery Clift had on Frank Sinatra.

"You can see the lessons Sinatra absorbed from Clift in his very physicality; from this film forward, Sinatra often adopted trademark Clift mannerisms of hunched shoulders, clenched fists, and a wounded look of vulnerability. Sinatra was here learning from the best, and it resulted in a fully fleshed-out characterization and a first-rate dramatic performance."[8] But Santopietro saw other subtle influences in Sinatra's transformation as a movie star. "By blending small parts of Cagney's toughness with Bogart's jaded but vulnerable wiseguy, and overlaying the mix with his own distinctly Italian-American physicality — a lovable underdog with a chip on his shoulder — Sinatra arrived at an entirely original screen persona."[9]

By the time the film was in the can, everyone knew this picture was special. After viewing rushes, Harry Cohn scheduled the film's premiere for August in New York City — an unheard of bit of arrogance. Nobody did premieres at the height of the summer in sweltering New York City, where theaters were not yet air conditioned. But Cohn was adamant.[10] The picture would overcome such obstacles, it was that good, and he wanted to launch it as soon as possible in the biggest market possible. Harry Cohn was right. *From Here to Eternity* would become the biggest moneymaker in the history of Columbia Pictures, and it would be nominated for 13 Academy Awards, winning eight of them. Its success wasn't due to any one member of the tight-knit team that had made the film, but the "lovable underdog with a chip on his shoulder," from Hoboken, New Jersey, could rightfully claim his share of the credit.

The Cohns threw a wrap party for the entire cast and crew. Everyone was in a celebratory mood — they all knew what they had accomplished. "There was something magic about that picture," one crew member said. "All of us went on to bigger and better things because of it." Frank Sinatra had more than the completion of the film to be happy about. He was going to be seeing Ava in "less than 16 hours," as he told everyone who would listen. "He thought he was married to the most exquisite creature on the face of the earth," Joan Cohn recalled, "and he was desperately in love with her. It was kind of sad because all the rest of us knew that the marriage was held together by mere threads at that point."[11]

* * *

On March 13, 1953, even before the *Eternity* cast and crew moved to Hawaii for the exterior shots at Schofield Barracks, Sinatra found a home as a recording artist at Capitol Records. He met that day with Capitol Vice President Alan Livingston in a Hollywood restaurant to sign the papers. Capitol had been in existence for less than 10 years and was making inroads into the pop record market, having signed Nat King Cole. Sinatra's agent at William Morris had reached out to Livingston on a cold call, found the record company executive to be interested, and was able to make a deal for the hard-to-market Sinatra, who was without a recording label since Columbia Records dropped him seven months earlier. Fortuitously, Capitol had recently added arranger Axel Stordahl to its staff, and Stordahl was quick to support the signing of his old pal. "Frank's singing great again," Stordahl told his bosses.[12]

The contract that Capitol offered was far from what Sinatra had commanded in the past; in fact, it was akin to what a recording novice might get, not a star of Sinatra's stature. But his recording successes were in the past, and even though he knew his voice was back, he also knew he had to once again prove his worth in a recording studio, just as he had taken on that challenge on a movie set. It was a seven-year contract, but with only one year guaranteed. The remaining years were all options, at the discretion of Capitol Records. If his recordings didn't sell, they could drop him just as swiftly as they signed him. He had until March 1954 to prove himself.

Frank had his first recording session with Capitol on April 2, 1953, just before leaving for Hawaii. He cut three sides, two of which were arranged by Axel Stordahl; none were particularly memorable. Four weeks later, Sinatra, back from Hawaii, was in the Capitol recording studio again, but with a new arranger and conductor, Nelson Riddle. At first, Sinatra resisted the idea of working with Riddle, as opposed to his friend, Axel Stordahl. But he was talked into giving it a try, helped along by Stordahl's having agreed to do a television program in New York with Eddie Fisher, Sinatra's singing nemesis at the time. Sinatra would use Stordahl's services in the future, but the recording magic between him and Riddle, producing as it did some of the greatest albums ever made, would overshadow the work done with Stordahl.

Sinatra and Riddle cut eight sides in their first two sessions together, on April 30 and May 2, including five sides that would bear the mark of Sinatra greatness for decades to come: "I've Got the World on a String," "South of the Border," "Don't Worry 'Bout Me," "My One and Only Love," and a song that was not part of the movie but was written to take advantage of the movie's expected success, "From Here to Eternity."[13] Sinatra was blown away from the moment Riddle began conducting "I've Got the World on a String." He had sung the song before, but always in a slow tempo, ballad-style. This was different. Once they had worked through the entire song, Sinatra had one word for Riddle, "beautiful." Later that night, after listening to the playback, Sinatra could hardly believe his ears. "Jesus Christ," he said, "I'm back! I'm back, baby! I'm back!"[14]

After his two Capitol sessions, Frank was riding high and looking forward to beginning an eight-week concert tour in Europe. Not only was his career *about-face* (to use a military term he had learned on the *Eternity* set) taking hold; he would also be seeing Ava. She planned on interrupting her

Knights of the Round Table shoot in England, with studio permission, to accompany him on part of the tour. Frank flew to London, where he picked up Ava, and together they continued to Italy, excited to be on what they deemed a "second honeymoon."[15] As was so often the case in Sinatra's life, he couldn't count on the good times lasting for long. One of Sinatra's enduring classics, which he recorded years later for his own Reprise label, had a line in its lyric that went something like this: "You're riding high in April, shot down in May."[16] May, in its fullness, would be anything but a merry month for Frank Sinatra.

* * *

Ava met Frank at London's Heathrow Airport, and, according to one source, they spent the next three days in bed.[17] Sex was never the problem between them, Ava once said. The problems commenced "on the way to the bidet," as she put it. The first stops on the tour were in Italy, presumably friendly territory for Sinatra, but getting there proved to be a hassle. Thanks to a flat tire, they missed their flight to Milan, where Frank's first appearance was scheduled, and had to take another flight, to Rome. The paparazzi were out in full force when the couple landed, and Frank, as usual, blew up at the sight of them, even engaging in a fistfight with one photographer that had to be broken up by Italian police.[18]

The Milan concert went off without incident, but attendance was not what Frank had hoped. When they arrived at the theater in Naples for the second tour event, on May 16, Ava was horrified to see her name on the bill, right alongside Frank's. The theater owner, hoping to take advantage of Ava's popularity in Italy and all over Europe, had promoted the concert as though it would be a joint appearance by both Sinatras. Ava refused to take the stage, and when a spotlight was suddenly turned on her in the audience and the half-filled theater began to chant her name, she fled the premises. Frank was furious and refused to go on with the performance. Police were called to put down the riot in the theater and to negotiate an accommodation between Frank and the owner. Sinatra could walk out and get paid nothing, or he could go on and get paid two-thirds of what had been promised him, since Ava wouldn't be appearing. He chose to go back on stage and sing, but it was altogether a miserable experience.

Gardner offered her own critique of her husband's European concerts. "I flew off to Italy to catch a few of Frank's gigs," she told Peter Evans, while they were collaborating on her biography in 1988. "I had to have been in love with him to sit through those performances. Let's say he was not at his best. He was playing to half-empty houses."[19]

Audience behavior improved when the tour moved to Denmark and Sweden, but the venues were still half-filled. The quality of the musicians the tour director had booked bothered Frank, and when he was bothered, he didn't perform well, on or off the stage. He cut his performance when it started to rain at an outdoor concert in Sweden, and blew off a news conference and photo shoot that had been scheduled. A newspaper lampooned him in a cartoon the next day, and ran an editorial with the headline "Mr. Sinatra, Go Home." Frank canceled the rest of the disastrous tour and returned to London with Ava, claiming to be suffering from "exhaustion."[20] A concert tour that had started with such promise, at a time when his voice was in good shape and when he needed a successful run, ended in another unexplainable failure. Frank managed to salvage something from his overseas trip. His manager hastily arranged a series of concerts in Great Britain, where Frank had always received a warm reception, along with a June BBC broadcast that garnered good reviews. He stayed with Ava while working these concerts until the beginning of August, when he had to depart for New York and the premiere of *From Here to Eternity*.

Arriving at Idlewild, Sinatra experienced the first effects of the buzz his new movie was creating, even before its first public showing. Gone was the airport reception he'd received six months earlier, when he had been detained by U.S. Customs and missed his flight to L.A. for the Maggio screen test. Now it was all hail-fellow-well-met as strangers called out to him with their congratulations. He checked into the Waldorf Astoria, and was inundated with calls from friends and well-wishers in advance of the *From Here to Eternity* premiere on August 5 at the Capitol Theatre. Demand for tickets was so great that the theater had to run around-the-clock showings, taking just an hour off pre-dawn to sweep out the place. The movie was an unabashed hit, with the box office and reviews to prove it. And the actor receiving the most critical praise was the guy with fifth billing in the credits.

"[Sinatra] does Private Maggio like nothing he has ever done before," *Time* magazine's reviewer said. "His face wears the calm of a man who is completely sure of what he is doing as he plays it straight from Little Italy." "Frank Sinatra is simply superb, comical, pitiful, childishly brave, pathetically defiant," said the *Los Angeles Times*, adding that "Sinatra makes his death scene one of the best ever photographed."[21] The *New York Post* was equally effusive in its praise. "For the first time, I find myself in the ranks of his ardent admirers," its critic wrote. "Instead of exploiting a personality, [Sinatra] proves he is an actor by playing the luckless Maggio with a kind of doomed gaiety that is both real and immensely touching."[22] "Frank Sinatra . . . is a first-rate actor," *The New Yorker* declared.[23]

Alone in New York while Ava was finishing up *Knights of the Round Table*,[24] Frank had his groove back as he made the rounds of his familiar haunts — Patsy's, Toots Shor's, Jilly's. He called Ava daily, reading each review and telling her about the offers that were pouring in. NBC wanted to talk to him about a radio and television package, and Milton Berle about another guest spot on his show, but this time for a hefty $6,000 appearance fee. Skinny D'Amato called from Atlantic City, offering a two-week gig at the 500 Club, at $10,000 per; Bill Miller's Riviera, the same — they had an opening for him in early September, if he could fit it in. Even his records were starting to sell again. Twentieth Century Fox wanted him for a new movie, *The Girl in Pink Tights*, co-starring Marilyn Monroe. And, best of all, he was being sized up for the lead role in an Elia Kazan-directed, Budd Schulberg-written picture about a crime-ridden longshoreman's union, to be filmed in Hoboken. He thought the picture tailor-made for him — he had worked those docks as a kid, for Christ's sake. Although he hadn't read the script yet, this seemed like the perfect follow-up to his Maggio performance.

It had been years since Sinatra experienced a seller's market like this, with both his singing and acting talents so much in demand. Ava must have detected a hint of the old arrogance in Frank's voice when they spoke, the side of him that never stopped bothering her. "When he was on top," Ava once said, "he was a sacred monster convinced there was no one in the world except himself." She "liked him better down and out."[25]

Frank wanted Ava back in the States when *Knights* wrapped, but if she were to end her residency *outside* the United States too soon, it would likely cost her $150,000 in additional taxes.[26] And so the bickering continued, by trans-Atlantic telephone, and the calls became less frequent. Sinatra had another smash run at The Five in Atlantic City, where Skinny D'Amato introduced him to Sam Giancana, one of Mafia boss Tony Accardo's top men in Chicago. Dolly and Marty showed up, and D'Amato treated them like the parents of royalty. Then it was back to New York for Frank, and another engagement at Bill Miller's Riviera — this time as the man of the hour and not as a supplicant.

Ava made a decision to return to the States. The New York premiere of *Mogambo* was set for October 1 (the picture would open in San Francisco a week earlier, to rave reviews for it and her), and she might as well be present for that, she thought. It was also time for her and Frank to have an adult conversation, if that was possible, about where their marriage was going. She had taken up again with Robert Taylor while they were filming *Knights*, more out of boredom and convenience — he had been a casual sex partner years earlier, before Frank — than passion. She was certain Frank was cheating on her, too — that was his nature, as he had proved over and over. And so she boarded a flight at Heathrow; but her immediate destination was Madrid, not New York. She was entitled to a little rest and relaxation before heading home to face the music, perhaps taking in a bullfight or two and, maybe, a bullfighter or two. While in Madrid, she met Luis Miguel Dominguín, Spain's finest toreador and a man Ernest Hemingway had referred to as "a combination Don Juan and Hamlet."[27]

When Ava finally arrived back in New York, there was no Frank to meet her, because she had not told him of her coming. She quietly checked into the Hampshire House (Frank was still at the Waldorf Astoria). Frank didn't learn about her arrival until he read about it in the newspaper the next day. On Frank's opening night at the Riviera, Ava went to a Broadway play with a girlfriend. The Riviera was packed to capacity, with more than 650 celebrities among the audience, including Montgomery Clift, all eager to share in Frank Sinatra's resurgence. Some were turned away, including Dean Martin and Jerry Lewis — there was simply no extra space at ringside in which to jam another table.[28]

Both Frank and Ava gave statements to the press, expressing bewilderment over their situation. "I didn't know she was in town," Frank said. "I don't understand it. I can't make a statement because I don't know what is going on." Ava said, "It's my marriage and my life," and left it at that.[29]

Frank must have reached out to his mother, because Dolly called Ava the next day and invited her to dinner at the elder Sinatras' new home in Weehawken, New Jersey, a few miles south of Fort Lee. She also told Frank to come to dinner that same night. "Who's gonna be there?" he asked, as if he didn't know. "Never mind," Dolly said, "just come." He would be able to make dinner between shows at the Riviera, the two locations being so close. Ava arrived a half-hour earlier than Frank and broke down in tears as Dolly hugged her. When Frank got there, he could barely contain his happiness. Dolly left the two of them alone in the kitchen, stirring her pot of gravy. Ava went back to the Riviera with Frank after dinner and sat through his second show. Frank moved into her Hampshire House suite the next day.[30]

The reconciliation would be short-lived, with a final break on the not-too-distant horizon. "The explosions continued," as Gardner biographer Lee Server put it. "One night he had promised to be back at the hotel by 2:00 A.M. and then wandered in at dawn. Another night at the club in Jersey, she went missing, her reserved table empty, destroying his concentration, ruining the show. It was the same old thing, of course, but somehow not the same — worse, because attrition was at work, the wounds no longer healed properly between battles."[31]

They attended the *Mogambo* premiere together on October 1 and flew to Los Angeles the next day. This was about the time that Sinatra learned he would not be getting the role he coveted almost as much as the Maggio role. Producer Sam Spiegel had been casting for *On the Waterfront*, a gritty drama set in an unnamed East Coast waterfront city, but to be filmed almost entirely in Hoboken, whose docks and warehouses and grimy buildings far surpassed anything Hollywood could have devised on a studio back lot. Right after the buzz began about his performance in *From Here to Eternity*, Spiegel had approached Sinatra about his picture's lead role — Terry Malloy, an ex-boxer who gets preferential treatment as a longshoreman because his older brother is connected to the mob that runs the union. When confronted with a moral dilemma, his girlfriend pushes him into making the right choice. Spiegel gave Sinatra a copy of the screenplay, and Sinatra, as he had with the Maggio role, became consumed by the prospect of playing Terry Malloy. In fact, he thought Spiegel had promised it to him.

Spiegel had other ideas. His first choice was Marlon Brando, eight years younger than Sinatra and, with Montgomery Clift, one of the movie industry's two best method actors. Brando also looked the part of a former professional fighter. Where Sinatra's very puniness had helped him to land the Maggio role, that physical attribute now worked against him. A tough longshoreman he was not, especially one who could use his fists. Brando was giving Spiegel a hard time, not because he didn't want the role, but because he didn't want to work with director Elia Kazan and writer Budd Schulberg. Brando's politics clashed with the director's and writer's, both of whom had cooperated with the House Un-American Activities Committee in ratting on their film industry colleagues who may have been involved in Communist-front organizations or the Party itself. Ironically, Sinatra had the same political leanings as Brando, but he wasn't about to let that get in the way of a good movie role. Finally, Spiegel convinced Brando to take the part of Terry Malloy, despite his misgivings. It was one of his best career decisions. The 1954 picture would go on to get 12 Academy Award nominations, winning eight of them, including a Best Actor Oscar for Brando.

The loss of the Malloy role must have contributed to the marital upset in the Sinatra household during the fall of 1953. Frank went off for an October engagement at the Sands in Las Vegas, while Ava stayed in L.A. for that city's *Mogambo* opening. When she didn't join Frank in Vegas afterward, he was steamed. Soon, photos began appearing in the Los Angeles papers of Frank arm and arm with Vegas showgirls. Frank Sinatra was "less than sulky with an unidentified girl in Vegas," Hedda Hopper reported.[32] Strictly publicity, he told Ava when she called him about it, but she wasn't buying his explanation — he looked too pleased with himself. Then Frank pulled a stunt he would later regret. He called and told her he was in bed right at that moment with a beautiful girl. *If I'm going to be blamed for fucking other women when I'm innocent,* he told her, *I might as well do it and get some pleasure out of it.*[33] It was the final straw.

On October 29, 1953, Ava had the publicity director at MGM issue a statement on her behalf that may, or may not, have been coordinated with Frank: "Ava Gardner and Frank Sinatra stated today that having reluctantly exhausted every effort to reconcile their differences, they could find no mutual basis on which to continue their marriage. Both expressed deep regret and deep respect for each other. Their separation is final and Miss Gardner will seek a divorce."[34]

Louella Parsons got into the picture when Frank confided to her, "I can't eat. I can't sleep. I love her."[35] Sinatra wouldn't, or couldn't, extinguish the torch. Peter Lawford, a casual friend at the time (he and Sinatra had worked together on *It Happened in Brooklyn*) and not yet the fellow Rat Packer he'd become in the late 1950s and early 1960s, made the mistake of having a drink with Ava Gardner, soon after the separation was announced. It was innocent enough — Lawford and his manager, Milt Ebbins, ran into Ava and her sister Bappie in a Beverly Hills restaurant and sat down at their table. A Louella Parsons stringer saw them and informed the Hearst columnist, who then wrote a piece implying that Lawford and Gardner had rekindled an old romance. In fact, the situation may have been exactly as Parsons reported it — a dinner date. Lawford gave conflicting versions of the tale. He and Ava had dated early in their careers, before Sinatra even knew Ava Gardner, so perhaps he was trying to catch a very desirable woman on the rebound. Lawford got a 2 a.m. call at his home from Sinatra, the day the Parsons story broke.

"Do you want your legs broken, you fucking asshole?" Sinatra screamed. "Well, you're going to get them broken if I ever hear you're out with Ava again. So help me, I'll kill you."[36] Lawford tried to explain, but the phone went dead in his hand.

Milt Ebbins, who knew Sinatra, later tried to calm the singer down. Lawford, his friend as well as his client, was truly afraid that Frank's threat was not an idle one. Ebbins told Sinatra there was nothing to the incident. It was just a drink . . . really. "Are you sure?" Sinatra said, more as a statement than a question. Lawford would suffer no bodily injury as a result of having incurred the Sinatra wrath, but Frank didn't speak to him — not a word — for the next five years.[37]

Somehow, Sinatra managed to pull it together for two recording sessions at the Capitol Records studio, on November 5 and 6. He cut eight Nelson Riddle-conducted sides, each of which warrants mention — they were that good: "A Foggy Day," "My Funny Valentine," "They Can't Take

That Away From Me," "Violets for Your Furs," "Like Someone in Love," "I Get as Kick Out of You," "Little Girl Blue," and "The Girl Next Door."[38] None of them would crack the Top 5 list on the *Billboard* charts as a single, but all endure as Sinatra classics. And, together, they were turned into Sinatra's first album for Capitol, *Songs for Young Lovers*, a 10-inch LP, with four songs on each side.

Frank Sinatra's collaboration with Nelson Riddle, an Oradell, New Jersey, native whose life story was, in many respects, similar to Sinatra's, produced an unprecedented run of hit albums at Capitol Records, first with a swinging theme but then embracing a genre that would define the Sinatra-Riddle collaboration: the ballad. Three of those memorable albums — *In the Wee Small Hours*, *No One Cares*, and *Only the Lonely* — all released in 1955, were unsurpassed in their chronicle of lost love, as author Ben Yagoda noted in his recent book, *The B-Side: The Death of Tin Pan Alley and the Rebirth of the Great American Song*. "The repertoire was ballads, most of them standards," Yagoda wrote, "but presented in a new and almost revolutionary way. The emotion was real and searing, never sentimental or formulaic."[39]

Nelson Riddle recognized Sinatra's special skill in this regard, and he knew how it had been achieved. "Ava taught him how to sing a torch song," Riddle observed. "She taught him the hard way."[40]

* * *

In mid-November 1953, Sinatra was still brooding over the abrupt end to his marriage. Ava hadn't yet taken steps leading to a divorce, but the signs all pointed in that direction. She wasn't answering his calls, and there seemed to be no hope of reconciliation. While awaiting an upcoming engagement at the Chase Hotel in St. Louis, Frank flew to New York to begin a new, twice-weekly radio show for NBC, called *To Be Perfectly Frank*. Each broadcast was only 15 minutes, so it didn't occupy much time. He stayed with Jimmy Van Heusen, whose company always brightened his spirits.

There had to have been other women in Sinatra's bed while he was in New York — Van Heusen was one of his prime procurers of women, mostly high-end call girls — so Frank wasn't missing female companionship. But he *was* missing Ava. Biographer Kitty Kelley described Sinatra's mood at this time: "He wandered around Manhattan like one of the damned, filled with remorse and self-pity, unable to focus on anything but his terrible personal loss."[41] When Frank wasn't wandering the streets, he padded around Van Heusen's apartment in his pajamas, drank and smoked, and watched television. He was oblivious to everything, even failing to show up for the premiere broadcast of his new radio show, which NBC wanted to do live. They substituted a prerecorded tape, but were furious with Sinatra.

On Monday, November 16, the trade papers had good news — for Ava Gardner and Marlon Brando, not for Frank Sinatra. Ava had signed to do a new picture, *The Barefoot Contessa*, to be filmed in Spain and Italy and co-starring Sinatra's friend and acting idol, Humphrey Bogart. She had clearly moved on, with a bright future that didn't include him. Brando had just started shooting *On the Waterfront* across the river in Hoboken, Sinatra's town. It was like being hit with both barrels of a sawed-off shotgun. Frank was due in St. Louis the next day to begin rehearsals for his engagement at the Chase Hotel, but was in no condition to even appear in public, let alone give a singing performance. Van Heusen was losing patience with him. All his friends were.

Tuesday night, Van Heusen returned home to his 57th Street apartment around 2 a.m. He had been playing piano and singing at the 21 Club, a celebrity hangout on 52nd Street, just west of Fifth Avenue. Ordinarily, he would have gone to a party afterward, but he didn't want to leave Sinatra alone for too long.

His instincts were good. Sinatra was lying on the kitchen floor, his left pajama sleeve soaked with blood. He was conscious but barely coherent. "Jimmy," he said, "I can't stop the bleeding."[42] He had cut his left wrist. Van Heusen hastily called friends and then rushed Frank to Mount Sinai Hospital, where he would remain for two days before checking himself out against medical advice. Sinatra's agent reported that he was "not seriously ill," and doctors went along with the coverup. Mr. Sinatra's medical problem, they said, was "complete physical exhaustion, severe loss of weight, and a tremendous amount of emotional strain." The wound on his left wrist was the result of "an accident with a broken glass."[43]

The Chase Hotel gig was canceled, and Frank headed back to the West

Coast. Van Heusen, unnerved by the suicide attempt, threatened to have nothing further to do with Sinatra, unless he sought psychiatric help. Sinatra reluctantly agreed. Arrangements were made for him to see Dr. Ralph Greenson, the brother-in-law of Mickey Rudin, Frank's new attorney after he signed with William Morris. Dr. Greenson was also treating Marilyn Monroe — not exactly a ringing endorsement of his psychiatric skill. In an effort to keep watch over Sinatra, the William Morris Agency assigned George E. Wood "to stay with him constantly, to do his bidding, to soothe and calm him and keep him from harming himself."[44] It was a good fit, perhaps because the two men had something in common. Wood "knew all the gangsters — Meyer Lansky, Vincent 'Jimmy Blue Eyes' Alo, Frank Costello — all of them!"[45]

Frank talked Ava into seeing him for dinner one night, at Bappie's house in Los Angeles. They were cordial to one another, but that was all. Over the Thanksgiving weekend, she flew off to Rome, to begin preparations — rehearsals, costume fittings, etc. — for *The Barefoot Contessa*. Frank spent the holiday with Nancy and the kids. On December 8 and 9, he was back in the recording studio;[46] one of the sides, "Young at Heart," would restore him to the top ranks of recording artists by becoming his first singles hit in seven years. The song would reach No. 2 on the *Billboard* pop charts in February 1954,[47] and inspire a movie of the same name, starring Sinatra and Doris Day.

He called Ava in Rome and practically begged permission to visit for her birthday and the Christmas holidays. She tried putting him off, but in the end relented. He flew to London, on the first leg of his trip, but before leaving Heathrow, found out she was in Madrid, not Rome, staying at the home of friends. Unable to get on a scheduled flight right away, he chartered a plane to take him to Madrid, unwilling to delay the reunion for even a day.

When they were finally alone, in her room at the friends' house, Ava told him that it was over, in a way that was sure to burn every bridge behind her. According to a Gardner friend, "Ava sat him down and she said something like, 'Look, I am in love with a bullfighter now. You gotta get over me, baby.'" Sinatra went ballistic, throwing lamps, pictures, and every other object he could get his hands on against the walls and thoroughly trashing the room. Gardner admitted to a friend that she actually feared for her life. "Stop it, baby, please," she cried. When his tantrum subsided, Sinatra grabbed a handful of bills from his pocket and threw them in her face. "This is for the damage, sweetheart," he said. "And, oh, by the way, if you ever call me baby again, I'll rip your tongue right out of your fucking mouth, you bitch."[48]

16

"Frank did me a great favor — he saved me from the disaster our marriage would have been."

N o matter what happens tomorrow," 13-year-old Nancy Jr. told her father, "you've already won *our* Oscar."[1] The Academy Award ceremonies would take place the next night, March 25, 1954, and Frank Sinatra was up against four actors who had delivered their own superb performances in the Best Actor in a Supporting Role category: Eddie Albert in *Roman Holiday*; Robert Strauss in *Stalag 17*; and Jack Palance and Brandon de Wilde, both in *Shane*. It had to have been the most nerve-racking night of his life, and Frank chose to spend it with his first wife, Nancy, and their three children.

It wasn't surprising. Ava had announced their separation five months earlier and was back in Europe shooting *The Barefoot Contessa*, which co-starred Frank's friend and acting idol, Humphrey Bogart. Frank was still carrying a torch for Ava and wouldn't finally douse that flame for another couple of years, but he could not have picked a better place to calm his pre-Oscar jitters — in the fold of the family he had abandoned, but which never had abandoned him.

In fact, after Nancy reluctantly agreed to the divorce, the Sinatras were never closer. He continued to provide for them, of course, by court order if not on his own volition; still, it went beyond that. There was now a comfortableness to the relationship. Nancy Sr. welcomed him whenever he decided to drop by, announced or not, and was always happy to cook up one of his favorite Italian dishes. Nancy Jr., the only child who remembered what it was like to have Frank home, learned, as she got older, to deal with the separation. She would be Daddy's girl for the rest of Frank's life. Frankie and Tina were too young to realize what was happening when their mother and father ceased living together — the new reality was the only reality they'd ever known. And so, when Frank came over that night, it almost seemed as though he had never left. There's no record of what they had for dinner, but one thing is certain: There was a lot of love on the menu. At the end of the meal, the children presented Frank with a religious medal. On one side was a likeness of St. Genesius, the patron saint of actors; on the reverse, an inscription: "Dad, We'll Love You From Here to Eternity."[2]

It must have seemed like an eternity, waiting for the Best Supporting category to be called the following night. The Oscar ceremonies were different then — all the top and even second-tier awards came at the end of the program. Frank's two guests at the theater — Nancy Jr. and 10-year-old Frankie — were probably getting a little sleepy by then. When actress Mercedes McCambridge announced Frank's name as the winner, the entire audience — many of them actual voters in the competition — roared its approval. Hollywood always liked a "comeback" story — it was good box office. Frank kissed both kids and rushed down the aisle of the Pantages Theater to claim his Oscar. This time, he truly was back, baby, back.[3]

The kids had already seen *From Here to Eternity* and knew it was all make-believe. That didn't stop young Frankie from being on the lookout for Ernest Borgnine at the ceremonies, the actor who had played Sgt. Fatso Judson, Private Angelo Maggio's tormentor at the post stockade. "Dad, when I see that man Fatso," Frankie said, "I'm going to kill him." With a smile, knowing how important the death scene in *Eternity* was to his success in the picture, big Frank replied, "No, son, you don't kill him — you kiss him. He helped me win the Academy Award."[4]

* * *

Ava Gardner once described Frank Sinatra as a "sacred monster"[5] when he was riding high, only thinking of himself and no one else. Success brought out an arrogance in him that was absent when he felt less sure of himself. And it also made him reckless.

In 1943, when Sinatra was dazzling audiences as a solo singing act and just beginning his movie career, swashbuckler Errol Flynn was on trial for his acting life. Two 17-year-old girls, Peggy Satterlee and Betty Hansen, had accused the 33-year-old Flynn of statutory rape — sexual relations with a minor, regardless of consent. "I'm bewildered. I can't understand it. I hardly touched the girl," Flynn had proclaimed, soon after his arrest. A jury of nine women and three men found the handsome star "not guilty" — a foregone conclusion, according to most observers. Famed Hollywood attorney Jerry Geisler represented Flynn and tore apart his two accusers with allegations of past immoral conduct — a defense that would not be permitted today. "I knew those women would acquit him," Peggy Satterlee said, after the verdict was read. "They just sat and looked adoringly at him as if he was their son or something."[6]

Sinatra should have learned something from the Errol Flynn episode. He didn't. In fact, his transgression was even greater than Flynn's. Frank Sinatra, fresh off his Oscar win, began a sexual relationship with a 15-year-old girl, a girl just two years older than his daughter Nancy. She was a child actress who had captured the hearts of all Americans seven years earlier, when she portrayed a little girl who didn't believe in Santa Claus, until a "miracle on 34th Street" convinced her to believe. Frank Sinatra began having sex with Natalie Wood. If the affair had gone public, it would have meant his ruin, at a time when he had erased seven years of career famine and was on the verge of a bright new future. Fortunately for him, this reckless behavior — perhaps the most egregious of his life, potentially more damaging than any alleged mob affiliation ever could have been — never came to light until after his death.

If there were just one source for this revolting detail in a famous man's life, it probably wouldn't be fair to mention it. Frank Sinatra never commented publicly about it and, as far as we know, neither did Natalie Wood. And unless they had engaged in relations in front of others, which they didn't, they were the only two who could have given a firsthand account.

But three people, otherwise in a position to know intimate details about Sinatra and Wood, did tell the tale, a tale that still has the ring of truth more than 60 years later.

George Jacobs was hired by Sinatra to be his personal valet in 1953, after Frank had completed his work in *From Here to Eternity* and was expecting big things to come from it. He needed someone to attend to his fastidious demands regarding clothing, food, housekeeping, and the like. He had men who attended to those needs when he was on the road — men like Tony Consiglio, Hank Sanicola, and Nick Sevano — but he wanted a body man, so to speak, in his household. Jacobs had been working in that same capacity for Swifty Lazar, the Hollywood agent and a neighbor of Sinatra's, and Sinatra liked what he saw, so he lured Jacobs away from Lazar. And he must have been satisfied with the man's work, including his discretion — he kept him employed in the most intimate setting in any public figure's life for 15 years.

Jacobs was present when Natalie Wood's mother — perhaps the vilest example of a Hollywood stage-door mother imaginable — first brought the 15-year-old girl to Sinatra's home, soon after he received his Academy Award for playing Maggio. Maria Gurdin, the mother, likely had one purpose in mind: to get Sinatra sexually involved with her daughter to boost her career. It was a tried and true Hollywood stratagem, though not often used with a subject so young. An early boyfriend of Natalie's, Scott Marlowe, once compared the mother to "a pimp."[7] Jacobs' description of the way Gurdin allowed her daughter to dress for her first meeting with Sinatra supports the overall impression.

"She had her kid all dolled up, total jailbait, in a form-fitting black party dress," Jacobs recalled, "and Mr. S [Jacobs' way of referring to Sinatra] went for it in a big way."[8]

Nothing sexual happened that first evening, with Jacobs and the mother present. But the stage was set. Natalie, with her mother's explicit permission, had two martinis and would have had a third, if Sinatra hadn't called a halt. They chatted about show business, and Frank played a few of his records. That was it, but the following week, Wood came over alone, after school at the movie studio.[9] And she kept coming over, wearing "skintight dresses, pushup bras, all the makeup that Saks could sell. She smoked and spoke like a world-weary New York sophisticate in a *Thin Man* movie," according to Jacobs.[10] The stated purpose for the frequent visits? "Singing lessons."[11]

"Mr. S would send me away when she was there," Jacobs said. " 'I don't want you to testify,' he joked. He wanted to be 'In like Flynn,' but he didn't want to be ruined for it."[12]

According to Natalie Wood biographer Suzanne Finstad, Natalie and her mother were in the Warner studio's commissary in May 1954 when Frank Sinatra walked in. Maria Gurdin encouraged her daughter to go over to Sinatra and introduce herself, which she did. Born on July 20, 1938, Wood was then 15. Sinatra, 38, was at the Warner Studios filming *Young at Heart*, with Doris Day and Gig Young. He was gracious to the girl and invited her and her mother over to his place.[13]

Actor Bobby Hyatt was then Natalie's co-star in an ABC sitcom, *The Pride of the Family*. He also had a crush on her and was as close to being her confidant as anyone at that time of her life, seeing her every day at studio school. "Natalie became a regular at Sinatra's that May and June," Hyatt would later recount. "When I asked her what was up between her and Sinatra, she said her mother told her not to say anything because if word got out that she was spending evenings at his house, it would ruin everything."[14]

Mary Ann Marinkovich, another close childhood friend of Natalie's, dating back to the 8th grade, was surprised that Wood's mother sent her alone to Sinatra's house: "She literally threw her to the lions," Marinkovich said. Marinkovich also believed that Wood and Sinatra were having an affair.[15]

The non-exclusive Sinatra-Wood relationship lasted for a number of years, well into Wood's adult life. Frank showered her with gifts and attention and at least one movie role, casting her as the female lead in his own production of *Kings Go Forth*, when she was just 19. She was already a rising star by then, based on her performances in *Rebel Without a Cause* and *The Searchers*. Sinatra was rehearsing at the 500 Club in Atlantic City when Wood was celebrating her 22nd birthday at a party in another state. Always a master of the grand gesture, he arranged for 22 fresh bouquets of flowers — bouquets, not individual flowers — to be sent to her at her party "every half-hour."[16]

Natalie Wood was a troubled young woman and would die in a mysterious drowning accident when she was just 43, having survived three earlier
suicide attempts.[17] Sinatra wasn't responsible for the tragic life of Natalie
Wood — he truly cared for her. Perhaps a *fatherly* touch would have done
the young woman more good.

* * *

Luis Miguel Dominguín was four years younger than Ava Gardner, and
she was as obsessively needy of him as Frank Sinatra was of her. She rented
an apartment in Rome, shortly after her arrival in that city to begin shooting
The Barefoot Contessa. Dominguín took a room at a nearby hotel, but the
two spent most of their nights in Ava's apartment. "I knew without a doubt
that he was for me," Ava said.[18]

She did not get along with her co-star, Humphrey Bogart — not at all.
He was constantly needling her, partly out of personal dislike but also
because Frank Sinatra was his friend, and Bogie was loyal to his friends. He
could see what was going on between Gardner and Dominguín, as could
everyone else — Ava made no effort to hide things. She was legally separated from Frank and could do as she pleased.

"I'll never figure you broads out," Bogart told Gardner one day on the
set. "Half the world's female population would throw themselves at Frank's
feet, and here you are flouncing around with guys who wear capes and little
ballerina slippers."[19]

"Aren't you being just a little bit nosy?" was Ava's only reply.[20]

Actually, Bogart had it wrong, perhaps out of friendship for Frank.
Dominguín was anything but effeminate. Gardner biographer Jane Ellen
Wayne described the bullfighter best, using Sinatra as a foil. "The splendidly
built Spaniard was all that Sinatra was not," Wayne wrote. "Luis had thick
black hair and Frank wore a toupee. Luis was fearless in and out of the bull-
ring. Frank's strength was his bodyguard. Luis was an attentive and romantic
companion. Frank wanted his cronies around him all the time. Dominguín's
close friends were Picasso and Stravinsky. Sinatra's pals were 'hoodlums.'"[21]

Bogie and Bacall got to know Frank Sinatra in 1952, during one of his
frequent estrangements from Ava, so they were his friends, not hers. They'd
been out to dinner with him a few times and initiated him into their

Holmby Hills Rat Pack. When Bogart left L.A. for Rome in January 1954, Lauren Bacall stayed behind a few weeks to be with the children, intending to join her husband in late January.

Arriving in New York on the first leg of her trip, Bacall took a hotel room to visit East Coast friends. While there, she got an unexpected call from Frank Sinatra. Would she mind delivering something to Ava in Rome? he asked, and Bacall readily agreed — perhaps too hastily. The "something" turned out to be a coconut cake, which arrived at Bacall's New York hotel room in a large white box the next day, before her departure for Rome and the *Contessa* shoot.[22] Coconut cake was apparently an Ava Gardner favorite, and this gesture on Frank's part was clearly an attempt to gain her attention once again. The Hollywood rumor mill wouldn't have let a thing like another Gardner romance with another bullfighter go unmentioned, no matter what distance it had to travel.

It's doubtful there could have been a more cumbersome object to transport in a commercial passenger plane, first to London, then Rome. It wasn't packable, but had to be carried and held or stored midflight where it wouldn't get crushed. But Bacall did it, for a friend who had no compunction about putting a friend through such an ordeal. Bogie met her at the Rome airport, where she explained the white box she was carrying and asked her husband to let Ava know, so she could pick it up at their hotel. And then she waited two days, but no Ava. Finally, Bacall decided she had to deliver Frank's present, before "it rotted." She had never met Gardner; still, the reception she got when she knocked on Ava's dressing room door at the studio was more than passing strange.[23]

"I felt like an idiot standing there with the bloody box — there were assorted people in the room and I was introduced to none of them," Bacall wrote, years later. "I said, 'I brought this cake for you — Frank sent it to me in New York, he thought you'd like it.' She couldn't have cared less. She wanted me to put it down on some table she indicated — not a thank-you, nothing. I stood there very much out of place and finally managed to get away." Later, Bacall realized that Gardner's coldness wasn't a reaction to her. It was Ava's reaction to Frank — "she was clearly through with him."[24]

"I never told Frank the coconut-cake saga," Lauren Bacall wrote. "He would have been too hurt."[25]

Frank began dating Judy Garland and Elizabeth Taylor in Los Angeles, while Ava, done with *Contessa*, rented a place on Lake Tahoe in May 1954 to establish Nevada residency for a divorce. Back in the notice of Hollywood gossip columnists, Ava told Hedda Hopper, "Sinatra and I are not going to be together again — ever." Dominguín flew over to be with her, but after he returned to Spain, Ava took up with Howard Hughes still again. Hughes, the most persistent of her suitors, after Sinatra, bought her a house in Palm Springs to use as her base in the United States. He also offered her a $250,000 bonus if she would agree to do a picture for his RKO studio. She told him to contact her agent, like everyone else. Independent as always, she left Nevada after fulfilling the residency requirement but didn't bother to file for divorce. No reason was given for the sudden change of heart.[26]

* * *

In November 1954, Frank Sinatra got involved in a cloak-and-dagger episode to help out his friend Joe DiMaggio, and it turned into another public relations mess — something his newly resurrected but still fragile career could ill afford.

DiMaggio had married Marilyn Monroe in January 1954, but the baseball hero-Hollywood star union wouldn't last the year. The rupture started on the honeymoon in Japan, where Monroe combined business with pleasure by entertaining the troops stationed there and in South Korea. As a sex symbol, Marilyn's concept of "entertaining" meant shaking and jiggling everything that would shake and jiggle, to make the boys happy. DiMaggio didn't like her using her voluptuous body that way and let her know it. It's hard to imagine what he thought she did for a living — he couldn't have married her ignorant of that. In any event, DiMaggio's forbearance reached its breaking point on September 14, 1954, in front of the Trans-Lux Theater on 52nd Street in New York City. Marilyn was filming a scene from *The Seven Year Itch* for director Billy Wilder, who decided to do it in front of a crowd of onlookers, including Joe DiMaggio. It was the "blowing skirt" scene, where Marilyn's dress is propelled upward by a blast of air as she's standing over a grate in the sidewalk. Her panties were completely exposed, to her delight and the crowd's. But not to DiMaggio's.

Joltin' Joe and the Blonde Bombshell had a blistering fight over the incident, right in the theater lobby, with gawkers pressed against the glass doors, watching everything. A month later, Marilyn engaged Hollywood attorney Jerry Geisler and filed for divorce.

Stewing over the breakup, DiMaggio hired a Keystone Kop crew of private detectives to get some dirt on his wife for the divorce battle. He was having dinner with Frank Sinatra on November 5 when the detectives brought him the goods — Marilyn was shacked up right at that moment with another woman, with whom she was having an affair. A reporter later described the scene in the restaurant. "It looked like a Sons of Italy meeting," the reporter said, "Sinatra, DiMaggio, and a few other *paisanos* . . . . I could see that DiMaggio was in a terrible mood."[27]

Joe, Frank, and the gumshoes, along with a photographer, rushed out of the restaurant at midnight and piled into two cars — Joe went with Frank in his Cadillac. They rushed to a West Hollywood apartment building, where the episode splinters into differing accounts. Frank said he stayed at the car and didn't go into the apartment building. Others who were there claim that Frank was a full participant throughout. The bottom line is that a group, with or without Frank, broke down the door of Marilyn's suspected tryst location, except that it was the wrong apartment. In what became know as the "wrong-door raid," the participants burst into the home of "Mrs. Florence K. Ross, a 39-year-old secretary, who didn't even know Monroe."[28]

In September 1955, *Confidential* magazine, that era's version of the tabloids that now line the supermarket checkout lanes, printed a story that put Frank Sinatra squarely in the group that entered Mrs. Ross' apartment. The source for the story was likely Philip Irwin, one of the men hired by DiMaggio. Days after the magazine hit the streets, unknown assailants administered a thorough beating to the 24-year-old Irwin, who attributed the assault to Sinatra's doing, as payback for Irwin's supposed involvement in leaking the information. Irwin also claimed that Sinatra lied under oath about the incident.[29]

The matter wouldn't die. In late 1955, a committee of the California Legislature began an investigation, although its jurisdiction seems questionable. Sinatra was subpoenaed to testify, under oath. "I drove DiMaggio to the general area," he said, "I never knew the address. I parked at a curb and DiMaggio met Mr. Ruditsky, a private investigator, and another man with a camera. I was not present. Someone later said they went into the wrong door."[30] No charges were filed against anyone as a result of the committee's investigation, but Sinatra and DiMaggio were sued for $200,000 over the incident. The case settled out of court.[31]

The ironic sequel to the wrong-door raid is that Marilyn Monroe and Frank Sinatra soon became fast friends and roommates, while the friendship between Joe DiMaggio and Sinatra faded to black. Marilyn and Frank began living together at Frank's place in late 1954, he pining for Ava, and she for Joe.[32] At first, it was strictly platonic, but Marilyn's habit of walking around nude, at almost any time of day, changed that. Frank went to the kitchen early one morning, and there she was, in the all-together, bending over to look in the fridge, a tableau hard to resist. They went at it right in the kitchen. Frank was drinking heavily at the time and having problems in bed. Over the ensuing weeks, Marilyn set him straight.[33]

They would remain friends and sometime lovers until Marilyn's tragic death in 1962. Joe DiMaggio handled the funeral arrangements for his former wife — there was no one else with a better claim of authority, and he still loved her, despite all that had transpired. Frank Sinatra was barred from attending.

* * *

Many longtime Sinatra fans consider his Capitol years, 1953-1962, the Golden Age of Sinatra, not only for the music he created but also for his masterful performances on the silver screen, in both dramatic and musical comedy roles. With Nelson Riddle doing most of the arranging and conducting in Capitol's Los Angeles studios, along with Billy May, Gordon Jenkins, and a few others, Sinatra turned out more than 300 sides and album cuts in 89 separate recording sessions.[34] They were events attended by a privileged few. Author Robin Douglas-Home was present at one session, on September 11, 1961, during which Sinatra recorded six songs, including "I'll Be Seeing You," "September Song," "Memories of You," "There Will Never Be Another You," and "When the World Was Young."[35] It was an experience he never forgot.

"I saw complete and utter involvement with the song he was singing," Douglas-Home wrote, "involvement so close that one might feel he was in the throes of composing both tune and lyric as he went along. When he controlled his breathing, he shuddered, almost painfully . . . ."[36]

These were the great years, with hit album following hit album. Sinatra's filmography over approximately the same span was equally impressive, averaging almost three pictures per year through 1964, including notable performances in *From Here to Eternity* (1953), of course, *Suddenly* (1954), *The Tender Trap* (1955), *Guys and Dolls* (1955), *The Man with the Golden Arm* (1955), *High Society* (1956), *The Joker Is Wild* (1957), *Pal Joey* (1957), *Some Came Running* (1958), *A Hole in the Head* (1959), *Can-Can* (1960), *Oceans 11* (1960), and *The Manchurian Candidate* (1962).[37]

Many film critics and fans, too, thought the role Sinatra truly deserved an Oscar for was that of Frankie Machine in *The Man with the Golden Arm*. Machine was a rehabilitated doper who gets thrown back onto the same mean streets that got him hooked in the first place. He wants to become a drummer, putting to use the manual skills he developed as a card dealer in illicit poker games. His drug dealer hooks him again and talks him into cheating players in a high-stakes game. The unlucky Machine gets caught, and the gamblers break his hands, ending his dream of becoming a drummer. Kim Novak played one of the female leads and helps Machine kick the habit once again, this time cold turkey. Sinatra's portrayal of a drug addict going through withdrawal ranks as one of the best pure acting performances ever put on film.

Nelson Algren wrote the 1949 novel on which the film was based, and it won the National Book Award in 1950. The author had misgivings about the movie. "I was afraid nobody out there could play it and that Preminger [the director] would crap it up," Algren said. "But Sinatra was Frankie Machine, just the way I wrote him in the book."[38]

Sinatra was nominated for an Academy Award in the Best Actor in a Leading Role category for his work in *The Man with the Golden Arm*, but he was up against even stiffer competition on March 21, 1956, than he had been two years earlier, when he won Best Supporting Actor for Maggio. Spencer Tracy, another acting idol and friend to Sinatra, had been nominated for *Bad Day at Black Rock*. James Dean, killed six months earlier in a car crash, gave a sterling performance in *East of Eden* and had to have been a sentimental choice, if nothing else. James Cagney, still another actor that Sinatra patterned himself after, was nominated for his portrayal of a Chicago hood in *Love Me or Leave Me*. But the recipient of the Best Acting Oscar that year may have been the most ironic choice of all. Ernest Borgnine, who played Sgt. Fatso Judson in *From Here to Eternity*, won for his portrayal of a plain-looking, kindhearted, shy-with-girls, old-school Italian butcher — the title role in *Marty*, which also won Best Picture. "I thought I won an Oscar for the wrong picture," Sinatra said, years later. "I did the finest work I ever did in my life on that film."[39]

But Frank didn't let his disappointment over the loss deter him. He was back in the recording studio for five sessions over the ensuing weeks. One of the sides he cut was a sad tune, "The End of a Love Affair"; he sang it beautifully, but he still wasn't ready to throw in the towel with Ava. In May 1956, he departed the United States for Spain to begin filming *The Pride and the Passion*, co-starring Cary Grant and Sophia Loren — an overblown costume epic that was more costume than epic. Ava was in Spain, and despite Frank's having brought with him a young singer, Peggy Connolly, as a traveling companion, he was anticipating one more try at resurrecting their marriage. He and Ava got together for a couple of nights, and Frank was on his best behavior.[40] No jealous outbursts — the bullfighter was safely tucked out of sight — no recriminations over past infidelities, although Ava wasn't thrilled about Peggy Connolly patiently waiting for Frank back at his rented villa. But the spark was finally dead. Frank left the *Pride and Passion* shoot weeks early and told the director he would finish his scenes back in Hollywood.[41] Ava realized it, too. A year later, she flew to Mexico and obtained a divorce. She and Frank would remain on friendly terms for the rest of her life — she died in 1990. After she went broke, from bad investments and bad financial advice, he paid her bills and did whatever he could to sustain her.

* * *

It became apparent on the set of *The Harder They Fall*, Humphrey Bogart's last film, in late 1955, that the actor was sick. He was coughing so much, but had resisted seeing a doctor about it. Finally, actress Greer Garson, a friend, dragged him to see her internist. Bogart was eventually diagnosed with cancer of the esophagus on February 29, 1956,[42] and underwent surgery, chemotherapy, and radiation treatment. During this ordeal, gossip columnist Dorothy Kilgallen wrote an article in which she said that Bogie was "fighting for his life," a phrase that made the actor livid.[43] The fact that Kilgallen had upset Bogie may have contributed to Frank Sinatra's enmity toward the columnist for the rest of her life.[44] Bacall was especially grateful for Sinatra's attention during her husband's illness.

"Frank was constant with his phone calls and visits to Bogie — and it wasn't easy for him," she wrote. "I don't think he could bear to see Bogie that way or bear to face the possibility of his death. Yet, he cheered Bogie up when he was with him — made him laugh — kept the ring-a-ding act in high gear for him. He did it all the only way he knew how, and he did it well."[45]

Bacall sidestepped the question of when she began her love affair with Frank Sinatra—whether after Bogart's death, on January 14, 1957, or before.[46] They were discreet, in any event, and did not become a public item until afterward. As their intimacy grew, Frank's moodiness began to take its toll.

"The simple truth was that I just didn't know where I stood," she wrote. "And though I tried not to push him in words, I must have been unable to stop myself. I don't know what I was afraid of — that he'd lose his temper? Not call me? I guess all of that. I was totally vulnerable then, my only thought was to please him. I was changed — he had changed me. But it hadn't changed Frank. He was still Frank — adoring one day, remote the next."[47]

In March 1958,[48] at Bacall's L.A. home, Sinatra proposed. She accepted without hesitation, and Frank suggested they go out to a Japanese restaurant to celebrate and invite their mutual friend Swifty Lazar to join them. While the three were toasting the happy event, a girl came over and asked for autographs. "Put down your new name," Sinatra told Bacall, and she wrote, "Betty Sinatra," *Betty* being the name all her friends used. Days later, while Frank was fulfilling a singing engagement at the Hotel Fontainebleau in Miami Beach, Lazar escorted Betty to a concert. During intermission, Louella Parsons stopped to chat with them and, while Bacall was in the ladies' room, pried out of Lazar the fact of the engagement. Her column headline the next day read "Sinatra to marry Bacall." Sinatra wasn't pleased when both Betty and Swifty called him that day to break the news, the news that the engagement was now public.[49] It was the kiss of death for the engagement, over almost before it began.

"He dumped her over the phone," George Jacobs later wrote. "That was as ruthless as I had seen Frank Sinatra at that point in our relationship. I was taken back by the cold way he cut Betty, whom he had truly cared about, completely dead." Perhaps worse, Sinatra then began denigrating his former fiancée to friends, calling her "cold" and a "bad kisser."[50]

Bacall took it hard, especially when Sinatra cut off all contact with her. All contact. "Actually, Frank did me a great favor — he saved me from the disaster our marriage would have been," she wrote later when the realization had sunk in of what life with Sinatra would have entailed. "The truth is he was probably smarter than I: he knew it couldn't work. But the truth also is that he behaved like a complete shit. He was too cowardly to tell the truth — that it was just too much for him, that he found he couldn't handle it."[51]

Frank Sinatra didn't speak to Betty Bacall for the next six years — not until he accidentally bumped into her at a party and asked how she was.

*   *   *

The old hubris was back, or maybe it never left. In early 1956, Dorothy Kilgallen published a piece in the *New York Journal-American*. "Success hasn't changed Frank Sinatra," she wrote. "When he was unappreciated and obscure, he was hot-tempered, egotistical, extravagant, and moody. Now that he is rich and famous, with the world on a string and sapphires in his cufflinks, he is still hot-tempered, egotistical, extravagant, and moody."[52]

17

"We're on our way to the White House, buddy boy."

D olly Sinatra taught her son to be "in" with the right people, the people who ran things — in the legitimate world as well as the underworld, and everywhere in between. Politicians were *in between*. At the tender age of 11, Frank saw how politics affected his family's well-being for the good when, in 1927, Dolly practically ordered the mayor of Hoboken to make an opening in the all-Irish Hoboken Fire Department for her unemployed husband, Marty. Marty didn't even have to take the written test, which he would have failed, being illiterate. Dolly had the political clout because she controlled 600 votes in the city's Italian voting precincts. It was all about power.

Once he became rich and famous, Sinatra didn't waste time or effort on local politicians, certainly not after his invitation to tea with President Franklin D. Roosevelt in 1944. He went all out for Roosevelt in that campaign year and stuck with the Democrats in most election cycles thereafter. He and Ava joined the "Madly for Adlai" campaign in 1952, when Adlai Stevenson ran against Eisenhower and Nixon. In fact, a Stevenson campaign rally in L.A. brought the two Sinatras together after one of their fights, albeit temporarily. Frank and Ava were separated by the time Stevenson ran for president a second time, in 1956. Ava was living in Europe by then, but Frank put his full support behind the former Illinois governor, attending the Democratic National Convention in Chicago and singing the National Anthem.[1]

At that event, Sinatra took notice of the attractive young senator from Massachusetts who was campaigning hard for the vice-presidential nomination. He'd already met the senator, casually, at a Hollywood party, but had never observed him in a political setting. Stevenson had ceded the vice presidential choice to the convention-at-large, instead of exercising the prerogative himself, as was customary. Senator John F. Kennedy narrowly lost the bid, but Sinatra was impressed by Kennedy's organization of bright family members and friends, including brother Bobby, and the way they worked the delegates like pros.[2] When the convention picked Senator Estes Kefauver from Tennessee, former chair of the Kefauver committee, to be Stevenson's running mate, Bobby Kennedy was overheard to say, "OK, that's it. Now we go to work for the next one."[3]

Peter Lawford — whom Sinatra hadn't spoken to since the fall of 1953, when the actor was seen keeping company with Ava — had married Pat Kennedy, Jack's sister, on April 24, 1954, and was among those working on Jack's behalf at the convention. Sinatra and Lawford didn't speak or otherwise come into contact with one another while there, but Lawford's obvious closeness to a potential president would have been part of Sinatra's calculation for the future.

After the convention, Frank headed to New York for a most improbable reunion. He appeared at the Paramount Theatre with his former bandleader and contract antagonist, Tommy Dorsey. The gig was successful; Tommy's brother Jimmy also appeared on the bill, and Frank's latest picture, *Johnny Concho*, one of his lesser movies, got a needed boost by being the featured film. The motivation for the joint appearance was strictly box office, not a true reconciliation. Tommy Dorsey died three months later, and Sinatra didn't attend the funeral. Jackie Gleason organized a televised tribute to Dorsey on December 1, 1956, but Sinatra declined an invitation to appear. When asked about the snub, Sinatra was blunt: "I didn't like him. It would be inappropriate for me to appear on a memorial show."[4]

Earlier, in November, *Metronome* magazine published its 1956 poll of jazz musicians, and Frank Sinatra was named the No. 1 choice — the "Musicians' Musician of the Year."[5] There's no record of how Tommy Dorsey voted in that poll. Five years later, Sinatra put out an album of Dorsey hits under his new Reprise label, titled *I Remember Tommy*. "I really think this album has some of the best work I've ever done," Sinatra said. "I feel sentimental over Dorsey. I tried to sing the songs the way he used to play them on the trombone."[6]

* * *

Sinatra's newfound success, after *From Here to Eternity* and *The Man with the Golden Arm*, also reestablished him as a target of opportunity for the press — no friend of his to begin with. Kilgallen did a multi-part, mostly derogatory newspaper series titled "The Frank Sinatra Story," which ran in Hearst newspapers across the country. When the series ended, Sinatra sent Kilgallen "a tombstone with her name on it"[7] — a gesture that said more about him than it did her. He also intensified his verbal attacks on her, making them a regular part of his nightclub act, at the Sands in Las Vegas, at the Copacabana during his last appearance there in December 1957-January 1958, and elsewhere.

Kilgallen had a weak chin, which Sinatra magnified into "the chinless wonder," an epithet, along with others, that devastated the emotionally fragile newspaperwoman and television game show panelist (*What's My Line?*). And he kept pouring it on, for years. A television critic in Las Vegas caught Sinatra's show at the Sands in 1961 and heard 20 minutes of invective against Kilgallen. The critic called Sinatra out on it, which threw the singer into a rage and sent a coffee pot crashing into the television set. Sinatra made a call and had the TV critic barred from the Sands. The banishment lasted four years,[8] but considering Sinatra's clout in Las Vegas at the time, the critic was lucky he kept his job.

Sinatra was relentless, especially if the object of his wrath was smaller, weaker, less able to fight back. Sheila Graham, another Hollywood gossip columnist, had her own run-ins with Sinatra and bore the scars to prove it. "Sinatra has a God complex," she once wrote. "Unless you're 100 percent praiseful of Frank, he's inclined to detest you. Sinatra is the only absolutely unforgiving enemy I've ever made."[9]

Look magazine got into the act in May 1957 and ran a three-part series, "The Life Story of Frank Sinatra — Talent, Tantrums and Torment." Writer Bill Davidson tried to capture the complexity of his subject. "There is a generous Sinatra and a cruel Sinatra," he wrote. "There is a Sinatra who fights for the underdog, and a Sinatra who bullies his underlings. There is a cocky Sinatra, a scared Sinatra, a gay Sinatra, a brooding Sinatra. There is Sinatra the devoted family man and Sinatra the libertine."[10]

And there was the litigious Sinatra, who sued *Look* magazine for libel; when that lawsuit was dropped, he sued again, for invasion of privacy. The second case was also dropped, on the advice of counsel. Libel and invasion of privacy are two causes of action that public figures have a hard time winning, thanks to court decisions setting a high bar — the need to prove not only falsity, but also actual malice. Despite the unflattering press coverage, the public never appreciated Frank Sinatra more.

In the mid-1950s, Frank and his Capitol recording team settled into a groove, cranking out one hit album after another, most embodying the Sinatra-invented idea of the "concept album" — all the selected songs contributing to a set theme or mood, as in *Come Fly with Me, Come Dance with Me, Where Are You?* and *Only the Lonely.* His movies weren't doing badly, either. A string of successful releases — *High Society* (1956), *The Joker is Wild* (1957), and *Pal Joey* (1957) — made up for clunkers sandwiched in between, like *Johnny Concho* (1956) and *The Pride and the Passion* (1957).[11] "All the Way," written by Sammy Cahn and Jimmy Van Heusen for *The Joker is Wild,* became one of Sinatra's biggest hits and won the Academy Award for Best Original Song. His nightclub act was the most sought-after ticket in Las Vegas and elsewhere. But in one particular medium, Sinatra was the *conqueree,* not the conqueror. He never achieved success as a regular television performer — almost inexplicable, given his talent and ability to connect with audiences.

Biographer Tom Santopietro analyzed the puzzling phenomenon this way. "Frank simply never appeared fully at ease on his own television series," Santopietro wrote, "his edgy, impatient personality conveying a pent-up energy on the verge of exploding, more than a warm easygoing presence one wanted to invite into a living room every week." Frank's fastidiousness about the way he looked for performances somehow didn't carry over to his television appearances, where he often went on camera *sans* toupee, his receding hairline in full view. Sinatra "was not an inviting figure like Perry Como or, decades later, Dean Martin," Santopietro continued. He "would go on to score brilliantly with television specials such as 1965's *A Man and His Music*, programs where he could conceptualize sequences and use the medium like an extended nightclub session. On a weekly basis, however, he was incapable of supplying the comfort food America wanted in the post-World War II era. The cold war was gathering force, and the somewhat-justified audience perception that Frank was making clever 'inside' remarks and leaving the audience out of the joke did not endear him to the viewing public."[12]

But in the fall of 1957, ABC television, the perennial third-place finisher in network ratings, was ready to take a chance on Sinatra. They signed him to a multiyear contract that would involve 21 hour-long musical shows, plus 10 half-hour dramatic shows. *The Frank Sinatra Show* premiered on Friday night, October 18, 1957. Despite an impressive lineup of guest stars that included "Bob Hope, Peggy Lee, Kim Novak, Dean Martin, Bing Crosby, Dinah Shore, Robert Mitchum, Sammy Davis, Eddie Fisher, Ethel Merman, Joey Bishop, Ella Fitzgerald and Natalie Wood"[13] — yes, Natalie Wood, all grown up at 19 — the show received poor reviews and dismal ratings. ABC canceled it after one season, and it would be the last time that Frank Sinatra had his own television series.

The Frank Sinatra Show may have claimed one unexpected victim. When CBS programmed *The Phil Silvers Show* for the same Friday-night time slot occupied by Sinatra's ABC show, Frank called Silvers to deliver a succinct message, before slamming down the phone: "You had to go Fridays, huh?" Silvers was the guy who wrote "Nancy (With the Laughing Face)," Sinatra's "good luck" song, in honor of Nancy Jr.'s fourth birthday, and Silvers was the guy who helped Sinatra overcome an undeserved but real draft-dodger reputation by shepherding the nervous singer through a USO tour in Italy after V-E Day. The comedian likely had no say in the CBS decision to schedule his show in competition with Sinatra's, but that didn't matter to Sinatra. He cut Silvers off, speaking not another word to him for the next 16 years.[14]

* * *

Frank Sinatra and Dean Martin became best buddies during the on-location filming of *Some Came Running* in Madison, Indiana, over a three-week period in August and September, 1958. The movie was based on James Jones' novel of the same name, but neither the book nor the movie achieved the success of *From Here to Eternity*. Sinatra played the role of Army vet Dave Hirsh, who returns to his hometown of "Parkman," Indiana, and finds that his older brother is now a leading citizen. The brother had abandoned Dave as a kid, after both were orphaned. When Dave doesn't conform to his brother's idea of a proper lifestyle, preferring to team up with Dean Martin's character, gambler Bama Dillert, to play poker for a living, they have a falling out. Shirley MacLaine, who later became the official "mascot" of Sinatra's Rat Pack, portrayed Dave's floozy love interest in the movie. Helped by Sinatra's alteration of the movie's ending — he had MacLaine's character die, in a heroic act that saved Dave's life — MacLaine received her first Academy Award nomination (Best Actress in a Supporting Role) for her work in the picture.

Chicago Mafia boss Sam Giancana and some of his boys spent part of that August-September time frame with Sinatra, in a rented house on location. Their chief entertainment in quiet Madison was gin rummy and playing practical jokes on one another, to include tossing cherry bombs under the chairs of unsuspecting victims, with the resulting explosion a cause for raucous laughter, no matter how many times the prank was repeated.[15] Sinatra and Giancana had been introduced five years earlier in Atlantic City by the 500 Club's Skinny D'Amato, and they would remain friends until Giancana's gangland murder, in June 1975, in his suburban Chicago home, while frying up one of his favorite dishes — sausage and peppers. Sinatra may have been closer to Sam Giancana than to any other Mafia figure, and he had met plenty of Mafiosi in his life.[16] Less than two years after their Madison, Indiana, sojourn, Frank Sinatra would ask Sam Giancana for the biggest favor imaginable. He would ask for Giancana's help in electing the next president of the United States.

＊ ＊ ＊

Jack Kennedy began hanging out in Hollywood soon after he returned from the war, even before getting involved in politics. He served three terms in the U.S. House of Representatives, then won a U.S. Senate seat in 1952. When Jack's sister Pat married actor Peter Lawford in 1954, the Lawfords' home in Santa Monica, California, became Jack Kennedy's West Coast base of operations, for political fundraising *and* for hell-raising. One of the first parties Kennedy attended at the Lawford residence — Jackie was with him on that trip, so his freedom of action was limited — had Marilyn Monroe and Joe DiMaggio on the guest list. Marilyn, whose marriage to Joe was already failing, soon became aware that she was the focus of Jack Kennedy's attention. She later told a friend, "He couldn't take his eyes off me." Monroe and Kennedy began their sexual relationship in 1955 and continued that intimate bond for the next seven years, right up to her death in August 1962.[17]

Frank Sinatra yearned for access to Kennedy's inner circle and saw a rapprochement with Peter Lawford as his ticket inside. His chance came in August 1958, at a party in Gary Cooper's home. Pat Kennedy Lawford was seated alone, and Sinatra engaged her in conversation. Peter showed up later and joined his wife and Sinatra. It was an awkward situation for a time — Peter remembered Sinatra's threat to have his legs broken, or worse, all because he'd had a drink with Ava Gardner. But with Sinatra in a good mood and now motivated by self-interest, peace prevailed. A week later, Pat invited Frank to dinner, and the redeemed friendship between Frank Sinatra and Peter Lawford flourished, for a time. When Pat gave birth to a daughter on November 4, 1958, the Lawfords' third child, they named the baby Victoria Francis Lawford — Victoria, in honor of Uncle Jack's Senate reelection victory on the very same day of her birth, and Francis (with an "i") in honor of their great friend, Francis Albert Sinatra. A year later, perhaps in a weak moment, Sinatra apologized to Lawford for his ill treatment over the Ava Gardner incident — an extremely rare occurrence. "Charlie," Sinatra said, "I'm sorry. I was dead wrong."[18]

Sammy Davis, Jr., had also had a drink with Ava Gardner, in 1954 after she'd separated from Frank. And he'd had the further misfortune of having his transgression recorded in *Confidential*, the era's see-all, tell-all magazine. Sinatra shut him out for a time, but relented after Davis' horrendous car crash, which cost the singer-dancer an eye. In 1959, however, Davis committed a larger offense — he disrespected Frank in an interview with

Chicago radio personality Jack Eigen. It was an unforced error, and Davis should have known better. You don't ever criticize or cross Frank Sinatra in public — not in the slightest degree — if you want to hold his friendship. It was a mortal sin, for which the penance was often severe. And mixing praise with the criticism, as Sheila Graham found out, was no remedy.

"I love Frank and he was the kindest man in the world to me when I lost my eye in an auto accident and wanted to kill myself," Davis told Eigen. "But there are many things he does that there are no excuses for. Talent is not an excuse for bad manners . . . it does not give you the right to step on people and treat them rotten. This is what he does occasionally."[19]

According to Peter Lawford, when Sinatra heard about Sammy's remarks, he went ballistic, calling Davis "a dirty nigger bastard."[20] He cut him off from personal contact, but, more financially devastating to Davis, he cut him out of a picture deal, too. Metro-Goldwyn-Mayer was producing a war picture starring Frank — the studio reestablished its relationship with him after the success of *From Here to Eternity* — and Frank, before this incident occurred, had insisted that MGM also hire Sammy Davis, Jr. for the picture, at $75,000, far above what Davis was commanding at the time.[21]

The Sammy Davis-Frank Sinatra relationship endured more ups and downs than any of Sinatra's other friendships, with Sinatra always forgiving in the end. The particularly loathsome racial epithet used in this instance should not be taken as racial bias on Sinatra's part. He was lashing out at someone who had, in his mind, betrayed him, and in those sorts of skirmishes, there were no rules of engagement for Sinatra: Any weapon or barb was fair use. Sinatra actually loved Davis. In the early 1970s, Davis became heavily dependent on cocaine, and it was Frank Sinatra who saved him, after first dropping him for three years, out of disgust. He finally confronted Davis: "Sam, I'm so fucking disappointed in you with that shit," Sinatra told him. "Dump it. You're breaking your friends' hearts." Davis promised to give up drugs, a promise he kept until his death in 1990, of throat cancer.[22] The love continued even after Davis' death. Davis died broke, with a $1 million IRS lien against the home he'd shared with his wife Altovise, their children, and Sammy's mother. Frank Sinatra paid off the lien in full. Quietly.[23]

But after the radio interview, Sammy Davis was dropped from *Never So Few* and replaced by actor Steve McQueen. Sammy would remain in purgatory — or perhaps his own personal hell, given his neediness for Frank's approval — until he made a groveling, public apology to Sinatra months later, and Sinatra took him back into the fold . . . and back into the Rat Pack.

In fact, the Rat Pack was being transformed, at least temporarily, into the "Jack Pack," in honor of its newest member, Senator John F. Kennedy, candidate for president. All the Packers had nicknames, and Kennedy's was "Chickie Baby," a reference to his interest in the chicks, or the ladies.[24] On every West Coast jaunt, campaign-related or not, Kennedy hung out with either the Lawfords, at their Santa Monica home (Pat arranged to be else-where or turned a blind eye to her brother's infidelities), or Frank Sinatra, at his Palm Springs compound. Author Ronald Brownstein studied the lure that Hollywood had for many Washington politicos, especially the Kennedy-Sinatra connection.

"The aspect of Hollywood life Kennedy seemed to admire most," Brownstein wrote, "was Sinatra's ability to produce an apparently number-less supply of beautiful and pliant women. Kennedy seemed to view Hollywood first as a cross between a fraternity and a brothel."[25] Years later, after he had fallen from favor with the Kennedys and with Sinatra, Peter Lawford referred to Sinatra as "Jack's pimp."[26]

One of the women Sinatra produced was Judy Campbell, a 26-year-old from L.A. and described as a prostitute by several sources,[27] although she never admitted that her sexual relations were paid for. She accepted gifts — that was all. One L.A. Mafioso, Aladena "Jimmy the Weasel" Fratianno, once described Judy as "a nicer Liz Taylor" in looks.[28] She first hooked up with Sinatra in November 1959 at Puccini's, Sinatra's own restaurant in Beverly Hills, and accepted an invitation to accompany him on a vacation to Hawaii the next day, along with Peter and Pat Lawford.[29] Sinatra intro-duced Judy to Kennedy on February 7, 1960, at the Sands Hotel in Las Vegas,[30] where the Rat Pack was then filming *Oceans 11* by day and per-forming in the Sands' Copa Room by night, with very little sleep in between. Kennedy became intimate with Campbell the next afternoon, in Sinatra's hotel suite. Teddy — Jack's younger brother, later to be known as Senator Edward M. Kennedy of Massachusetts — was the first of the broth-ers to hit on her that night of February 7, Judy Campbell revealed in an autobiography written under her married name, Judith Exner. She rebuffed Teddy and was rewarded with first prize — the future president.[31]

One week after meeting Jack Kennedy, Judy Campbell was in Florida. So was Frank Sinatra and so was Sam Giancana. Sinatra introduced Judy to his friend "Sam Flood," one of Giancana's aliases. Also present was a man called "Joe Fish," as Joe Fischetti was known.[32] She became intimate with Giancana almost immediately, another indication of her professional status. More important, she would continue ongoing sexual relations with both Kennedy and Giancana over the same time span, lasting through early 1962, when circumstances forced Kennedy to terminate his relationship not only with Judith Campbell, but also, less completely, with Frank Sinatra. But that was in the future.

According to Sinatra biographer Kitty Kelley, the two-year affair between Judy Campbell and Jack Kennedy "included twice-a-day phone calls, a four-day stay at the Plaza Hotel in New York City, and romantic interludes in Palm Beach, Chicago, Los Angeles, and Jack Kennedy's home in Georgetown while Jackie was away. They met twenty times for intimate lunches in the White House in 1961, and telephone records show that Judith called him seventy times."[33] Kennedy "knew all about" her simultaneous relationship with Sam Giancana, Campbell said. In fact, he was "jealous."[34]

Columnist Walter Winchell hinted at the scandal: "Judy Campbell of Palm Springs and Beverly Hills is Topic Number One in Romantic Political Circles," he wrote.[35] Winchell's power was on the wane, but even at its height, he wouldn't have dared mention Jack Kennedy by name. It was a different time.

* * *

As the Kennedy team geared up for the 1960 presidential run, Frank Sinatra was flattered to be included in the strategy sessions at Peter and Pat Lawford's home, beginning in 1959. He would give all the help he was capable of, including recruitment of celebrity friends to join the cause, raising money at concerts benefitting the campaign, and singing a campaign jingle based on a song — "High Hopes" — from his latest movie, *A Hole in the Head.* But patriarch Joe Kennedy had another role in mind for Sinatra, one that Sinatra would have undoubtedly considered beneath him, had not Joe Kennedy been the one asking and had not the prize — a friend in the White House — been so tantalizing. Old Joe wanted Frank to use his mob connections on Jack's behalf. In other words, to act as a "go-between."[36]

The presidential nominating process was different back then. Just 16 states held primary elections to determine which candidate's slate of delegates would go to the Democratic Party's convention. Party bosses in the remaining 34 states selected the delegates, and those party bosses needed to be cajoled, coaxed, bribed with promises of favors, or otherwise persuaded to come over to Jack Kennedy's side. Because there was no incumbent in the race, the Democratic field was wide open and, in addition to Kennedy, featured Senate Majority Leader Lyndon B. Johnson of Texas, Senator Hubert Humphrey of Minnesota, and "favorite sons" Governor Pat Brown of California, Senator George Smathers of Florida, and Governor Michael DiSalle of Ohio. Even Adlai Stevenson was hopeful a deadlocked convention might turn to him as the party's standard bearer for a third time.

Kennedy was young, attractive, and a war hero — qualities that would have ordinarily made him a standout candidate. But he was also a Roman Catholic, and a Catholic, in mostly Protestant America, had never been elected president. He would have to win impressively in the early primaries to convince the bosses that he was their man, that he could overcome the religion handicap to win the presidency. Jack won the first-in-the-nation New Hampshire primary on March 8, 1960, and was campaigning hard in Wisconsin, when Frank Sinatra almost got himself dropped from the Kennedy fold.

Sinatra was producing some of his own movies by then and bought the rights to a play, *The Execution of Private Slovik*, about the only U.S. soldier to be executed for desertion in World War II, with the idea of turning it into a movie. He hired Robert Parish to direct the film and Steve McQueen to star in the title role. But his choice of a screenwriter for the project turned out to be problematic.

Albert Maltz had written the screenplay for *The House I Live In*, the film short that won an Academy Award for Sinatra and its producers in 1945. The problem was that Maltz was also one of the "Hollywood Ten" —

directors, producers, and screenwriters who refused to testify before the House Un-American Activities Committee in 1947 and who were jailed for contempt of Congress. They were subsequently blacklisted in the motion picture industry — no one would hire them because of the Communist Party taint. No one, that is, but Frank Sinatra, who purposely wanted to stick his thumb in the eye of the blacklist and destroy it forever.

When *The New York Times* broke the story on March 12, 1960, of Sinatra hiring Maltz, the ensuing furor threatened to hurt the Kennedy campaign because of its close association with Sinatra. Actor John Wayne, a staunch Republican, took a cheap shot at both Sinatra and Kennedy. "I wonder how Sinatra's crony, Senator John Kennedy, feels about him hiring such a man," Wayne was quoted as saying.[37] The right-wing Hearst chain of papers took up the cause, blasting Sinatra for standing by Maltz. Harry Cohn, the head of Columbia Pictures, urged his former *From Here to Eternity* star to get rid of Maltz: "They're calling you a fucking Communist," Cohn said.[38]

Finally, Sinatra backed down and dropped the project altogether, having the good grace, nonetheless, to pay Maltz the full $75,000 writing fee he had been promised. Frank took out a newspaper ad, stating, in part, that "Mr. Maltz had an affirmative, pro-American approach to the story. But the American public has indicated it feels the morality of hiring Albert Maltz is the more crucial matter and I will accept this majority opinion."[39]

In a 1985 interview, Maltz praised Sinatra's initial stance, but condemned his later collapse under the intense pressure. "Sinatra threw down the gauntlet against the blacklist," Maltz said. "He was prepared to fight. His eyes were open. The ad firing me was ridiculous. The American people had not spoken, only the Hearst press and the American Legion had. Something had come from behind that caused him to change his position." In his pocket, Maltz had a newspaper clipping of a Dorothy Kilgallen column from 1960. "The real credit," Kilgallen had written about Sinatra's reversal, "belongs to former Ambassador Joseph P. Kennedy. Unquestionably anti-Communist, Dad Kennedy would have invited Frank to jump off the Kennedy bandwagon if he hadn't unloaded Mr. Maltz."[40]

Indeed, Joe Kennedy had consulted with the cardinals in Boston and New York; both archbishops told him that Catholics were in an uproar over the situation and that if it continued, Jack was sure to lose support among strongly anti-Communist Catholics [41]— something the campaign could ill afford. It wouldn't be the last time Sinatra compromised principle and backed down to the Kennedys, to keep his standing with them.

Meanwhile, Jack Kennedy was rolling along. He followed up his New Hampshire primary victory with a win in Wisconsin, Hubert Humphrey's neck of the woods, besting the Minnesotan 56 percent to 44 percent. Still, it wasn't impressive enough. Humphrey won most of the precincts in the state, with Kennedy accumulating enough votes in the cities, where Catholics predominated, to gain the majority. The key contest would be a head-to-head matchup between Kennedy and Humphrey in West Virginia, on May 10. Only 5 percent of that Appalachian state's voters were Catholic. The vast majority was not only Protestant, it was anti-Catholic as well, fearful of a Papist in the White House, controlled by Rome.

It was in that context that Joe Kennedy asked for Sinatra's help. West Virginia was heavily unionized, and the mob controlled most of the unions. Would Sinatra go to Sam Giancana and get him behind Jack in West Virginia? Joe Kennedy asked. Tina Sinatra, Frank's younger daughter, would later confirm that Joe Kennedy approached her father on that very issue — getting Giancana's help with the Teamsters Union in West Virginia, as well as in the general election, should Jack get the nomination.[42] Nancy Sinatra also wrote about the meeting between Joe Kennedy and her father (she placed it in February 1960) and the elder Kennedy's request that Sinatra reach out to Giancana for help in West Virginia. Calling Giancana "an old acquaintance" of her father's, Nancy credited the gangster with getting 120,000 votes and the win for Jack Kennedy in West Virginia.[43]

Giancana went all out for Kennedy, and not just with the unions. He sent Skinny D'Amato into the state with $50,000 in cash to pass around, giving special attention to county sheriffs, who were the power base in West Virginia. Those same county sheriffs were frequent visitors to D'Amato's 500 Club in Atlantic City and its illegal casino, so he knew most of them . . . and knew they could be bought.[44]

When the stakes were high, the Kennedys were not ones to rely on just one hole card. Indeed, in West Virginia they had another power working for them — the power of Franklin D. Roosevelt's continuing favor among

West Virginians 15 years after his death. Old Joe got FDR, Jr., to work the coal miners, whose love of FDR Sr., and Eleanor Roosevelt as well, was unsurpassed.[45] On May 10, Jack Kennedy trounced Hubert Humphrey, knocking him out of the race.

The Democratic National Convention opened in Los Angeles on July 11, 1960, with Kennedy just 61 votes shy of the majority. Dolly Sinatra had already done her part to help Jack Kennedy . . . and her son; using her connections, she got Jersey City Mayor John V. Kenny and the Hudson County political machine behind Kennedy and, eventually, the entire New Jersey Democratic organization.[46] Bobby led the effort to corral the remaining delegates needed to put his brother over the top, before the vote actually occurred, on July 13. Frank Sinatra, Sammy Davis, Jr., Dean Martin, Peter Lawford, Tony Curtis, and Janet Leigh were all onstage at the start, leading the delegates in the singing of the "Star-Spangled Banner." During the National Anthem, the Alabama delegation was close to the stage and began heckling Davis, who was almost brought to tears by their taunts. Standing close by, Sinatra heard the racial slurs and whispered to his friend, "Those dirty sons of bitches. Don't let them get to you, Charlie."[47]

Jackie Kennedy did not attend the convention with her husband; she was home, pregnant. But Jack did not lack for companionship. He spent the first night of the convention with Judy Campbell. She left, but was replaced for the remaining nights by Marilyn Monroe.[48]

On July 13, Jack Kennedy received 806 votes, or 53 percent of the total, and won the presidential nomination. He chose Lyndon B. Johnson, the second-place finisher, as his running mate. Frank Sinatra was present, beaming at his friend's victory. He leaned over to Peter Lawford, patted him on the back, and said, "We're on our way to the White House, buddy boy."[49]

* * *

The 1960 presidential campaign is one of the most studied in U.S. history. It represented a changing of the guard, from one generation to the next, as Kennedy would note in his stirring inaugural address. Televised debates brought the candidates into American homes for the first time — the perspiring, five-o'clock-shadowed Nixon, who had spurned the use of makeup for the event, versus the cool, collected Kennedy, less impressive on the issues, however, more attractive physically. Those who listened to the debates on radio thought Nixon had won; those who watched them on television deemed Kennedy the winner. The "dirty tricks" of the 1968 Nixon campaign were still in the future but may have had their genesis in a little known facet of the 1960 campaign, one that didn't come to light until decades later and, even then, remained a little known footnote in history. And Frank Sinatra was involved, directly and indirectly.

In 1986, Kitty Kelley revealed that Sinatra hired a private investigator during the campaign to dig up dirt on Nixon, thinking it would help Kennedy if anything surfaced. And something did: Richard Nixon had been, for a time, under the care of a New York psychiatrist, Dr. Arnold Hutschnecker — a fact that would have effectively ended his candidacy if the public had gotten wind of it. Americans were still in the Dark Ages when it came to mental health and its treatment. Frank turned over the investigator's report to Bobby Kennedy, who was Jack's campaign manager. According to a Bobby Kennedy aide, Bobby "sat on the report and refused to make it public." In fact, the document remained in his office safe for the duration.[50]

Kelley offered no explanation for Bobby Kennedy's suppression of the damaging report. Did he not think it was important? If anything, Bobby was a political animal, clearly versed in every bare-knuckled aspect of the game, as tough as old Joe Kennedy. Did he have scruples against such tactics? Not likely in a man known as Jack's ruthless enforcer, the guy who pulled out all the stops to get his brother elected. It wasn't until the 1991 publication of James Spada's biography of Peter Lawford that the probable cause of Bobby Kennedy's forbearance came to light. Nixon had dirt on Jack Kennedy, too.

In 1959, private investigator Fred Otash secretly installed a listening device in the Santa Monica home of Pat and Peter Lawford — not to catch the Lawfords in any indiscretion but to gain intelligence about Jack Kennedy, who was known to be using the place for campaign meetings, as well as for his sexual trysts. According to Otash, "some people within the Republican Party" approached him to do the job. They "were trying to find things out about the Kennedys," Otash later said. "It was a political bugging to try to develop a derogatory profile on the Kennedys. Not regarding women, that came later. Just some inside information about what they were doing generally, their strategy for the 1960 campaign, that sort of thing."[51] Spada reports that "Nixon was aware that Bobby Kennedy knew but had decided not to leak the fact that Nixon had sought psychiatric counseling in the 1950s."[52]

It was like the "mutual assured destruction" strategy of the 1960s, '70s and '80s, when both the Soviet Union and United States had nuclear arsenals capable of bombing each other, and the world, back into the Stone Age. Each side — the Nixon camp and the Kennedy camp — had the ability to destroy the other, and so neither side pulled the trigger.

* * *

During the 1960 general election campaign, Sammy Davis, Jr., saved Frank Sinatra from still another embarrassment at the hands of the Kennedys. Davis was planning to marry May Britt,[53] a Swedish actress he had been courting, on October 16, 1960, about three weeks before the general election. Frank was going to be his best man. It was a time of racial intolerance in America, of *de facto* segregation and of an insensitivity that would shock the conscience of most Americans today. When news of the Davis-Britt wedding became public, some columnists openly mocked the couple and tied Davis to Kennedy's campaign. One mused that, if Kennedy were elected, would he appoint Davis as ambassador to Israel (Davis had converted to Judaism) or the Congo. Others speculated that if Sinatra were to participate in the wedding as best man, it would cost Kennedy votes in the upcoming election.[54] Kennedy insiders agreed.

Davis knew that Sinatra would be under pressure from the Kennedys to skip the wedding, and he wanted to save his friend from having to make that choice, without being asked to. He called Sinatra at his Palm Beach home — Peter Lawford was there at the time — and gave some made-up excuse to Sinatra about postponing the wedding. The following conversation ensued.

> SINATRA: "You're lying, Charlie."
> DAVIS: "Look, it's best that we postpone until after the
> election."

SINATRA: "You don't have to do that."

DAVIS: "I want to. All the talk ..."

SINATRA: "Screw the talk."

DAVIS: "I know, but it's better this way."

SINATRA: "I'll be there, whenever it is. You know that, don't you?"

DAVIS: "I know that, Frank."

SINATRA: "I'd never ask you to do a thing like this. Not your wedding. I'd never ask that."

DAVIS: "That's why it is up to me to be saying it."

SINATRA: "You're a better man than I am, Charlie. I don't know if I could do this for you, or for anyone . . ."

The next thing Sammy Davis heard was Peter Lawford on the line. "Frank can't talk anymore," Lawford said. Sinatra was overcome by emotion at his friend's gesture, a gesture that had saved him from making a difficult choice. A choice he probably knew would have gone against his conscience, simply to accommodate those whose power he sought to share. The next day, Sammy issued a press release. He and May Britt postponed their wedding, he said, because of technicalities involving Britt's prior divorce.[55]

Frank Sinatra didn't know it at the time, but Sammy Davis wasn't the only person being talked about and being disrespected within the Kennedy campaign organization. John Siegenthaler, a JFK aide, wrote a memo expressing the hope "that Sinatra would . . . keep his distance from the senator" at an event they were both to attend. He suggested that Sinatra be sent to Harlem to campaign, "where he is recognized as a hero of the cause of the Negro."[56] Jack Kennedy himself disparaged Sinatra, even as Sinatra was working hard for his election, according to one unnamed Kennedy aide. "We were discussing Frank one day," the aide said, "and all that he was doing for the campaign, and Jack said to a group of us, 'Look, make no mistake about it. Sinatra's a thug. Let's face it. Let's be aware of it and then let's try to use him to our advantage.'"[57]

John F. Kennedy went on to win the 1960 general election by one of the closest margins in U.S. history. In the key state of Illinois, Nixon won

93 of 102 counties, but lost the popular vote by less than 9,000 votes, thanks to the large majorities that Kennedy had rung up in Cook County,[58] Sam Giancana's home base. There were other suspected improprieties in the election, notably in Texas, where Lyndon B. Johnson's formidable political machine had eked out a two-percentage-point victory for the Kennedy-Johnson ticket. If Illinois and Texas had gone the other way, Richard Nixon would have won a bare Electoral College majority.

The silly ditty that Frank Sinatra sang during the campaign was written by Sammy Cahn and used Jimmy Van Heusen's original melody from *A Hole in the Head*. It went something like this:

> *Everyone is voting for Jack, because he has what all the others lack.*
> *Everyone wants to back Jack/Jack is on the right track.*
> *'Cause he's got high hopes, he's got high hopes,*
> *1960's the year for his high hopes . . .*

Frank Sinatra had high hopes, too. They lasted two years, at which time Sinatra's reputation and Jack Kennedy's reckless behavior caught up with both men. Only Sinatra suffered consequences.

18

"The guy got off on breaking things, as if it were sex."

Three days before the January 20, 1960, inauguration, Sammy Davis, Jr., got a call from Evelyn Lincoln, President-elect Kennedy's private secretary. "Mr. Davis . . . Sammy," Lincoln began, "the president has asked me to tell you that he does not want you to be present at his inauguration. There is a situation into which he is being forced and to fight it would be counterproductive to the goals he's set. He very much hopes you will understand."[1]

One can almost picture Evelyn Lincoln reading from a carefully crafted script, likely produced by a committee of Kennedy staffers with one purpose in mind: keep the black guy with the white wife away from the spotlight of the inauguration, at all costs. Sammy Davis had married May Britt in Las Vegas on November 13, 1960, five days after the election. Frank Sinatra was the best man. The Kennedys couldn't invite Sammy to the inauguration and not his wife — too obvious. If they could be diplomatic and somewhat ambiguous about the stated reasons given to Davis, letting everyone avoid hurt feelings and bruised egos, well, that would be good. If they couldn't, that was okay, too.

The South was still a loyal Democratic voting bloc in those days —

Kennedy wouldn't have won the election without it — but it was also still heavily segregated, despite inroads by a young Baptist minister in Montgomery, Alabama. Some states still had laws against interracial marriages. The Kennedys had to already be thinking about Jack's reelection bid four years later. There was trouble enough looming in the South. A Page One photo, in any of a dozen Southern newspapers, of President Kennedy greeting Mr. and Mrs. Sammy Davis, Jr. at his inauguration would have sounded the death knell for a second term.

Sammy was momentarily stunned when he heard Evelyn Lincoln's short recital. He had worked tirelessly for Jack's election, doing everything that was asked of him, and more. They had used him to get black votes, but that was okay. He'd campaigned with Ethel Kennedy, Bobby's wife, and Bobby, too, when he was available, in the Watts neighborhood of South Los Angeles and in 20 other large cities across the country.[2] And now, to be treated this way — *after* the election, with no repercussions possible from the voting public. Sammy had postponed his wedding so as not to hurt Jack's chances, and this was his payback? Where was their courage? Where were their balls? He felt used, discarded.

He thought about how he should respond to Evelyn Lincoln. He knew how he wanted to respond — "If John can do this to me, then tell him I hate him" — but, instead, he went quietly, as the Kennedy team knew he would. "I understand," he said, his voice choking up, barely audible. "Thank you for calling."[3] He was crushed, humiliated . . . and here he was, thanking the person who had delivered the devastating news.

Peter Lawford called right afterward. "Bobby argued for you," Lawford said,[4] as though that should be a source of comfort. Sammy knew that no decision was made in the Kennedy camp without Bobby's approval. Even Jack was reluctant to override his younger brother, in whose hands he had placed his destiny. Jack would have been consulted, but in the end he would have deferred to Bobby's decision.

And where was Frank? Frank, who was organizing the entertainment for the pre-inauguration gala and Democratic Party fundraiser. He hadn't even called Sammy; he hadn't the guts to deliver the news himself. The Kennedys, or one of their underlings, had to have told Frank about their decision not to invite Sammy and May — not soliciting Frank's approval, but merely informing him of a *fait accompli*. What did Frank say when they told him? Did he display the same high standard of loyalty he demanded of everyone else? Did he say, "Take your inauguration and shove it — you're not going to do this to a friend of mine"?

Apparently not.

"Though deeply troubled by the Kennedys' treatment of his friend Sammy," Nancy Sinatra later wrote, "the inaugural celebration was a milestone event for my father, not only as a lifelong Democrat but as a close personal friend of the man who was being sworn into the presidency of the United States. For the son of an immigrant Italian couple who had risen from the streets of Hoboken to become the biggest and most powerful star in show business, it was a moment to savor for a lifetime."[5]

Gloria Cahn Franks, who was married to songwriter Sammy Cahn at the time, attended a dinner party Sinatra was hosting (on the night of the actual inauguration) for the celebrities who had performed at the gala. Jack Kennedy, who was making the rounds of the several post-inauguration balls, put in a late appearance at Frank's dinner. Gloria noticed that Kennedy's arrival triggered something in Sinatra. He was "beaming, beaming" after Jack Kennedy arrived, she said, following him around from table to table and "grinning like the Cheshire Cat."[6] Frank Sinatra was in his own *Alice's Adventures in Wonderland* world. It was, to him, a world of unlimited possibilities. Maybe Dolly and Marty would get to spend a night in the White House. Maybe Frank could be the ambassador to Italy, as everyone had joked about. Sammy would get over this insult, and Frank would make it up to him later, with a couple of movie roles or something. Sammy wouldn't want Frank to throw everything away over a little thing like this. He'd understand.

As the pre-inaugural gala wound to a close in the early morning hours of January 20, President Kennedy took to the stage and thanked the celebrities who'd performed and the well-heeled audience who, by their purchase of tickets to the event, had replenished the election-depleted party coffers. The president singled out one man for special praise.

"I know we're all indebted to a great friend — Frank Sinatra," Kennedy said. "Long before he could sing, he used to poll a Democratic precinct back in New Jersey. That precinct has grown to cover a country. But long after he has ceased to sing, he is going to be standing up and speaking for the Democratic Party, and I thank him on behalf of all of you tonight."[7]

Sinatra had a recording made of Kennedy's remarks. Weeks later, while he was performing at the Sands in Las Vegas, Frank would invite guests to his hotel suite and play the recording for them. "We all had to sit around . . . and listen to that record of Kennedy thanking him," a live-in girlfriend of Jimmy Van Heusen later remarked. "Frank would stand by the mantel and play it, over and over, and we had to sit there for hours on end listening to every word."[8]

One week after the inauguration, Frank, Dean, and Sammy were onstage at Carnegie Hall, performing at a benefit concert for Dr. Martin Luther King Jr.'s Southern Christian Leadership Conference. All had been forgiven.

* * *

Nineteen sixty-one was a banner year for Frank Sinatra, in almost every respect. Following the inauguration, his two-week engagement at the Sands and a similar stint at the Fontainebleau in Miami Beach were sold out for every show. High rollers in Vegas had trouble getting a table. In Miami Beach, Sam Giancana was there and pressed Sinatra to speak to Joe Kennedy and ask him to get his son Bobby, the attorney general, to lay off. The expected easing of FBI scrutiny of mob activities, after the mob's help in getting Jack Kennedy elected, had never materialized; in fact, things got worse. Frank promised Giancana he would handle it. "Don't worry about it," Frank told the mob boss. "If I can't talk to the old man [Joe Kennedy], I'm gonna talk to the man [Jack Kennedy]." It was a promise he'd come to regret.[9]

Sinatra's film output in 1961 was meager, his only release being the mediocre *The Devil at 4 O'Clock*, co-starring Spencer Tracy. His record output was a different story. Frank was ending his association with Capitol Records. It had been a good run, but he had now formed Reprise, his own record label, and would be earning even more money, as both recording artist and record label owner. *Ring-a-Ding-Ding*, Sinatra's first Reprise album, was recorded in three sessions in December 1960 and released in March 1961. It rose to No. 4 and stayed on the charts for 35 weeks. Still,

Frank had remaining obligations to Capitol Records and spent March 21, 22, and 23 cutting 12 sides that would turn into the Capitol album *Come Swing With Me*. He doubled that effort less than two months later, all on behalf of the Reprise label. He spent May 1, 2, and 3 recording the *I Remember Tommy* album, using Dorsey's former arranger Sy Oliver for the orchestration, then worked May 18, 19, and 23 to produce the Billy May-arranged album *Sinatra Swings* — originally titled *Sing Along With Me*, but changed at Capitol's insistence because of its similarity to that label's swing album released earlier in the year.[10] "Granada," from the Reprise album, was released as a single and became a minor hit for Sinatra.

In August 1961, Sinatra, through Park Lane Enterprises, Inc., bought the Cal-Neva Lodge, a rustic resort at Lake Tahoe straddling the border between California and Nevada, with its casino legally situated in Nevada. The other shareholders were Hank Sanicola and Sanford Waterman.[11] Sam Giancana was reportedly a silent partner in the venture.[12]

August also brought Frank a welcome call from Joe Kennedy, who wanted to thank him, belatedly, for his help in the campaign and also to invite him to the Kennedy compound in Hyannis Port, on Cape Cod in Massachusetts.[13] Sinatra was thrilled — it was the type of access he'd hoped his work on the Kennedy campaign would bring. The visit would take place the following month, but before Frank had time to revel in anticipation, Sam Giancana was on his case once again about getting Bobby Kennedy to call off the FBI. There was a heated exchange between the two, with Giancana reminding Sinatra about the debt that was owed. Sinatra said he would try to do something, but there is no evidence that he did anything at all, except, perhaps, to get Peter Lawford to approach Bobby on the issue. Sinatra was "in his glory" at Hyannis Port, with the president, attorney general, Pat and Peter Lawford, and Ted Kennedy all present. They went cruising one afternoon aboard the *Honey Fitz*, the presidential yacht Kennedy renamed after his maternal grandfather, a two-term Boston mayor in the early 1900s.[14]

According to one Kennedy aide, Jack was rather cool toward Frank, but that didn't seem to bother Frank, if he noticed at all. Sinatra did persuade "Peter to talk to Bobby Kennedy about laying off of Giancana," that same aide said. "Lawford did talk to Bobby and was told to mind his own business." Lawford expected Sinatra to get angry over the rebuff, but Sinatra took it in stride. He wasn't about to tangle with Bobby Kennedy over Sam Giancana's problem and ruin his relationship with the Kennedys in the bargain. Besides, he was having too good a time to get upset.[15]

Mafioso Johnny Roselli, Sam Giancana's man in Los Angeles, stopped by Sinatra's Palm Springs home, after the singer got back from his visit with the Kennedys. It was a social call — the two were friendly from Frank's early days in L.A.— but was likely part business, too. Roselli was there to check up on Frank's mission. Did he talk to Bobby Kennedy on Giancana's behalf, and, if yes, what was the result? We actually have a firsthand account of that conversation, thanks to an illegal listening device the FBI had planted in Giancana's home.[16]

Johnny Roselli was at Giancana's house on December 6, 1961, and the conversation turned to Sinatra's failure to deliver the goods.[17] Roselli related to Giancana part of his conversation with Sinatra about the way Sinatra said he handled the issue with Bobby Kennedy. "Johnny," Sinatra told Roselli, "I took Sam's name and wrote it down and told Bobby Kennedy, 'This is my buddy, this is my buddy. This is what I want you to know, Bob.' "[18]

Sinatra's story smacked of a lie, and Giancana spotted it right away when Roselli recounted the tale. "One minute he says he talked to Robert," Giancana told Roselli, "and the next minute he says he hasn't talked to him. So he never did talk to him. It's a lot of [expletive deleted]. Either he did or he didn't. Forget about it. Why lie to me? I haven't got that coming."[19]

Sinatra had other things on his mind in December and January — a construction project at his Palm Springs compound. He was building what he hoped would become the Western White House — Jack Kennedy's getaway spot when he wanted to leave Washington for rest and relaxation. Frank had already erected a shrine of sorts in the main house. Kennedy had stayed with him in November 1959; soon after, Frank filled the house with framed Jack Kennedy photos and put a solid-gold plaque on the door of the then-senator's room: "John F. Kennedy Slept Here, November 6 and 7, 1960." He got the year wrong.

This latest project was more elaborate than setting aside a bedroom for the president. Sinatra began constructing a separate building, large enough to accommodate the president's entourage and seat 40 for dinner, with still another outbuilding for the Secret Service detail and their communications gear. He also erected a special flagpole on which to fly the presidential flag when Kennedy was in residence. And to make travel more convenient, he installed a concrete heliport. In January, Sinatra got a call from Peter Lawford. His dream was about to come true. Jack Kennedy would be coming West in March, Lawford said, and wanted to know if he could stay with Frank in Palm Springs.[20] Brimming with joy, Frank put the construction crews on overtime and spared no expense in getting the special accommodations ready.

He still made time for a vigorous sex life, with some of Hollywood's most beautiful women. Dorothy Provine filled that role for a while, until he met Juliet Prowse, a long-legged dancer from South Africa, on the set of *Can-Can* in 1960 and began a semi-serious affair with her. It would get more serious later, but Frank had a problematic Marilyn Monroe on his hands . . . and in his bed.

Marilyn had obtained a Mexican divorce in January 1961 from her third husband, playwright Arthur Miller, and had been on the loose and hungry for love ever since. She latched on to Sinatra, or vice-versa, and Frank had set her up in a West Hollywood apartment, in the building where George Jacobs, Sinatra's valet, lived when he wasn't staying with his boss in Palm Springs. Sinatra wasn't about to bring Marilyn into his own home this time, a mistake he'd made after her breakup with Joe DiMaggio. Fastidious in the extreme, Sinatra couldn't abide Marilyn's personal habits.

"She was a total mess," George Jacobs recalled, years after both Marilyn Monroe and Frank Sinatra were gone. "She was usually drunk, which [Sinatra] could deal with. She was also usually filthy, which he couldn't. She was frequently too depressed to bathe or wash her hair, she ate in bed and slept among the crumbs and scraps, she would wear the same stained pants for days."[21] Jacobs was frequently in Monroe's apartment, mostly to transport her to and from Sinatra's place in L.A.. She propositioned him once, while standing nude in front of him, sipping champagne. He had the good sense not to get involved. "The image was glorious; the reality was squalid," Jacobs said. "Mr. S claimed he didn't even want to sleep with her. Of course, that rarely stopped him from doing it."[22]

In June 1961, Sinatra was performing at the Sands, and Marilyn was there with him. So were Peter and Pat Lawford, Eddie Fisher and Liz Taylor, and Dean and Jeanne Martin. They were together to celebrate Dean's 44th birthday. With all of Frank's friends at a ringside table during one of his shows, Marilyn became drunk and disorderly, leaning on the stage and speaking so loudly that half the audience could hear her. At an after party, the bad behavior continued, until Frank had her whisked away by one of his underlings. In August, Marilyn spent a weekend with Frank on his yacht, along with Jeanne Martin and Gloria Romanoff, restaurateur Mike Romanoff's wife. Marilyn was using drugs throughout the weekend, to the extent that she became incoherent one minute and almost comatose the next. The cruise was cut short. Frank wasn't about to give Marilyn an engagement ring, but he did give her a small white poodle, which she named "Maf," for Mafia, just to bug him.[23]

When Frank became formally engaged to Juliet Prowse (the engagement would last 43 days) in February 1962, Sammy Davis, Jr. ascribed Frank's motivation to his wanting to rid himself of Marilyn Monroe. Sinatra was never good at face-to-face confrontations, especially with women, as Lauren Bacall and others found out. The simplest way for Frank to end Marilyn's dependence on him was to get engaged to someone else. "Marilyn was a sweetheart," Davis said, "but Frank had his hands full with her."[24]

On May 19, 1962, Marilyn sang a sultry, almost breathless "Happy Birthday" tribute to President Kennedy at a Washington celebration of his 45th birthday. The crowd cheered the beautiful Hollywood star, dressed in a skin-tight gown that she literally had to be sewn into (she never wore underwear), as she paid homage to the man of the hour. Jacqueline Kennedy had stayed home, perhaps knowing what was in store. Those who were aware of Marilyn's special relationship with Jack smiled knowingly as she came to the final lines — "Happy birthday, Mr. Pres-i-dent, happy birthday to you" — and sprang to attention, rendering a full salute to the commander in chief — one that threatened to burst the seams of her dress.[25]

* * *

In January 1962, Judy Campbell went to Sam Giancana for help. Giancana was romantically involved with singer Phyllis McGuire at the time, but had maintained friendly relations with Campbell. Judy told him that she was pregnant with John F. Kennedy's baby. The timing of the pregnancy made her certain that Kennedy was the one — she had not had intercourse with any other man at the time conception would have taken place, during her last visit to the White House in December. She told Giancana that she'd discussed her condition with Kennedy and that he suggested she go to Sam for help. So, that's what she was doing.

Giancana had the Kennedys right where he wanted them, with information that could destroy both Jack and brother Bobby. They couldn't afford to let Jack's reckless sexual dalliances become public. They would have to play ball and call off the FBI's investigators. Still, it would involve putting Judy through hell, and Sam, one of the most ruthless mobsters Chicago had ever produced, decided he didn't want to destroy the girl in the process of getting even with the Kennedys. He arranged for her to go to Chicago's Grant Hospital on January 26, 1962, where she had an abortion, illegal at the time but doable for a man with Giancana's power.[26]

Another powerful man, FBI Director J. Edgar Hoover, wasn't above using his knowledge of the Jack Kennedy-Judy Campbell affair to solidify his standing within the Kennedy administration. Hoover was known to keep secret files on any number of famous Americans, holding back information until it became useful for him to leak it. Those secret files were filled with rumors and innuendo, not worth the paper they were printed on. But Hoover had the real goods on John F. Kennedy. If Kennedy was going to be around for eight years, Hoover, whose office was a presidential appointment, wanted to make sure he was around, too. The key was to make the Kennedys aware that he (Hoover) knew all about the Campbell affair, as well as the mob connections of Frank Sinatra, the president's particular friend, but to do so without seeming insubordinate or threatening.

On February 10, 1961, just three weeks after the inauguration and perhaps inspired by Sinatra's prominent role in that event, Hoover sent his first briefing memo to Attorney General Robert Kennedy. It reported that Sinatra, accompanied by actor George Raft, visited a known Washington, D.C., private gambling club over the weekend of January 21, 1961. Both men lost heavily at craps. An enclosure to Hoover's memo provided a summary of Sinatra's FBI dossier, including his association with mob figures.[27]

On November 24, 1961, and December 11, 1961, Hoover sent two more memos to the attorney general. Both memos were based on conversations overheard in various mob locations by illegally placed FBI bugs. The first memo established a Sinatra-Giancana friendship by relating their interactions when Sinatra was in Chicago. It also stated that "Giancana is one of the individuals selected as a target for early prosecution" by the Justice Department, confirming Sam Giancana's firmly held suspicion in that regard. The second memo, marked "Personal," was the more revealing of the two.

"Information has been received," Hoover wrote, "indicating that Samuel M. Giancana, a hoodlum figure, has sought to enlist Frank Sinatra to act as an intermediary to intercede on Giancana's behalf with the Attorney General. In this regard, consideration was allegedly given to making such overtures through the father of the Attorney General. However, Sinatra is reported to have rejected this idea." The memo went on to describe Giancana's pique at "not getting his money's worth" for the contributions he made to Jack Kennedy's presidential campaign.[28]

It's interesting to note that the second memo, mentioning Joe Kennedy as a possible conduit to the attorney general, was delivered to Bobby just eight days before his father suffered a debilitating stroke that left him unable to speak and partially paralyzed. One can't help wondering if Bobby warned the 73-year-old man about being a possible go-between in this matter, upsetting him in the process. It would seem a natural thing for Bobby to do — warning his dad — when faced with the knowledge that Hoover was aware not just of the Giancana-Sinatra connection, but also of the Giancana-Kennedy connection. Bobby had been Jack's campaign manager, and Joe Kennedy surely told Bobby about efforts to get mob help in West Virginia and elsewhere. It had been a crucial turning point in the campaign.

But it was a third pair of Hoover memos, dated February 26 and 27, 1962, that spelled doom for Frank Sinatra's hopes for a future as a Kennedy insider, if such hopes ever had real traction. "Judith E. Campbell" was brought into the picture and named as an associate of Johnny Roselli and Sam Giancana. "A review of the telephone toll calls from Campbell's Los Angeles residence," Hoover advised Bobby Kennedy, "discloses that on November 7 and 15, 1961, calls were made to Evelyn Lincoln, the President's secretary at the White House." Hoover then added a sentence so transparently false that its opposite meaning was clearly what the FBI director had in mind: "The relationship between Campbell and Mrs. Lincoln or the purpose of these calls is not known." Hoover knew beyond any doubt why Judy Campbell was calling the president's private secretary . . . and he knew that Bobby Kennedy would get the message and would transmit it to the president. To be certain about that last point, Hoover told Bobby that he was copying Special Assistant to the President Kenneth O'Donnell on the memo, Jack Kennedy's closest adviser — maybe even closer than Bobby.[29]

The potential for public scandal was quite clear, as were the disastrous consequences it would have on the president's young administration. At a Justice Department staff meeting, one of the attorneys said, in Bobby's presence, "We are out front fighting organized crime at every level and here the President is associating with Sinatra, who is in bed with those guys."[30]

On March 22, 1962, FBI Director Hoover and President Kennedy met privately in the Oval Office.[31] There is no record of what they discussed or of who initiated the meeting. The subject of the meeting had to have been both Sinatra's known mob associations and Judy Campbell, although Kennedy, astute politician that he was, would not have made any damaging admissions to Hoover. But he would have pumped his FBI director to extract every bit of information. And Hoover, most likely, would have given the president every assurance of confidentiality. Afterward, Bobby Kennedy told his brother, "Johnny, you just can't associate with this guy [Sinatra]."[32] Later that same day, the president phoned Judy Campbell from the White House,[33] perhaps to warn her about calling him and to begin the process of disengaging himself.

Bobby called Peter Lawford, just days before the impending trip, and told Lawford to inform Sinatra that the president would not be staying with him. Knowing that Frank had every detail of the visit meticulously planned, Lawford begged Bobby to reconsider, but Bobby was adamant. The Sinatra visit was canceled, and Peter, who had become the Kennedys' toady, had to be the one to deliver the news. ("Peter sold his soul to the Kennedys," remarked Patricia Seaton Kennedy, Lawford's fourth and final wife — he died the same year he married her, 1984.[34]) In desperation, Peter phoned the president directly, to see if he could turn this around. He knew instinctively that Sinatra would blame him, personally, for the change in plans. But Jack's mind was made up. "I can't stay there while Bobby's handling the [Giancana] investigation," the president told Lawford. "See if you can find me someplace else. You can handle it, Peter. We'll take care of the Frank situation when we get to it."[35]

Lawford made the call and told Sinatra that Jack Kennedy would not be making the visit. George Jacobs was with his boss in Palm Springs, helping him get ready for the presidential visit, so he was an eyewitness to what had to have been the most humiliating experience in Frank Sinatra's life. "We worked for weeks getting everything perfect," Jacobs later wrote, "planning parties, doing guest lists, trying to include everyone and not piss anyone off." When Lawford related the news, Sinatra's first thought was that government business was delaying the trip, but Lawford said that wasn't the case — Jack was still coming to California, but just not coming to Frank's place. Sinatra, his voice rising, demanded to know the reason. Lawford took a shot at calming his friend and offered a story he'd concocted beforehand. The Secret Service detail, Peter said, had raised security concerns about the location of Frank's compound and their ability to protect the president in such exposed surroundings.[36] An incredulous Frank Sinatra wasn't buying it. Pressed, Lawford finally admitted the truth. Bobby Kennedy had torpedoed the visit because Frank was friendly with so many mobsters. The conversation ended abruptly when Sinatra smashed the phone he was holding against the wall.[37] Jacobs was used to Sinatra smashing things. "The guy got off on breaking things, as if it were sex,"[38] Jacobs later remarked.

Sinatra then called Bobby in Washington, using another phone in the house. When Bobby got on the line, Sinatra started the conversation with, "What is this shit?" He repeated that phrase several times, according to Jacobs, who ascertained that Bobby was refusing to have the president stay at Sinatra's home because Sam Giancana had been a frequent guest there. *What do you mean?* Sinatra screamed — Jack had already stayed with him, Giancana or no Giancana. The decision was final, Bobby said, before abruptly hanging up. "There went another phone," Jacobs said, "smashed to smithereens."[39] Anger wasn't the only emotion consuming Sinatra. "Nearly in tears," Frank called Peter Lawford on still another phone, only to learn of the unkindest cut.[40]

It wasn't part of Frank Sinatra's nature to be a supplicant, but he began pleading with Lawford to do something with Peter's Kennedy in-laws to save him (Frank) from this almost unbearable loss of face. It was too late, Peter told Frank. The president had already made other arrangements. President Kennedy would be staying at the Palm Springs home of Bing Crosby, Sinatra's lifetime rival in the music business. Sinatra was in shock. The president was snubbing him, perhaps the biggest supporter of the Democratic Party among the Hollywood crowd, to stay at the home of a Republican, "an Eisenhower, Nixon guy." Sinatra let the phone slide from his hand and just "stood there staring out at the desert, as if someone had told him his folks had died."[41] It was the calm before the storm.

"Once the import of the last call to Lawford had sunk in," Jacobs said, "Mr. S went on the most violent rampage I had seen." Lawford kept clothing and golf clubs at Frank's place. Sinatra tore the clothes to shreds and bent Lawford's clubs over his knee, before ordering Jacobs to take the stuff to a nearby garbage dump. When Jacobs returned, "the whole compound was a sea of glass shards. Mr. S had smashed every Kennedy photo. He had also kicked the bedroom door in, but somehow he couldn't pry the 'Kennedy Slept Here' plaque off of it, and it would remain as a bitter reminder of how he had been used and dumped."[42] Later, Sinatra took a sledgehammer to the concrete heliport.[43] "I followed Mr. S around on his search-and-destroy mission," Jacobs said, "just to make sure he didn't die of a cerebral hemorrhage, his blood pressure was off the charts. I didn't dare try to stop him, or even say, 'Cool it, boss. This ain't worth it.' He probably would have killed me."[44]

After Jack Kennedy arrived in Los Angeles, Peter Lawford begged him to give Sinatra a call, which he did. The conversation was pleasant enough, and neither man mentioned the 800-pound elephant in the room — the president's snub of his "great friend — Frank Sinatra," as Kennedy had referred to him at the inaugural gala. The phone call did not mollify Sinatra. Jimmy Van Heusen had the misfortune of having a house next to Crosby's Palm Springs home and rented it to the Secret Service detail, so they could be close to the president. As a result, Sinatra shunned Van Heusen for the next several weeks.[45] Peter Lawford wasn't so lucky. Sinatra removed him from two Rat Pack movies that were in the works — *4 for Texas* and *Robin and the 7 Hoods* — and, except for one occasion, didn't speak to Lawford for the next 22 years, the remainder of Lawford's life.[46]

Richard Goodwin, a JFK speechwriter, once commented on the president's attitude concerning the break with Sinatra: "It meant nothing to [him]," Goodwin said. "If Kennedy thought about it in any way, if he thought it would even in the slightest wound his presidency, of course he would cut it off; he would cut off people a lot closer than Sinatra if he had to."[47]

As one might expect, the president's West Coast trip received extensive coverage in all media, adding to Sinatra's embarrassment within the Hollywood community and among men in his other, less glamorous world. Giancana had an "I told you so" look about him when he next stayed at Sinatra's Palm Springs home. In an earlier conversation between Johnny Roselli and Sam Giancana, recorded by the FBI, Roselli had summed up, accurately, how the Kennedys and their cronies viewed Frank Sinatra: They treat him "like they treat a whore," Roselli said.[48]

* * *

The news of Jack Kennedy's assassination reached Frank Sinatra while he was on a Warner Bros. soundstage shooting a scene for *Robin and the 7 Hoods*, a musical farce about Mafia-controlled Chicago in the 1930s. It was also his latest Rat Pack movie — the second since he banished Peter Lawford over the Western White House debacle. Frank quietly left the set and, for the first time in anyone's memory, went to a church and prayed. Later, he called the White House and spoke with Pat Lawford to express his condolences. "Frank was pretty broken up when he talked to Pat," according to Peter Lawford, whom Frank did not ask to speak with, "and would have given anything to come back to Washington for Jack's funeral, but it just wasn't possible to invite him. He'd already been too much of an embarrassment to the family."[49]

Sinatra would watch the Kennedy funeral, with all its ceremonial trappings, on television, just like the rest of us. And he would quietly grieve, just like the rest of us, over the loss of a youthful, attractive president, learning on the job and becoming a better leader with each passing day. Sinatra had made two movies dealing with presidential assassinations: one — *Suddenly* (1954) — in which he was the unsuccessful assassin, and one — *The Manchurian Candidate* (1962) — in which he was the hero, striving to prevent an assassination. He pulled both pictures from further distribution or rerelease.

On December 8, 1963, none of that would matter to Frank Sinatra. It was the day he learned that his 19-year-old son, Frankie, just starting out as a singer, had been kidnapped from his room at a Lake Tahoe resort, where he was performing. Sinatra's first instinct was to call Peter Lawford and ask for his help in getting Bobby Kennedy and the FBI on the case.

19

"I stretched Frank out on the sand and gave him artificial respiration."

When my family lived on Toluca Lake," Tina Sinatra wrote in her haunting 2000 memoir, *My Father's Daughter*, "Frankie was my father's little appendage. If my father was showering instead of taking a bath, Frankie wanted to shower. If Dad was shaving, Frankie would insist on lathering up, then shave with an empty razor. Sometimes they'd head out for a fishing expedition on the lake — 'Come on, son' — and Frankie would trudge lockstep with Dad to the rowboat, then ape his technique: same stance, same pose, same expression."[1]

Frankie was 6 when Nancy Sr., on Valentine's Day, 1950, finally locked Frank Sr. out of the house. He had taken his affair with Ava Gardner public, being seen with her at a Broadway show in December and a Houston restaurant in January. For the next 12 years, Nancy would harbor the forlorn hope that Frank would come back, but they never again would live as a family under the same roof.

"My brother understood just enough to draw the loss inside," Tina Sinatra wrote. "He felt bewildered and abandoned and quietly traumatized." As Frankie grew older, he turned into a brooding loner. "My dad truly loved Frankie," Tina wrote. "But he was also perplexed by his introverted middle child . . . ." [2]

In his early teens, Frankie fell under the sway of an older boy, a "black-leather-jacket type." Frankie and the other boy were caught shooting out street lamps with a BB gun, and, on one occasion, Nancy Sr. had to go to the police station at 2 a.m. to pick Frankie up after he'd been taken into custody. "Where Nancy idolized our father after he left home, and I just forged ahead without him," Tina wrote, "Frankie struggled for Dad's attention by acting out." Nancy Sr. wanted her son out of the house, for his own good, and he was shipped off to the Desert Sun School, a private co-ed boarding school not far from Palm Springs. Frankie would later refer to it as "Stalag 17." [3]

Besides bearing a striking resemblance to his father, Frank Jr. also possessed an appreciation of and talent for music. After graduation from Desert Sun, he decided to forego college and become a singer. He started out much as his father had, perhaps with the advantage of his name and the connections that came with it. He made his singing debut on September 12, 1963, at the Americana Hotel in New York, in a room packed with his father's celebrity friends. Frank Sr. stayed away opening night, not wanting to draw attention from his son. But he did show on a subsequent night and praised his son's performance, going so far as to acknowledge that, at similar stages in their respective careers, his son's voice was better than his had been. [4]

Three months later, 19-year-old Frankie was appearing at Harrah's Club in Lake Tahoe with the Tommy Dorsey band — not the original, but a pickup group of musicians with a claim to that billing. Around 9:30 p.m. on December 8, Frankie and John Foss, one of the musicians, were having dinner in Frankie's room at the lodge where the entertainers stayed; Frankie was in his underwear, not wanting to wrinkle his tuxedo before going onstage for a later show. There was a knock at the door, and a voice outside said, "Package for you, sir." Frankie opened the door, only to be pushed back inside by two men dressed in ski parkas. One of the men was armed with a .38 caliber revolver.

Barry Keenan and Joseph Amsler, both 23 and both former classmates of Nancy Sinatra at University High School in West Los Angeles, were the two intruders; their aim was to kidnap Frank Sinatra Jr. and hold him for ransom. There was a third conspirator, John Irwin, 42, waiting in Los Angeles for Keenan and Amsler to return with Frank Jr.

Irwin, with his deeper, more mature voice, would make the calls to Frank Sr. to arrange the ransom payment. Keenan, a "washed-up stockbroker" by his own admission, was the ringleader. It was he who hatched the plot and recruited the hapless Amsler and Irwin to join it. Their object was money — they didn't intend to harm Frank Jr., but saw him as someone easily manageable.[5]

In the lodge at Harrah's, Keenan and Amsler told Frankie to get dressed, while they bound and gagged John Foss. They gave their actions the appearance of a robbery — Frankie had $20, which was the extent of their immediate proceeds — and told Frankie they were taking him along as a hostage to ensure their safe getaway, promising to let him go afterward. They taped Frankie's hands behind his back, blindfolded him, and put him into their car. He went along quietly.[6]

After the intruders left, Foss managed to break free and notified the hotel staff about the abduction of Frank Sinatra Jr. at gunpoint. A hotel official summoned the authorities — there was a blizzard raging outside, so everything was moving at a slow pace — and told Frankie's road manger, Tino Barzie, to notify Frank Sinatra Sr. of his son's kidnapping. Instead, Barzie called Nancy Sinatra at her home. Nancy reacted with shock but managed to call Frank with the horrible news. He immediately reached out to Peter Lawford, asking him to contact Bobby Kennedy to request FBI involvement.

Bobby had remained attorney general after President Kennedy's assassination, but would soon leave the Johnson administration to run for a U.S. Senate seat, representing New York State. Despite continuing grief over losing his brother, Bobby called Sinatra and assured him that the full resources of the FBI and Justice Department would work to free Frankie. Later, Sam Giancana called Frank to offer his help, but Sinatra told Giancana, "Please. Don't do a damn thing. Let the FBI handle this."[7] J. Edgar Hoover also called the worried father and offered both reassurance and advice, the gist of which was to not make any public statements and to allow the bureau to do its work.[8] FBI agents were with the family throughout, including a detail that was dispatched to guard Nancy Jr., who was in New Orleans with her husband, singer Tommy Sands.

Despite Frank Sr.'s attempt to appear strong, his daughter Tina saw something in him that sent a chill through her. "My father did his best to conceal his emotions," she later wrote. "He wanted to lead by example, not exacerbate the problem. But he couldn't fool his daughter, and it was tough for me to watch him wrestle with his fear. 'Why haven't they called?' he kept muttering through the afternoon. 'Why haven't they *called?*' He was getting angry, which was good, because it made the rest of us a little stronger."[9]

The first call from the kidnappers came a day after the abduction. It was Irwin who made the call, and he let Frankie get on the line to briefly speak to his father. Subsequent calls from Irwin detailed the arrangements that were to be followed. The kidnappers wanted $240,000 in small bills — Frank would get the cash from a banker friend — and issued purposely convoluted instructions for the delivery of the money, promising to let Frankie go as soon as it was in their hands.[10] Barry Keenan and John Amsler went out together to get the ransom money, which had been delivered according to their instructions. In the process, Amsler got cold feet and ran off, on foot. With the money in hand, Keenan stopped to phone Irwin and relay that news. Irwin, who had bonded with Frankie as he held him captive, didn't wait for Keenan's return. He drove Frankie to a specific release point, not far from the Sinatra home, then called Frank Sr. and told him where he could find his son. Frank rushed out, but Frankie was not in the spot where the kidnapper said he would be. The father returned home crestfallen, something he couldn't hide from his former wife. It turned out that Frankie had been released at the promised location, but he had hidden himself on the side of the road, in case the kidnappers changed their minds and doubled back to get him. Frankie finally made contact with a security guard who was passing by and explained his situation to the guard, who delivered him back home. It was December 11, and Frankie had been missing for 56 hours.[11]

Joseph Amsler was the first of the kidnappers to be caught — his own brother turned him in to the FBI — and he soon implicated Keenan and Irwin. All three were in custody by December 14 and gave statements admitting their participation in the crime. At their trial, their attorneys put forth a contrived defense — Keenan admitted the lie, years later — in which Frank Sinatra Jr. was allegedly a participant in the incident. It was a hoax, they said, for Frankie to gain publicity for his singing career. The jury didn't buy the defense's theory and convicted all three men. Keenan and Amsler received life sentences, with Irwin getting a lesser, 16-year term because of his reduced role. When it was later discovered that the prosecution had withheld information from the defense team — namely, that Barry Keenan may have had a legitimate insanity defense — the trial judge was so incensed by the misbehavior that he drastically reduced the sentences of all three men. They each ended up serving less than five years.

Unfortunately, the made-up story of Frank Sinatra Jr.'s involvement in a faked kidnapping, all to help his singing career, gained traction with some members of the press. Rona Barrett, a friend of Nancy Jr.'s who had spent nights in the Sinatra home as she and Nancy were growing up, probably delivered the nastiest blow to the family and to young Frank when she later wrote, "Although there isn't any hard evidence, in my heart of hearts I always felt that Frank Jr. had staged his own kidnapping. Not for money. Not for publicity. But for the attention of his father."[12]

Indeed, there was no evidence to support the hoax theory, which was subsequently disavowed by the man who invented it, Barry Keenan. Yet the rumors persisted, to Frank Jr.'s detriment and, probably, to the detriment of his career. The apparent alienation between Frank Jr. and Frank Sr. for much of their lives — they came together near the end of Frank Sr.'s performing life, when Frank Jr. acted as his conductor — also fueled speculation. Nelson Riddle, a friend to both Sinatra singers, once commented on the strained relationship between father and son.

"Poor Frankie. He's had it tough being Frank's son," Riddle said. "Frankie's not an athlete like Dean Martin's son; he's not a great student; he's not a comedian or a back-slapper. He's an introspective little guy. Broods a lot. Frank has never taken the time to know his son, and what he does know, he doesn't like." Acknowledging that Frank Sr. always took financial responsibility for Nancy and the kids, Riddle went on to say that "a son needs more than that. He needs a man he can look up to. I've talked to Frankie a lot and I know he doesn't like his dad but deep down he wants to be loved by him. He can't get that love though. He knows it. He doesn't fawn like the girls do. He's been left out ever since he was a little kid."[13]

Frank Sinatra was immensely grateful to the FBI agents who worked to get Frankie back safe and sound and to apprehend the kidnappers. All of the ransom money, except for a few thousand, was recovered. After it was over, Sinatra had gold watches specially made in France, each costing $2,000 (or $15,000 in today's dollars), and sent them to the agents who had participated. The watches were returned to Sinatra by the senior FBI agent in charge of the investigation, with a note of thanks but no thanks. FBI agents, he explained, were not allowed to accept gifts. Sinatra then had one additional watch crafted for FBI Director J. Edgar Hoover and sent it, along with all the other watches, and a letter of appreciation to Hoover in Washington. This time the watches were not returned.[14] Neither was their receipt noted in Hoover's secret FBI file on Frank Sinatra or in any other official record.

* * *

In May 1964, Frank Sinatra was producing and directing another World War II drama,[15] on location in Kauai, Hawaii. *None But the Brave* (1965) told the story of two platoons of soldiers — one American and one Japanese — stranded together on a desert island in the Pacific and forced to cooperate for their own survival. The movie was noteworthy, thanks to Sinatra's penchant for ethnic and racial tolerance, for its portrayal of Japanese fighting men as real human beings, rather than as part of a Yellow Horde shouting "Banzai! Banzai!" while bayoneting unarmed prisoners or committing other acts of treachery.

Sinatra had rented a beach house on Kauai where he, his cronies, and other members of the cast and crew could relax on days when no shooting was to take place. May 10 was such a day, and Sinatra and friends were on the beach enjoying the splendid weather, among them executive producer Howard Koch and his wife, Ruth; Jilly Rizzo and his wife, Honey; and Brad Dexter, a hulking actor whom Sinatra had taken a liking to, both as a bar-hopping crony and an ever-ready bodyguard, should one be needed. Murray Wolf, part of Sinatra's entourage, was at the house, just 50 yards away and within sight of the folks sunning on the beach.

"It was a sun-drenched afternoon and we were all on the beach enjoying the ocean and that great tropical sun," Brad Dexter later recalled. "The waves were billowing higher and higher, though, and I noticed a treacherous riptide developing with a very strong undertow. I warned everyone to be careful in the water. Frank asked me to go to the house to bring him some wine and soda, so I went on up. While I was collecting everything in the kitchen I heard Murray screaming hysterically from the living room that Frank was drowning. I ran in and found Murray framed in front of the huge bay window in an emotional frenzy, pleading with me to save Frank's life."[16]

Dexter dropped everything and rushed headlong to the water's edge, where he caught glimpses of Sinatra and Ruth Koch out in the surf and struggling to keep their heads above water. Everyone on shore seemed frozen in place. Dexter plunged into the ocean and swiftly swam to Ruth Koch, the closer of the two. "Save Frank," she said, "I can't go on." Dexter tried to shake her into survival mode. "Nobody's going to die," he said. "C'mon, fight. C'mon. You're going to be okay."[17]

Clutching Ruth under one arm, Dexter took several powerful strokes to reach Sinatra, all the while shouting to him to hold on. Sinatra cried out, "I can hear you, but I can't see you," perhaps losing vision as a result of oxygen deprivation.

It must be noted that Sinatra and Brad Dexter parted company two years after this incident, on bad terms, so Dexter's recollection more than 20 years later may have been clouded not only by the elapsed time but also by lingering bad blood.

"Frank was pathetic, helpless like a baby," Dexter told Sinatra biographer Kitty Kelley, "and he kept sputtering to me, 'I'm going to die. I'm finished. It's all over, over. Please take care of my kids. I'm going to die. My kids. I'm going to die.' I tried to instill in him the will to fight for his life. I kept slapping him repeatedly on the face and back with stinging blows. I pulled him up and out of the water, over and over again, but he was as limp and lifeless as a rag doll. It was like grabbing a handful of jelly. He was so soft — there was no muscle tone, no firmness to hang on to, only squishy flesh. I yelled at him to help save himself, but he kept saying, 'I'm going to die, I'm going to die.' I tried to get him angry enough to start fighting back by calling him a fucking, lily-livered coward. A spineless, gutless shit. [Dexter appears to be laying it on a bit thick here.] But he didn't react. He seemed like he wanted to die, like he had no will to live. He just caved in.

"With one hand, I grabbed him by his ass and pulled him up and out of the water, but his body was a dead weight," Dexter continued. "Then I realized that he was unconscious, and so was Ruth. I had to fight continuously to hold them up and out of the crashing waves, praying that someone on the beach would summon help soon. I kept slapping them, pulling them out of the water, hoisting them up for air, but they were two dead weights. I cradled one in each of my arms and treaded water, trying to keep us all afloat, knowing that time was running out."[18]

Brad Dexter was big and strong, but no superman. Some of the feats he described in his account to Kitty Kelley are hard to believe, especially his "hoisting" of "two dead weights" while "treading water." They also violate a basic law of physics: For every action, there is an equal and opposite reaction. As Dexter "bench-pressed" Sinatra and Ruth Koch, their combined weight and Dexter's upper thrust would have sent him to the bottom. Still, most insiders, including Ruth Koch, did credit Dexter with saving Frank Sinatra's life.[19] "If Brad hadn't been there,," Ruth Koch said, years later, "I don't think Mr. Sinatra would have survived."[20]

Lifeguards came to the rescue, strapped Sinatra and Koch to surfboards, and paddled back to shore, leaving Dexter to fend for himself. He made it back, too, and saw that both Sinatra and Koch were unconscious. "I stretched Frank out on the sand and gave him artificial respiration," Dexter said. "Once he started vomiting the water out of his lungs, I turned him over to the lifeguards. Jilly Rizzo ran up to me and shouted, 'You're a hero, Brad. You're a hero. Without you, Frank would be dead.'"[21]

Hours later, after Dexter had rested and regained his strength, he went to Sinatra's rented beach house and saw the singer in bathrobe and slippers, seated and speaking on the phone with his daughter Nancy, who was on the island of Oahu with her husband, Tommy Sands, also an actor in the picture. Sinatra was reassuring Nancy that he was okay. The house, crowded with reporters, photographers, and other members of the cast and crew, as well as state officials and Red Cross members, looked like a madhouse. A Hawaii radio station mistakenly reported that Frank Sinatra had actually drowned,[22] likely causing pandemonium all over the islands.

"He looked up at me when I entered the room," Dexter said, "and I realized he was still in a state of shock. His eyes were bloodshot and he had the expression of a felled ox. When our eyes locked, it seemed that he didn't know what to say. He was embarrassed. He hung up the telephone and said, 'My family thanks you.' It was such a strange remark, almost as if I had put him in the uncomfortable position of having to thank me for saving his life. He never thanked me then or later, and I realize now that my rescue efforts probably severed the friendship right then and there by depriving him of the big-benefactor role, which is the one he liked to play with his friends."[23]

Sinatra would reward Dexter with an executive position in his movie production company and a prominent role in *Von Ryan's Express* (1965), which would begin shooting in Italy within months. Their association lasted two more years, breaking up while the Sinatra production company was filming *The Naked Runner* (1967) in England. Despite Dexter's exaggerations regarding his rescue of Sinatra that day in Kauai, he wasn't far off the mark in his analysis of Sinatra's reaction to *being* rescued. Other Sinatra intimates, including Shirley MacLaine, have noticed that same trait in the man.

"That's the way it was with Frank," Shirley MacLaine wrote in 1995, while Sinatra was still alive. "If you helped him more than he helped you, the friendship was doomed because the balance he wanted had been tipped. And if you worked for Frank and attempted to protect him from himself, you committed the most heinous of crimes. He was the godfather, indisputably. He knew not only what was best for himself, but also what was best for you."[24]

Joey Bishop had had his Rat Pack membership revoked well before the incident on Kauai. Bishop was a happily married man, faithful to his wife and not part of Sinatra's post-performance, booze-and-broads culture in the early 1960s. He also objected to the racial and ethnic slurs that Sinatra and Dean Martin tossed out for laughs during the famed "Summit" nightclub shows at the Sands and elsewhere. When Bishop learned of Sinatra's brush with death, he sent Sinatra a seven-word telegram: "I thought you could walk on water."[25] The comedian was immediately restored to Sinatra's good graces.

* * *

Sometime in 1953, Frank Sinatra and movie director John Farrow were having dinner at Romanoff's, the Beverly Hills restaurant owned by Frank's friend, Mike Romanoff. At the time, Sinatra was unaware of the brief affair Farrow had had with Ava Gardner (then, still Mrs. Frank Sinatra) while Farrow was directing Gardner in *Ride, Vaquero!* — a forgettable Western partially shot on location in Utah. At that dinner, Farrow's daughter, 8-year-old Mia, bounded up to the table to say hello to her dad. After Mia returned to her own table, shared with the person who'd brought her to the restaurant, Frank told John, "Pretty girl." Farrow's response was at once swift and prescient: "You stay away from her," Farrow said.[26] John Farrow would die, at 58, in January 1963 of a massive heart attack,[27] two years before a 19-year-old Mia Farrow and a 49-year-old Frank Sinatra began their relationship.

They had their first adult encounter at Stage 5 on the 20th Century Fox Studios lot, where Sinatra was finishing up *Von Ryan's Express*, after the on-location shoot in Italy. Mia was at a nearby sound stage, working on the television adaptation of *Peyton Place*, also produced by Fox as a follow-up to the studio's hugely successful 1957 movie of the same name. Farrow played the role of Allison MacKenzie in the prime-time soap opera during the first two years of its run, which began in September 1964.

Mia wandered over to Stage 5 during a break in her television production and watched Sinatra film a scene from his picture, thinking to herself, "What a beautiful face . . . full of pain and somehow familiar."[28] She may actually have been setting her sights on Sinatra — one report has her wearing "a transparent gown" she'd "borrowed from the wardrobe department" to the *Von Ryan* set.[29] "I love older men," Farrow had said, prior to her encounter with Sinatra, "I feel much more comfortable with them. They're exciting. They've lived. They have marvelous experiences to share." She might have been describing Frank Sinatra, of whom she said, "I liked him instantly. He rings true. He is what he is."[30]

On a second visit to the *Von Ryan* set, she saw Frank sitting and talking with a group of men — "boisterous" was how she characterized the group. Sinatra must have noticed her, too — perhaps this was the day she wore the "transparent gown" — because he sent one of his go-fers to ask her a strange question: "Hi," the man said, "we were wondering how old you were," as though to check on her *legality* — that is, being above the age of consent. "Nineteen," she responded, whereupon she was invited to join Sinatra and his cronies. The "jail bait" concerns of the boisterous group were justified. Mia Farrow was waif-like in her appearance, standing 5 feet, 5 inches and weighing under 100 pounds. She once jokingly referred to her measurements as "20-20-20," with the truth not far off from the jest.[31]

She was nervous, she said, and spilled the contents of her handbag as soon as she reached the group of men. Frank knelt beside her and helped pick everything up. "It might have been right then," Farrow later reported, "as our eyes met, that I began to love him . . . ."[32]

Later, Frank walked her to the door of the soundstage and asked her to join him for a private screening of *None But the Brave*, his first (and what would be his last) directorial effort, due for release in late February 1965. Mia accepted the invitation, and during the screening, two days later, Frank held her hand. She didn't remember much else about that first "date," except that Sinatra asked her to go to Palm Springs with him that very night. She got flustered and made an excuse about having to arrange for her cat to be cared for. "How about tomorrow," Frank responded. "I'll send my plane for you. You can bring the cat." She said yes.[33]

Sinatra was waiting for her at his Palm Springs home when she arrived the next day and showed her the impressive compound he had built, including its JFK room. At the pool, she saw actor Yul Brynner, dressed in a white terry-cloth robe and quietly talking to a striking redhead, who was crying. Sinatra hurried past them without speaking, as he was showing Mia around. "Later," Mia said, "I learned that she [the redhead] had originally been invited by Frank to be *his* date for the weekend, but as plans changed (me) he had simply passed her along to Yul . . . ." Mia slept with Frank that first night.[34]

It was a strange relationship that began that weekend, one that can best be illustrated by this exchange between Sinatra and his newly acquired 19-year-old girlfriend. He was telling her about his life and how he sang with "Tommy." Mia wrote about it this way: "'Who's Tommy?' I asked, and Frank just stared at me." She had never "listened to a Sinatra song or seen any of his movies," she said. "People my age were listening to the Beatles . . . ."[35]

"Ours was an intimate, intense existence," Farrow wrote, one that the lovers tried to keep secret. "A speculative line or two occasionally crept into the gossip columns, but Frank's publicist and Fox Studios effectively dispelled any rumors."³⁶

Sinatra was clearly worried about what his friends and family might think about the May-December romance. Mia was younger than two of his children. Frank introduced Mia to Shirley MacLaine and later asked MacLaine to "pass judgment on her. He asked what I thought," MacLaine remembered, "and I think I said something like, 'What do you say about someone who looks like a twelve-year-old boy?' "³⁷

Gossip columnist Sheila Graham, observing Mia on the set of *Peyton Place*, saw that the young actress was getting calls from someone; Graham guessed it was Sinatra. Later, in the studio commissary, Mia told Graham, "I just got a call from the man I love." Graham asked, "Frank Sinatra?" and Mia said, "Yes." Graham broke the story in her November 30 column, provoking the expected Sinatra outburst and an order to one of his publicists: "Shut that dame up. Jesus Christ."³⁸

Frank and Mia came out of the closet at a Hollywood charity gala, where Mia mingled, for the first time in public, with some of Frank's closest friends, including Sammy Davis, Jr. Dean Martin toasted her from the stage, with a singular comment: "Hey, I've got a bottle of Scotch that's older than you."³⁹

In April and May, 1965, Frank recorded songs that would become one of his best albums ever — *The September of My Years* — including "The September of My Years," "Hello Young Lovers," "Last Night When We Were Young," "September Song," and "It Was a Very Good Year."⁴⁰ The album would win four Grammys, but the theme was destined to call even more attention to the Sinatra-Farrow romance. The press wouldn't leave them alone, hounding them throughout their relationship, primarily over the age difference. "I kept thinking," Mia said, "they have it all wrong, they don't really know him. They can't see the wounding tenderness that even he can't bear to acknowledge — except when he sings."⁴¹

In August, Sinatra invited eight of his A-list friends — Bill and Edie Goetz; actress Rosalind Russell and her husband, Freddie Brisson; actress Claudette Colbert and her husband, Joel Pressman; and Armand Deutsch and his wife, he being heir to the Sears, Roebuck & Co. retail fortune — to join him and Mia on a month-long cruise in New England waters. He chartered a 168-foot yacht, with a crew of 20, for the excursion, which included a stop at the Kennedy compound in Hyannis Port so that Frank and Mia could visit with Joe Kennedy, still incapacitated by the stroke he had suffered in late 1961. There was rampant speculation that this was a wedding cruise, and reporters crowded into every port the vessel visited. The cruise ended abruptly off Martha's Vineyard when one of the crew members died in a drowning accident.

Nancy Sr., Nancy Jr., and Tina threw a 50th birthday party for Frank on December 12, 1965; although the family was willing to invite Mia, Frank insisted that she stay away, so as not to embarrass his former wife. Frank was not in a good mood to begin with. CBS had aired a special program the month before — *Sinatra: A CBS News Documentary.* Frank had cooperated and had even sat for an interview with newsman Walter Cronkite, but some subjects were supposed to be off limits, like Sinatra's personal life and his alleged mob connections. Cronkite went there anyway, almost precipitating a walkout by Sinatra. He completed the interview, and the show wasn't as bad as feared. But it wasn't good — those questions still got asked. At the birthday celebration, Sinatra got drunk . . . and emotional. Frank Jr. had not attended and had not called to congratulate his father. Alone in the ballroom with Brad Dexter, Frank lamented his poor relationship with Frankie. "My son never calls me," he said. "He puts as much distance between us as he possibly can." Later, when Frank got to Mia's apartment, he was in for a shock. Mia had chopped off her long blond hair — almost all of it. "I got bored with me," she said, but the action may well have been tied directly to the fact that Frank hadn't wanted her at his birthday celebration.

Frank's two daughters did their best to be supportive of his relationship with Mia. "As I began to spend time with Mia and Pop," Nancy wrote, "I realized how good she was for him."[42] Tina, 3½ years younger than her father's new flame, was more dubious. "I really liked Mia," Tina Sinatra said. "I just never thought that she and Dad would last."[43] Attempting to explain the romance, Tina said that "Mia needed nurturing, and Dad had a crying need to nurture,"[44] after the multiple upsets of the early 1960s — the Kennedy snub in Palm Springs in 1962 and, in 1963, Jack's assassination and Frankie's kidnapping.

Mia's mother, actress Maureen O'Sullivan, recognized an almost calculating side to her daughter. "Men had an instinctive desire to protect Mia," O'Sullivan said. "That's the secret." Edie Goetz, a Hollywood socialite (she was Louis B. Mayer's daughter) and close friend to Frank Sinatra, was more direct in her assessment. "Mia was a very clever young lady and she knew exactly what she was about and what she wanted," Goetz said. "She was crazy about Frank and she intended to marry him."[45]

* * *

Easily given to violent outbursts, Sinatra was involved in an incident, in the early morning hours of June 8, 1966, that could have cost a man his life. Frank, Dean Martin, Jilly Rizzo, actor Richard Conte, and five others were all at a table in the Polo Lounge of the Beverly Hills Hotel celebrating Dean's 49th birthday. One might easily assume that copious amounts of liquor were being consumed. Frederick Weisman, 54, president of Hunt's Foods, came into the lounge with Franklin Fox, a Boston businessman. The two men had just come from a rehearsal dinner — their children were getting married the next day — and wanted to celebrate with a nightcap. They took a table near Sinatra's party, but found the noise so loud they couldn't carry on a conversation. Weisman asked Sinatra to hold it down, and Sinatra lashed out: "You're out of line, buddy," he said. As Weisman sat down, Sinatra was heard by Franklin Fox to utter an anti-Semitic remark, which Weisman took as an insult. Weisman got up and was about to say something, but Sinatra and his party were already moving toward the exit, so he sat down again, upset but not wanting to press it. Minutes later, Sinatra came rushing back to Weisman's table, in an obvious rage. Franklin Fox described what happened next.

"He [Sinatra] came back to vent his anger, and Fred stood up," according to Fox. "My efforts were simply to keep Sinatra away from him and I did that by sidearming him. I was standing in front of Fred when Sinatra threw the telephone . . . . Dean Martin was trying to get him out of there, and the next thing I knew, Fred was lying on the ground, and Sinatra and his party had walked out. I was trying to help Fred on the floor . . . . When we weren't able to revive him, we called an ambulance and he was carried out of the room on a stretcher."[46]

Weisman almost died. He underwent cranial surgery on June 11 and remained in serious condition for weeks after the incident. Sinatra went into seclusion at his Palm Springs home. He had phoned police and given a statement denying any involvement in Weisman's injury, instead claiming that Weisman was the aggressor and that Weisman injured himself when he fell over a table and to the floor. "I at no time saw anyone hit him," Sinatra said, "and I certainly did not."[47] Dean Martin, who had gone on to Lake Tahoe, told police, "I never saw a thing."[48]

The story at Sinatra's Palm Springs digs, according to George Jacobs, his valet, was that Jilly administered the near-fatal blow to Weisman, not Sinatra,[49] but Jack Entratter's wife, Corinne, who was there with Jack and Mia, seemed to be of the opinion that Frank was on the hook. "That's the only time I think I ever saw that man scared," she said.[50]

Weisman's family initially demanded an investigation and charges against Sinatra, but after it was clear that Weisman would recover, they changed their mind. Kitty Kelley reported that the Weismans told friends they received threatening phone calls, but that was never stated publicly or proven. Weisman's attorney later confirmed his client's wish to call a halt: "He wants the case closed. A further investigation as to whether he was hit, pushed, or fell is not warranted." The Los Angeles District Attorney had no other choice but to announce, on June 30, 1966, that the investigation was over: "In the absence of any other evidence," he said, "we have concluded no prosecution is indicated."[51]

To celebrate his "exoneration," Sinatra bought a 9-carat diamond engagement ring for Mia. They were wed on July 19, 1966, in Jack Entratter's suite at the Sands Hotel. Dolly would later remark to George Jacobs, "She's a little nothing. Is that the best he can do?"[52]

Before the wedding ceremony, Frank told his daughter Nancy, "I don't know, maybe we'll only have a couple of years together. She's so young. But we have to try."[53]

* * *

Howard Hughes, Sinatra's old rival for Ava Gardner's affection, began a casino-buying spree in Las Vegas in 1967, snapping up, among others, the Sands Hotel and Casino in July of that year — Sinatra's performing venue. It was a different atmosphere under Hughes, and Sinatra soon decided to

switch his loyalty to the new and opulent Caesar's Palace. He began negotiating with Caesar's, but still had an early September engagement to fulfill
at the Sands. Claiming to be suffering from "desert throat," Sinatra bailed
out of that obligation for the Labor Day weekend, the casino's busiest, and
spent it with Mia in Palm Springs. Sammy Davis substituted for him. Sinatra had, by this time, negotiated a new deal with Caesar's Palace, one that
would make him, at $100,000 per week, the highest-paid performer in
Vegas.

The Sands management was unhappy with Sinatra's feigned health
emergency, but lived with it. Sinatra returned a few days later to complete
the engagement, but became enraged when his credit was cut off in the
casino after he had lost $50,000. Mia was with him. They both got into a
golf cart — it was about 5 a.m., she remembered — and were heading back
to their suite along an outdoor route. Sinatra, who was driving the cart, suddenly steered it toward a plate-glass window in the hotel, speeding up as
much as he could. He swerved at the last moment but still crashed into the
window, smashing it. Mia was seated next to him but was not hurt. Some
of the glass did injure a security guard. Screaming obscenities, Sinatra then
gathered furniture into a pile and tried, unsuccessfully, to light the items
on fire with his lighter.[54] His rage undiminished, he demanded to see Carl
Cohen, a Sands executive, and was finally put through to Cohen's room by
phone. It was 5:45 a.m. Cohen agreed to meet Sinatra in the hotel's empty
coffee shop. Once there, Sinatra hurled an unending stream of obscenities
at Cohen, including anti-Semitic slurs. Cohen got up to leave, unwilling to
put up with the tirade. Sinatra then threw betting chips in Cohen's face and
tipped a table's contents into his lap. "I'll get a guy to bury you, you son of
a bitch motherfucker," Sinatra screamed. "You kike."[55]

Cohen reached his limit. He threw a hard right to Sinatra's face, cutting
his lip and knocking the caps off two of the singer's teeth. Sinatra screamed
at Jilly Rizzo, who was there with Sinatra, to go after Cohen, but for some
unknown reason, the normally loyal Rizzo didn't move. Cohen then walked
away, leaving Sinatra shouting threats and curses in his wake. The Clark
County District Attorney investigated, but no one pressed charges, and that
was the end of the matter. Except for Carl Cohen's enhanced status as the
guy who gave Frank Sinatra what he deserved. Hotel and casino workers all

over Las Vegas were thrilled that Sinatra had received this comeuppance. Posters of Sinatra, minus his two front teeth, went up around the city, with notations at the bottom: "Hooray for Carl Cohen. Elect Carl Cohen Mayor."[56]

It also marked the beginning of the end for the Sinatra-Farrow marriage. Mia was beginning to have her fill of Frank's boorish behavior. They would eventually go their separate ways, Sinatra to film *The Detective* with co-star Lee Remick, with whom he would have an affair. Mia Farrow began work on *Rosemary's Baby*, perhaps her most widely acclaimed film. While she was on the set of that film, Mickey Rudin, Sinatra's attorney, paid her a visit, with divorce papers in hand. Mia willingly signed everything, without reading a page and without asking for any settlement. They were divorced in August 1968, fulfilling Frank's prophesy to his daughter — "Maybe we'll only have a couple of years together."

* * *

After Lyndon Johnson became one more casualty of the Vietnam War and declared that he would not seek reelection in 1968, the race for the Democratic nomination wound down to two candidates: Senator Bobby Kennedy from New York and Vice President Hubert Humphrey. Sinatra still had nothing but hatred for Bobby Kennedy for ruining his relationship with Jack. Bobby's help with the kidnapping case did nothing to diminish those emotions, and Frank naturally gravitated toward Humphrey's campaign, something the Happy Warrior from Minnesota at first welcomed. But once again, Sinatra's mob connections surfaced and forced Humphrey to distance himself from Sinatra. Joseph Nellis, the former Kefauver committee attorney who had questioned Sinatra in March 1951 about his Mafia ties, was serving on Humphrey's campaign committee and was among those urging Humphrey to cut his ties to the singer. When Humphrey stopped taking Sinatra's calls late in the campaign, after Bobby Kennedy had been assassinated and was no longer a threat, Sinatra got the message.

Frank never gave a thought to President Richard Nixon's inauguration on January 20, 1969. He was with his father at Methodist Hospital in Houston, where Marty was being treated by Dr. Michael DeBakey, the renowned heart surgeon. The elder Sinatra had been suffering with an "aortic aneurysm," but the condition was too far gone for DeBakey to save him. Marty died on January 24, 1969, with his wife and son by his side. The body was flown back to Fort Lee, New Jersey, for a funeral Mass at the Church of the Madonna and interment at Holy Name Cemetery in Jersey City. Frank had grown closer to his father over the last 10 years of the man's life, frequently flying both Marty and Dolly out to California to spend time with them. Not long after Marty's passing, Frank decided to move his mother to Palm Springs and bought a house for her on property adjoining his compound. As a condition of moving, Dolly insisted that Marty's grave go West with her. Frank made the arrangements and reburied his father in Palm Springs.

Soured by the treatment he had been receiving from the Democratic Party, Frank Sinatra was ripe for the picking. Republican Ronald Reagan gained Sinatra's support in his reelection campaign for California governor in 1970 and would continue to get Sinatra's strong backing in his presidential runs later on. The Nixon White House wasn't bashful about picking up the support of an entertainer with Sinatra's standing, even though Sinatra had shown a distinct aversion to their man in the past. Sinatra's shady associations with underworld figures didn't bother them at all.

The Nixon camp assigned Vice President Spiro Agnew the task of cozying up to Frank Sinatra. Agnew was the son of Greek immigrants, and so shared a Mediterranean heritage with Sinatra. Agnew, an avid golfer, began running into Sinatra at the country club in Palm Springs, and they soon became more than mere acquaintances. Agnew became a frequent guest at Sinatra's Palm Springs compound, and when Agnew and his wife spent the Thanksgiving weekend with Frank, November 25-27, 1971, in the cottage that had been constructed for John Kennedy's aborted visit in 1962, the Sinatra-Agnew friendship was cemented.

"There was instant chemistry — personally and politically — between Sinatra and Agnew," Peter Malatesta, Agnew's special assistant, said, "and because of that we started spending a lot of time with Frank in Palm Springs. He treated the Vice-President like royalty." Sinatra filled the place with laughter, music, and good cheer whenever the Agnews were present. Guests often included "the Ronald Reagans, Roz Russell and Freddie Brisson, Jimmy Van Heusen, the Milton Berles, the Bennett Cerfs, Dr. Michael

DeBakey, Jilly Rizzo, and Barbara and Zeppo Marx,"[57] who lived just across a fairway from Sinatra's home. Zeppo was one of the famed Marx Brothers and had married Barbara Blakely Oliver, a Las Vegas showgirl, late in life. Soon, Barbara Marx started coming alone to the parties. One morning, Mrs. Agnew spotted Barbara slipping out of the main house and caught on that she had stayed over. A bit taken back by the blatancy of it and the fact that Zeppo was supposedly a friend of Frank's, she said something to Peter Malatesta, who brought the matter to Frank's attention. Frank told Malatesta that he couldn't let Barbara Marx go home late at night "because a coyote might get her."

20

"*I don't want no whore coming into this family.*"

Richard Nixon, arguably the most corrupt president in United States history, may have been indirectly responsible for cleaning up New Jersey, then the most corrupt state in the nation. Nixon named Frederick B. Lacey as the United States attorney for the District of New Jersey, but the appointment did not receive Senate confirmation until late August 1969. Within a year, Lacey's office, following up on work begun by the previous U.S. attorney, David M. Satz Jr., had indicted 62 public officials and mobsters, all of whom were subsequently convicted.[1] When Lacey left office in late 1970 to accept a federal judgeship, he was succeeded by his hand-picked first assistant, Herbert J. Stern, who continued to build on the record of his predecessor.[2] It was Angelo "Gyp" DeCarlo's unfortunate destiny to be caught up in this law enforcement juggernaut. DeCarlo had risen in the New Jersey mob hierarchy by this time, thanks in part to the fall of Willie Moretti, Longy Zwillman, and Vito Genovese.

In what fellow mobsters characterized as a "mercy killing,"[3] Willie Moretti was gunned down on October 4, 1951, in Joe's Elbow Room, a Cliffside Park, New Jersey, restaurant. The "hit" was ordered by Vito Genovese,[4] probably with Frank Costello's okay — not out of malice, but almost in the way that a caring master puts down a terminally ill pet. Moretti, suffering from untreated syphilis and the mental instability engendered by that disease, had been called earlier that year before the U.S. Senate's Special Committee to Investigate Crime in Interstate Commerce, headed by Senator Estes Kefauver of Tennessee. The Kefauver committee, operating between May 10, 1950, and May 1, 1951, televised most of its hearings, causing a sensation across America. The public, treated to a succession of 600 mostly disreputable witnesses, learned an expression that would become forever embedded in popular culture — "taking the Fifth," as one mobster after another relied on his Fifth Amendment right against self-incrimination. Willie Moretti, perhaps owing to his diminished mental capacity, did not take the Fifth; in fact, he was outright garrulous in front of the committee, not necessarily responsive to the committee's questions, but far too talkative for his colleagues in crime. And so Moretti had to go, for fear that his ramblings might disclose something important in the future.[5]

Longy Zwillman was subpoenaed to testify before a similar committee in 1959, the McClellan Select Senate Committee investigating organized crime and labor. But days before he was scheduled to testify, he was found hanging in his home in West Orange, New Jersey, on February 27, 1959, an apparent suicide. There were suspicious circumstances, however, that pointed to Zwillman's death being murder, although no one was ever charged with the crime. Later that same year, Vito Genovese was convicted on a heroin charge and sentenced to 15 years in prison. Gerardo "Jerry" Catena (1902-2000) took over as boss of the Genovese crime family and named his three underbosses: Anthony "Tony Pro" Provenzano (1917-1988), Ruggiero "Richie the Boot" Boiardo (1890-1984), and Angelo "Gyp" DeCarlo (1902-1973).[6]

Robert F. Kennedy "made his bones," so to speak, as a relentless foe of organized crime while serving as counsel to the McClellan Select Senate Committee. RFK continued that crusade upon taking office as United States attorney general, during the administration of his brother, President John F. Kennedy, and, for a while, under President Lyndon B. Johnson, before he resigned in 1964 to run for a seat in the U.S. Senate representing New York. Prior to RFK's tenure as attorney general, the Federal Bureau of

Investigation, though supposedly under the jurisdiction of the Department of Justice, took its marching orders from Director J. Edgar Hoover, who operated the law enforcement agency as his own personal fiefdom. Bobby Kennedy, more than any other predecessor, brought Hoover under the control of the U.S. attorney general, due in large measure to his added power as "First Brother."[7]

For whatever reason, J. Edgar Hoover had been in denial as to the existence of a nationwide crime syndicate and wouldn't use the term "Mafia" in his discourse. That changed on November 14, 1957, when more than 100 members of the Mafia gathered for a summit meeting in Apalachin, New York.[8] Thanks to an alert state trooper, who noticed lots of black limousines traveling the usually deserted country roads, the meeting was compromised and dozens of the syndicate's leaders were arrested. After that event, Hoover could no longer ignore reality; and so, when committed Mafia foe Bobby Kennedy took office as attorney general, in early 1961, the stars were aligned for a new initiative in the fight against organized crime. Fortunately or unfortunately, depending on one's view of an ends-justify-the-means argument or on one's level of adherence to the U.S. Constitution, this new anti-crime initiative put forth by Hoover — most certainly with the approval and concurrence of Bobby Kennedy — was blatantly illegal.

The chief law enforcement agency in the country embarked on a series of burglaries — breaking and entering into the homes, offices, and hangouts of organized crime figures throughout the county — to install listening devices, or "bugs," allowing FBI agents to monitor and record conversations from a secure location offsite. They were called "black-bag jobs" by the bureau and continued for five or six years, until Attorney General Ramsey Clark (in office 1965-1967, under President Lyndon Johnson) put a stop to them.[9] None of the information gathered through these black-bag jobs was admissible in court against the individuals being bugged because of the protections under the Fourth Amendment, prohibiting unreasonable searches and seizures. The bugs were installed without a warrant and without probable cause: They were simply put into place to see what developed and to act as an intelligence-gathering program. Among the Mafia leaders bugged were Sam Giancana in Chicago,[10] Simone "Sam the Plumber" DeCavalcante,[11] boss of New Jersey's "sixth family," and Angelo "Gyp" DeCarlo, at his headquarters, located in a club called "The Barn," on Route 22 in Mountainside, New Jersey.[12]

While none of the illegally recorded "tapes"[13] could be used in evidence, they did expose the extent to which the Mafia controlled government officials, especially in New Jersey. Before joining the U.S. Attorney's Office, Herbert J. Stern received advice from Henry E. Peterson, chief of the organized crime and racketeering section, U.S. Department of Justice. "There are some things you need to know about northern New Jersey," Peterson told Stern. "Other places have mobs and some have corrupt politicians. But New Jersey is unique, in that the mob controls the political bosses."[14]

In pursuit of that corrupt combination of mobsters and crooked politicians, the U.S. Attorney's Office for New Jersey — first under Lacey, then Stern — was able to obtain indictments against Essex County and Hudson County officials (including former U.S. Congressman and Newark Mayor Hugh Addonizio and the Hudson County *de facto* Democratic boss, John V. Kenny),[15] as well as the Mafia operatives who worked hand-in-glove with them. The indictments were developed from independently gathered information, apart from the illegal bugs. Among those prosecuted by crime-busting U.S. Attorney Stern was Gyp DeCarlo, a man who figured prominently in the career of Frank Sinatra.

Angelo "Gyp" DeCarlo was indicted and convicted on extortion charges, arising from criminal activity not directly related to political corruption. On March 4, 1970, DeCarlo was sentenced to 12 years in prison,[16] but would end up serving less than three years, thanks to what may have been — or what may not have been, depending on one's point of view — the intervention of Frank Sinatra.

On December 22, 1972, Stern was attending his office's Christmas party when a reporter informed him that Gyp DeCarlo's prison sentence had just been commuted by President Nixon to time served and that the gangster had been freed from prison. Stern was shocked that so dangerous a criminal would be given such preferential treatment, especially since his office had not been consulted on any application for leniency. One would think that before a convicted criminal would be granted a pardon or commutation of sentence, the U.S. attorney who had obtained the conviction would be notified and given a chance to comment. Stern had heard nothing from Washington. The reporter supplied an intriguing insight into the strange occurrence: "The word on the street is that Frank Sinatra, DeCarlo's cousin, arranged for the commutation through his pal, Vice President Spiro Agnew."[17]

Frank Sinatra's political evolution had led him from being an almost worshipful supporter of liberal Democratic President Franklin D. Roosevelt (he named his only son after FDR) to a diehard Nixon and, later, Reagan stalwart. His support of Nixon, whom he initially disliked personally, was fueled by his close friendship with Spiro Agnew. Sinatra and his eventual fourth wife, Barbara Marx Sinatra, spent a lot of time with the Spiro Agnews, including the 1971 Thanksgiving holidays; Sinatra went so far as to name one of the guest bungalows at his Palm Springs, California, compound the "Agnew House."

Stern wasn't about to ignore Gyp DeCarlo's release. In January 1973, he tried to investigate the Nixon administration's action, but the FBI director at the time, L. Patrick Gray, would not agree to the request, requiring Stern to first get permission from Attorney General Richard Kleindienst. Stern fired off a letter to the attorney general, asking for the go-ahead. And then he heard nothing for six months.[18]

Meanwhile, Kleindienst resigned his office during the Watergate investigation — he was not touched personally by that particular scandal, but resigned as a matter of principle — and was replaced by Elliot Richardson, with Archibald Cox also coming on board as special prosecutor for Watergate. Richardson happened upon Stern's earlier request for permission to investigate the DeCarlo matter and, in June, gave his approval for that investigation to proceed. As Stern would put it, after getting the green light, "So it is now up to me to determine how a notorious murdering criminal persuaded the President of the United States to grant him a commutation of sentence."[19]

Also in June, Archibald Cox called Stern and agreed that Stern would send FBI investigators to interview all potential witnesses, including the "pardons attorney" who handled the DeCarlo commutation for the Department of Justice, the White House people involved, Vice President Agnew, and Frank Sinatra, "to determine whether Sinatra used his connections with Agnew to obtain a White House commutation of DeCarlo's sentence."[20]

Stern would later conclude, based on what was reported to him, that nothing "dirty" occurred in the process and that Sinatra had "no involvement." The man Stern had asked to look into the matter was FBI Special Agent Fred McMahon, about whose integrity and professionalism, Stern later said, he had no doubt.[21] McMahon determined that the commutation request originated with the warden at Atlanta Penitentiary, the maximum-security prison where DeCarlo was being held. DeCarlo was terminally ill with cancer, and the warden didn't want the mobster dying in his facility.[22]

Yet a different scenario can be drawn, based on an FBI report contained in *The Sinatra Files*, an examination of FBI files complied by editors Tom Kuntz and Phil Kuntz in 2000.

On April 30, 1973, William Ruckelshaus took over as acting FBI director, and one of his first acts was to order up a report on Frank Sinatra. The impetus for Ruckelshaus' request is unknown, but it preceded by more than a month the conversations that Stern had with Attorney General Richardson, who took office in May 1973, and with Special Watergate Prosecutor Archibald Cox, who also took office in May. Stern has said that his conversations with Richardson and Cox on the DeCarlo commutation issue both took place in June 1973, so it appears that the investigation instigated by Ruckelshaus in Washington was independent of the one conducted by SA Fred McMahon, on behalf of the U.S. attorney for New Jersey.

On May 24, 1973, Acting Director Ruckelshaus received a report that, in part, portrayed the Sinatra connection to the DeCarlo sentence commutation in a different light from what was revealed in Stern's 2012 book, *Diary of a DA*. The report relied on sources "who have supplied reliable information in the past," an investigatory tool that law enforcement officers regularly use in their work and that judges regularly rely upon in issuing warrants based on probable cause.

According to that May 24 report, a reliable source told agents "that DeCarlo's release came as no real surprise to certain associates of DeCarlo, as they had been informed by someone very close to DeCarlo that he was expected to be released before Christmas." The report continued, "This source further stated that these same associates are attributing DeCarlo's release to the intervention of singer Frank Sinatra, whose close personal relationship with Vice President Spiro Agnew allegedly served as the necessary 'contact.' The source stated that Sinatra's efforts had been in the works for 'at least a couple of months.'" [23]

The author of the May 24, 1973, report to Acting Director Ruckelshaus is identified as "J. Keith." Portions of his report were redacted to keep the identity of sources confidential, for their own safety and to maintain their continued usefulness to the FBI. On May 18, Jonathan Goldstein, first assistant U.S. attorney under Herbert Stern (and the person who would succeed Stern in 1974), told J. Keith that he had been contacted the day before by [redacted], who "claimed to have information indicating that initial contact to secure the release of Angelo DeCarlo from Federal custody was made in April, 1972, by DeCarlo to a singer with a rock group performing at the Atlanta Federal Penitentiary. This singer (Frankie Valli of the Four Seasons Quartet) was allegedly requested to contact Frank Sinatra and have him intercede with Vice President Agnew for DeCarlo's release. This request was ostensibly related to Mrs. [Dolly] Sinatra who in turn supposedly forwarded [it] to Frank Sinatra."[24]

This scheme, allegedly involving Frankie Valli and Dolly Sinatra as conduits, has plausibility. Gyp DeCarlo was close to Frankie Valli and to Tommy DeVito, another member of the Four Seasons, an association that was depicted in the Broadway musical *Jersey Boys.* Valli has confirmed his relationship with DeCarlo, likening him to a father.[25] Also, Dolly had known DeCarlo, a Hoboken native, all his life and had even babysat him when he was a child. In fact, they were related by marriage: DeCarlo's sister-in-law was married to Dolly's nephew.

The report goes on to convey an allegation by the same redacted source that Sinatra "turned over $100,000 cash to Maurice Stans, [then finance chairman of the Committee to Re-elect the President], as an unrecorded contribution." Because Vice President Agnew had been "stripped of his authority by White House aides," in the words of the unnamed source, a former Agnew staff assistant went directly to then-White House Counsel John Dean and "got him to make the necessary arrangements to forward the request to the Justice Department." Then, according to the source, Sinatra "made a $50,000 contribution to the President's campaign fund sometime during December 1972. DeCarlo's release followed."[26]

Without doubting for a moment the integrity of Herbert J. Stern, who would later be appointed to a federal judgeship, questions remain. The unnamed source in the FBI report offered many details, including names of the people involved. Would he have created so elaborate a scheme or have provided the witnesses to refute his story, if it were not true? Also, who were the people interviewed in this matter? The public record is silent on that, except for a notation in Stern's book that Dolly Sinatra was one of the interviewees and that she had no relevant information. The only interesting items ascertained from Dolly were that she was related to DeCarlo and had babysat for him. But there's no information as to whether Agnew and Sinatra were interviewed, or which White House operatives were questioned. Was John Dean interviewed? Or the former Agnew aide who approached John Dean? Did Frankie Valli perform at the Atlanta Federal Penitentiary and did he have contact then with Gyp DeCarlo? The Watergate-related resignations/dismissals of John Dean and Nixon aides John Ehrlichman and H.R. Haldeman on April 30, 1973, as well as the pending criminal charges, might have prevented those individuals from cooperating in the DeCarlo commutation inquiry, but was any attempt made? And what about Agnew and Sinatra, themselves — the central figures? Were they approached? Did they cooperate or refuse to cooperate?

Edwin Stier was chief of the criminal division in the U.S. Attorney's Office in New Jersey when the case against Angelo DeCarlo was made, largely through his and FBI Agent Fred McMahon's efforts. Stier left the U.S. Attorney's Office to become co-director of a new unit in the New Jersey State Attorney General's Office — the organized crime and special prosecutions section — before the DeCarlo case came to trial, so he was unable to handle the matter himself. That task fell to U.S. Attorney Frederick Lacey and First Assistant Herbert Stern, both of whom did a masterful job with a very difficult prosecution, according to Stier. But Stier did follow the progress of the case, and he, too, was dismayed when President Nixon commuted DeCarlo's sentence.

"Gyp DeCarlo beat the victim to an inch of his life," Stier said in a recent interview, "not DeCarlo, personally, but his guys." Stier described DeCarlo as "a man of great violence" and "a major racketeer in North Jersey," noted for "bribing public officials" and "corrupting public institutions. It would take a lot to convince any president to commute his sentence," Stier added. "It had to be someone with access to Nixon" who made it happen. Stier said he would have reservations about the warden's story that DeCarlo was released from prison as a humanitarian gesture, because of his terminal cancer. Lots of prisoners die of cancer and other diseases every year — it would be "extraordinarily unusual in my experience," Stier said, for a president to allow a criminal with DeCarlo's violent past to get out of prison on that basis.[27]

But Edwin Stier also suggested that the Nixon administration was corrupt enough to make a deal with someone to spring DeCarlo from prison — it was in that administration's DNA. Nixon had made a deal with the Teamsters union to let Jimmy Hoffa out of jail in exchange for that union's political support, so a DeCarlo deal would hardly have taxed Nixon's sense of honor. "I'd bet my bottom dollar," Stier said, "that Fred [McMahon] didn't interview Frank Sinatra or knock on the president's door at the White House" when he investigated the circumstances surrounding DeCarlo's release.[28]

It boils down to this, one must suppose. As the Watergate scandal unfolded, any inquiry into the DeCarlo sentence commutation became small potatoes, not worth anyone's time or attention. And so, we are unlikely to ever know the complete truth of the matter. But the story does have a *commonsensical* ring of truth. All the pieces fit. The role of every participant — from DeCarlo to Sinatra's mother, Dolly, to Frank Sinatra himself to Spiro Agnew to John Dean and, finally, to Richard Nixon — is in keeping with that person's character. The suggestion that Frank Sinatra was behind Angelo "Gyp" DeCarlo's release from prison is eminently conceivable; in fact, there's a kind of poetic symmetry to the whole idea, if one considers the part DeCarlo played in Sinatra's early professional life. Here was Frank Sinatra, to whom loyalty meant everything, pulling out all the stops to return the favor, some 30-odd years later, by freeing his long-ago benefactor from prison. Pure poetry indeed.

* * *

Frank Sinatra refrained from attacking three newspaper columnists:

Louella Parsons, Hedda Hopper, and Walter Winchell. Each of them reached 10 million or more Americans every week. They were too powerful for Sinatra to tangle with, and he knew it. Los Angeles-based Parsons and Hopper could make or break a movie, or a movie star. Studio heads, producers, directors — everyone in the motion picture industry — tiptoed around these two women, afraid to say anything derogatory, even in a presumably private setting, for fear that a stringer might overhear. If not that, trusted friends might betray confidences and trade them to Louella or Hedda in exchange for their own favorable treatment. The same held true for Walter Winchell on the East Coast. *Sweet Smell of Success*, a 1957 movie co-starring Burt Lancaster and Tony Curtis, portrayed the seamy New York world of a Winchell-like gossip columnist (Lancaster) and an unscrupulous press agent (Curtis). It remains a *film noir* classic to this day.

But if a newspaper reporter or columnist were not powerful, he or she would be fair game for Sinatra, literally and figuratively. In April 1947, Sinatra beat Lee Mortimer outside Ciro's nightclub in Hollywood, after the Hearst columnist printed references to Sinatra's Mafia ties and panned one of his movies. Sinatra paid out more than $15,000 ($160,000 today) in damages and attorneys' fees when he was hauled into court to answer for the attack. But Sinatra never answered for the relentless verbal attacks he made on female columnists in his nightclub act. To Sinatra, Barbara Walters was "the ugliest broad on television." Rona Barrett earned his enmity when she questioned the legitimacy of Frank Jr.'s kidnapping. She had been a friend of Nancy Jr.'s and had spent nights in the Sinatra home. That didn't save her. "What can you say about her," Sinatra said, referring to Barrett, "that hasn't already been said . . . about leprosy?" Entertainment reporter Liz Smith, according to Sinatra, was "so ugly she has to lie on an analyst's couch face down."[29] Dorothy Kilgallen may have been his favorite target for as long as she remained alive. He called her "the chinless wonder," referring to her most unfortunate facial feature, or explained to audiences why she couldn't be with them — "She's out shopping for a chin." When he was told of Kilgallen's death in November 1965, his response was, "Well, I guess I got to change my act."

Radio personality Jonathan Schwartz — perhaps the most knowledgeable person alive, or who ever lived, on the subject of Sinatra's music —

was mildly critical in 1980 of Sinatra's *Trilogy* album. Schwartz had been hosting *Sinatra Saturday* on New York's WNEW radio for more than 10 years. Hearing about the comment, Sinatra allegedly called the station owner and demanded that Schwartz be taken off the air. He was banned from the show for six weeks, which prompted *New York Daily News* columnist Liz Smith to rally to Schwartz's defense. "I don't care how fabulous the singer is . . ." she wrote. "What kind of world is it when critics are not safe to criticize freely?" It earned her a snarling telegram from Sinatra, and his lasting enmity.[30]

"He believes in punishment," Schwartz later said of Sinatra. "He's a bully."[31]

Washington Post columnist Maxine Cheshire may have suffered the most humiliating of Frank Sinatra's verbal assaults. Cheshire, twice nominated for a Pulitzer, was a "respectable and respected syndicated columnist . . . married and the mother of four,"[32] according to *New York Post* columnist Earl Wilson, himself the recipient of a five-year banishment to Sinatra Siberia, after 25 years in the singer's good graces, for one off-handed comment.[33] The Cheshire incident was really a two-parter: Sinatra handled himself perfectly in his first encounter with Cheshire, then allowed his violent temper, never far from the surface, to take charge in the second, almost resulting in Sinatra's alienation from President Nixon.

The Nixon-Agnew Republican ticket had trounced the McGovern-Shriver Democratic ticket in November 1972. It was the first presidential election in which Frank Sinatra had openly supported the Republican candidates, due in no small measure to his burgeoning friendship with Vice President Spiro "Ted" Agnew. As a result, Sinatra was flying high once again and on everyone's guest list in Washington circles — just like the old days, before Bobby Kennedy ruined everything.

Not long after the election, Sinatra was invited to a dinner at the State Department hosted by Vice President Agnew and arrived in California Governor Ronald Reagan's limousine. As he was getting out of the limo, Maxine Cheshire approached and asked one question: "Mr. Sinatra, do you think that your alleged association with the Mafia will prove to be the same kind of embarrassment to Vice President Agnew as it was to the Kennedy administration?"[34]

It was a *gotcha* question, particularly under the circumstances, and must have startled the unsuspecting Sinatra. He handled it like a perfect gentleman. "No," Sinatra responded, "I don't worry about things like that,"[35] and then he went in to the dinner. That could have been the end of the story — no harm, no foul — but that is not the way things happen in Sinatra world.

On January 19, 1973, the night before Nixon's second-term inauguration, Sinatra and Barbara Marx, his almost-constant companion, were attending a cocktail party in the lobby of Washington's Fairfax Hotel. They were separated as they mingled with the other guests. When Frank looked for Barbara, he saw her talking with Maxine Cheshire. He rushed over and let loose a tirade that turned the heads of guests within a 20- or 30-yard radius.

"Get away from me, you scum," Sinatra shouted, his voice rising in anger. "Go home and take a bath. Print that, Miss Cheshire." Turning to the startled guests around him, their attention immediately drawn to the unfolding scene, Sinatra addressed them: "You know Miss Cheshire, don't you? That stench is coming from her." Back to Cheshire: "You're nothing but a two-dollar cunt. C-U-N-T, know what that means? You've been laying down for two dollars all your life." Sinatra put two dollars in the drink cup Cheshire was holding and stormed out of the party, pulling Barbara Marx with him.[36]

The media exploded the next day, fueled by the affront to one of their own. A few, despite their own decency codes, actually printed the most offensive word in Sinatra's rant; others used euphemisms that left little doubt as to what was said. Then European papers began calling Cheshire for comment.

Sinatra worried that the incident might precipitate another White House banishment and asked Ted Agnew to sound out the president. Agnew reported back that Nixon was, indeed, "mad as hell." But Agnew played up one big hole card with his boss: Nixon hated the *Washington Post* with a passion, as the paper was beginning to get nosier and nosier in its Watergate reporting . . . and closer and closer.[37] Sinatra was safe. Indeed, President Richard M. Nixon would soon honor Francis Albert Sinatra with the thing he had coveted most, something the Kennedys had denied him in the three years of Camelot: an invitation to a formal state dinner at the White House.

Giulio Andreotti, prime minister of Italy, was the guest of honor, and Sinatra was asked to sing. It was prearranged, of course — you don't perform at the White House without material and rehearsal. Frank sang for 40 minutes, to an enthralled audience, including the First Couple. Ironically, it was the first time Sinatra had sung in public in almost two years. He'd retired suddenly in 1971, while still relatively young (55) and in fine voice, and had shocked the entertainment world.

In March 1971, Frank's daughter Tina had come upon him sitting poolside in Palm Springs and doodling over a statement, with phrases like "for reflection, reading, self-examination" and "for a fallow period, a long pause." Her father's "throat was tired, his soul was tired," Tina wrote. "He needed time to recover, reenergize."[38] The news broke a few days later, along with the announcement that Sinatra's last public performance would take place on June 13, 1971, at the Los Angeles Music Center, in a benefit for the Motion Picture and Television Relief Fund. That night, Rosalind Russell gave a tearful introduction of her friend, Francis Albert Sinatra, as he took the stage for what was likely his last performance.

Frank sang eight songs, all handpicked by him and designed almost as a retrospective of his career. His first number, "All or Nothing at All," was his first hit recording, done when he was with Harry James, and he prefaced his singing of it with the spoken words "Here's how it started."[39] Other tunes included "My Way" and "That's Life." Tina Sinatra, who was there, described how the night ended.

"Dad's final selection was 'Angel Eyes,' the saloon song he sang like no one else. All lights were doused, save for one pin spot on his profile. As he sang the last line ('Scuse me . . . while I disappear . . .'), Dad stepped out of the spot. When the lights came on, he was gone. The audience leapt to their feet, screaming for more, but he never came back."[40]

It was a masterful exit for a performer, but it wouldn't — couldn't — last. After Frank's White House performance, President Nixon went to the microphone to thank him. "Once in a while," Nixon said, "there is a moment when there is magic in this room, when a singer is able to move us and capture us all, and Frank Sinatra has done that and we thank him. This house is honored to have a man whose parents were born in Italy, but yet from humble beginnings went to the very top in entertainment."[41] Frank said a few words of appreciation, but then went around to the side of the bandstand, where he hoped he was out of view. He took a handkerchief from his pocket and was seen "dabbing at his eyes."[42] The president encouraged Sinatra to rethink his retirement decision, and it wouldn't be long before he did just that.

The comeback started with Frank's return to a Reprise recording studio for the first time since early November 1970. Over four sessions in June 1973 and two more in August, Sinatra recorded 12 songs that would become his *Ol' Blues Eyes Is Back* album; among the songs were "Let Me Try Again," "Send in the Clowns," "You Will Be My Music," "You're So Right (For What's Wrong in My Life)," and "Dream Away." Gordon Jenkins arranged most of the material (Don Costa arranged a few) and conducted the orchestra.[43] The album was a prelude to a television special of the same name — one of Sinatra's most successful. The show was taped on September 20, 1973, before a live audience of invited guests. Gene Kelly appeared with Sinatra, and Nancy Jr.'s husband, Hugh Lambert, did the choreography and staging for the event. The show aired on NBC on November 18, 1973, to much acclaim. Kay Gardella, reporter for the *New York Daily News*, wrote, "I thought we were through writing love letters to Frank Sinatra. Here we go again."[44]

While Sinatra was planning and executing his comeback, his friend, Vice President Spiro "Ted" Agnew, was experiencing *his* downfall. In a deal with prosecutors, Agnew resigned his office on October 10, 1973, and pleaded *nolo contendere* to one count of income tax evasion, thereby avoiding prison time. The bribery incident underlying this deal had occurred while Agnew was governor of Maryland, before being elected to the vice-presidency.[45] Sinatra had urged his friend not to resign, to fight it out,[46] but Agnew did the honorable thing in the end, perhaps anticipating what loomed ahead for the Nixon administration and the county. The Senate's Watergate investigation was already underway. Frank Sinatra was loyal to Agnew throughout the ordeal. When it was over, he did his best to get the former vice president back on his feet, emotionally and financially, sending him $30,000 for his tax-evasion fine and much more for his other needs, including a $200,000 load for back taxes. Sinatra and Agnew would remain close until Agnew's death in 1996.

Despite his sadness over Agnew's troubles, Sinatra went full bore on the comeback trail. He made a triumphant return to Caesar's Palace. A bitter encounter there in 1970 with a Caesar's executive may have contributed to Frank's retirement decision, but that executive was gone. Las Vegas' showiest venue agreed to pay Sinatra the then-unheard of sum of $400,000 per week for his return engagement. The showroom was filled to capacity on opening night, January 25, 1974, mostly with celebrities. Each attendee received a medallion with the inscription "Hail Sinatra, The Noblest Roman Has Returned." Frank Jr. had "a previous engagement" and did not attend.[47]

In April 1974, Sinatra began a 10-concert stateside tour to benefit Variety Clubs International, and its success encouraged him to branch out, first to Europe, then, in July, to the Far East. After tour dates in Japan, Sinatra arrived in Melbourne, Australia, for a scheduled concert there; unfortunately, his penchant for doing battle with the press almost left him up the creek without a paddle. Frank and his bodyguards reached a new high for boorish behavior Down Under. Frank spat at a reporter, whose only sin was a desire to interview him. A Sinatra bodyguard wrapped an electric cord around the neck of a cameraman, warning him, "Things are going to get physical."[48]

Still, the Australians loved him; a sold-out crowd of 8,000 cheered his every song and every gesture onstage at Festival Hall in Melbourne. Perhaps buoyed by that reception, Sinatra let loose against the Australian press corps during a pause in the concert.

"They are bums and parasites who have never done an honest day's work," Sinatra said, referring to the male reporters he'd encountered. "Most of them are a bunch of fags, anyway." As to the female reporters, they were "broads and buck-and-a-half hookers. " He apologized to the audience, saying he was tired "because of the parasites who chased us." He went on in that vein, ending with, "We who have God-given talent say to hell with them . . . ."[49]

The next day, all of Australia lined up against Sinatra and his entourage, but especially the labor unions. In solidarity, they refused to do anything in support of Sinatra's concert tour or his physical comfort. The stagehands would not work his remaining concerts, forcing their cancellation and the loss of $650,000 in expected proceeds. The waiters union refused service, so his group could get no food in their hotel rooms. At the airport, workers wouldn't refuel his airplane, effectively grounding him. All the unions demanded that Sinatra apologize for his remarks before they would allow their members to assist his departure. Sinatra wouldn't give in; instead, he complained about "fifteen years of abuse" that he had "taken from the world press" — hardly a conciliatory statement. Mickey Rudin, Sinatra's lawyer, pleaded with union leaders, asking them to allow Sinatra to leave. He could go, they said, "if he can walk on water."[50]

Finally, a compromise was reached. Mickey Rudin read a non-apology apology from Sinatra, and his group was permitted to leave the county. Comedians back home had a field day with the incident. "They finally let Frank out of the country," Bob Hope told one audience, "right after the head of the union down there woke up one morning and saw a kangaroo's head on the next pillow."[51]

Back home and out of reach of the Australians, Sinatra began lacing his nightclub act with barbs. He apologized to "all the hookers" who sold their bodies, comparing them favorably to newspaperwomen, who sold their souls because no one wanted their bodies. On October 13, 1974, he appeared at Madison Square Garden in New York for a live television special, billed as "The Main Event." The producer was worried about Sinatra continuing his anti-reporter diatribe over nationwide television, but, fortunately, he was able to persuade Sinatra to hold back on any such attacks until the commercial breaks in the program, when he was free to regale the live audience with his venom. He held to that plan.

"A funny thing happened in Australia," Sinatra told the crowd. "I made a mistake and got off the plane. You think we've got trouble with one Rona Barrett, but they've got twenty in Australia, and each one is uglier than the other . . . . Those nickel-and-dime garbage dealers make Rona Barrett look like a nun."[52]

* * *

Frank Sinatra had given little thought to vows of fidelity through three marriages, but as he passed the age of 55 and approached 60, being married again seemed much on his mind. He didn't want to be alone in his old age. Frank proposed to English beauty Pamela Churchill Hayward in March 1971, after her husband, producer Leland Hayward, died. She'd once been married to Winston Churchill's son, Randolph, and would have represented Sinatra's entrée into English aristocracy, assuming they would have him. Pamela turned him down and married multimillionaire W. Averell Harriman before the year was out. Edie Goetz's husband died in 1969, and it wasn't long before Frank sought a serious relationship with her. Edie's father, Louis B. Mayer, entitled her by birth to a place in Hollywood's aristocracy, such as it was. When Frank asked Edie to marry him, she was startled for a moment, then said, "Why Frank, I couldn't marry you. Why . . . why . . . you're nothing but a hoodlum." Sinatra never spoke to her again.[53] He began dating actress Lois Nettleton later in 1971 and proposed to her after a year (she said yes), but then dumped her before he even bought a ring.[54]

It was in that context that Frank began seeing Barbara Marx, while she was still married to Zeppo (wags in the business called Zeppo the "unfunny Marx Brother"). The Marxes lived across the 17th fairway from Sinatra in the Tamarisk Country Club district of Palm Springs.

Barbara, divorced and the mother of a young son, was a showgirl at the Riviera in Las Vegas when she met Zeppo, 26 years her senior. In those days, part of the job was to dress in something attractive and hang out in the hotel's high-roller cocktail lounge after the last show. If a guy asked one of the girls to bring him luck at the tables, she was expected to comply. Anything beyond that was up to the girl. Like most of the showgirls on the Vegas strip, Barbara was looking for a ticket out of the rat race — in other words, she was looking for the right man. She left Vegas before she found him and went to California to start up a modeling school, but that wasn't working out, either. Then Zeppo called her.

"Come to Palm Springs," he said. "I'll set you and Bobby [her son] up in your own place. You can commute back to L.A. to model whenever you want." Barbara accepted, feeling she had no other option. "I fell in love with Palm Springs during the winter of 1958," she later wrote, "but not with Zeppo Marx." On September 18, 1959, she became Mrs. Zeppo Marx.[55]

One of the centers of Palm Springs social life was the Frank Sinatra compound, and the Marxes were invited guests on occasion. Zeppo and Frank were friends from way back, ever since Frank had starred in a 1951 movie with Groucho Marx. After the Agnews became part of Frank's circle, Barbara was at the compound more often, filling in as a doubles partner for Spiro Agnew or just sitting poolside. Soon, the flirtation between Frank and his beautiful blond neighbor began — a look here, a quip there. The first kiss followed soon after.

She and Zeppo were at a dinner party at Frank's house with a bunch of other people. It was during the Dinah Shore golf tournament, she remembered. Frank offered to mix a martini for her, but had to do it in the den. Zeppo was playing gin rummy in another room. She went with Frank, and as soon as they were alone, he pulled her into his arms and kissed her. "I was caught completely off guard," she said, "but I found myself returning his kiss with just as much ardor. There was no way to avoid that flirtation. Besides, I was as lost and lonely as he was."[56]

Nothing more happened for a while, but then, in May 1972, Barbara and Frank learned that they were both going to be in Monaco at the same time — she while on a trip to visit her son, Bobby, who was living in Europe, and he . . . well, he most likely had no reason to be in Monaco, except the opportunity to be alone with Barbara.[57]

They became sexually intimate in Monaco and began the relationship that would last until the end of Frank's life. It would be bumpy at times — she had to end her marriage once it became clear that Frank was serious. Zeppo was jealous of Frank and suspected the affair. He suggested they separate, which Barbara agreed to on the spot. (The divorce became final in 1973.) She moved out of Zeppo's house and into a place Frank bought for her. And she and Frank began to be seen openly as a couple.

Barbara accompanied Frank to Washington for the Nixon inauguration in January 1973 and was present when the Maxine Cheshire furor occurred. She would also be with Frank for all his subsequent nightclub engagements and concert tours, including the unpleasantness in Australia.

There was one fly in the ointment: Dolly Sinatra. Dolly, now living next door to her son, detested Barbara once she saw that her son was becoming serious about the relationship. She was openly hostile, at times causing Barbara to run from the dinner table in tears. Frank would not go against his mother, which rankled Barbara even more. It became an issue between them, as did Frank's foot-dragging on the subject of marriage. They separated for a time, in 1974. But the mutual attraction and Frank's need for a permanent companion were too strong to keep them apart. On May 18, 1976, he proposed, spectacularly. Frank presented Barbara with a 17-carat diamond engagement ring. It had set him back $360,000 ($1.5 million in today's dollars). Dolly's reaction — "I don't want no whore coming into this family"[58] — did not bode well for harmony in the Sinatra compound.

When Frank and Barbara set the date — the wedding would be on July 11, 1976 — Frank sent his lawyer, Mickey Rudin, over to Dolly's house to break the news to her, rather than tell her himself. Later, she confronted him.

Dolly: "You fucking no-good bastard, you were going to get married and not even tell me, weren't you."

Frank, meekly: "You know, I can't tell you because you always give me hell, Mama."[59]

On the morning of her wedding day, Barbara heard a knock at her door. It was Mickey Rudin, and he asked her to accompany him to one of Frank's guesthouses. Once there, he put a document in front of her, handed her a pen, and said, "You have to sign this, Barbara, before you marry Frank." It was a prenuptial agreement — something Frank had never discussed with her. She flipped through it, then pushed it away, saying that she'd rather not sign. Rudin set her straight. "Unless you do," he said, "there'll be no wedding." She signed.[60]

The wedding ceremony took place at Sunnylands, the beautiful Rancho Mirage, California, estate of diplomat and philanthropist Walter Annenberg. Dolly was there, resigned to the reality of her son's marriage to a woman she still intensely disliked, but determined to make the best of it. The guest list included a small but select group of friends. Frank Jr. was invited but did not attend.

* * *

Sinatra's engagement at Caesar's Palace was set to begin on January 6, 1977. He and Barbara flew from Palm Springs to Vegas in his larger jet on the day of the opening. He asked his mother to come along with them on the same flight, but Dolly, who loved to gamble, demurred. She and Anna Carbone, a visiting friend from New Jersey, would go later, she told her son. Frank arranged for a twin-engine Lear Jet to transport his mother and her friend later in the day. At 5 p.m., when the two older women boarded the small jet, the weather was starting to close in. Visibility was poor when the plane left Palm Springs airport for the 20-minute flight to Las Vegas. The tower lost contact with the Lear pilot two minutes into the flight. The plane had crashed into the San Gorgonio Mountains, killing everyone aboard.

The charter service contacted Mickey Rudin about the missing flight, and Mickey flew to Las Vegas to tell Frank in person. There was little hope that the outcome would be good, but Frank went onstage anyway for the first show. The house was packed with fans, oblivious to the pain consuming the man performing for them. They erupted into a standing ovation when he finished, but there were no encores. Frank canceled the rest of the engagement and flew back to Palm Springs, still hoping that his mother had escaped death. They found the wreckage three days later, so scattered that it was clear there would be no survivors. The bodies were eventually recovered, and Frank buried his mother next to his father, in Desert Memorial Park in Palm Springs. And he grieved for the rest of his life.

On June 22, 1977, the Hoboken Public Library dedicated a section of its facility at 500 Park Avenue for a Sinatra collection. Dignitaries, including Mayor Steve Cappiello, were on hand to unveil a portrait of Frank and Dolly Sinatra. Fred "Tamby" Tamburro and James "Skelly" Petrozelli were there, hoping to see their old Hoboken Four pal. Frank had been invited to the event. He was in Paramus, New Jersey, about 18 miles away, filming a scene for his first made-for-TV movie, *Contract on Cherry Street*. When he failed to show for the event, the headline in the *New York Daily News* the next day read "No Homecoming for Ol' Blue Eyes; Hoboken Heartbroken He Stands 'Em Up."

21

"My father did not die. He escaped."

Frank Sinatra's mob ties threatened, once again, to derail his access to a president of the United States, but Ronald Reagan proved more loyal to Frank than Jack Kennedy had been. Sinatra campaigned vigorously for Reagan in 1980, just as he had in 1976, when President Gerald Ford beat off the challenge of the California governor and secured the Republican nomination. But Sinatra wasn't always in Reagan's corner. He had supported Democratic incumbent Edmund G. "Pat" Brown against Reagan in the 1966 race for governor. Reagan, a Barry Goldwater backer and TV pitchman in the 1964 presidential election, used that platform to launch his first run for elective office against Brown, who was running for a third term. Capitalizing on his celebrity as an actor and on Californians' desire for change, Reagan trounced Brown by close to 1 million votes.

In that 1966 race, Sinatra made no secret of his antipathy toward Reagan. According to a girlfriend of Sinatra pal Jimmy Van Heusen, Sinatra "hated the guy, just hated him." Frank would snap his fingers at whoever was in his entourage and leave a party whenever Ron and Nancy Reagan showed up.

"This happened time and time again," the same woman recalled, "because he could not abide being in the same room with the Reagans.

Every time they walked in, we'd have to walk out, and each time we'd have to listen to Frank's diatribe against Reagan all over again."[1]

Comedian Shecky Greene described a similar experience. He and Sinatra were watching television one night when Ronald Reagan put in an appearance on the show they were watching. "Frank immediately got crazy and started screaming things and calling Reagan every name in the book. He hated the guy and cursed him out all night long."[2]

The intense reaction Reagan evoked in Sinatra may be traceable to one particular event, on September 19, 1959. Soviet Premier Nikita Khrushchev was touring Hollywood while on a trip to the United States (the first by any Soviet premier) and was invited to the set of *Can-Can*, a Twentieth Century Fox picture starring Frank Sinatra, Shirley MacLaine, and Maurice Chevalier. Fox had asked Sinatra to host a luncheon for Khrushchev that day, and Sinatra threw himself into the project. Four hundred Hollywood stars turned out for the event. Actor Ronald Reagan, an unrelenting anti-Communist crusader, refused to attend the luncheon.[3] Whether that was the trigger for Sinatra's antipathy is unclear, but it would certainly qualify, as dozens of Sinatra's friends and acquaintances could have attested to. Any affront, real or imagined, to Sinatra's self-image as *il padrone*, the boss, could lead to years of backlash.

But old wounds had healed by the time of Reagan's 1970 reelection campaign in California, and Sinatra, perhaps seeing Reagan as having presidential potential, jumped on his bandwagon and stayed on it during every subsequent Reagan bid for elective office. In the 1980 presidential campaign, Sinatra played a prominent role, provoking an angry letter from at least one Reagan supporter, who complained about Reagan's embrace of mob-connected Frank Sinatra. Reagan responded in a letter that has been preserved for history.

"I have known Frank Sinatra and Barbara Marx for a number of years," Reagan wrote. "I'm aware of the incidents, highly publicized, quarrels with photographers, nightclub scrapes, etcetera and admit it is a lifestyle I neither emulate or approve. However, there is a less publicized side to Mr. Sinatra, which in simple justice must be recognized. It is a side he has worked very hard to keep hidden and unpublicized. I know of no one who has done more in the field of charity than Frank Sinatra."[4]

President-elect Ronald Reagan named Frank Sinatra to head up his inaugural gala just days after his victory on November 4, 1980. It was déjà vu all over again, except that this production, according to one critic, resembled not Camelot, but "a tacky combination of a Hollywood awards show, a Kiwanis club talent contest, and a telethon stocked with fewer greats than near-greats and even more mediocrities." Another critic called the gala "a cross between Dial-a-Joke and *Hee Haw*."[5] There were few positive reviews.

The Sinatra temper, always primed to recognize the slightest insult or show of disrespect, threatened to blow the next day, at the actual inauguration. His name wasn't included on the select list of 100 guests invited to sit with the presidential party on a raised platform. Instead, he and Barbara were directed to the second place of honor, on the lawn right in front of the U.S. Capitol, where the ceremony would take place. Frank was incensed at being passed over for the honored position and relegated to the cheap seats, so to speak. He escorted Barbara to her assigned seat, then brazened his way onto the platform where Ronald and Nancy Reagan, their relatives, and friends were sitting. A White House photographer described the scene. "He didn't have an authorized ticket, but he *ballsed* his way through, ramming past the Secret Service and the Capitol police. No one had the nerve to stop him. No one!"[6]

* * *

The Sinatras were not a religious family. Nominally Roman Catholic, they had flouted some of the church's strictest canons. Dolly and Marty were married in a civil ceremony on Valentine's Day, 1913, so, technically, they were living in sin, according to church doctrine, until they repeated their nuptials later, in front of a priest. Part of Dolly's livelihood while Frank was growing up came from performing abortions. In fact, the Sinatra women of the second and third generations — Nancy Barbato Sinatra, Nancy Jr., and Tina — had abortions or, in Tina's case, a surgically induced miscarriage, prior to the U.S. Supreme Court making abortions legal under *Roe v. Wade* (1973).[7] Frank Sr.'s adulterous conduct, also a sin under Catholicism, has been well documented. But this is not a commentary on the subject of abortion or marital infidelity; rather, its purpose is to demonstrate the lack of religious fervor among the Sinatras, at least as it related to the teachings of the Catholic Church.

In a February 1963 *Playboy* interview, writer Joe Hyams asked Sinatra about his religious principles. "Are you a religious man?" Hyams inquired. "Do you believe in God?"

"I think I can sum up my religious feelings in a couple of paragraphs," Sinatra replied. "First: I believe in you and me. I'm like Albert Schweitzer and Bertrand Russell and Albert Einstein in that I have a respect for life — in any form. I believe in nature, in the birds, the sea, the sky, in everything I can see or that there is real evidence for. If these things are what you mean by God, then I believe in God. But I don't believe in a personal God to whom I look for comfort or for a natural on the next roll of the dice.

"I'm not unmindful of man's seeming need for faith; I'm for anything that gets you through the night, be it prayer, tranquilizers, or a bottle of Jack Daniel's. But to me religion is a deeply personal thing in which man and God go it alone together, without the witch doctor in the middle. The witch doctor tries to convince us that we have to ask God for help, to spell out to him what we need, even to bribe him with prayer or cash on the line. Well, I believe that God knows what each of us wants and needs. It's not necessary for us to make it to church on Sunday to reach Him. You can find Him any-place. And if that sounds heretical, my source is pretty good: Matthew, Five to Seven, The Sermon on the Mount."

Sometimes it takes a tragedy to bring people back to religion. Dolly's death in January 1977 did it for Frank. When Nancy Jr. arrived at the compound in Palm Springs soon after the plane crash, to keep vigil with her father, a private Catholic Mass was in progress in the living room. Nancy saw her father seated, reading from a missal.[8] Dolly had become a devout Catholic in later years, despite her abortion trade early on. Frank's sudden return to the religion of his youth fulfilled a need to remain close to the mother he'd just lost.

Barbara Sinatra got religion, too, even before Dolly died. She decided to convert to Catholicism (she'd been raised a Protestant) and enlisted Dolly's help in learning about the faith — something that pleased Frank. It was good to see his mother and his wife studying the catechism together instead of insulting one another.

"Ever since Dolly's death, Frank seemed to find solace in the religion his mother had taught him and then me," Barbara Sinatra wrote in her 2011 memoir, *Lady Blue Eyes: My Life with Frank.* "He began to attend Mass with me more often . . . . One thing that kept haunting him, though, was that we had never been officially married in the eyes of our church. The more Frank thought about that, the more the omission bugged him. Still grieving for his dead mother, he told me morosely, 'She'd have wanted that.' " [9]

It's hard to imagine Frank Sinatra being "haunted" by guilt over his non-church wedding, no matter how much he was grieving for his mother. He knew Dolly better than anyone. She had treated Barbara to a steady stream of abuse, before and after the marriage, and wouldn't have cared a whit about the type of wedding ceremony that had joined her son to that "whore." The more likely scenario is that the desire for a wedding within the Catholic Church was Barbara's idea and that the idea had sprung from her need to strengthen the bond of marriage, to make it less susceptible to breakage. She and Frank had had their periodic flare-ups before they were married. He had once slapped her across the face, in front of friends, when she laughed at something he was angry about, and there had been other indignities she was forced to endure, if she wanted to gain the eventual prize of becoming Mrs. Frank Sinatra. Now that she had attained that status, she didn't want to make it easy for Frank to divorce her, should it come to that.

Ending a civil marriage, especially one that involved a prenuptial agreement, was a simple matter; but with Frank's newfound religion, he wouldn't have such an easy time of ending a marriage that had been sanctioned by the church, by his mother's church. That being said, the only way for Frank and Barbara to marry in a religious ceremony was to get his marriage to Nancy Barbato Sinatra annulled by the Catholic Church that had consecrated it. Frank was still married to Nancy under church law, which didn't recognize divorce or subsequent civil marriages. It was as though the Ava Gardner and Mia Farrow marriages never happened. If something could be done about Frank's first marriage, Barbara would be able to cement her hold on Frank. Fortunately, a friendly priest was at hand to facilitate Barbara's plan.

Father Tom Rooney headed up a charity called the World Mercy Fund, and Barbara and Frank Sinatra were among its biggest financial backers.

Barbara has stated that it was Frank who sought the help of Father Rooney, "a family friend," on the subject of annulment, but that isn't likely. In his home life, as opposed to his professional and public life, Sinatra always "followed the path of least resistance."[10] He didn't make waves as far as his family was concerned and would agree to just about anything, as long as it didn't create a hassle for him. An annulment would be a giant hassle, certain to cause Nancy Sr., for whom Frank still had feelings, great pain and certain to create a furor with his three children. No, Frank Sinatra would not have initiated any talk of an annulment, nor would he have gone to Father Rooney for help. That was Barbara's doing. And once the plot was hatched, Frank would have gone along with it, because that was the path of least resistance in the home occupied by him and Barbara, who could turn on the silent treatment for days on end to bend Frank to her will.

Father Rooney explained how easy getting an annulment would be, and they didn't even have to get Nancy's consent. "I loved the idea of being properly married in the eyes of the church I'd embraced as my own," Barbara wrote, "but I knew the suggestion of an annulment would be controversial, and I had no intention of getting involved. I hadn't been with Frank all those years [they'd had an intimate relationship for four years before their marriage] and learned nothing about keeping my nose out of his private affairs. In the end, he went ahead and organized it himself. I think it was something he needed to do for Dolly."[11]

"Father Rooney would play Dad like a Stradivarius," Tina Sinatra wrote. "My father was sixty-two years old and feeling terribly vulnerable. Like many men of his age and background, he was riddled with half-suppressed Catholic guilt. Soon he was attending Mass more often. At Father Rooney's suggestion, Dad wrote a handsome check to the World Mercy Fund. Barbara got her church wedding."[12] The annulment and subsequent church wedding was Barbara Sinatra's attempt, Tina Sinatra believed, to "control father's future by erasing his past."[13]

Still another rift arose between Barbara and Frank's children, and once again, Barbara alleges that it was Frank who instigated the idea. "As part of the healing process after Dolly's death, Frank made another decision that came as a complete surprise," Barbara wrote. She and Frank were returning home on his private plane "from somewhere when he scribbled a note and handed it to me. 'I want to adopt Bobby [Barbara's son by her first husband, Bob Oliver]. I love him and I want him to be my son. He deserves to be part of a bigger family.'" When Barbara demurred, saying that Bobby was a "fully grown man" (he was 25 at the time), Frank insisted. "I've made up my mind," he said. "I want to do this for you and for him." Frank summoned Mickey Rudin, who was on the same flight, and told him about his plan to adopt Barbara's son. Rudin was shocked and tried to dissuade his boss from such a crazy idea. "Just do it," Sinatra snapped at his lawyer of many years.[14]

The Sinatra kids learned about the impending adoption when Mickey Rudin called Tina and told her, "Your dad needs help and you're just the girl for the job. Your father's inches away from adopting Bobby." Tina was incredulous, but Rudin told her it was no joke. "I'm dead serious," he said. "I'm doing all I can to stop it, but I'm not making a dent. You better step in, and quick."[15]

Nancy Jr., her father's favorite, made the first call to Frank, but couldn't budge him. Tina called next. "Are you out of your mind?" she said. "The Sinatra name is a birthright and a bloodline and a major responsibility, and you can't just give it away."[16] Tina actually accepted Barbara's claim that the adoption was Frank's idea — he was big-hearted about such things and genuinely liked Bobby — but believed that Barbara planted that seed in her father's head. Tina also worried about the impact of the adoption on her father's natural son, Frankie, whose relations with their father had been strained for some time.[17]

Finally, it came down to Nancy Sr., whom Mickey Rudin had also called. "There's still time," Rudin told her, "but you better get involved, or it's going through." Nancy telephoned Frank immediately. "If it's not too late," she said, "I'd appreciate it if you would stop this — for my children's sake as well as mine." Nancy's call brought her husband to his senses. "Okay," he said, "I'll see what I can do."[18] And that was that. There would be no adoption.

* * *

The Frank Sinatra saga did not end well. The last 20 years of his life were filled with the kinds of turmoil that had dogged his earlier years, but he became increasingly less able to deal with that turmoil, physically and mentally. His relationship with Barbara Sinatra was a double-edged sword. She went everywhere with him, but that companionship he so desperately needed came at a price. They fought constantly, in public and in the privacy of their home. Their housekeeper, a woman named Vine, fed information back to Tina and Nancy Sinatra about their father's battles with his fourth wife. They'd go at it toe-to-toe, but by the next morning, Frank would "be ready to make up." Barbara learned, early on, how to control the guy who was uncontrollable in any other setting. "She'd withhold her congeniality and conversation," Tina wrote. "She'd dish out the ultimate punishment, the one thing my father hated: the silent treatment. Barbara could sustain her grudge for days, until Dad was so sad and unsettled that he seemed angry with the world. He'd wear his pain on his face, and it was a piteous thing to see."[19]

In 1983, at a time Frank was alone in Palm Springs — Barbara was in England for Wimbledon — he called Nancy Sr. late at night, feeling sorry for himself, to tell her how "miserable" he was. "I never should have left you — I never should have left home," he told her while crying.[20]

If his home life was problematic, politics was still a strong diversion for Sinatra. President Reagan called upon him for help in the 1984 reelection campaign. The president wanted to gain the support of blue-collar Democrats,[21] and there were lots of them in Hoboken. Frank hadn't made a public appearance in his hometown in 32 years, not since the embarrassing night at the Union Club, when attendees at his father's fire department dinner had shown disrespect while he was singing, causing him to walk out. Reagan asked Sinatra to accompany him to the St. Anne's Church festival on July 26. It was an annual event that drew large crowds. Frank agreed to do it — he couldn't refuse Reagan. They flew to Newark Airport, then helicoptered to Hoboken, where Sinatra introduced Reagan to the large crowd in front of the church. It was an uncomfortable experience for Frank; many in the crowd knew all about Dolly's abortion business in the city decades earlier, and here was her son, introducing an anti-abortion president. Reagan would stay for a spaghetti dinner in the church basement, but Sinatra fled the city as quickly as he could.[22]

President Reagan remained Frank Sinatra's loyal and devoted friend throughout his eight years in office. On May 23, 1985, at a White House ceremony, the president presented Sinatra with one of the nation's highest civilian awards — the Medal of Freedom. Ten other citizens of great repute received the same award that day. But the day held a second high honor for Frank Sinatra, one bestowed by the Stevens Institute of Technology, in Hoboken. On the afternoon of May 23, Frank was there to receive an Honorary Doctor of Engineering degree, but it was not without controversy. Some students protested the giving of an engineering honor to a man who hadn't even completed high school, calling it a stain on their college. But the crowd at the graduation exercises and most of the students were on Sinatra's side and cheered the obviously pleased new doctor of engineering.

* * *

If he were a younger man, he'd get out of his marriage to Barbara, Frank confided to a friend. But he wasn't young anymore, and he didn't want to grow old alone. Things were happening over which he had no control — the ultimate blow to a control freak like Sinatra. The mob associations were still plaguing Frank, as he was hauled before several government agencies during the 1970s and '80s to explore those connections in hearings that produced more heat than light.

In October 1986, Kitty Kelley, whose genre was "tell-all" biographies, published her Sinatra book — *His Way: The Unauthorized Biography of Frank Sinatra* — which rose to the top of *The New York Times* bestseller list almost immediately. Frank was devastated by the revelations it contained and, at the same time, furious with the people in Hoboken who had cooperated with Kelley in her latest exposé. The single item that caused the most pain for Frank was the revelation, for the first time in public, that Dolly Sinatra had been an abortionist. The proof Kelley had dug up was irrefutable, so there was no way Sinatra could deny what he already knew to be true. Frank started two separate lawsuits against Kelley when he found out, before its publication, what the book contained; both suits were dropped on the advice of counsel. Fame has its consequences, one of which is a greatly reduced legal right to sue for libel or invasion of privacy.

The stress over the Kelley book may have caused Sinatra's hospitalization in November 1986. He was performing at the Golden Nugget in

Atlantic City when he was beset by sharp abdominal pains so severe that he canceled the rest of his engagement and flew home to check into the Eisenhower Medical Center in Palm Springs. He had an infection in the lower colon and had to undergo surgery to remove part of it. It also required a temporary colostomy, which Frank had to endure for a while. Despite the discomfort and inconvenience of "the bag," it didn't slow Sinatra down. In January, he flew to Hawaii to make a guest appearance on Tom Selleck's *Magnum P.I.* show.[23]

On March 20, 1987, Dean Martin lost his son, Dean Paul Martin, when the Air National Guard Reserve pilot crashed his Phantom jet into the San Gorgonio Mountains — ironically, the same mountains that had claimed the life of Dolly Sinatra in 1977. It was a personal tragedy for both families — the Martins and the Sinatras. The children had grown up together and looked upon each other as "cousins," as family. Dean Martin would never recover, despite Sinatra's efforts to get the man he had called "brother" back on his feet through work. Sinatra had his agents book a concert tour the following year, starring Frank, Dean, and Sammy Davis, Jr. It was billed as the "Ultimate Event," and was going to be the former Rat Pack ers final, triumphal tour, but Dean wasn't up to it. He left the tour on its first leg, and would never be a force in the entertainment world again. Sinatra had to get Liza Minnelli to take Dean's place in the tour. The show went on, to enthusiastic receptions everywhere.

Mickey Rudin, Sinatra's longtime lawyer and manager, quit in a huff in late 1987, possibly pushed by Barbara Sinatra,[24] who most likely blamed Rudin for gumming up the adoption try. Tina started noticing her father's frequent bouts with depression. He was relying heavily on prescription drugs, including the antidepressant Elavil, which Barbara was regulating "to level [his] mood swings." But Tina noticed that her father "became strangely tractable and subdued. He expressed neither joy nor sadness; he was smack in the middle plane of nowhere."[25] Tina went to Reno to see her father perform — something she had missed for a while — and was shocked by what she observed onstage. "The consummate performer was *unsure*," she later wrote, "tentative in his demeanor, unsteady of voice." She could "barely bring" herself to watch.[26]

Around this time, the financial agreements Sinatra and Mickey Rudin had carefully put in place prior to Frank's marriage to Barbara Marx began to unravel. Three months after Rudin quit, Frank and Barbara executed an "Agreement to Rescind Pre-Nuptial Agreement," effectively tearing up that protection for Frank's heirs. Then, Frank changed the ownership mechanism for many of his real estate parcels to a joint tenancy with Barbara, a device that would automatically transfer those properties to her when he died, without them devolving through his will.[27] Tina arranged a meeting with her father and his lawyers. Aware of the changes she had been seeing in her father, she asked him directly if he understood what he had signed and if he had the advice of an attorney. He answered no on both counts, but Tina saw she wasn't going to get anywhere and left the meeting more saddened for her father than angry.[28]

Frank's friends, many of them younger than he, were dying off, leaving him even more depressed. Nelson Riddle died in 1985, as did Hugh Lambert, Nancy's husband, of cancer. Frank was close to his son-in-law, the father of his two granddaughters. Ava Gardner, the love of Frank's life, died on January 25, 1990, a month after her 67th birthday; Jimmy Van Heusen died 12 days later. Sammy went on May 16, 1990, suffering terribly from throat cancer. Jilly Rizzo died a horrible death on May 5, 1992, after a drunken driver struck the sports car he was driving. Jilly was trapped in his car as it burst into flames. Songwriter Sammy Cahn, the other half of the Cahn-Van Heusen duo that had written so many hits for Frank, died on January 15, 1993; and finally Dean Martin, perhaps the worst blow of all, died a broken man in 1995 on the most joyous of days, Christmas.

And yet, Sinatra continued to work at a younger man's pace, even though his eyesight and hearing were deteriorating, as well as his memory. Teleprompters had to be set up around the stages wherever he performed — he couldn't remember words to many standards he'd been singing for 50 or more years.

Frank had 65 singing appearances in 1990, including an engagement at the Brendan Byrne Arena in East Rutherford, New Jersey, on December 12, 1990 — his 75th birthday — after which he went on the road in what was billed as his Diamond Jubilee Tour, with Steve Lawrence and Edie Gormé. The husband-and-wife team helped cover for him when he forgot the lyrics to a song.[29] Audiences were understanding and supportive, often finishing a familiar song when he couldn't.

Comedian Charlie Callas was Sinatra's opening act for two years in the 1980s and almost two years in the 1990s. Even with his personal problems, Sinatra maintained a kind and generous relationship with the performers in his shows. Sinatra gave them equal billing, Callas said, and when Callas got a case of nerves the first time he performed with Sinatra, at the Spectrum in Philadelphia, Frank came out of his dressing room to wish the comedian luck. Frank stood by while the announcer introduced Callas with these words: "Ladies and gentlemen, Frank Sinatra presents his friend, Charlie Callas." As Callas was about to take the stage, Sinatra leaned over and said to him, "You're my friend, you know. Go get 'em tiger," and sent him out with a pat on his rear end.[30]

Sinatra did 71 engagements in 1991, but topped even that with 84 in 1992. Tina saw him perform at the Desert Inn in Las Vegas and suggested to him that he might want to think about retirement. "No, I can't stop," he said. "I've got to earn more money, got to earn more money. I have to make sure that everyone's taken care of."[31]

Shirley MacLaine was on tour with Frank in 1992 and remembered his memory losses — not only the lyrics to songs he'd sung hundreds if not thousands of times, but also her name, at times, when introducing her, though he'd known her for almost 40 years. "Frank's state of mind, what he ate, how long he slept, whom he talked to, how much he drank, and whether or not he was in a good mood were the subject of concern and conversation among everyone who worked around him" MacLaine said. "They had reconciled with his demons, and his musical genius demanded their respect.[32]

Sinatra's *Duets* album, his first album in nine years, was released under the Capitol label in November 1993 and became Sinatra's all-time best-selling album, despite mixed reviews from critics and Sinatra's own misgivings about his performances on the album.[33] All the songs were duets with younger singers of different musical backgrounds, but each track was recorded separately by Frank and by his duet partner; then the two recordings were combined electronically to produce the final product. It was a unique effect, pulled off to the satisfaction of 3 million album purchasers. A sequel, *Duets II*, was released in 1994 to a good but lesser reception.

Murray Kempton, one of Sinatra's favorite writers and a friend, commented on the changes in Frank's demeanor when he was presented with a Tower of Achievement award by Capitol Records in June 1993. "Sinatra's part in the ceremonies was rationed down to the five minutes he spent doubly lifting and lowering his award as the photographers bade him. When he was told it was time to leave, he complied with an amiable, 'O.K., you're the general.'"[34] Frank received the Legend Award on March 2, 1994, at the Grammys. "Dad came out to a loving bedlam of applause and was overwhelmed," Tina said. "As he rambled through his acceptance speech, I could tell he was in one of his fogs. There was no one in the wings to save him; they finally cued the orchestra to cut him off. It was awful."[35]

And still he performed. On March 6, 1994, Sinatra collapsed onstage in Richmond, Virginia. Frank Jr. was conducting for him and tried to reach him before he fell, but he was too late. Sinatra was conscious as they waited for the ambulance to arrive. As he was being wheeled out, the Chairman of the Board waved to the audience, amid their cheers. He was diagnosed at the hospital as being dehydrated. They pumped him full of fluids, and he was back on the road within days. In December 1994, Frank appeared at the MGM Grand Hotel in Las Vegas. He was so pitiful one night, because of memory loss, that he asked management to give everyone in the audience his or her money back. Sinatra gave his last singing performance as a solo act on February 25, 1995, at the Marriott Desert Spring Hotel. It was a benefit concert for the Barbara Sinatra Children's Center in Palm Springs. The audience was charitable.

In March 1995, the compound in Palm Springs was sold, but Frank refused to leave after the closing. The new owners were kind and gave the Sinatras an extension — time for Frank to get acclimated to the changes swirling around him. "He was grieving like someone had died," Tina said. Frank's children wanted to get their father "out of the public eye." They didn't want to see him embarrassed anymore, but there was one final embarrassment in store, an ABC Television special in honor of his 80th birthday. The event was pushed by Barbara, who was perhaps incentivized by the large contribution the network was making to her children's center.[36]

Sinatra had a heart attack on November 2, 1996, and was hospitalized at Cedars-Sinai Hospital, where he remained for eight days. Tina, who had been estranged from her father for almost a year, rushed to his bedside and immediately noticed further deterioration, both physically and mentally, from the last time she'd seen him. Later that month, Frank's doctor visited him at home and talked with the family. Sinatra's heart attack had been worse than they'd first thought, he said. There was also a question of dementia.[37] Frank was back in the hospital two months later with high blood pressure.[38]

On Sinatra's 82nd birthday, the U.S, Congress voted to award Francis Albert Sinatra the Gold Medal of Honor, its highest civilian award. Frank was too ill to attend, but watched the proceedings on television. And the Empire State Building in New York was bathed in blue light, as a further tribute.[39]

Barbara Sinatra was out to dinner with friends the night Sinatra's condition worsened (her fourth consecutive night out[40]), but she'd left word where she could be reached. She rushed home when Frank's caretaker told her he didn't have a pulse. The ambulance had already left for the hospital by the time she reached home, so someone drove her there. Three doctors were working on her husband when she arrived. He was still alive, but barely. She got close to him and held his hand for the remainder of his life.

Francis Albert Sinatra died at 10:50 p.m. on May 14, 1998. He was 82 years old. Barbara was the only family member with Frank when he died — no one had thought to call his children, who could have arrived in time to be with their father before he passed on. The first notification they got that something was wrong was a call from Frank's doctor to Tina, at 11:10 p.m., 20 minutes after he'd died.

Frank Sinatra's last words, according to Barbara, were, "I can't."[41]

"My father was the strongest, bravest man I'd ever known," Tina wrote, two years later. "He seemed indestructible to me; he was not one to quit. I believe that he was ready to go. He was so tired and lonely and broken. His soul had expired years before that stubborn body gave way. His future held nothing but pain. He could never be at peace, never stop running until he *stopped*.

"My father did not die. He escaped."[42]

EPILOGUE

"The only thing you owe the public is a good performance."

A s of this writing, the political phenomenon of 2015 has been, unquestionably, the Donald Trump candidacy for president of the United States. In late summer, a cable news network hosted a forum of Trump supporters in New Hampshire, the first primary state in the presidential election cycle.[1] The moderator began questioning those supporters, testing, in some cases, their actual knowledge of Trump's positions on key issues. It was a relevant approach to understanding Trump's appeal — he was the front-runner for the Republican nomination when the forum was held and had been purposely vague about the policies he would implement as president. Like most candidates, he wouldn't be nailed down on specifics, speaking instead in broad strokes about "making America great again" and his own negotiating skills. He touted *The Art of the Deal*, his 1987 book about negotiating business contracts, as the second-greatest book ever written, surpassed only by the Bible.

The moderator reached out to one particularly ardent Donald Trump fan and thought he would toss her a zinger. "Did you know," he asked the middle-aged woman, "that Mr. Trump once praised Hillary Clinton as an excellent secretary of state and the best person to negotiate with Iran?"

An allegation like that, lodged against any other Republican candidate in any other political year, would have spelled doom for that candidate's prospects. But not for Trump, and not in this election year. The woman's blunt response to the moderator was, "I don't care."

He tried again. "Did you know that Mr. Trump donated to the campaigns of Nancy Pelosi and Harry Reid, two of the most liberal Democrats in the House and Senate?" And he got the same response: "I don't care." And so it went, with this woman and most of the other Trump supporters in the room. They simply didn't care about any inconsistencies with conservative principles that might exist in Trump's past. He was their guy, no matter what.

It's sort of that way with Frank Sinatra fans. They love the way he sang . . . and they don't give a hoot about anything else — his mob connections; his extramarital sex life; his temper tantrums; his demeaning treatment of journalists, especially female journalists; his bullying of underlings and others less powerful than he was; and his often boorish and coarse behavior. None of that matters to most Sinatra fans. They love the man's music and, in most instances, they also have a soft spot for the man, too. Ol' Blue Eyes.

It's not hard to like the man behind the voice, if one concentrates on the good stuff, of which there was plenty. His generous nature has been well documented, in this book and elsewhere. Whenever he and his entourage walked into any restaurant or club, every employee in the joint, from the busboy to the maitre d', knew he or she was going to get at least a hundred-dollar bill as a tip. Not from Sinatra's hands, but from one of the lackeys following in his wake. "Duke 'em a C-note," Frank would say to Jilly or Nick Sevano or Hank Sanicola or Brad Dexter — whoever was the designated guy for that night — and it would get done. When a parking lot attendant retrieved his Dual Ghia one night outside a Hollywood club, Sinatra peeled off three hundreds and handed them to the kid. "I'll bet you never got a tip that big," Sinatra said. "No, *sir!*" the happy kid replied. Pressing, Sinatra asked the kid, "What was the biggest tip you ever got before this?" Turns out, it was a generous $200 tip. Sinatra was amazed. "Who the hell gave you that?" he wanted to know. "You did, Mr. Sinatra, last week."

Sinatra's generosity extended well beyond tipping, and knew no bounds. He took care of dozens of friends who'd fallen on hard times, particularly when they needed help with medical bills. Boxer Joe Louis, actor Lee J. Cobb, singer Peggy Lee, and drummer Buddy Rich were all in that category. In 1964, Bill Miller, Frank's pianist, was spending a quiet evening at home with his wife and daughter. A nearby reservoir dam burst, and the resulting deluge swept away Miller's house, with him and his family inside. His daughter escaped without injury but his wife was lost. Miller suffered extensive injuries and had to stay in the hospital for two weeks. Frank went down to the morgue and identified Mrs. Miller's body, then made sure Bill Miller received the finest medical care. When the pianist was ready to leave the hospital, Frank paid the bill and set Miller up in a new apartment, furnishing it throughout.[2] It would be impossible to list all the people and causes that Sinatra helped financially in a one-volume biography, but the Bill Miller episode is illustrative of that generosity.

Was there a pathological side to this aspect of Frank Sinatra? Shirley MacLaine, who was close to Sinatra for the last 40 years of his life, apparently thought so. "That's the way it was with Frank," MacLaine wrote in her 1995 memoir. "If you helped him more than he helped you, the friendship was doomed because the balance he wanted had been tipped."[3] Brad Dexter noticed a change in Sinatra's demeanor toward him, after he'd saved the singer from drowning in May 1964. How do you top saving a guy's life? Sinatra didn't have a prayer of getting the right balance back with Dexter, although he tried. The two men parted ways two years later, bad blood between them.

Gift-giving may have been a defensive gambit Frank used as a boy. He was a puny kid, small of stature but also weakened by medical issues — two mastoid operations and an appendectomy before he was 12. Dolly always made sure he had pocket money to treat friends to ice cream or candy — friends who were bigger than he was, like Tony Macagnano, and who could protect him if called upon. Doing favors or giving benefits of any kind was a way of buying loyalty, after all, much in the way that a Mafia don, a "godfather," bestows gifts and favors upon his loyal followers. According to singer Eddie Fisher, Sinatra once expressed to him a preference: He would rather be a Mafia don than president of the United States. If Sinatra made that statement to Fisher, it was nothing more than a wistful fantasy. But there's no denying Sinatra's fascination with those men who seemingly possessed unlimited power over all those around them. As Sinatra got bigger, his entourage got bigger, ready to ask "How high?" if Sinatra said jump.

Wielding unrestrained power can have a corrupting influence on the wielder. Frank never apologized for anything he did or said. If he felt guilty about something afterward, he might make amends by gifting, his old standby way of buying goodwill, but that would be the extent of the self-recrimination. Jimmy Van Heusen considered Frank Sinatra his best friend, but he had a behind-the-back nickname for him: "the monster." One incident demonstrates the appropriateness of that sobriquet.

Jimmy and Frank were at a restaurant when Desi Arnaz walked in with two bodyguards. Arnaz was being cautious while his Desilu Studios produced *The Untouchables*, a television program about the Chicago mob. Word was out on the street that Sam Giancana, who had been a driver for Al Capone in the old days, didn't like the program. Arnaz knew that Sinatra was a pal of Giancana's, and when Sinatra said something to him, like "Why don't you lay off the Italians," Arnaz told him to go stuff it. Sinatra held his rage in check — he didn't have his bodyguards with him, while Arnaz was fully prepared. After Frank and Jimmy got back to Jimmy's place, Frank let loose.

Van Heusen had an original portrait, given to him by Norman Rockwell. Sinatra knew how much Van Heusen treasured that painting, but he had to take out his fury on something and chose Van Heusen's portrait as that something. He destroyed it as Van Heusen stood by, frozen in place. The next day, a courier delivered a jeweled watch to Van Heusen's apartment, courtesy of Frank Sinatra. The watch was easily worth two or three times what the Rockwell painting would have brought on the market. But the painting's personal value to Van Heusen was irreplaceable.[4]

Sinatra's mood swings were well known, in Hollywood and elsewhere, and were often triggered by the most trivial of circumstances. Intimates could usually recognize the signs. Tony Consiglio had met Frank when Frank was 15 and acted as his road valet, off and on, for 30 years. "When Frank came out of his bedroom," Consiglio said, "I could tell just by his walk if we were going to have a good day or a bad day."[5]

"I'm not the kind of guy," Sinatra once said about himself, "who does a lot of brainwork about why or how I happen to get into something. I get an idea — maybe I get sore about something. And when I get sore enough, I do something about it."[6]

Is volatility of this nature something we must expect in an exceptional performer, part of his or her *sine qua non* of stardom? In a BBC television interview, British actor Richard Attenborough, a friend of Sinatra's, talked about "great artists" and the temperament that makes them tick. "They have within them," Attenborough said, "a feeling of an explosion. What makes them stars is that you feel that they might, in fact, blow the whole place to pieces, emotionally, at any particular moment."[7]

George Jacobs, Sinatra's valet at home, saw his boss go berserk on numerous occasions, including the one time when Jacobs was on the receiving end. They were in Hawaii, and Sinatra had invited Spencer Tracy and Katharine Hepburn to his house for dinner. Sinatra idolized Tracy and had co-starred with him in *The Devil at 4 O'Clock*, which had been filmed in Hawaii in 1960. One might think Frank would have been on his best behavior under the circumstances, but no. Sinatra, Tracy, and Hepburn were all seated at the dinner table when George brought out the pasta dish.

"When I served the spaghetti marinara, which I had made a million times for him," Jacobs wrote, "he tasted it, started raving that it wasn't *al dente*, and picked up the bowl and threw the pasta all over me and my white jacket. This was the only time that he had ever abused me, but once was enough. Tracy and Hepburn were so appalled that they left immediately, while Sinatra cleared the table by smashing all the dishes."[8]

Sometimes, the fallout from a Sinatra wilding was not so contained as a bruised employee ego and soiled white serving jacket. Peter Lawford, before he was banished forever from Sinatra's presence over the aborted Kennedy visit in 1962, spent many hours with his Rat Pack chieftain, many wary hours.

"You have no idea of that temper," Lawford recalled later in life. "He can get so mad that he's driven to real violence, especially if he's been drinking. I know. I've seen it. One time at a party in Palm Springs, he got so mad at some poor girl that he slammed her through a plate-glass window. There was shattered glass and blood all over the place and the girl's arm was nearly severed from her body. Jimmy Van Heusen rushed her to the hospital. Frank paid her off and the whole thing was hushed up, of course, but I remember Judy Garland and I looking at each other and shivering in fright at the time. I did everything I could to avoid setting off that temper."[9]

Sinatra may have come closer to killing someone on June 8, 1966, when he hit businessman Frederick Weisman over the head with a telephone in the Polo Lounge at the Beverly Hills Hotel and put him in a coma for two weeks. Sinatra always got away with those violent outbursts, seldom paying the slightest consequence because he was always surrounded by a coterie of protectors and flunkies. In the Polo Lounge incident, Jilly Rizzo was ready to take the fall, if it came to that.

"When Sinatra says that something unseemly did not happen, why, then it did not happen," Jonathan Schwartz wrote in a June 1989 *Gentlemen's Quarterly* article. "There might have been seven or eight guys standing around who saw it happen, but they are the palace guards, they ain't talking."[10]

Is there a mental illness issue here? How else can one explain Frank Sinatra's four faked or botched suicide attempts, all staged to repair a faltering relationship with Ava Gardner? How else can one explain the extreme recklessness, not to mention the immorality, of Frank Sinatra, a 38-year-old man, having sex with Natalie Wood, a 15-year-old girl, within months of his winning an Academy Award and rescuing a career on life support? Sinatra risked everything — prison, the end of his movie and singing careers, the embarrassment to his family, and nationwide condemnation — for a roll in the hay with a girl-woman, when he likely had the pick of hundreds of willing female stars, all beautiful and all of legal age. How else can one explain the mood swings, the hair-trigger temper, the frequent bouts with depression, the predilection for violence?

And what of his obsessive-compulsive behavior? The fastidiousness, carried to the extreme? Irving Mansfield produced seven or eight weekly broadcasts of *The Frank Sinatra Show* for CBS in late 1950 until he quit the show, unable to work with Sinatra. Mansfield observed rather erratic behavior on the part of his star. "Frank was always washing his hands, constantly washing, washing, washing, as if he was trying to wash his life away or something," Mansfield told Kitty Kelley in an interview. "When he wasn't washing his hands, he was changing his shorts. He would drop his pants to the floor, take off his drawers, and kick them up in the air with his foot.

Some flunky would chase those dirty shorts around the room while Frank put on a clean pair. He must have changed his shorts every twenty minutes. I've never seen anything like it in my life."[11]

This is not intended to be a psychiatric evaluation of Frank Sinatra, but from a layman's point of view, wasn't there something wrong with the man? And even if there was, what business is it of ours, if he could sing like no one else?

In a 1965 interview by Walter Cronkite for a CBS television special, Frank Sinatra talked about advice that Humphrey Bogart had once given him. "The only thing you owe the public," Bogie opined, "is a good performance." If that's the case, Sinatra gave us thousands of good performances, so maybe we should be giving him the privacy he always craved.

Actor Anthony Quinn acknowledged that "there is a cruel streak in Frank, no question about it, but I still love the guy. He's what all men are and not one man in a million ever is. Thomas Wolfe said that. I guess what I love is the Frank that sings. That's when he's really himself. I love what he says in his songs. I don't love everything that Frank does or the way he treats people at times, but anyone who sings like he does cannot be a really bad man."[12]

Is it possible to love the music and dismiss the man? Wasn't Sinatra's music informed by every painful experience of his life? Bruce Springsteen thought so.

Sinatra's "was a voice filled with bad attitude, life, beauty, excitement . . . and a sad knowledge of the world," Springsteen said at Sinatra's 80th birthday celebration in 1995. "It was the deep bluesness of Frank's voice that affected me the most, and while his music became synonymous with black tie, good life, the best booze, women, sophistication, his blues voice was always the sound of hard luck and men late at night with the last ten dollars in their pockets trying to figure a way out."[13]

ACKNOWLEDGMENTS

I've enjoyed a 15-year relationship with my publisher, North Jersey Media Group (North Jersey), mostly as a freelance contributor to *The Record*, North Jersey's outstanding daily newspaper. Amre Youssef, North Jersey director of content syndications and archives, was the publisher's representative for this book project, and working with him has been one of the most rewarding publishing experiences I've had. The team he assembled to work on this project couldn't have been better. My editor, Kim Kline, has made this book much better than my original manuscript, and the cover and interior design by Glenn Garvie give the book and the subject matter the class they deserve. Zhanna Gitana whipped the photo insert into shape, always offering useful suggestions to improve that aspect of the book. I also must thank Maggie Grande for her expert marketing program.

Tackling a project as complex as a Frank Sinatra biography wouldn't be possible without the help of some very knowledgeable people. Robert Foster, director of the Hoboken Museum, was one of my first interviews, and he provided a wealth of information and contacts. The museum's online resources are fantastic. I visited the Hoboken Public Library on many occasions and availed myself of its wonderful Sinatra collection. My thanks to the helpful library staff. James Farina, city clerk for the city of Hoboken and nephew of James Petrozelli, one of the Hoboken Four, provided me with background information I couldn't have gotten anywhere else. Jerry Lore, deputy clerk for Hoboken, was kind enough to help me along with information I needed, fulfilling every request without delay. Mike "Brother"

Yaccarino, son of Biggie's founder Joe Yaccarino, chatted with me while he opened clams for his customers in Biggie's original location at 318 Madison Street in Hoboken. His daughter, Rose Marie Ranuro, set up the interview. He offered insights into the Sinatra family and his visits to Dolly Sinatra's house when he was a kid to help his father cater parties. By the way, the clams Brother kept passing my way were the freshest I've ever tasted, and I am a raw bar aficionado. Pat Samperi's grandfather Joseph Samperi owned the Union Club in Hoboken, where Frank Sinatra had his first full-time singing job as a solo act in 1938. Her father, Paul Samperi, wrote an unpublished memoir about Joseph, his father, and about the Union Club. Pat was kind enough to share with me excerpts that pertained to Sinatra.

Tom Meyers, Fort Lee cultural and heritage affairs administrator and curator at the Fort Lee Museum, provided invaluable assistance, especially about the Riviera in Fort Lee, where Sinatra performed. He also provided recorded interviews with Rocky Vitetta, the Riviera's house barber, and with Lou Gallo, one of its waiters. I also viewed a taped interview with Irene Bruno Orifice, whose father, Jack Bruno, was a key executive at the Riviera under both Ben Marden's and Bill Miller's ownership. Her mother also worked at the club as a hatcheck girl in the late 1930s and early 1940s.I knew the Bruno family — Jack; his wife, Mary; and Irene and her sister Diane — while growing up. Jack was a partner with my father and mother, M. Richard Muti and Mafalda Muti, in the 1950s. They made the Milano in Ramsey, my hometown, one of the finest Italian restaurants in our area. I know, because my mother was the cook. I also interviewed Irene in person, and it was fun to renew our acquaintance. Irene provided me with information about a Frank Sinatra event that appears in no other Sinatra biography.

I interviewed Patricia Politis and her daughter Dale Monaco at Pat's restaurant, GP's, in Guttenberg, New Jersey. Pat was married to Dolly Sinatra's nephew, the son of Josie Garaventa Monaco, Dolly's sister and Frank Sinatra's favorite aunt. Both Pat and Dale had stories that have made it into my book. I thank them for their time and their hospitality — I got a great dinner at GP's out of the interview, as well as information.

Herbert J. Stern, a retired federal judge and former U.S. attorney for the District of New Jersey, has few peers in the annals of criminal prosecution anywhere in this country. His book *Diary of a DA: The True Story of the Prosecutor Who Took on the Mob, Fought Corruption, and Won* is an eye-opener about the corruption that was rampant in New Jersey when Stern's boss, Frederick Lacey, became U.S. attorney in 1969, to be succeeded by Stern himself. Judge Stern kindly sat for an interview with me and read some of the passages in this book about organized crime, providing a useful critique. Attorney Edwin Stier, now in private practice, but a former assistant U.S. attorney in the New Jersey office and ranking official in the New Jersey Attorney General's Office, provided important information about Sinatra's possible link to President Richard M. Nixon's commutation of the prison sentence of Angelo "Gyp' DeCarlo, a key Mafia benefactor of Frank Sinatra. I can't thank him enough. Albert Wunsch III, Esq., was a friend and confidant of comedian Charlie Callas, who worked with Sinatra in the late 1980s and early 1990s. Mr. Wunsch, who is the historian for the borough of Englewood Cliffs, New Jersey, where the Rustic Cabin was once located, provided a fine historical perspective, as well as remembrances of Charlie Callas (now deceased) of his time with Sinatra. Geri Fallo, cultural affairs director for the city of Hoboken, hosted the annual Sinatra Idol contest in Hoboken. More than a dozen Sinatra sound-alikes sang their hearts out and their fedoras off on June 11 in Hoboken. It was one of my most delightful evenings spent researching this book. Ms. Fallo also put me in touch with Dale Monaco, facilitating that interview.

I interviewed Tom Austin, who is an author himself and who knows more about the Riviera nightclub than anyone else — his father worked there when Tom was a youth, so Tom got to enjoy many of the delights of the club. Tom and co-author Ron Kase wrote the definitive book about the Riviera and that era of nightclub entertainment: *Bill Miller's Riviera: America's Showplace in Fort Lee, New Jersey.*

Finally, I cannot fail to acknowledge my wife, Lorraine, who not only put up with a sometimes (she would say, always) cranky author working on deadline, but also read parts of the book to ensure clarity and served as an unpaid research assistant. Also, I must say a word about a constant companion I had in my home office throughout my many marathon writing sessions, often lasting into the wee hours of the morning, and this companion can't even read. I'm talking about Miss Moneypenny ("Penny"), our golden retriever, who listened to my clicking keyboard without complaint and who always knew the right time for us to take a break and "walk it off" in the back yard.

Other books by Richard Muti

NON-FICTION

The Charmer: *The True Story of Robert Reldan—Rapist, Murderer,*
and Millionaire—and the Women who Fell Victim to his Allure
(Written with Charles Buckley)
(PRINT* AND E-BOOK EDITIONS)

Essays for my Father: *A legacy of passion, politics,*
and patriotism in small-town America
(PRINT* AND E-BOOK EDITIONS)

Passion, Politics and Patriotism in Small-Town America:
Confessions of a plain-talking independent mayor
(PRINT EDITION ONLY)

A Tale of Two Christies: *Essays about Gov. Chris Christie*
and Jersey-style politics, the national political scene,
unnecessary wars and wrongheaded government
(E-BOOK EDITION ONLY)

FICTION

Good Lawyer, Dead Lawyer: *A Novel*
(PRINT AND E-BOOK EDITIONS)

*Available at **www.shoptherecord.com/muti**
and wherever books are sold

SELECTED
BIBLIOGRAPHY

Austin, Tom, and Ron Kase, *Bill Miller's Riviera: America's Showplace in Fort Lee, New Jersey*, The History Press, 2011.

Bacall, Lauren, *By Myself and Then Some*, Harper Entertainment, 2005.

Badham, Keith, *Marilyn Monroe: The Final Years*, Thomas Dunne Books, 2010.

Barbas, Samantha, *The First Lady of Hollywood: A Biography of Louella Parsons*, University of California Press, 2005.

Barrett, Rona, *Miss Rona: An Autobiography*, Nash Publishing, 1974.

Britt, Stan, *sinatra: a celebration*, Schirmir Books, an imprint of Simon & Schuster Macmillan, 1995.

Brownstein, Ronald, *The Power and the Glitter: The Hollywood-Washington Connection*, Pantheon Books, 1990.

Cahn, Sammy, *I Should Care: The Sammy Cahn Story*, Arbor House, 1974.

Clarke, Donald. *All or Nothing at All: A Life of Sinatra*, Fromm International, 1997.

Consiglio, Tony, as told to Franz Douskey, *Sinatra and Me: The Very Good Years*, Tantor Media, Inc., 2012.

Davis, Jr., Sammy, and Jane and Burt Boyar, *Sammy: An Autobiography*, Farrar, Straus and Giroux, 2000.

Day, Doris, and A.E. Hotchner, *Doris Day: Her Own Story*, William Morrow and Company, 1975.

Demaris, Ovid, *The Boardwalk Jungle: How greed, corruption, and the Mafia turned Atlantic City into . . .*, Bantam Books, 1986.

De Palma, Jr., Anthony, "Stranger in the Night: The story of Sinatra and Hoboken and what went wrong," *New Jersey Monthly*, February 1982.

Dick, Bernard F., *The Merchant Prince of Poverty Row: Harry Cohn of Columbia Pictures*, The University Press of Kentucky, 1993.

Dominis, John, and Richard B. Stolley, *Sinatra: An Intimate Portrait of a Very Good Year*, Stewart, Tabori and Chang, 2002.

Douglas-Home, Robin, *Sinatra*, Grosset & Dunlap, 1962.

Hawes, Esme, *The Life and Times of Frank Sinatra*, Chelsea House Publishers, 1998.

Evanier, David, *The Jimmy Roselli Story: Making the Wiseguys Weep*, Farrar, Straus and Giroux, 1998.

Evans, Peter, and Ava Gardner, *Ava Gardner: The Secret Conversations*, Simon & Schuster, 2013.

Exner, Judith (Campbell), as told to Ovid Demaris, *My Story*, Grove Press, 1977.

Falcone, Vincent, and Bob Popyk, *Frankly Just Between Us: My Life Conducting Frank Sinatra's Music,* Hal Leonard Corporation, 2005.

Farrow, Mia, *What Falls Away: A Memoir,* Nan A. Talese, Publisher, an imprint of Doubleday, 1997.

Finstad, Suzanne, *Natasha: The Biography of Natalie Wood,* Harmony Books, 2001.

Freedland, Michael, *All the Way: A Biography of Frank Sinatra, 1915-1998,* St. Martin's Press, 1997.

Frew, Tim, *Sinatra,* élan press, 1998.

Frost, Jennifer, *Hedda Hopper's Hollywood: Celebrity Gossip and American Conservatism,* New York University Press, 2011.

Fuchs, Jeanne, and Ruth Prigozy, Editors, *Frank Sinatra: the Man, the Music, the Legend,* University of Rochester Press/Hofstra University, 2007.

Gardner, Ava, *Ava: My Story,* Bantam Books, 1990.

Giancana, Antoinette, and Thomas C. Renner, *Mafia Princess: Growing Up in Sam Giancana's Family,* William Morrow and Company, Inc., 1984.

Goddard, Peter, *Frank Sinatra: the Man, the Myth, and the Music,* Greywood Publishing Limited, 1973.

Hamill, Pete, *Why Sinatra Matters,* Little, Brown and Company, 1998.

Hawes, Esme, *The Life and Times of Frank Sinatra,* Chelsea House Publishers, 1998.

Hodge, Jessica, *Frank Sinatra,* Chartwell Books, Inc., 1998.

Irwin, Lew, *Sinatra: A Life Remembered,* Courage Books, an Imprint of Running Press, 1997.

Israel, Lee, *Kilgallen: A Biography of Dorothy Kilgallen,* Delacorte Press, 1979.

Jacobs, George, and William Stadiem, *Mr. S: My Life with Frank Sinatra,* Harper Entertainment, 2003.

Kaplan, James, *Frank: The Voice,* Doubleday, 2010.

Kelley, Kitty, *His Way: The Unauthorized Biography of Frank Sinatra,* Bantam Books, 1986.

Kelly, Robert J., *Encyclopedia of Organized Crime in the United States,* Greenwood Press, 2000.

Knight, Timothy, *Sinatra: Hollywood His Way,* Running Press, 2010.

Kuntz, Tom, and Phil Kuntz, Editors, *The Sinatra Files: The Life of an American Icon under Government Surveillance,* Three Rivers Press, 2000.

Lahr, John, *Sinatra: The Artist and the Man,* Random House, 1997.

Lawford, Patricia Seaton, with Ted Schwartz, *The Peter Lawford Story: Life with the Kennedys, Monroe and the Rat Pack,* Carroll & Graf Publishers, Inc., 1988.

Lee, Peggy, *Miss Peggy Lee: An Autobiography,* Donald I. Fine, Inc., 1984.

Levinson, Peter J., *Tommy Dorsey: Livin' in a Great Big Way,* Da Capo Press, 2005.

Levy, Shawn, *Rat Pack Confidential: Frank, Dean, Sammy, Peter, Joey and the Last Great Showbiz Party,* Doubleday, 1998.

Lewis, Jerry, and James Kaplan, *Dean and Me (A Love Story),* Doubleday, 2005.

Linnett, Richard, *In the Godfather Garden: The Long Life and Times of Richie "the Boot" Boiardo,"* Rutgers University Press, 2013.

MacLaine, Shirley, *My Lucky Stars: A Hollywood Memoir,* Bantam Books, 1995.

MacLaine, Shirley, *I'm All Over That: And Other Confessions,* Atria Books, 2011.

McNally, Karen, *When Frankie Went to Hollywood: Frank Sinatra and the American Male Identity,* University of Illinois Press, 2008.

Mortimer, Lee, "Frank Sinatra Confidential: Gangsters in the Night Clubs," *The American Mercury,* August 1951.

Petkov, Steven, and Leonard Mustazza, Editors, *The Frank Sinatra Reader,* Oxford University Press, 1995.

Podell-Raber, Mickey, with Charles Pignon, *The Copa: Jules Podell and the Hottest Club North of Havana,* Collins, an imprint of Harper Collins Publishers, 2007.

Pugliese, Stanislao G., Editor, *Frank Sinatra: History, Identity, and Italian American Culture,* Palgrave Macmillan, 2004.

Quirk, Lawrence J. and William Schoell, *The Rat Pack: The Hey-Hey Days of Frank and the Boys*, Taylor Publishing Company, 1998.

Romero, Gerry, *Sinatra's Women*, Manor Books, Inc., 1976.

Rooney, Mickey, *Life Is Too Short*, Villard Books, 1991.

Samperi, Paul A., *The Courage to Come Up on Top: The Runner and the Steamship*, an unpublished manuscript.

Santopietro, Tom, *Sinatra in Hollywood*, Thomas Dunne Books, St. Martin's Press, 2008.

Server, Lee, *Ava Gardner: "Love Is Nothing,"* St. Martin's Press, 2006.

Sifakis, Carl, *The Mafia Encyclopedia, from Accardo to Zwillman*, 3rd. Ed., Facts on File, Inc., 2005.

Sinatra, Barbara, with Wendy Holden, *Lady Blue Eyes: My Life With Frank*, Crown Archetype, an imprint of the Crown Publishing group, 2011.

Sinatra, Nancy, *Frank Sinatra: An American Legend*, W. Quay Hays, Publisher, 1995, 1998.

Sinatra, Tina, with Jeff Coplon, *My Father's Daughter: A Memoir*, Simon & Schuster, 2000.

Spada, James, *Peter Lawford: The Man Who Kept the Secrets*, Bantam Books, 1991.

Starr, Michael Seth, *Mouse in the Rat Pack: The Joey Bishop Story*, Taylor Trade Publishing, 2002.

Stern, Herbert J., *Diary of a DA: The True Story of the Prosecutor Who Took on the Mob, Fought Corruption, and Won*, Skyhorse Publishing, 2012.

Summers, Anthony, and Robbyn Swan, *Sinatra: The Life*, Alfred A. Knopf, 2005.

Summers, Anthony, *Goddess: The Secret Lives of Marilyn Monroe*, Macmillan Publishing Company, 1985.

Talese, Gay, "Frank Sinatra Has a Cold," *Esquire*, April 1966.

Taraborrelli, J. Randy, *Sinatra: Behind the Legend*, Carol Publishing Group, 1997.

Taraborrelli, J. Randy, *The Secret Life of Marilyn Monroe*, Grand Central Publishing, 2009.

Thomas, Bob, *King Cohn: The Life and Times of Harry Cohn*, G.P. Putnam & Sons, 1967.

Tormé, Mel, *Traps the Drum Wonder: The Life of Buddy Rich*, Oxford University Press, 1991.

Turner, Lana, *Lana: the Lady, the Legend, the Truth*, E.P. Dutton, Inc., 1982.

Vare, Ethlie Ann, Editor, *Legend: Frank Sinatra and the American Dream*, Boulevard Books, 1995.

Wayne, Jane Ellen, *Ava's Men: The Private Life of Ava Gardner*, St. Martin's Press, 1990.

Wilson, Earl, *Sinatra: An Unauthorized Biography*, Macmillan Publishing Co., Inc., 1976.

Yagoda, Ben, *The B-Side: The Death of Tin Pan Alley and the Rebirth of the Great American Song*, Riverhead Books, 2015.

Zehme, Bill, *The Way You Wear Your Hat: Frank Sinatra and the Lost Art of Livin'*, Harper Collins, 1997.

NOTES

PREFACE

1 McPhee, John, "The Writing Life: Frame of Reference," in *The New Yorker*, March 9, 2015, p. 42.

2 Summers, Anthony, and Robbyn Swan, *Sinatra: The Life*, Alfred A. Knopf, 2005, pp. 301-302.

3 Tormé, Mel, *Traps the Drum Wonder: The Life of Buddy Rich*, Oxford University Press, 1991, p. 92. Other sources put the figure at $40,000, but Tormé, Rich's close friend as well as his biographer, is probably the most accurate reporter. Whatever the amount, it was Sinatra's gesture that mattered.

4 Taraborrelli, J. Randy, *Sinatra: Behind the Legend*, Carol Publishing Group, p. 185.

5 McNally, Karen, *When Frankie Went to Hollywood: Frank Sinatra and the American Male Identity*, University of Illinois Press, 2008, p. 71.

6 Taraborrelli, pp. 468-469.

7 Levy, Shawn, *Rat Pack Confidential: Frank, Dean, Sammy, Peter, Joey and the Last Great Showbiz Party*, Doubleday, 1998, p. 114. Here are just two of Sinatra's offstage remarks to Sammy Davis, Jr. while Davis was performing onstage: (1) with the lighting low, "Keep smiling so they can see you, Smokey"; and, (2) "Hurry up, Sam, the watermelon's getting warm." Comedian Joey Bishop was a Rat Pack member but didn't approve of the ethnic "jokes" Sinatra and Martin used in their act. Lawford went along with whatever Sinatra wanted.

8 Jacobs, George, and William Stadiem, *Mr. S: My Life with Frank Sinatra*, Harper Entertainment, 2003, p. 3.

9 Ibid., p. 50.

10 Ibid., pp. 41-42.

11 Bacall, Lauren, *By Myself and Then Some*, Harper Entertainment, 2005, p. 249.

12 Ibid., p. 241.

13 Frew, Tim, *Sinatra*, élan press, 1998, p. 55, claiming the affair started in 1956, when Sinatra was filming *The Joker is Wild*. Bacall was silent in her memoir on that particular point.

14 Farrow, Mia, *What Falls Away: A Memoir*, Nan A. Talese/Doubleday, 1997, pp. 110-111.

15 Goddard, Peter, *Frank Sinatra: The Man, The Myth and The Music*, Greywood Publishing Limited, 1973, p. 49.

[16] Kaplan, James, *Frank: The Voice*, Doubleday, 2010, p. 184.

[17] Summers and Swan, p. 135.

[18] Although the character of Vito Corleone in *The Godfather* was probably a composite of several New York mob figures, Frank Costello was likely the principal "role model," according to numerous popular culture sources. Like the fictional godfather, Costello had a raspy voice, was opposed to the drug trade, exercised power over politicians, and was the target of an unsuccessful assassination attempt.

[19] Interview, James Farina, Clerk, City of Hoboken, April 10, 2015. Farina was a nephew of James Petrozelli, a member of the Hoboken Four.

[20] De Palma, Jr., Anthony, "Stranger in the Night: The story of Sinatra and Hoboken and what went wrong," in *New Jersey Monthly*, February 1982, p. 52. See also, Summers and Swan, pp. 29-31.

[21] Douglas-Home, Robin, *Sinatra*, Grosset & Dunlap, 1962, p. 23. See also, Hamill, Pete, *Why Sinatra Matters*, Little Brown and Company, 1998, p.107.

[22] Levinson, Peter J., *Tommy Dorsey: Livin' in a Big Way*, Da Capo Press, 2005, p. 95.

[23] Petkov, Steven, and Leonard Mustazza, *The Frank Sinatra Reader*, Oxford University Press, 1995, p. 15, taken from *The Great American Popular Singers*, by Henry Pleasants, 1974.

CHAPTER 1

[1] "Casino fined, Sinatra dealt sharp rebuke," *The Jersey Journal*, August 2, 1984.

[2] Ibid.

[3] "Casino fined, Sinatra dealt sharp rebuke," *The Jersey Journal*, August 2, 1984.

[4] "Casino czar blasted on Sinatra charges," *The Jersey Journal*, August 8, 1984.

[5] Demaris, Ovid, *The Boardwalk Jungle: How greed, corruption, and the Mafia turned Atlantic City into . . .*, Bantam Books, 1986, pp. 39-40.

[6] Ibid.

[7] "Sinatra doesn't like us anymore," *The Jersey Journal*, September 4, 1984.

[8] Ibid.

[9] Sinatra remained true to his word for 14 months, but then relented and returned to do a seven-show engagement, October 9-13, 1985, again at the Golden Nugget in Atlantic City. In the remaining nine years of his performing career, he would entertain in New Jersey a few more times: at the Golden Nugget, whose owner, Steve Wynn, was a friend; at the Sands Hotel and Casino, also in Atlantic City; at the Brendan Byrne (Meadowlands) Arena in East Rutherford; and at the Garden State Arts Center in Holmdel.

[10] Gardner, Ava, *Ava: My Story*, Bantam Books, 1990, p. 150.

[11] MacLaine, Shirley, *My Lucky Stars: A Hollywood Memoir*, Bantam Books, 1995, p.85.

[12] Ibid., p. 87.

[13] Hamill, Pete, *Why Sinatra Matters*, Little, Brown and Company, 1998, p.78.

[14] A number of Sinatra biographers have spelled Dolly's maiden name as "Garavente," including Frank's daughter Nancy, or as "Garavante," used by Kitty Kelley in her bestselling 1986 biography. My search of Ellis Island records indicates no results for immigrants with the surname "Garavente," which appears to be a misnomer, and just two hits (neither of them Frank Sinatra's forebears) for "Garavante." In contrast, there were hundreds of immigrants with the surname "Garaventa," which is likely the correct spelling of Dolly's family name. More recent Sinatra biographers — Anthony Summers and Robbyn Swan, in 2005, and James Kaplan, in 2010, in particular — used the "Garaventa" spelling, as I do in this book. An interview with Pat Politis and Dale Monaco, daughter-in-law and granddaughter, respectively, of Josie Garaventa Monaco, Dolly's sister, con-

firmed the Garaventa spelling.

[15] McNally, Karen, *When Frankie Went to Hollywood: Frank Sinatra and the American Male Identity,* University of Illinois Press, 2008, p. 51.

[16] There were Irish and German sections, too, and some with residents of different heritages. Immigrants — not just in Hoboken, but all over — mostly preferred living with their own kind — human nature, I suppose, as well as the convenience of a common first language and food markets, in close proximity, selling home-country staples.

[17] De Palma, Jr., p. 55. These were not necessarily substandard accommodations in 1913, when many families had only an outhouse for their basic sanitary needs, or, as broken-English-speaking Italians called that rear-yard facility, the *back-housa.*

[18] Later in life, Frank would give his birth weight as 12¾ pounds, but virtually every biography of the man agrees with the 13½ pound figure. Either way, the baby's size was staggering, especially coming from a 90-pound mother.

[19] Irwin, Lew, *Sinatra: A Life Remembered,* Courage Books, an Imprint of Running Press, 1997, p.10.

[20] Frank Sinatra made a scene his son's christening ceremony in 1944 when his choice for Frank Jr.'s godfather, Manie Sacks, head of Columbia Records and Frank's friend and mentor, was disputed by the priest because Sacks was Jewish.

[21] One uncle, Lawrence "Babe" Garaventa, had more than 20 arrests and would later serve a long prison sentence for driving the getaway car in a botched robbery-murder. Dominick Garaventa, the boxer, had a bootlegging past and was also arrested but not prosecuted in connection with brother Babe's robbery incident. A third brother, Gustavo, was a numbers runner. See Summers and Swan, p. 12.

[22] Dolly herself would become godmother to 87 Hoboken children, an indication of the influence she had within the Italian community. See Talese, Gay, "Frank Sinatra Has a Cold," *Esquire,* April 1966. See also, Petkov, Steven, and Leonard Mustazza, Editors, *The Frank Sinatra Reader,* Oxford University Press, 1995, p. 115.

[23] De Palma, Jr., p. 56.

[24] Most of the congregation at this church was Italian, it being in the Italian section of the city. It is Stop No. 2 on the Hoboken Museum's "Frank Sinatra, The Voice" walking tour, in honor of the city's most famous son. See, https://www.hobokenmuseum.org/self-guided-walking-tours/frank-sinatra-the-voice.

[25] Sinatra, Nancy, *Frank Sinatra: An American Legend,* W. Quay Hays, Publisher, 1995, 1998, p. 17. Ms. Sinatra included a copy of the original birth certificate in her book.

[26] Sinatra, pp. 17, 21.Frank's junior high school diploma, dated January 18, 1931, gave his name as "Francis Albert Sinatra."

[27] Sinatra tried to block the book's publication, because of unsavory details it revealed about his life and, in particular, the damage it did to his deceased mother's reputation. He was unsuccessful, as his lawyers probably persuaded him would be the case. He never carried through with any lawsuit for libel or defamation, but had nothing but contempt for Hoboken friends and acquaintances who had cooperated with Kelley by giving interviews and telling tales "out-of-school."

[28] Talese, Gay, "Frank Sinatra Has a Cold," *Esquire,* April 1966. See also, Gennari, John, in "Mammissimo: Dolly and Frankie Sinatra and the Italian American Mother/Son Thing, " in the anthology *Frank Sinatra: History, Identity, and Italian American Culture,* Stanislao G. Pugliese, Editor, Palgrave Macmillan, 2004, p. 128.

[29] Taraborrelli, J. Randy, *Sinatra: Behind the Legend,* A Birch Lane Press Book, published by Carol Publishing Group, 1997, p. 10.

[30] Kelley, pp. 17-18.

[31] See, http://hoboken.pastperfectonline.com/32340cgi/mweb.exe?request=image&hex=20012260001.jpg, link to Hoboken Museum photo.

CHAPTER 2

[1] McNally, Karen, *When Frankie Went to Hollywood: Frank Sinatra and the American Male Identity*, University of Illinois Press, 2008, p.45.

[2] Santopietro, Tom, *Sinatra in Hollywood*, Thomas Dunne Books, St. Martin's Press, 2008, p. 21.

[3] Vare, Ethlie Ann, Editor, *Legend: Frank Sinatra and the American Dream*, Boulevard Books, 1995, p. 3.

[4] Jacklosky, Rob, "Someone to Watch Over Him: Images of Class and Gender Vulnerability in Early Sinatra," an essay in *Frank Sinatra: History, Identity, and Italian American Culture*, Stanislao G. Pugliese, Editor, Palgrave Macmillan, 2004, p. 95.

[5] Farrow, Mia, *What Falls Away: A Memoir*, Nan A. Talese, Publisher, an imprint of Doubleday, 1997, p. 95.

[6] Frank Sinatra, The Voice of the Century, Part 1 of a YouTube tribute to the singer after his death, online at https://www.youtube.com/watch?v=g5d6B_TkwBw, quoting Sinatra in Sinatra's own voice. Sinatra's daughter Tina cites her father's 1965 interview with CBS' Walter Cronkite as the source of this quote. See Sinatra, Tina, with Jeff Coplon, *My Father's Daughter*, Simon & Schuster, 2000, p. 95.

[7] De Palma, Jr., Anthony, "Stranger in the Night: The story of Sinatra and Hoboken and what went wrong," *New Jersey Monthly*, February 1982, p. 56.

[8] Kelley, Kitty, *His Way: The Unauthorized Biography of Frank Sinatra*, Bantam Books, 1986, pp. 18, 20.

[9] Ibid., p. 21.

[10] Hodge, Jessica, *Frank Sinatra*, Chartwell Books, Inc., 1998, p. 8.

[11] Sinatra, Nancy, *Frank Sinatra: An American Legend*, W. Quay Hays, Publisher, 1995, 1998, p. 21. Ms. Sinatra included a copy of her father's junior high diploma in her book. Sinatra had just turned 15 the month before. The diploma shows the first "official" use of the full name that would become the most famous in entertainment history. A mid-school-year graduation date seems strange to us today, but it may very well have been a way to transition students to the greater rigors of high school — both social and academic — by having them complete the first half of ninth grade in the less demanding junior high setting.

[12] Britt, Stan, *sinatra: a celebration*, Schirmir Books, an imprint of Simon & Schuster Macmillan, 1995, p.21.

[13] Kelley, p. 27.

[14] Sinatra, p. 20.

[15] Consiglio, Tony, as told to Franz Douskey, *Sinatra and Me: The Very Good Years*, Tantor Media, Inc., 2012. Consiglio died on June 24, 2008. In the book, he reveals much about Sinatra's private life, but there is no meanness of spirit in his accounts; rather, the affection he held for his friend and boss is apparent in every story he tells.

[16] Ibid., p. 14.

[17] Ibid., p. 286.

[18] Sinatra, p. 21.

[19] Kelley, p. 28.

[20] Ibid.

[21] Ibid.

[22] Ibid., p. 29.

[23] Lahr, John, *Sinatra: The Artist and the Man*, Random House, 1997, p. 14.

[24] Ibid., p. 7.

[25] Sinatra, p. 27.

[26] Irwin, Lew, *Sinatra: A Life Remembered*, Courage Books, 1997, p.15.

[27] Freedland, Michael, *All the Way: A Biography of Frank Sinatra, 1915-1998*, St. Martin's Press, 1997, p. 29. Film shorts were a popular add-on in movie theaters of the day, as fillers to the featured motion pictures on the bill.

[28] *The New York Post*, May 16, 1998.

[29] Freedland, p. 31.

[30] *The New York Post*, May 16, 1998.

[31] Clarke, Donald, *All or Nothing at All: A Life of Sinatra*, Fromm International, 1997, pp. 20-21. The other three members of the Hoboken Four — Tamby, Skelly, and Patty — would also quit the tour shortly thereafter. None of them would go on to careers in the entertainment business

[32] Freedland, p. 36.

[33] Clarke, p. 21.

[34] Samperi, Paul A., *The Courage to Come Up on Top: The Runner and the Steamship*, an unpublished manuscript about the author's father, Joseph Samperi, pp. 196-198. Furnished through the courtesy of Patricia Samperi.

[35] The "singing waiter" concept, a holdover from the late 1800s, was not uncommon in restaurants of the day, but it would soon become an entertainment anachronism.

[36] Information about the Rustic Cabin furnished by Tom Austin, who, as a teenager, was employed as a parking lot attendant at the roadhouse, and by Albert H. Wunsch III, local historian for the Borough of Englewood Cliffs, New Jersey.

[37] Kelley, p. 42.

[38] Sinatra, p. 30.

CHAPTER 3

[1] Kelley, Kitty, *His Way: The Unauthorized Biography of Frank Sinatra*, Bantam Books, 1986, p. 6.

[2] Kuntz, Tom, and Phil Kuntz, Editors, *The Sinatra Files: The Life of an American Icon under Government Surveillance*, Three Rivers Press, 2000, p. 15, quoting language from the actual criminal complaint, as contained in a report in Frank Sinatra's FBI file, dated February 17, 1944.

[3] Kuntz and Kuntz, p. 15.

[4] Kelley, p. 7.

[5] *Jersey Observer*, December 26, 1938.

[6] Summers, Anthony, and Robbyn Swan, *Sinatra: The Life*, Alfred A. Knopf, 2005, p. 54.

[7] Kuntz and Kuntz, p. 16.

[8] Sinatra, Nancy, *Frank Sinatra: An American Legend*, W. Quay Hays, Publisher, 1995, 1998, p. 32. Ms. Sinatra included a copy of the wedding invitation in her book.

[9] Clarke, Donald, *All or Nothing at All: A Life of Sinatra*, Fromm International, 1997, p. 26.

[10] Hodge, Jessica, *Frank Sinatra*, Chartwell Books, Inc, 1998, p. 11.

[11] Clarke, pp. 28-29.

[12] Kaplan, James, *Frank: The Voice*, Doubleday, 2010, p. 74.

[13] Pugliese, Stanislao G., Editor, *Frank Sinatra: History, Identity, and Italian American Culture*, Palgrave Macmillan, 2004, p. 180, taken from "I Get No Kick from Assimilation, or 'My' Frank Sinatra Problem," by Rocco Marinaccio.

[14] Goddard, Peter, *Frank Sinatra: the Man, the Myth, and the Music*, Greywood Publishing Limited, 1973, p.28.

[15] Britt, Stan, *sinatra: a celebration*, Schirmir Books, an imprint of Simon & Schuster/Macmillan, 1995, p. 27.

[16] Kaplan, p. 78.

[17] Goddard, p. 30.

[18] The record's reception among show-business professionals was much keener than it was, initially, with the public. Jazz singer Mel Tormé was especially enthusiastic. "Sinatra's record of 'All or Nothing at All' with James raised eyebrows in the music business," Tormé said. "He had a fresh, original sound, astonishing breath control, perfect intonation, spotless enunciation, and a warm vocal quality . . . ." See, Tormé. Mel, *Traps the Drum Wonder: The Life of Buddy Rich*, Oxford University Press, 1991, p. 52.

[19] Levinson, Peter J., *Tommy Dorsey: Livin' in a Great Big Way*, Da Capo Press, 2005, p. 110.

[20] Ibid.

[21] Freedland, Michael, *All the Way: A Biography of Frank Sinatra, 1915-1998*, St. Martin's Press, 1997, p. 52. It was common practice for theater managers to book a '5 of acts on each bill — something for everyone.

[22] Clarke, pp. 44-45.

[23] Ibid., pp. 50-58, 61.

[24] Tormé, Mel, *Traps the Drum Wonder: The Life of Buddy Rich*, Oxford University Press, 1991, pp. 56, 57.

[25] Levinson, p. 119.

[26] Clarke, pp. 44-45.

[27] Tormé, pp. 56-57.

[28] Ibid., pp. 58-59.

[29] Ibid., pp. 60-61.

[30] Clarke, pp. 55-56.

[31] Kaplan, pp. 117.

[32] Tormé, p. 62.

[33] Ibid., pp. 62-63.

[34] Ibid., p. 63.

[35] Ibid.

[36] Clarke, p. 55.

[37] Britt, p. 31.

[38] Lahr, John, *Sinatra: The Artist and the Man*, Random House, 1997, p. 54.

[39] Clarke, p. 76. There was a musicians' union strike against record companies just as Sinatra started out, so his earlier Columbia recordings had no music, so to speak. They were of Sinatra singing *a cappella*, with vocal groups providing the accompaniment.

[40] Levinson, p. 156.

[41] Vare, Ethlie Ann, Editor, *Legend: Frank Sinatra and the American Dream*, Boulevard Books, 1995, p. 36, from "Star-Spangled Octopus," by David G. Wittels, *Saturday Evening Post*, August 1946.

[42] Clarke, p. 75.

[43] Vare, p. 36.

[44] Irwin, Lew, *Sinatra: A Life Remembered*, Courage Books, an imprint of Running Press, 1997, p. 26. Other sources have Goodman using a saltier expletive. See Britt, p. 45.

[45] Lee, Peggy, *Miss Peggy Lee: An Autobiography*, Donald I. Fine, Inc., 1984, p. 19.

[46] Pugliese, p. 78, from "Why the Bobby Soxers?" by Janice L. Booker.

[47] Ibid., p. 76.

[48] Kuntz and Kuntz, p. 25.

[49] Petkov, Stephen, and Leonard Mustazza, Editors, *The Frank Sinatra Reader*, Oxford University Press, 1995, p. 48, quoting from "The Bobby Sox Have Wilted, But the Memory Remains Fresh," *The New York Times*, October 13, 1974. See also, Clarke, p. 71.

CHAPTER 4

[1] Frew, Tim, *Sinatra*, élan press, 1998, p. 31.

[2] Knight, Timothy, *Sinatra: Hollywood His Way*, Running Press, 2010, *passim*.

[3] Summers, Anthony, and Robbyn Swan, *Sinatra: The Life*, Alfred A. Knopf, 2005, p. 91.

[4] Freedland, Michael, *All the Way: A Biography of Frank Sinatra, 1915-1998*, St. Martin's Press, 1997, p. 81.

[5] Kuntz, Tom, and Phil Kuntz, Editors, *The Sinatra Files: The Life of an American Icon under Government Surveillance*, Three Rivers Press, 2000, p. 11.

[6] Summers and Swan, pp. 92-93.

[7] Freedland, p. 95.

[8] From a December 20, 1943, *Newsweek* article, included in *Legend: Frank Sinatra and the American Dream*, Ethlie Ann Vare, Editor, Boulevard Books, 1995, p. 18.

[9] Attorney General Robert F. Kennedy signed off on Hoover's request to carry on enhanced and illegal surveillance of Dr. King, in what many would come to regard as the low point in RFK's public service.

[10] Kuntz and Kuntz, p. *xi*.

[11] Ibid., pp. 5-6.

[12] Ibid., p. 7.

[13] Ibid., pp. 10-11.

[14] Ibid., pp. 9-10.

[15] Ibid., p. 10.

[16] Ibid., pp. 18-19.

[17] Ibid.

[18] Ibid., p. 20.

[19] Sinatra, Nancy, *Frank Sinatra: An American Legend*, W. Quay Hays, Publisher, 1995, 1998, p. 67.

[20] Kuntz and Kuntz, pp. 69-71.

[21] Freedland, p. 96.

[22] Sinatra, pp. 55-59.

[23] Lahr, John, *Sinatra: The Artist and the Man*, Random House, Inc., 1997, p. 34.

[24] Freedland, p. 95.

[25] Frew, p. 32.

[26] Quirk, Lawrence J. and William Schoell, *The Rat Pack: The Hey-Hey Days of Frank and the Boys*, Taylor Publishing Company, 1998, p. 31-32.

[27] Dominis, John, and Richard B. Stolley, *Sinatra: An Intimate Portrait of a Very Good Year*, Stewart, Tabori and Chang, 2002, p. 90.

[28] Quirk and Schoell, p. 32.

[29] Irwin, Lew, *Sinatra: A Life Remembered*, Courage Books, an Imprint of Running Press, 1997, p. 35.

[30] Kelley, Kitty, *His Way: The Unauthorized Biography of Frank Sinatra*, Bantam Books, 1986, p. 104.

[31] Gay Talese used this Italian term in his widely acclaimed article "Frank Sinatra Has a Cold," in the April 1966 issue of *Esquire*.

CHAPTER 5

[1] Hamill, Pete, *Why Sinatra Matters*, Little, Brown and Company, 1998, p. 146.

[2] Ibid.

[3] In 1978, the year after his mother's untimely desath, Sinatra had thoughts about writing his autobiography. He and sidekick Jilly Rizzo traveled to New Jersey to visit his aunt, Josie Monaco, Dolly's sister. Frank had a tape recorder with him and asked his aunt about her memories of the family and his youth in Hoboken. Nothing came of that autobiographical effort. Source: Josie's granddaughter, Dale Monaco, who, as a young adult, was present at her grandmother's house during Sinatra's visit.

[4] Evanier, David, *The Jimmy Roselli Story: Making the Wiseguys Weep*, Farrar, Straus and Giroux, 1998, pp. 64-65.

[5] Hamill, p. 146.

[6] Levinson, Peter J., *Tommy Dorsey: Livin' in a Great Big Way*, Da Capo Press, 2005, p. 161.

[7] Sifakis, Carl, *The Mafia Encyclopedia, from Accardo to Zwillman*, 3rd. Ed., Facts on File, Inc., 2005, p. 190. Giancana's earlier mob nickname was "Mooney," an appellation rooted in his craziness and unpredictability, as in "lunatic"—*luna* being the Italian for *moon*. Giancana didn't like that nickname, a fact that led his associates, wisely, to discontinue its use.

[8] Spada, James, *Peter Lawford: The Man Who Kept the Secrets*, Bantam Books, 1991, p. 208.

[9] Levy, Shawn, *Rat Pack Confidential: Frank, Dean, Sammy, Peter, Joey and the Last Great Showbiz Party*, Doubleday, 1998, p. 137.

[10] MacLaine, Shirley, *I'm All Over That: And Other Confessions*, Atria Books, 2011, p. 23.

[11] MacLaine, Shirley, *My Lucky Stars: a Hollywood Memoir*, Bantam Books, 1995, p. 62.

[12] Ibid., p. 63. Non-stop practical joking prevailed during the making of this movie, often instigated by Giancana, to the delight of Sinatra. Mostly, it would involve cherry bombs placed under an unsuspecting victim's chair. MacLaine tells of an incident involving her and Giancana. She surprised him with a toy gun, which she pointed in his direction. In response, Giancana calmly pulled out the real thing and waved it at her, in fun but with a hint of malice.

[13] Jacobs, George, and William Stadiem, *Mr. S: My Life with Frank Sinatra*, Harper Entertainment, 2003, pp. 3-4. Apparently, Sinatra got the cherry bomb habit from Sam Giancana (see Levy, p. 141) and would often send Jacobs on a run to Tijuana to buy the mini-explosives. He

"was obsessed with stupid practical jokes," Jacobs said (p. 6). After an attack on one of his friends, the singer would gleefully exclaim, "The Hoboken bomber strikes again!" (pp. 74-75).

[14] Linnett, Richard, *In the Godfather Garden: The Long Life and Times of Richie "the Boot" Boiardo,"* Rutgers University Press, 2013, pp. 62-63.

[15] Ibid., p. 109.

[16] Summers, Anthony, and Robbyn Swan, *Sinatra: The Life*, Alfred A. Knopf, 2005, pp. 7-8. The grandfather died in the mid-1940s, and Frank was often in his company growing up; but there's no indication they ever talked about Francesco's common roots with the nation's No. 1 mob figure.

[17] According to two sources — Nancy Sinatra and Pete Hamill — Jewish mobster Waxey Gordon, a Lucky Luciano underling, was a regular at the bar run by Dolly and Marty Sinatra and was probably their source for illegal liquor. See Summers and Swan, pp. 20-21.

[18] Linnett, p. 63. Costello was gunned down by a Genovese henchman, Vincent "Vinny the Chin" Gigante, but survived the shooting and wisely decided to retire.

[19] Ibid., *passim.*

[20] Ibid., p. 26-27. At 6 feet, 2 inches, Zwillman stood almost a foot taller than most of his Italian associates — hence, "Longy."

[21] Sifakis, p. 47.

[22] Ibid., p. 314.

[23] Linnett, pp. 31-32.

[24] DeCarlo hated the nickname "Gyp," much preferring to be called "Ray" by his associates. See Stern, Herbert J., *Diary of a DA: The True Story of the Prosecutor Who Took on the Mob, Fought Corruption, and Won*, Skyhorse Publishing, 2012, p. 85.

[25] Summers and Swan, p. 47.

[26] Stern, pp. 506-507.

[27] Mortimer, Lee, "Frank Sinatra Confidential: Gangsters in the Night Clubs," *The American Mercury*, August 1951, p. 32.

[28] Summers and Swan, pp. 47-48.

[29] Ibid., p. 49.

[30] Ibid., pp. 49-50.

[31] *Sunday Star-Ledger*, December 13, 1981. Lorenzo's reference to Frank not singing "for once" was probably grounded in her observations of him growing up, when he sang at every opportunity, invited or not. According to Pat Politis, once married to Dolly's nephew, Frank Monaco, the type of ravioli that Dolly was famous for was Genoese-style, from her native province of Genoa, Italy. It was a difficult and time-consuming recipe, but it was also Frankie's favorite, so Dolly made it on just about every special occasion involving her son.

[32] Levinson, p. 155.

[33] Ibid., pp. 155-156. In the release deal, Dorsey also lent $17,000 in cash to Sinatra, to tide him and his family over until he started earning as a solo act. See Levinson, p. 162.

[34] Ibid.

[35] Tormé, Mel, *Traps the Drum Wonder: The Life of Buddy Rich*, Oxford University Press, 1991, p. 75.

[36] Consiglio, Tony, as told to Franz Douskey, *Sinatra and Me: The Very Good Years*, Tantor Media, 2012, p. 23.

[37] Britt, Stan, *sinatra: a celebration*, Schirmir Books, an imprint of Simon & Schuster/Macmillan,

340   *Richard Muti*

1995, p. 49.

[38] Cahn, Sammy, *I Should Care: The Sammy Cahn Story*, Arbor House, 1974, p. 132.

[39] MacLaine, Shirley, *My Lucky Stars: A Hollywood Memoir*, Bantam Books, 1995, p. 73.

[40] Vare, Ethlie Ann, Editor, *Legend: Frank Sinatra and the American Dream*, Boulevard Books, 1995, p. 37, taken from "Star Spangled Octopus," an article by David G. Wittels that first appeared in the *Saturday Evening Post* in August 1946.

[41] This had to have been a happy time in the marital home, however fleeting. Nancy became pregnant and would give birth on January 10, 1944, to the couple's second child, a son — Franklin (after FDR) Wayne Emanuel (after Manie Sacks) Sinatra. In a 2015 HBO television special, Frank Jr. denied that his given name was "Franklin," stating that he has always been "Francis." As with the arrival of Nancy Jr. in 1940, Frank was not around for the birth of his son, but was in Hollywood.

[42] Britt, p. 49.

[43] Levinson, p. 163.

[44] Goddard, Peter, *Frank Sinatra: The Man, The Myth and The Music*, Greywood Publishing Limited, 1973, p. 49. See also, Hodge, Jessica, *Frank Sinatra*, Chartwell Books, inc., 1998, p. 20; and Britt, p. 50. Frank Cooper had recommended to Sinatra that he hire Evans as his publicist. It turned out to be one of the best hires Sinatra ever made. See Levinson, p. 163.

[45] Santopietro, Tom, *Sinatra in Hollywood*, Thomas Dunne Books, St. Martin's Press, 2008, p. 37. See also, Levinson, p. 163. Santopietro gives Jaffe's first name as "Henry," but others, including Sinatra himself, have referred to the attorney as Saul Jaffe, the name used here. There actually were two Jaffes, Saul *and* Henry — brothers and partners in a law practice. Both probably represented Sinatra, at one time or another.

[46] Levinson, p. 164.

[47] Kaplan, James, *Frank: The Voice*, Doubleday, 2010, p. 184.

[48] Mortimer, Lee, "Frank Sinatra Confidential: Gangsters in the Night Clubs," in *The American Mercury*, August 1951, p. 33. The magazine was popular during the 1924-1960 period.

[49] Hamill, p. 139. After Lee Mortimer died, in March, 1963, Sinatra took some measure of revenge. Following a night of drinking, he "found Mortimer's grave and pissed on it" while declaiming, "I'll bury the bastards. I'll bury them all." See Lahr, John, *Sinatra: The Artist and the Man*, Random House, 1997, p. 43.

[50] Dolly Sinatra attended Dorsey's November 1956 wake. Television star Jackie Gleason hosted a memorial show for Dorsey on December 1, 1956, but Sinatra did not participate. Dorsey had been the godfather of then-16-year-old Nancy Jr. See Levinson, 303-304.

[51] Summers and Swan, p. 75.

[52] Ibid., referencing the January 12, 1964, issue of *Parade*.

[53] Levinson, p. 161.

[54] Hamill, p. 141.

[55] Sinatra, p. 127.

[56] Clarke, Donald, *All or Nothing at All: A Life of Sinatra*, Fromm International, 1997, p. 65.

CHAPTER 6

[1] Rooney, Mickey, *Life Is Too Short*, Villard Books, 1991, p. 153. Rooney's description of DeHaven is *delicious*: "blonde, buxom, a fine broth of a girl."

[2] Tormé, Mel, *Traps the Drum Wonder: The Life of Buddy Rich*, Oxford University Press, 1991, p. 64.

3 Levinson, Peter J., *Tommy Dorsey: Livin' in a Great Big Way*, Da Capo Press, 2005, p. 143.

4 Kaplan, James, *Frank: The Voice*, Doubleday, 2010, pp. 120-121.

5 Kelley, Kitty, *His Way: The Unauthorized Biography of Frank Sinatra*, Bantam Books, 1986, p. 56.

6 Zehme, Bill, *The Way You Wear Your Hat: Frank Sinatra and the Lost Art of Livin'*, Harper Collins, 1997, p. 142.

7 Sinatra included both joints in special lyrics for a record he did with Sammy Davis Jr. — "Me and My Shadow." The reference went, "We'll wind up at Jilly's right after Toots Shor." That was the Sinatra habit when in New York City — touching all the nightspots he liked, but "winding up at Jilly's, right after Toots Shor."

8 Falcone, Vincent, and Bob Popyk, *Frankly Just Between Us: My Life Conducting Frank Sinatra's Music*, Hal Leonard Corporation, 2005, p. 79.

9 Hawes, Esme, *The Life and Times of Frank Sinatra*, Chelsea House Publishers, 1998, p. 18.

10 Pugliese, Stanislao G., Editor, *Frank Sinatra: History, Identity, and Italian American Culture*, Palgrave Macmillan, 2004, p. 50, taken from "Frank Sinatra and Presidential Politics," by Michael Nelson.

11 Ibid., p. 51.

12 Freedland, Michael, *All the Way: A Biography of Frank Sinatra, 1915-1998*, St. Martin's Press, 1997, p. 105.

13 Turner, Lana, *Lana: the Lady, the Legend, the Truth*, E.P. Dutton, Inc., 1982, p. 34.

14 Mickey Rooney dated Lana Turner soon after she signed with MGM and described her as having "the nicest set of knockers" he had ever seen. Turner later told Rooney that during their passionate affair, he had gotten her pregnant and that she had obtained an abortion. See Rooney, pp. 98-99.

15 Turner, p. 73.

16 Spada, James, *Peter Lawford: The Man Who Kept the Secrets*, Bantam Books, 1991, pp. 88-89; see also, Romero, Gerry, *Sinatra's Women*, Manor Books, Inc., 1976, p. 78.

17 Turner, pp. 98, 184-185.

18 Summers and Swan, pp. 124-125; see also, Taraborrelli, p. 85.

19 Romero, p. 71.

20 Kelley, p. 116.

21 Kaplan, p. 239.

22 Some accounts say that Frank was in the car, too, teaching Nancy how to drive, but that scenario leaves little room for what followed.

23 Sinatra, Nancy, *Sinatra: An American Legend*, W. Quay Hays, Publisher, 1995, 1998, p. 73. Ms. Sinatra gets the year wrong, reporting this particularly memorable New Year's Eve party as happening on December 31, 1946, instead of 1945. The Maxwell-Sinatra affair was over by the summer of 1946.

24 Sinatra met future Rat Packer Lawford for the first time in 1945, at a Hollywood party in the home of Louis B. Mayer. Ironically, Lawford was there with Marilyn Maxwell, who introduced him to Sinatra. See Spada, p. 110.

25 The only two intervening motion pictures were *The House I Live In*, the 1945 film short, and a 1946 performance of "Ol' Man River" in *Till the Clouds Roll By*, a Jerome Kern biopic.

26 Santopietro, Tom, *Sinatra in Hollywood*, Thomas Dunne Books, 2008, pp. 84-90.

27 Irwin, Lew, *Sinatra: A Life Remembered*, Courage Books, an Imprint of Running Press, 1997, p.

114.

[28] Clarke, Donald, *All or Nothing at All: A Life of Frank Sinatra*, Fromm International, 1997, p. 84.

[29] Taraborrelli, pp. 80-81.

[30] Podell-Raber, Mickey, with Charles Pignon, *The Copa: Jules Podell and the Hottest Club North of Havana*, Collins, an Imprint of Harper Collins Publishers, 2007, p.34.

[31] Sinatra, p. 72-73.

[32] Turner, p. 134.

[33] Freedland, p. 129.

[34] Hamill, Pete, *Why Sinatra Matters*, Little, Brown and Company, 1998, p. 139.

[35] Barbas, Samantha, *The First Lady of Hollywood: A Biography of Louella Parsons*, University of California Press, 2005, p. 269.

[36] Ibid., p. 270.

[37] Kelley, p. 120.

[38] Frost, Jennifer, *Hedda Hopper's Hollywood: Celebrity Gossip and American Conservatism*, New York University Press, 2011, p. 1.

[39] Ibid., pp. 167-168.

[40] Ibid., pp. 175-176.

[41] Ibid., p. 177.

[42] Summers and Swan, p. 124.

[43] As a boxer, Rosenbloom rose to become the Light Heavyweight Champion of the world in the early 1930s. His open-glove style of punching caused famed sports writer Damon Runyon to nickname him "Slapsie Maxie" Rosenbloom, and the name stuck throughout Rosenbloom's boxing and acting careers. For some reason, the nightclub that bore his name changed the spelling to "Slapsy Maxie's," according to archive photos of the establishment, which went out of business after its heyday in the 1940s and '50s.

[44] Barbas, p. 270.

[45] Ibid.

[46] Hamill, p. 147.

CHAPTER 7

[1] Austin, Tom, and Ron Kase, *Bill Miller's Riviera: America's Showplace in Fort Lee, New Jersey*, The History Press, 2011, p. 36. Author Mario Puzo had those same words uttered by Hyman Roth in his novel *The Godfather*. Hyman Roth was the Meyer Lansky-like character in both the novel and the movie of the same name.

[2] Kelly, Robert J., *Encyclopedia of Organized Crime in the United States*, Greenwood Press, 2000, p. 4.

[3] Sifakis, Carl, *The Mafia Encyclopedia, from Accardo to Zwillman*, 3rd. Ed., Facts on File, Inc., 2005, pp. 214-215. See also, Summers, Anthony, and Robbyn Swan, *Sinatra: The Life*, Alfred A. Knopf, 2005, p. 130; Kaplan, James, *Frank: The Voice*, Doubleday, 2010, p. 319; and Levy, Shawn, *Rat Pack Confidential: Frank, Dean, Sammy, Peter, Joey and the Last Great Showbiz Party*, Doubleday, 1998, pp. 127-128.

[4] Brownstein, Ronald, *The Power and the Glitter: The Hollywood-Washington Connection*, Pantheon Books, 1990, p. 163.

[5] Summers and Swan, p. 181.

⁶ Ibid., p. 130.

⁷ Kuntz, Tom, and Phil Kuntz, Editors, *The Sinatra Files: The Life of an American Icon under Government Surveillance*, Three Rivers Press, 2000, pp. 93, 95.

⁸ Summers and Swan, p. 130.

⁹ Ibid., pp. 130-131.

¹⁰ "AKA Frank Sinatra," by Jeff Leen, *The Washington Post Magazine*, March 7, 1999, p. M6. See also, Mortimer, Lee, "Frank Sinatra Confidential: Gangsters in the Night Clubs," in *The American Mercury*, August 1951, p. 33-34; and Kuntz and Kuntz, p. 109.

¹¹ Lee Mortimer met with Clyde Tolson, J. Edgar Hoover's right-hand man at the FBI, on May 13, 1947 — about a month after he suffered a beating by Sinatra outside Ciro's nightclub. He showed Tolson a photo of Sinatra walking from the plane in Havana three months earlier, probably obtained from Ruark, and asked the FBI's help in identifying the man walking next to Sinatra. Tolson did not offer any assistance in that regard, but the person Mortimer inquired about was later identified as Joe Fischetti. See Kuntz and Kuntz, pp. 31-32.

¹² Summers and Swan, p. 131 and note on page 444.

¹³ Ibid.

¹⁴ Ibid.

¹⁵ Ibid.

¹⁶ Sifakis, p. 215.

¹⁷ Jo-Carroll Silvers, the first wife of comedian Phil Silvers, recalled the discussions her husband and Frank Sinatra had about Bugsy Siegel: "They would brag about Bugsy and what he had done and how many people he had killed," she said. "I will always remember the awe Frank had in his voice when he talked about him. He wanted to emulate Bugsy." See Kaplan, p. 258.

¹⁸ Kaplan, pp. 318-319. See also, Sifakis, p. 215.

¹⁹ Levy, p. 129.

²⁰ Hamill, Pete, *Why Sinatra Matters*, Little, Brown and Company, 1998, p. 143.

²¹ *The New York Times* derided Sinatra's performance in *Higher and Higher* (1943), re-titling the picture "Lower and Lower." The paper went on to note that "Frankie is no Gable, or Barrymore." Other reviews were more favorable, and Sinatra's acting would improve. See Frew, Tim, *Sinatra*, élan press, 1998, p. 28.

²² Kelley, Kitty, *His Way: The Unauthorized Biography of Frank Sinatra*, Bantam Books, 1986, p. 105.

²³ Pugliese, Stanislao G., Editor, *Frank Sinatra: History, Identity, and Italian American Culture*, Palgrave Macmillan, 2004, pp. 52-53, taken from "Frank Sinatra and Presidential Politics," by Michael Nelson.

²⁴ Frew, p. 38.

²⁵ Freedland, Michael, *All the Way: A Biography of Frank Sinatra, 1915-1998*, St. Martin's Press, 1997, pp. 134-135.

²⁶ Ibid., p. 135.

²⁷ Kelley, p. 127.

²⁸ Freedland, pp. 136-137.

²⁹ Barbas, Samantha, *The First Lady of Hollywood: A Biography of Louella Parsons*, University of California Press, 2005, p. 270.

³⁰ Kelley, p. 128.

³¹ Irwin, Lew, *Sinatra: A Life Remembered*, Courage Books, an Imprint of Running Press, 1997, p.

44.

[32] Clarke, Donald, *All or Nothing at All: A Life of Sinatra*, Fromm International, 1997, p. 95.

[33] Irwin, p. 114.

[34] Freedland, p. 139.

[35] Sinatra, Nancy, *Sinatra: An American Legend*, W. Quay Hays, Publisher, 1995, 1998, p. 81. This would be Sinatra's second stint on the long-running radio show.

[36] Ibid., p. 234.

[37] Santopietro, Tom, *Sinatra in Hollywood*, Thomas Dunne Books, 2008, pp. 92-93.

[38] Quirk, Lawrence J. and William Schoell, *The Rat Pack: The Hey-Hey Days of Frank and the Boys*, Taylor Publishing Company, 1998, p. 36.

[39] Freedland, p. 144.

[40] Hamill, Pete, *Why Sinatra Matters*, Little, Brown and Company, 1995, p. 51.

[41] Hoboken mayoral history courtesy of Jerry Lore, Deputy City Clerk, City of Hoboken. Including DeSapio, eight of the next 11 Hoboken mayors would be of Italian descent. Under that city's charter, non-partisan local elections take place in May, not in November.

[42] De Palma, Jr., Anthony, "Stranger in the Night: The story of Sinatra and Hoboken and what went wrong," *New Jersey Monthly*, February 1982, pp. 81-82.

[43] Irwin, p. 114.

[44] Hoboken City Clerk James Farina produced a replica of the Sinatra "Key to the City," during an interview with the author, on April 10, 2015.

[45] De Palma, Jr., p. 82.

[46] Summers, Anthony, and Robbyn Swan, *Sinatra: The Life*, Alfred A. Knopf, 2005, p. 146; also, Freedland, p. 141.

[47] De Palma, Jr. p. 82.

[48] Turner, Lana, *Lana: the Lady, the Legend, the Truth*, E.P. Dutton, Inc., 1982, pp. 120-121.

[49] Irwin, p. 39.

[50] Summers and Swan, p. 116.

[51] Clarke, pp. 103-104.

[52] There was one technological development at Columbia Records in mid-1948 that would have tremendous ramifications for Sinatra's recording career. An engineer with that company invented the "LP" — a "plastic, microgroove long-playing record," paving the way for Sinatra's huge album success at Capitol Records. See Clarke, p. 102.

[53] Sinatra, p. 85.

CHAPTER 8

[1] It is impossible to fix the date of this shocking episode in the Sinatra-Gardner affair with complete accuracy. The principal players are dead, of course, and all records have been destroyed. Biographers of both Sinatra and Gardner are all over the place when it comes to their reporting. Kitty Kelley didn't even try to come up with a date; she merely described the events as happening "one night." Kelley, Kitty, *His Way: The Unauthorized Biography of Frank Sinatra*, Bantam Books, 1986, p. 133. Summers and Swan said it happened "early in the romance," again with no attempt to date it more precisely than that — perhaps a wise move. Summers, Anthony, and Robbyn Swan, *Sinatra: The Life*, Alfred A. Knopf, 2005, p. 154. Taraborrelli said the singular event happened two weeks after the December 8, 1949, premiere of the Broadway musical *Gentlemen Prefer Blondes*, which would have put it much later in the affair. Taraborrelli, J. Randy,

Sinatra: Behind the Legend, Carol Publishing Group, 1997, pp. 105-106. James Kaplan places the event in the fall of 1948, too early by a year. Kaplan, pp. 369-376. Almost all accounts confirm that it happened *after* MGM assembled its stars for the group photo on the studio's 25th anniversary. That photo was taken in January 1949. In her autobiography, Ava Gardner leaves out any account of the more reckless aspects of the incident (she would confirm those details in a later, as-told-to book), but places it "sometime early in 1949." Gardner, Ava, *Ava: My Story*, Bantam Books, 1990, p. 124. Nancy Sinatra establishes the date as "February 1949." Sinatra, Nancy, *Frank Sinatra: An American Legend*, W. Quay Hays, Publisher, 1995, 1998, p. 87. Gardner biographer Lee Server called the time frame as "Autumn 1949." Server, Lee, *Ava Gardner: "Love Is Nothing,"* St. Martin's Press, 2006, pp. 174-176. Given that these two celebrities were on the radar screen of every gossip columnist and freelance photographer in the country, there would have been more public accounts of a romance between the two if, indeed, they were an item very much prior to the summer of 1949. The reasonable approach, in this author's opinion, is to place the occurrence "sometime during the spring or summer of 1949."

[2] Server, Lee, *Ava Gardner: "Love Is Nothing,"* St. Martin's Press, 2006, p. 176.

[3] Ibid., pp. 64-71.

[4] Ibid., p. 72.

[5] Gardner, Ava, *Ava: My Story*, Bantam Books, 1990, p. 122.

[6] Evans, Peter, and Ava Gardner, *Ava Gardner: The Secret Conversations*, Simon & Schuster, 2013, p. 223.

[7] Ibid.

[8] Server, p. 110.

[9] Gardner, p. 80.

[10] Server, *passim*.

[11] Ibid., p. 145.

[12] Ibid., p. 174.

[13] Evans, p. 224.

[14] Kelley, Kitty, *His Way: The Unauthorized Biography of Frank Sinatra*, Bantam Books, 1986, p. 134.

[15] Lewis, Jerry, and James Kaplan, *Dean and Me (A Love Story)*, Doubleday, 2005, p. 69.

[16] Hawes, Esme, *The Life and Times of Frank Sinatra*, Chelsea House Publishers, 1998, pp. 23-25. See also, Kelley, pp. 134-135.

[17] Kelley, p. 135.

[18] Gardner, p. 122.

[19] According to one source, "[Ava] was as close to being a nymphomaniac as a Hollywood star could be in the early fifties without losing her contract. Her flings with various men were the subject of constant Hollywood gossip." See Freedland, Michael, *All the Way: A Biography of Frank Sinatra, 1915-1998*, St. Martin's Press, 1997, p. 165.

[20] Wayne, Jane Ellen, *Ava's Men: The Private Life of Ava Gardner*, St. Martin's Press, 1990, p. 109.

[21] Gardner, p. 123.

[22] Ibid., p. 124.

[23] Sinatra valet George Jacobs said that singing was Sinatra's career and what concerned him most. "Movies . . . were a crapshoot out of his control." Jacobs, George, and William Stadiem, *Mr. S: My Life with Frank Sinatra*, Harper Entertainment, 2003, p. 57.

[24] Freedland, p. 150.

25 Ibid., p. 151.

26 Freedland, p. 161.

27 Santopietro, Tom, *Sinatra in Hollywood*, Thomas Dunne Books, St. Martin's Press, 2008, p. 101.

28 Ibid., p. 105.

29 Ibid., p. 106.

30 Ibid., p. 112.

31 Sinatra, p. 95.

32 Later in his career, when he was more comfortable with his status, Sinatra was generous about billing, often giving a less commanding actor or actress an equal spot in a movie's credits.

33 Freedland, p. 169.

34 Clarke, pp. 98-99.

35 Server, pp. 182-183.

36 Gardner, pp. 126-127.

37 Kelley, p. 143.

38 Wayne, p. 111.

39 Gardner, p. 127.

CHAPTER 9

1 Podell-Raber, Mickey, with Charles Pignon, *The Copa: Jules Podell and the Hottest Club North of Havana*, Collins, an imprint of Harper Collins Publishers, 2007, pp. 31, 34.

2 Frank did play the straight man for Phil Silvers at the Copa in September 1946, but that was an unannounced one-night gig to help out a friend.

3 Kelley, Kitty, *His Way: The Unauthorized Biography of Frank Sinatra*, Bantam Books, 1986, p. 146.

4 Taraborrelli, J. Randy, *Sinatra: Behind the Legend*, A Birch Lane Press Book, published by Carol Publishing Group, 1997, pp. 114-115.

5 Ibid., p. 115.

6 Ibid.

7 Ibid., p. 117.

8 Kaplan, James, *Frank: The Voice*, Doubleday, 2010, p. 411.

9 Taraborrelli, p. 116.

10 Ibid., pp. 115-116.

11 Kelley, pp. 146-147; see also, Kaplan, p. 412.

12 Kelley, p. 147. Ava Gardner denied being upset over this song's place in Frank's repertoire. "I always thought it was a beautiful song," Ava would later write, "and contrary to what everyone seems to believe, it was never the reason for a single quarrel between us. Unfortunately, we never had any trouble inventing other reasons to be at each other's throats." See Gardner, Ava, *Ava: My Story*, Bantam Books, 1990, p. 128.

13 Taraborrelli, p. 116.

14 Kelley, p. 147; see also, Kaplan, p. 413.

15 Taraborrelli, pp. 116-117.

16 Kelley, p. 147. As is the case for much of this history, we often do not know the dates of various occurrences, because no one bothered to note them as they were happening, preferring in many

cases to blur the facts or deny them entirely. Kelley's placement of this particular incident — 11 days after Sinatra's opening night at the Copa, or April 7, 1950 — is as good as any.

[17] Gardner, p. 129.

[18] Hank Sanicola had the title of Frank's personal manager, but he was really a glorified bodyguard, according to Tony Consiglio, Sinatra's road valet for more than 30 years, off and on. See Consiglio, Tony, as told to Franz Douskey, *Sinatra and Me: The Very Good Years*, Tantor Media, Inc., 2012, p. 112.

[19] Gardner, p. 130.

[20] Ibid., p. 131.

[21] Ibid.

[22] Taraborrelli, p. 119.

[23] Sebastian Junger's 1997 bestseller, *The Perfect Storm*, and the motion picture of the same name portrayed a scenario in which separate storms over the North Atlantic merged to create a phenomenon — the "perfect storm" — whose destructive magnitude exceeded the sum of its parts. The term has entered colloquial usage to describe overlapping forces that bring about a disastrous effect, otherwise unachievable by any single one of them alone.

[24] Freedland, Michael, *All the Way: A Biography of Frank Sinatra, 1915-1998*, St. Martin's Press, 1997, p. 176.

[25] Singer Paul Anka wrote the lyrics to "My Way" specifically for Frank Sinatra.

[26] Hedda Hopper's February 15 *Los Angeles Times* column carried the headline "Frank Sinatra's wife decides on separation." Kaplan, p. 407. See also, Taraborrelli, p. 113.

[27] Summers, Anthony, and Robbyn Swan, *Sinatra: The Life*, Alfred A. Knopf, 2005, p. 470n.

[28] Clarke, Donald, *All or Nothing at All: A Life of Frank Sinatra*, Fromm International, 1997, pp. 106-107.

[29] Ibid., p. 108.

[30] Kelley, pp. 154-155.

[31] Clarke, pp. 110-111.

[32] Irwin, Lew, *Sinatra: A Life Remembered*, Courage Books, an imprint of Running Press, 1997, pp. 114-115.

[33] Yagoda, Ben, *The B-Side: The Death of Tin Pan Alley and the Rebirth of the Great American Song*, Riverhead Books, 2015, p. 25.

[34] Kelley, p. 154.

[35] Kaplan, pp. 425-426.

[36] Taraborrelli, p. 107.

[37] McNally, Karen, *When Frankie Went to Hollywood: Frank Sinatra and the American Male Identity*, University of Illinois Press, 2008, p. 101.

[38] Kelley, pp. 150-151.

[39] Gardner, pp. 137-138.

[40] Server, Lee, *Ava Gardner: "Love is Nothing,"* St. Martin's Press, 2006, p. 203.

[41] Kaplan, pp. 428-429, 742n. Kelley dates this occurrence as April 26 (see Kelley, p. 151), but Kaplan's timing seems to be more accurate. He quotes an *International News Service* report of May 4, 1950, as substantiation.

[42] Kelley, p. 151.

[43] Kaplan, pp. 428-429.

[44] Kaplan, p. 429.

[45] If Fischetti had anything to do with the acquisition of the bracelet, this might not have been the last time Sinatra used his underworld contacts to supply jewelry. Photographer John Dominis spent a year with Sinatra (1964-1965) taking pictures for a *Life* magazine spread in honor of Frank's 50th birthday. Sinatra gave him unfettered access, but on one occasion, Dominis wisely decided not to take a photo. Here is how he described what took place in a Florida hotel room that day. "Some guys came in with a string bag full of jewels they emptied on the bed, pearls and diamonds, a big pile. Frank picked out two or three diamonds, a necklace, and a brooch. The guys put the rest back in the bag and left. I didn't know if the jewels were hot, or if Frank was going to pay for them, or if it was just a friendly gesture. I decided not to ask and not to shoot." See Dominis, John, and Richard B. Stolley, *Sinatra: An Intimate Portrait of a Very Good Year*, Stewart, Tambori & Chang, 2002, p. 6.

[46] Server, p. 206.

[47] Taraborrelli, pp. 122-123.

[48] Ibid., p. 123.

[49] Ibid., p. 124.

CHAPTER 10

[1] Kaplan, James, *Frank: The Voice*, Doubleday, 2010, pp. 435-436.

[2] Sinatra, Nancy, *Frank Sinatra: An American Legend*, W. Quay Hays, Publisher, 1995, 1998, p. 97.

[3] Kaplan, p. 438, quoting Peter Richmond in his biography of Peggy Lee, Sinatra's fellow guest on the show.

[4] Ibid., p. 439.

[5] Ibid., pp. 439-440.

[6] Kelley, Kitty, *His Way: The Unauthorized Biography of Frank Sinatra*, Bantam Books, 1986, p. 155. See also, Kaplan, p. 440, although Kaplan says the CBS deal was for five years, not three. It seems unlikely that CBS would commit itself to five years, given Sinatra's standing at the time. Neither author gave sourcing for this information.

[7] While Frank Sinatra's career was taking a momentary turn for the better, the fortunes of the United States and the world, for that matter, were not. Communist North Korea, with the approval of its patron, the Soviet Union, sent its troops and tanks rushing through the 38th Parallel and into South Korea, overwhelming its less militaristic neighbor. In what would be termed a "Police Action," the Truman administration got United Nations approval to oppose North Korea's aggression — a move that would result in a military draw three years later, at a cost of 36,500 American lives and more than 100,000 wounded.

[8] Kaplan, p. 441.

[9] Ibid.

[10] Taraborrelli, J. Randy, *Sinatra: Behind the Legend*, A Birch Lane Press Book, published by Carol Publishing Group, 1997, p. 125.

[11] Kaplan, pp. 441-442.

[12] Gardner, Ava, *Ava: My Story*, Bantam Books, 1990, p. 140.

[13] Ibid., p. 142.

[14] Consiglio, Tony, as told to Franz Douskey, *Sinatra and Me: The Very Good Years*, Tantor Media, Inc., 2012, p. 245.

[15] Taraborrelli, p. 125.

[16] Wayne, Jane Ellen, *Ava's Men: The Private Life of Ava Gardner,* St. Martin's Press, 1990, p. 125.

[17] Taraborrelli, pp. 125-126.

[18] Server, Lee, *Ava Gardner: "Love is Nothing,"* St. Martin's Press, 2006, p. 217. Studio executives would later hire singer Annette Warren to dub Gardner's two songs, not willing to take a chance on their star's own voice. Through a series of legal advisories, they were stuck, however, when it came to the original cast album. Because Gardner's image was on the album cover, they had to use her voice on the record inside. See Gardner, p. 144.

[19] Kelley, p. 155. Kitty Kelley interviewed Irving Mansfield on seven separate occasions in 1983 and 1984.

[20] Ibid., pp. 155-156. Barton and Sanicola were partners with Sinatra in a music publishing company. Silvani, an ex-boxing manager, was principally a bodyguard and go-fer for the singer.

[21] Dominis, John, and Richard B. Stolley, *Sinatra: An Intimate Portrait of a Very Good Year,* Stewart, Tabori & Chang, 2002, p. 114.

[22] Fuchs, Jeanne, and Ruth Prigozy, Editors, *Frank Sinatra: the Man, the Music, the Legend,* University of Rochester Press/Hofstra University, 2007, p. 2

[23] Kelley, p. 156.

[24] Ibid., p. 157.

[25] Summers, Anthony, and Robbyn Swan, *Sinatra: The Life,* Alfred A. Knopf, 2005, p. 158.

[26] Server, pp. 215-216.

[27] Ibid.

[28] Kefauver would ride the fame he garnered as chair of this special committee to the Democratic nomination for vice president in 1956, defeating an up-and-coming young senator from Massachusetts, John F. Kennedy, for the right to be Adlai Stevenson's running mate. A graduate of Yale Law School, Kefauver loved to show off his back-home, backwoods credentials by sporting a coonskin cap, à la Davy Crockett, then being featured in a popular, Disney-produced television show.

[29] http://www.senate.gov/artandhistory/history/common/investigations/Kefauver.htm; see also, Kaplan, p.459.

[30] Kelley, p. 159.

CHAPTER 11

[1] Summers, Anthony, and Robbyn Swan, *Sinatra: The Life,* Alfred A. Knopf, 2005, p. 133.

[2] Obituary of Joseph L. Nellis, *The Washington Post,* July 16, 2004.

[3] Kelley, Kitty, *His Way: The Unauthorized Biography of Frank Sinatra,* Bantam Books, 1986, pp. 159-160. Kelley interviewed Joseph L. Nellis, now deceased, on three different occasions in February 1984. See Kelly, p. 525n. The photos would later disappear from Sinatra's government file. See Summers, Anthony, and Robbyn Swan, p. 445n.

[4] Kaplan, James, *Frank: The Voice,* Doubleday, 2010, p. 460.

[5] Irwin, Lew, *Sinatra: A Life Remembered,* Courage Books, an imprint of Running Press, 1997, p. 115; see also, Sinatra, Nancy, *Frank Sinatra: An American Legend,* W. Quay Hays, Publisher, 1995, 1998, p. 98.

[6] Summers and Swan, p. 159; see also, Kaplan, p. 458. Nancy Sinatra, in her 1995 biography of her father, places this incident in the summer of 1952, but Summers and Swan, as well as Kaplan, seem to be more reliable in fixing the time frame. Nancy Sinatra also reported the Nellis interview of her father as having occurred in December 1950, rather than the actual date, March 1, 1951. See Sinatra, pp. 97, 105. Kelley doesn't mention the incident at all.

7 Kelley, p. 160.

8 Kaplan, p. 462.

9 Ibid. Kaplan quotes from the transcript of Sinatra's sworn testimony to Nellis.

10 Ibid.

11 Ibid.

12 Ibid., pp. 462-463.

13 Frank did indeed have a planned joint vacation in Mexico with Nancy — a reconciliation attempt after the Marilyn Maxwell/Lana Turner affairs. It was in Mexico that Nancy told him she had aborted his child, out of frustration over the status of their marriage.

14 Kaplan, p. 463.

15 Mortimer, Lee, "Frank Sinatra Confidential: Gangsters in the Night Clubs," *The American Mercury*, August 1951, p. 33-34.

16 Ibid., p. 34.

17 Kelley, p. 160.

18 Kaplan, pp. 463-464.

19 Ibid., p. 464.

20 Kelley, p. 161; see also, Kaplan, p. 464.

21 Summers and Swan, p. 183.

22 Kaplan, pp. 464-465; see also, Kelley, pp. 161-162.

23 Summers and Swan, p. 183.

24 Kaplan, pp. 465-466; see also, Kelley, pp. 162-163.

25 Kaplan, p. 468.

26 Irwin, p. 115.

27 Kaplan, p. 469.

28 Irwin, p. 115.

29 Clarke, Donald, *All or Nothing at All: A Life of Frank Sinatra*, Fromm International, 1997, p. 112.

30 Kaplan, p. 471.

31 Zehme, Bill, *The Way You Wear Your Hat: Frank Sinatra and the Lost Art of Livin'*, Harper Collins, 1997, pp. 161-162.

CHAPTER 12

1 Gardner, Ava, *Ava: My Story*, Bantam Books, 1990, p. 33.

2 Ibid., p. 28.

3 Ibid., pp. 32-33.

4 Ibid., pp. 33-34.

5 Gardner, p. 192.

6 Freedland, Michael, *All the Way: A Biography of Frank Sinatra, 1915-1998*, St. Martin's Press, 1997, p. 165.

7 Jacobs, George, and William Stadiem, *Mr. S: My Life with Frank Sinatra*, Harper Entertainment, 2003, *passim*; Frew, Tim, *Sinatra*, élan press, 1998, pp. 56, 64; Quirk, Lawrence J., and William Schoell, *The Rat Pack: The Hey-Hey Days of Frank and the Boys*, Taylor Publishing

Company, 1998, p. 166; Romero, Gerry, *Sinatra's Women*, Manor Books, Inc., *passim*; Consiglio, Tony, as told to Franz Douskey, *Sinatra and Me: The Very Good Years*, Tantor Media, Inc., 2012, *passim*; Zehme, Bill, *The Way You Wear Your Hat: Frank Sinatra and the Lost Art of Livin'*, Harper Collins, 1997, p. 147; Lahr, John, *Sinatra: The Artist and the Man*, Random House, 1997, pp. 74-75; Wayne, Jane Ellen, *Ava's Men: The Private Life of Ava Gardner*, St. Martin's Press, 1990, p. 173; Wilson, Earl, *Sinatra: An Unauthorized Biography*, Macmillan Publishing Co., Inc., 1976, p. 141.

[8] Jacobs and Stadiem, p. 67.

[9] Taraborrelli, J. Randy, *Sinatra: Behind the Legend*, A Birch Lane Press Book, published by Carol Publishing Group, 1997, p. 142.

[10] Kaplan, James, *Frank: The Voice*, Doubleday, 2010, p. 397.

[11] MacLaine, Shirley, *My Lucky Stars: A Hollywood Memoir*, Bantam Books, 1995, p. 85.

[12] Evans, Peter, and Ava Gardner, *Ava Gardner: The Secret Conversations*, Simon & Schuster, 2013, p. 5.

[13] Ibid. Ava's resolve in disregarding Sinatra's feelings about the project would eventually weaken. "Frank's not going to be happy when he finds out I'm writing a fucking book," she told Evans. See p. 175. Sinatra had helped her financially when she had her stroke. Ultimately, Sinatra did kill Gardner's collaboration with Evans on the book, which would be published only after Gardner, Sinatra, and Evans had all died.

[14] Ibid., p. 15.

[15] Ibid., p. 16. Viertel suggested to Evans that Gardner would try to seduce him during the collaboration, despite her stroke and age. He was right. When Evans showed up at her London apartment for the first meeting, she answered the door "wearing nothing but an angry scowl and a towel." Later, she told Evans she just wanted to see his reaction. See Evans and Gardner, p. 18.

[16] Server, Lee, *Ava Gardner: "Love is Nothing,"* St. Martin's Press, 2006, pp. 222-225.

[17] Ibid., p. 225.

[18] Ibid.

[19] Ibid.

[20] Ibid.

[21] Clarke, Donald, *All or Nothing at All: A Life of Frank Sinatra*, Fromm International, 1997, pp. 100-101.

[22] Santopietro, p. 25.

[23] Clarke, pp. 112-113.

[24] Frost, Jennifer, *Hedda Hopper's Hollywood: Celebrity Gossip and American Conservatism*, New York University Press, 2011, p. 178.

[25] Kaplan, p. 479.

[26] Ibid.

[27] "The parallel is inescapable," remarked the *Los Angeles Times* when the film premiered. See Kelley, p. 165.

[28] Santopietro, p. 124.

[29] Ibid., pp. 124-128.

[30] Kelley, Kitty, *His Way: The Unauthorized Biography of Frank Sinatra*, Bantam Books, 1986, p. 165.

[31] Kaplan, pp. 482-483.

[32] It was the club where Dean Martin and Jerry Lewis first teamed up — they were billed as sepa-

rate acts, but started invading each other's space during a night's show, to the audience's great delight. At the end of the run, they became a comedy duo, scoring big in the movies and on the nightclub circuit until their split-up.

[33] Demaris, Ovid, *The Boardwalk Jungle: How greed, corruption, and the Mafia turned Atlantic City into . . .*, Bantam Books, 1986, p. 32. When D'Amato died, in June 1984, Frank Sinatra was the only celebrity, out of the scores who had performed at the 500 Club, to show up at his funeral. See Demaris, p. 357.

[34] McNally, Karen, *When Frankie Went to Hollywood: Frank Sinatra and the American Male Identity*, University of Illinois Press, 2008, p. 43.

[35] Ibid., quoting from *The Last Good Time*, by Jonathan Van Meter.

[36] Gardner, p. 156.

[37] Ibid., p. 157. When the press got hold of the story, Frank attributed the incident to "a bellyache." He'd taken "two sleeping pills," he said, and had "two or three brandies." The combination made him sick, but a doctor was called and nothing else happened. "That was all there was to it," he said, "honest." See Kaplan, p. 491.

[38] Evans and Gardner, p. 179.

[39] Composer Jimmy Van Heusen was in attendance for the Desert Inn engagement, to lend moral support to his pal Sinatra. While there in Vegas, Van Heusen heard pianist Bill Miller playing another room and introduced himself. The two hit it off. Van Heusen knew that Sinatra was looking for a regular pianist. He brought Miller to Sinatra's attention, and Miller and Sinatra began a decades-long association. See Kaplan, pp. 494-495.

[40] Sifakis, Carl, *The Mafia Encyclopedia: From Accardo to Zwillman*, 3rd Ed., 2005, p. 132. See also, Kelly, Robert J., *Encyclopedia of Organized Crime in the United States*, Greenwood Press, 2000, p. 187.

[41] Levy, Shawn, *Rat Pack Confidential: Frank, Dean, Sammy, Peter, Joey and the Last Great Showbiz Party*, Doubleday, 1998, pp. 87, 89, 91. The added 7 percent was actually a gift from Genovese crime family member Vincent "Jimmy Blue Eyes" Alo.

[42] Sifakis, p. 256.

[43] Gardner, p. 159.

[44] Ibid., pp. 160-161.

[45] Server, p. 238.

[46] As a consequence of the movie's dismal reception, Universal International dropped its option to use Sinatra in a second film, and he was without a movie studio once again.

[47] Santopietro, p. 129.

[48] Server, pp. 241-242; see also, Santopietro, p. 129.

[49] Santopietro, p. 129.

[50] Ibid.

[51] Ibid.

[52] Ibid.

CHAPTER 13

[1] Hamill, Pete, *Why Sinatra Matters*, Little, Brown and Company, 1998, p. 161.

[2] Server, Lee, *Ava Gardner: "Love is Nothing,"* St. Martin's Press, 2006, p. 242. See also, Kaplan, James, *Frank: The Voice*, Doubleday, 2010, p. 530.

[3] Server, pp. 242-243.

[4] Kelley, Kitty, *His Way: The Unauthorized Biography of Frank Sinatra*, Bantam Books, 1986, p. 176.

[5] Kaplan, pp. 527-528.

[6] Server, p. 245.

[7] Irwin, Lew, *Sinatra: A Life Remembered*, Courage Books, an imprint of Running Press, 1997, p. 115.

[8] Sinatra, Nancy, *Frank Sinatra: An American Legend*, W. Quay Hays, Publisher, 1995, 1998, p. 104.

[9] Singer Paul Anka wrote the lyrics for "My Way" specifically with Frank Sinatra in mind.

[10] Kelley, p. 178.

[11] Ibid.

[12] Ibid.

[13] Ibid., pp. 178-179.

[14] Ibid., p. 179.

[15] Sinatra, p. 104.

[16] Server, p. 243.

[17] Farrow, Mia, *What Falls Away: A Memoir*, Nan A. Talese, Doubleday, 1997, p. 27.

[18] Turner and Gardner had remained friends, despite their common interest in Sinatra, albeit at different times. When Ava first took up with Frank, a couple of years after the Turner-Sinatra affair had ended, Lana advised her to not get involved with him, advice that Ava ignored.

[19] Server, pp. 245-246.

[20] This "Bill Miller" is a different person from the "Bill Miller" who became Frank's longtime pianist.

[21] Austin Tom, and Ron Kase, *Bill Miller's Riviera: America's Showplace in Fort Lee, New Jersey*, The History Press, 2011, p. 36. Austin and Kase's book provides an outstanding history of the club, where Austin's father worked as a security guard.

[22] Austin and Kase, *passim*. Also, interview with Tom Meyers of the Fort Lee Historical Society on May 5, 2015.

[23] Ibid., p. 66.

[24] Lewis, Jerry, and James Kaplan, *Dean and Me (A Love Story)*, Doubleday, 2005, p. 150; see also, Austin and Kase, p. 27.

[25] Ibid., p. 113.

[26] Orifice, Irene Bruno, interview at the Fort Lee Museum, December 6, 2013; also, interview with the author, on August 21, 2015.

[27] Summers, Anthony, and Robbyn Swan, *Sinatra: The Life*, Alfred A. Knopf, 2005, p. 49.

[28] Kaplan, p. 534.

[29] Kelley, pp. 180-181.

[30] Kaplan, pp. 535-536. Days later, when a Columbia executive asked Mitch Miller how Frank was doing, Miller replied, "Fuck him. He's a has-been." See Summers and Swan, p. 164.

[31] Kaplan, p. 538.

[32] Server, p. 247.

[33] Turner, Lana, *Lana: the Lady, the Legend, the Truth*, E.P. Dutton, Inc., 1982, p. 165.

[34] Server, p. 247. In her 1990 memoir, Ava explained that she was uncomfortable being seen in the

nude, even by her lovers. That was pure baloney. She had willingly done a nude swimming scene in *Pandora and the Flying Dutchman*, after the director offered to use a body double, and would also parade around nude on the African set of *Mogambo*, in front of the native workers, on the way to her bath.

[35] Wayne, Jane Ellen, *Lana: The Life and Loves of Lana Turner*, St. Martin's Press, 1995, p. 95.

[36] Turner, pp. 166-167.

[37] Server, p. 248.

[38] Ibid.

[39] Kelley, pp. 183-184; see also, Server, pp. 248-249.

[40] Taraborrelli, J. Randy, *Sinatra: Behind the Legend*, A Birch Lane Press Book, Carol Publishing Group, 1997, p. 149.

[41] Israel, Lee, *Kilgallen: A Biography of Dorothy Kilgallen*, Delacorte Press, 1979, p. 221.

[42] Taraborrelli, p. 149.

[43] Kelley, p. 184.

[44] Thomas, Bob, *King Cohn: The Life and Times of Harry Cohn*, G.P. Putnam & Sons, 1967, p. 315.

[45] Wayne, p. 153.

[46] Kelley, p. 187.

CHAPTER 14

[1] Day, Doris, and A.E. Hotchner, *Doris Day: Her Own Story*, William Morrow and Company, 1975, pp. 146-147.

[2] Thomas, Bob, *King Cohn: The Life and Times of Harry Cohn*, G.P. Putnam & Sons, 1967, pp. 305-306.

[3] Kelley, Kitty, *His Way: The Unauthorized Biography of Frank Sinatra*, Bantam Books, 1986, p. 187.

[4] Ibid., pp. 187-188.

[5] Ibid., p. 188.

[6] Ibid.

[7] Ibid.

[8] Ibid.

[9] Taraborrelli, J. Randy, *Sinatra: Behind the Legend*, A Birch Lane Press Book, Carol Publishing Group, 1997, p. 146.

[10] Kelley, p. 185.

[11] Ibid.

[12] Ibid., pp. 185-186.

[13] Ibid., pp. 188-189.

[14] Gardner, Ava, *Ava: My Story*, Bantam Books, 1990, pp. 187-188; see also, Kaplan, James, *Frank: The Voice*, Doubleday, 2010, pp. 541-542.

[15] Kelley, p. 190.

[16] Server, Lee, *Ava Gardner: "Love is Nothing,"* St. Martin's Press, 2006, p. 253.

[17] Summers, Anthony, and Robbyn Swan, *Sinatra: The Life*, Alfred A. Knopf, 2005, pp. 171-172.

[18] Kelly, soon to be known as Princess Grace of Monaco, had started what would turn into a habit:

having affairs with her leading men. Gable was second in that series of conquests, after Gary Cooper in *High Noon.*

[19] Wayne, Jane Ellen, *Ava's Men: The Private Life of Ava Gardner*, St. Martin's Press, 1990, p. 156.

[20] Server, p. 256.

[21] Gardner, pp. 184-185.

[22] Wayne, p. 157.

[23] Ibid., pp. 185-186.

[24] Kelley, p. 191.

[25] Ibid.

[26] Ibid.

[27] Ibid.

[28] Gardner, p. 186.

[29] Kelley, p. 192.

[30] Ibid., p. 193.

[31] Ibid.

[32] Summers and Swan, p. 46.

[33] Sifakis, Carl, *The Mafia Encyclopedia: From Accardo to Zwillman*, 3rd Ed., Facts on File, Inc., 2005, p. 392.

[34] Thomas, Bob, *King Cohn: The Life and Times of Harry Cohn*, G.P. Putnam & Sons, 1967, p. 198; see also, Dick, Bernard F., *The Merchant Prince of Poverty Row: Harry Cohn of Columbia Pictures*, The University Press of Kentucky, 1993, p. 54. In Thomas's book, Johnny Roselli is referred to by a pseudonym, Charlie Lombard. Dick's book makes that connection.

[35] Kelley, pp. 194-195.

CHAPTER 15

[1] Kelley, Kitty, *His Way: The Unauthorized Biography of Frank Sinatra*, Bantam Books, 1986, p. 197.

[2] Kaplan, James, *Frank: The Voice*, Doubleday, 2010, pp. 585-586.

[3] Wayne, Jane Ellen, *Ava's Men: The Private Life of Ava Gardner*, St. Martin's Press, 1990, p. 163.

[4] Gardner, Ava, *Ava: My Story*, Bantam Books, 1990, p. 187.

[5] Kelley, p. 197.

[6] Ibid.

[7] Kaplan, p. 590.

[8] Santopietro, Tom, *Sinatra in Hollywood*, Thomas Dunne Books, 2008, p. 136.

[9] Ibid., pp. 137-138.

[10] Kelley, p. 200.

[11] Ibid., p. 201.

[12] Kaplan, p. 600.

[13] Irwin, Lew, *Sinatra: A Life Remembered*, Courage Books, an imprint of Running Press, 1997, p. 115.

[14] Kaplan, pp. 616, 620.

[15] Server, Lee, *Ava Gardner: "Love is Nothing,"* St. Martin's Press, 2006, pp. 263-264.

[16] "That's Life," with words and music by Kelly Gordon and Dean Kay, became a Top 5 hit in 1966.

[17] Kaplan, p. 625.

[18] Ibid., pp. 625-626. The term "paparazzi" would not come into popular use for another decade, but it accurately describes the feeding frenzy the press engaged in with celebrities, in Italy and elsewhere.

[19] Evans, Peter, and Ava Gardner, *Ava Gardner: The Secret Conversations*, Simon & Schuster, 2014, p. 176.

[20] Kelley, p. 203; see also, Kaplan, pp. 627-628.

[21] Ibid.

[22] Kaplan, p. 633.

[23] Santopietro, p. 140.

[24] "It stinks," she told a reporter, when asked for her assessment of the picture.

[25] Wayne, p. 160.

[26] Server, p. 265.

[27] Wayne, p. 166.

[28] Archived interview with Lou Gallo, a Riviera waiter who was there that night. Courtesy of the Fort Lee Museum.

[29] Wayne, p. 167.

[30] Ibid.

[31] Server, pp. 266-267.

[32] Wayne, p. 168.

[33] Server, p. 268.

[34] Gardner, p. 191.

[35] Zehme, Bill, *The Way You Wear Your Hat: Frank Sinatra and the Lost Art of Livin'*, Harper Collins, 1997, p. 160.

[36] Spada, James, *Peter Lawford: The Man Who Kept the Secrets*, Bantam Books, 1991, pp. 154-155.

[37] Ibid., p. 155.

[38] Irwin, p. 115.

[39] Yagoda, Ben, *The B-Side: The Death of Tin Pan Alley and the Rebirth of the Great American Song*, Riverhead Books, 2015, p. 228.

[40] Santopietro, Tom, *Sinatra in Hollywood*, Thomas Dunne Books/St. Martin's Press, 2008, p. 118.

[41] Kelley, p. 207.

[42] Server, p. 273.

[43] Kelley, p. 208.

[44] Ibid.

[45] Ibid.

[46] Irwin, p. 115.

[47] Clarke, Donald, *All or Nothing at All: A Life of Frank Sinatra*, Fromm International, 1997, p. 125.

[48] Taraborrelli, J. Randy, *Sinatra: Behind the Legend*, A Birch Lane Press Book, Carol Publishing Group, 1997, p. 173.

CHAPTER 16

1 Zehme, Bill, *The Way You Wear Your Hat: Frank Sinatra and the Lost Art of Livin'*, Harper Collins, 1997, p. 185.

2 Ibid.

3 Ava Gardner had also been nominated for an Oscar — for Best Actress in a Leading Role — for her performance in *Mogambo*. She lost to Audrey Hepburn, in *Roman Holiday*. Ava did not attend the ceremonies.

4 Zehme, p. 185.

5 Wayne, Jane Ellen, *Ava's Men: The Private Life of Ava Gardner*, St. Martin's Press, 1990, p. 160.

6 http://www.hollywoodreporter.com/news/throwback-thursday-errol-flynn-stood-699299.

7 Finstad, Suzanne, *Natasha: The Biography of Natalie Wood*, Harmony Books, 2001, p. 121.

8 Jacobs, George, and William Stadiem, *Mr. S: My Life with Frank Sinatra*, Harper Entertainment, 2003, p. 70.

9 Most studios ran academic exercises for their child actors, to comply with state law more than anything else.

10 Jacobs and Stadiem, p. 70.

11 Ibid.

12 Ibid. Sinatra summarily fired Jacobs in 1968, after Jacobs was seen at the Candy Store, a Beverly Hills disco, dancing with Mia Farrow, Sinatra's estranged wife, whom he had served with divorce papers while she was filming *Rosemary's Baby*, in November 1967. See Jacobs and Stadiem, p. 11. While the firing might indicate bias on Jacobs' part, thereby tainting his account of the Natalie Wood-Sinatra affair, Jacobs' memoir is so friendly to Sinatra in most other respects that the firing seems unlikely to have motivated Jacobs to lie.

13 Finstad, p. 121.

14 Ibid., p. 122.

15 Ibid., pp. 121-123.

16 Ibid., p. 228.

17 Ibid., p. 271.

18 Gardner, Ava, *Ava: My Story*, Bantam Books, 1990, p. 201.

19 Wayne, p. 171.

20 Ibid.

21 Ibid., p. 173.

22 Bacall, Lauren, *By Myself and Then Some*, Harper Entertainment, 1978, 2005, p. 241.

23 Ibid., pp. 241-242.

24 Ibid., p. 242.

25 Ibid.

26 Wayne, pp. 175-176.

27 Summers, Anthony, and Robbyn Swan, *Sinatra: The Life*, Alfred A. Knopf, 2005, pp. 309-310.

28 Sinatra, Nancy, *Frank Sinatra: An American Legend*, W. Quay Hays, Publisher, 1995, 1998, p. 119.

29 Ibid., pp. 122-123.

30 Ibid., p. 123.

31 Freedland, Michael, *All the Way: A Biography of Frank Sinatra, 1915-1998*, St. Martin's Press,

1997, p. 234.

[32] During the *Contessa* filming, Gardner posed for a life-size sculpture, which would be used in one of the final scenes of the picture. Her character, an Italian countess, dies and is buried in the family plot, with the sculpture adorning the gravesite. After the film wrapped, Frank Sinatra purchased the Gardner sculpture from the production company, had it shipped to L.A., and set it up in the backyard of his home, shrine-like. See Server, Lee, *Ava Gardner: "Love is Nothing,"* St. Martin's Press, 2006, p. 278.

[33] Taraborrelli, J. Randy, *The Secret Life of Marilyn Monroe*, Grand Central Publishing, 2009, pp. 251-252.

[34] Irwin, Lew, *Sinatra: A Life Remembered*, Courage Books, an imprint of Running Press, 1997, pp. 115-116.

[35] Ibid., p. 116.

[36] Douglas-Home, Robin, *Sinatra*, Grosset & Dunlap, 1962, pp. 15-16.

[37] Irwin, p. 119.

[38] Vare, Ethlie Ann, Editor, *Legend: Frank Sinatra and the American Dream*, Boulevard Books, 1995, p. 209, taken from "Secrets of Sinatra: Inside Tales of his Life and Career," by Budd Schulberg, first published in *New Choices for Retirement Living*, (December 1993/January 1994).

[39] Santopietro, Tom, *Sinatra in Hollywood*, Thomas Dunne Books/St. Martin's Press, 2008, p. 195.

[40] Wayne, p. 187.

[41] Ibid., p. 216.

[42] Sinatra, p. 125.

[43] Bacall, p. 272.

[44] Sinatra began taking potshots at Dorothy Kilgallen during his nightclub act, usually at the expense of her worst feature, a noticeably weak chin. "Dorothy Kilgallen couldn't make it tonight," he'd tell his audiences," she's out shopping for a new chin." When Sinatra was informed of the columnist's death, in November 1965, he was heard to mutter, "Well, I guess I got to change my act." See Petkov, Steven, and Leonard Mustazza, Editors, *The Frank Sinatra Reader*, Oxford University Press, 1995, p. 109, quoting from "Frank Sinatra Has a Cold," by Gay Talese, in *Esquire*, April 1966.

[45] Bacall, p. 275.

[46] Several friends believed the affair started before Bogart died, but kept quit about it out of respect for Bogie. See Taraborrelli, pp. 198-200.

[47] Ibid., pp. 317-318.

[48] Sinatra, p. 136.

[49] Bacall, pp. 320-321.

[50] Jacobs and Stadiem, p. 115.

[51] Bacall, p. 324.

[52] Israel, Lee, *Kilgallen: A Biography of Dorothy Kilgallen*, Delacorte Press, 1979, p. 284.

CHAPTER 17

[1] After Sinatra finished singing the "Star-Spangled Banner" and stepped down from the stage, Sam Rayburn, speaker of the U.S. House of Representatives and the second most powerful man in Washington, grabbed his arm as he walked past the Texas delegation. Rayburn wanted to ask Sinatra to also sing "The Yellow Rose of Texas," but was taken aback when the singer turned to him and snarled, "Get your hands off the suit, creep." It was an affront Rayburn never forgot and one that Rayburn's chief protégé in Washington never forgot, either. When Sinatra visited Lyn-

don B. Johnson in the White House a decade later, Johnson treated him as brusquely as Sinatra had treated Rayburn, Johnson's mentor and a father figure. See Levy, Shawn, *Rat-Pack Confidential: Frank, Dean, Sammy, Peter, Joey and the Last Great Showbiz Party,* Doubleday, 1998, p. 69.

2   Spada, James, *Peter Lawford: The Man Who Kept the Secrets,* Bantam Books, 1991, p. 203.

3   Sinatra, Nancy, *Frank Sinatra: An American Legend,* W. Quay Hays, Publisher, 1995, 1998, p. 127.

4   Levinson, Peter J., *Tommy Dorsey: Livin' in a Great Big Way,* Da Capo Press, 2005, p. 303. Five years later, Sinatra put out an album of Dorsey hits under his new Reprise label, titled *I Remember Tommy.*

5   Sinatra, p. 128.

6   Sinatra, p. 157.

7   Taraborrelli, J. Randy, *Sinatra: Behind the Legend,* A Birch Lane Press Book, Carol Publishing Co., 1997, p. 201.

8   Ibid., p. 202.

9   Goddard, Peter, *Frank Sinatra: The Man, The Myth and The Music,* Greywood Publishing Limited, 1973, p. 145.

10   Sinatra, p. 130, quoting from the *Look* magazine article by Bill Davidson.

11   Irwin, Lew, *Sinatra: A Man Remembered,* Courage Books, an imprint of Running Press, 1997, p. 119.

12   Santopietro, Tom, *Sinatra in Hollywood,* Thomas Dunne Books/St. Martin's Press, 2008, p. 113.

13   Sinatra, p. 133.

14   Lahr, John, *Sinatra: The Artist and the Man,* Random House, 1997, p. 74.

15   MacLaine, Shirley, *My Lucky Stars: A Hollywood Memoir,* Bantam Books, 1995, pp. 62-63.

16   Frank invited Giancana and his then-girlfriend, singer Phyllis McGuire, to his parents' home in New Jersey for a Dolly-cooked Italian dinner — something no other Mafia figure in Sinatra's life had the pleasure of experiencing.

17   Spada, pp. 188-189.

18   Ibid., pp. 203-204.

19   Quirk, Lawrence J., and William Schoell, *The Rat Pack: The Hey-Hey Days of Frank and the Boys,* Taylor Publishing Company, 1998, p. 170.

20   Levy, Shawn, *Rat Pack Confidential: Frank, Dean, Sammy, Peter, Joey and the Last Great Showbiz Party,* Doubleday, 1998, pp. 73-74.

21   Quirk and Schoell, pp. 171-172; see also, Levy, p. 74.

22   Zehme, Bill, *The Way You Wear Your Hat: Frank Sinatra and the Lost Art of Livin',* Harper Collins, 1997, p. 81.

23   Consiglio, Tony, as told to Franz Douskey, *Sinatra and Me: The Very Good Years,* Tantor Media, 2012, p. 204.

24   Frew, Tim, *Sinatra,* élan press, 1998, p. 63.

25   Brownstein, Ronald, *The Power and the Glitter: The Hollywood-Washington Connection,* Pantheon Books, 1990, p. 145.

26   Summers, Anthony, and Robbyn Swan, *Sinatra: The Life,* Alfred A. Knopf, 2005, p. 260.

27   See Jacobs, George, and William Stadiem, *Mr. S: My Life with Frank Sinatra,* Harper Entertainment, 2003, p. 133. Jacobs, Sinatra's personal valet during this time, alleged that Sinatra also used Judy Campbell to provide sexual favors to Joseph Kennedy, Jack's father, when the elder Kennedy visited the Palm Springs compound. See also, Summers and Swan, pp. 264-266.

[28] Spada, p. 226.

[29] Ibid.

[30] Brownstein, p. 151.

[31] Exner, Judith (Campbell), as told to Ovid Demaris, *My Story*, Grove Press, 1977, pp. 50, 86.

[32] Ibid., p. 116.

[33] Kelley, Kitty, *His Way: The Unauthorized Biography of Frank Sinatra*, Bantam Books, 1986, p. 269.

[34] Ibid.

[35] Brownstein, p. 157.

[36] Summers and Swan, p. 270.

[37] Levy, pp. 157-158.

[38] Vare, Ethlie Ann, Editor, *Legend: Frank Sinatra and the American Dream*, Boulevard Books, 1995, p, 67, from an article titled "When Old Blues Eyes Was Red," by Jon Wiener, originally published in *The New Republic* on March 31, 1986.

[39] Ibid.

[40] Ibid., pp. 67-68.

[41] Levy, p. 158.

[42] Pugliese, Stanislao G., Editor, *Frank Sinatra: History, Identity and Italian American Culture*, Palgrave Macmillan, 2004, p. 57, from the essay, "Frank Sinatra and Presidential Politics," by Michael Nelson. Giancana hated Bobby Kennedy, who as chief counsel for the U.S. Senate's McClellan Committee, had ridiculed him unmercifully just a month earlier, when the mobster was subpoenaed and repeatedly took the Fifth before the committee. Each time Giancana invoked his right not to incriminate himself, he giggled nervously, which Bobby publicly compared to the actions of a little girl. Ironically, the McClellan Committee was investigating organized crime's influence over labor, the very quality that Joe Kennedy enlisted to help elect Jack to the presidency. Hypocrisy was not something the Kennedy family bothered about. Giancana and Jack Kennedy were sharing Judy Campbell at this time. The mobster actually liked Jack. Although there is no substantiated record of them ever meeting, Nick Sevano, Sinatra's on-and-off go-fer, claims he was present at a dinner attended by both Giancana and then-Senator Jack Kennedy. See Summers and Swan, p. 267. Campbell would later allege that she carried messages between the two, but there's no corroboration of that, either. The Chicago mob boss's hope was that if Jack became president, the FBI would take a softer approach in its investigation of mob activities. It was a pipe dream, especially after Jack installed his brother as the attorney general of the United States and head of the Department of Justice, under whose jurisdiction the FBI fell.

[43] Sinatra, p. 146.

[44] Demaris, Ovid, *The Boardwalk Jungle: How greed, corruption, and the Mafia turned Atlantic City into . . . .,"* Bantam Books, 1986, p. 33; see also, Levy, pp. 160-162.

[45] Levy, pp. 160-162.

[46] Sinatra, p. 146.

[47] Spada, p. 228.

[48] Ibid., pp. 228-229.

[49] Ibid., p. 230.

[50] Kelley, p. 279.

[51] Spada, p. 235.

[52] Ibid., pp. 234-235.

[53] Britt initially went by a different spelling of her first name — "Mai" — but switched to May around this time.

[54] Davis, Jr., Sammy, and Jane and Burt Boyar, *Sammy: An Autobiography*, Farrar, Straus and Giroux, 2000, pp. 374, 377.

[55] Ibid., pp. 378-380.

[56] Pugliese, Stanislao G., Editor, *Frank Sinatra: History, Identity and Italian American Culture*, Palgrave Macmillan, 2004, p. 58, from the essay "Frank Sinatra and Presidential Politics," by Michael Nelson.

[57] Taraborrelli, p. 223.

[58] Spada, p. 234.

CHAPTER 18

[1] Davis, Jr., Sammy, and Jane and Burt Boyar, *Sammy: An Autobiography*, Farrar, Straus and Giroux, 2000, p. 388.

[2] Ibid., p. 377.

[3] Ibid., p. 388.

[4] Ibid., p. 389.

[5] Sinatra, Nancy, *Frank Sinatra: An American Legend*, W. Quay Hays, Publisher, 1995, 1998, p. 151.

[6] Brownstein, Ronald, *The Power and the Glitter: The Hollywood-Washington Connection*, Pantheon Books, 1990, p. 159.

[7] Kelley, Kitty, *His Way: The Unauthorized Biography of Frank Sinatra*, Bantam Books, 1986, p. 285.

[8] Ibid., p. 286.

[9] Taraborrelli, J. Randy, *Sinatra: Behind the Legend*, A Birch Lane Press Book, published by Carol Publishing Group, 1997, p. 243.

[10] Irwin, Lew, *Sinatra: A Life Remembered*, Courage Books, an imprint of Running Press, 1997, p. 116; see also, Sinatra, pp. 150, 157-159.

[11] Sinatra, p. 158.

[12] Summers, Anthony, *Goddess: The Secret Lives of Marilyn Monroe*, Macmillan Publishing Company, 1985, p. 230; see also, Kelley, p. 279. Giancana and Sinatra brought in their friend Paul "Skinny" D'Amato from the 500 Club in Atlantic City to run the Cal-Neva Lodge for them. In July 1962, a drugged-up Marilyn Monroe visited Sinatra at the Cal-Neva, just days before she would commit suicide back in Los Angeles. She made a suicide attempt while at the Cal-Neva and had to be rushed to a hospital to have her stomach pumped. Sam Giancana was there as well, causing a permanent rift between Sinatra and his longtime road manager/bodyguard, Hank Sanicola, who was also a partner in the Cal-Neva. Giancana, as a known mob figure, was barred from all Nevada casinos by that state's gaming commission. See Kelley, p. 314. Giancana would make a return visit to the Cal-Neva in late July 1963 to be with his girlfriend, Phyllis McGuire, who was performing there as part of the popular McGuire Sisters singing trio. This time, the FBI had Giancana under surveillance and reported his presence to the Nevada Gaming Commission. The commission later held hearings and revoked Sinatra's gaming license because of Giancana being allowed on the premises, forcing Sinatra to sell his interest in the resort. See Kelley, pp. 319-324.

[13] On December 19, 1961, 73-year-old Joseph Kennedy, Sr. suffered a debilitating stroke, leaving him unable to speak and rendering him partially paralyzed. It would end his active reign as patri-

arch of the Kennedy family, although he would live eight more years and see two of his sons assassinated. See Spada, James, *Peter Lawford: The Man Who Kept the Secrets*, Bantam Books, 1991, p. 281.

[14] Taraborrelli, *Sinatra: Behind the Legend*, pp. 243-244.

[15] Ibid., p. 244.

[16] See Chapter 19 for a detailed discussion of these so-called "black-bag jobs" by the FBI — placing bugs in the homes and offices of selected mobsters to gather intelligence, illegal because it was done without a warrant. The program started during Robert Kennedy's tenure as attorney general and had to have been approved by him. FBI Director J. Edgar Hoover wouldn't have chanced it otherwise.

[17] Giancana, Antoinette, and Thomas C. Renner, *Mafia Princess: Growing Up in Sam Giancana's Family*, William Morrow and Company, Inc., 1984, p. 224.

[18] Kuntz, Tom, and Phil Kuntz, Editors, *The Sinatra Files: The Life of an American Icon under Government Surveillance*, Three Rivers Press, 2000, p. 152. See also, Giancana, p. 224. The FBI couldn't say for sure if it was Johnny Roselli or another Chicago hood, Johnny Formosa, who was engaging in this conversation with Giancana, but Sam's daughter Antoinette Giancana confirms that it was Roselli. Given Roselli's earlier meeting with Sinatra on this very subject, Roselli had the knowledge about the issue being discussed, so it was likely he who was present.

[19] Kuntz and Kuntz, p. 153.

[20] Spada, p. 292.

[21] Jacobs, George, and William Stadiem, *Mr. S: My Life with Frank Sinatra*, Harper Entertainment, 2003, p. 133.

[22] Ibid.

[23] Badham, Keith, *Marilyn Monroe: The Final Years*, Thomas Dunne Books, 2010, p. 26.

[24] Taraborrelli, J. Randy, *The Secret Life of Marilyn Monroe*, Grand Central Publishing, 2009, p. 380n.

[25] Less than three months after the birthday party, Marilyn Monroe would be dead, by her own hand. Joe DiMaggio took charge of her arrangements. He blamed Sinatra and the Kennedys for her death and barred them from Marilyn's funeral on August 8, 1962. See Taraborrelli, *The Secret Life of Marilyn Monroe*, p. 480.

[26] Judith Campbell went public with the incident, after reporter Liz Smith uncovered the sordid details in December 1996. Campbell, then going by her married name, Exner, appeared on the ABC program 20/20 and told the world about her affair with Jack Kennedy and the baby he had fathered. It did little to diminish the man's reputation, at a time when another White House occupant, Bill Clinton, was also accused of carrying on with a young woman. Both men, Kennedy and Clinton, are, to this day, among the most popular former presidents in every poll.

[27] Kuntz and Kuntz, pp. 146-149.

[28] Kuntz and Kuntz, pp. 154-155.

[29] Ibid., pp. 158-159.

[30] Spada, p. 292.

[31] Kuntz and Kuntz, p. 164.

[32] Pugliese, Stanislao G., Editor, *Frank Sinatra: History, Identity and Italian American Culture*, Palgrave Macmillan, 2004, p. 60, from the essay "Frank Sinatra and Presidential Politics," by Michael Nelson.

[33] Ibid.

[34] Lawford, Patricia Seaton, with Ted Schwartz, *The Peter Lawford Story: Life with the Kennedys,*

Monroe and the Rat Pack, Carroll & Graf Publishers, Inc., 1988, p. 135.

[35] Spada, p. 293.

[36] Ibid.

[37] Jacobs and Stadiem, p. 163. Years later, Nancy Sinatra reported that President Kennedy's planned visit to her father's Palm Springs compound was canceled because of security concerns, or so said Kenny O'Donnell, the president's special assistant and friend. O'Donnell said that it was strictly a decision by the Secret Service and that Bobby Kennedy had tried to persuade Jack to stay with Sinatra. See Sinatra, p. 162. The clear evidence is to the contrary. Security had nothing to do with the decision, unless it was the security of "Camelot."

[38] Jacobs and Stadiem, p. 187.

[39] Ibid., p. 163.

[40] Ibid., pp. 163-164.

[41] Ibid., p. 164.

[42] Ibid., p. 165.

[43] Spada, p. 294.

[44] Jacobs and Stadiem, p. 165.

[45] Lawford, p. 150.

[46] Kelley, p. 302. See also, Spada, pp. 294-295, who wrote, "The Sinatra debacle sent Peter reeling into a depression, one punctuated by bouts of heavy drinking."

[47] Brownstein, p. 166.

[48] Kuntz and Kuntz, p. 155.

[49] Kelley, p. 328.

CHAPTER 19

[1] Sinatra, Tina, with Jeff Coplon, *My Father's Daughter: A Memoir,* Simon & Schuster, 2000, p. 61.

[2] Ibid., p. 62-63.

[3] Ibid., pp. 69-70.

[4] Taraborrelli, J. Randy, *Sinatra: The Legend,* A Birch Lane Press Book, published by Carol Publishing Company, 1997, p. 294

[5] Ibid., pp. 294-296.

[6] Ibid., pp. 297-298.

[7] Ibid., p. 300.

[8] Ibid., p. 302.

[9] Sinatra, Tina, and Jeff Coplon, pp. 86-87.

[10] Taraborrelli, pp. 304-305.

[11] Ibid., pp. 306-308.

[12] Barrett, Rona, *Miss Rona: An Autobiography,* Nash Publishing, 1974, p. 197.

[13] Kelley, Kitty, *His Way: The Unauthorized Biography of Frank Sinatra,* Bantam Books, 1986, p. 261.

[14] Ibid., pp. 331-332.

[15] Ironically, Sinatra and John Wayne probably made more war-based movies than any other pair of Hollywood actors, though neither one of them ever spent a day in actual military service.

[16] Kelley, p. 324. Kitty Kelley interviewed Brad Dexter, who died in 2002, on multiple occasions in 1984 and 1985.

[17] Ibid.

[18] Ibid., pp. 334-335.

[19] Taraborrelli, p. 319.

[20] Summers, Anthony, and Robbyn Swan, *Sinatra: A Life*, Alfred A. Knopf, 2005, pp. 297-298.

[21] Kelley, p. 335.

[22] Wilson, Earl, *Sinatra: An Unauthorized Biography*, Macmillan Publishing Co., Inc., 1976, p. 182.

[23] Kelley, pp. 335-336.

[24] MacLaine, Shirley, *My Lucky Stars: A Hollywood Memoir*, Bantam Books, 1995, p. 87.

[25] Starr, Michael Seth, *Mouse in the Rat Pack: The Joey Bishop Story*, Taylor Trade Publishing, 2002, p. 115.

[26] Farrow, Mia, *What Falls Away: A Memoir*, Nan A. Talese/Doubleday, 1997, p. 87.

[27] Obituary of John Farrow, *Los Angeles Times*, January 29, 1963.

[28] Farrow, p. 86.

[29] Kelley, p. 344.

[30] Ibid., pp. 343-344.

[31] Ibid., p. 344.

[32] Farrow, p. 87.

[33] Ibid., pp. 87-88.

[34] Ibid., p. 91.

[35] Ibid., pp. 95, 97.

[36] Ibid., p. 98.

[37] Summers and Swan, pp. 315-316. When told about the Frank-Mia relationship, Ava Gardner responded similarly: "Hah! I always knew Frank would end up in bed with a boy." Summers and Swan, p. 316.

[38] Taraborrelli, p. 331.

[39] Farrow, pp. 98-99.

[40] Irwin, Lew, *Sinatra: A Life Remembered*, Courage Books, an imprint of Running Press, 1997, p. 117.

[41] Farrow, p. 99.

[42] Sinatra, Nancy, *Frank Sinatra: An American Legend*, W. Quay Hays, Publisher, 1995, 1998, p. 194.

[43] Sinatra, Tina, and Jeff Coplon, p. 113.

[44] Ibid., p. 111.

[45] Kelley, p. 345.

[46] Ibid., p. 353.

[47] Ibid., p. 354.

[48] Wilson, p. 233.

[49] Jacobs, George, and William Stadiem, *Mr. S: My Life with Frank Sinatra*, Harper Entertainment, 2003, p. 230.

[50] Kelley, p. 354.

[51] Ibid., p. 355.

[52] Jacobs and Stadiem, p. 236.

[53] Sinatra, Nancy, p. 199.

[54] Demaris, Ovid, *The Boardwalk Jungle: How greed, corruption, and the Mafia turned Atlantic City into . . .*, Bantam Books, 1986, p. 240; see also Farrow, pp. 110-111.

[55] Kelley, p. 373.

[56] Ibid., p. 375.

[57] Kelley, p. 402.

CHAPTER 20

[1] Demaris, Ovid, *The Boardwalk Jungle: How greed, corruption, and the Mafia turned Atlantic City into . . .*, Bantam Books, 1986, pp. 40-41.

[2] This is the opinion of former U.S. Attorney for New Jersey Herbert J. Stern, later a federal judge in that state. See Stern, Herbert J., *Diary of a DA: The True Story of the Prosecutor Who Took on the Mob, Fought Corruption, and Won*, Skyhorse Publishing, 2012, p. 520. U.S. Senator Clifford Case (R-NJ) once referred to his home state in this way: "I am tired of having New Jersey a stench in the nostrils and an offense to the vision of the world and of ourselves." See Stern, p. 241.

[3] Sifakis, Carl, *The Mafia Encyclopedia: From Accardo to Zwillman*, 3rd. Ed., Facts on File, Inc., 2005, p. 316.

[4] Ibid., p. 186.

[5] Ibid., pp. 240-242.

[6] Linnett, Richard, *In the Godfather Garden: The Long Life and Times of Richie "the Boot" Boiardo,"* Rutgers University Press, 2013, pp. 72-74. See also, Sifakis, p. 488.

[7] Stern, p. 85.

[8] Interview of Herbert J. Stern, June 18, 2015.

[9] Stern, pp. 227, 239.

[10] Kuntz, Tom, and Phil Kuntz, Editors, *The Sinatra Files: The Life of an American Icon under Government Surveillance*, Three Rivers Press, 2000, pp. 152-156.

[11] Stern, p. 229.

[12] Ibid., pp. 227, 239.

[13] Technically, the transcripts later made public were not verbatim recordings or tapes; rather, they were excerpts of conversations in the bugged facilities, selected by the listening FBI agents as being relevant to the criminal enterprises being engaged in. They would be referred to as "tapes" in media accounts.

[14] Stern, p. 91.

[15] Kelly, Robert J., *Encyclopedia of Organized Crime in the United States*, Greenwood Press, 2000, p. 92.

[16] Stern, p. 290.

[17] Ibid., pp. 473-474.

[18] Stern, p. 475.

[19] Ibid., p. 502.

[20] Ibid., p. 503.

[21] Interview of Herbert J. Stern, June 18, 2015.

[22] Stern, pp. 506-507.

[23] Kuntz and Kuntz, p. 227.

[24] Ibid., pp. 227-228.

[25] See link, http://www.historyvshollywood.com/reelfaces/jersey-boys/, citing a *Parade Magazine* interview with Frankie Valli. Other sources confirm the accuracy of the close bond between Valli and DeCarlo.

[26] Kuntz and Kuntz, p. 228. Sinatra biographer Kitty Kelley also reported on this incident, although in considerably less detail. See Kelley, Kitty, *His Way: The Unauthorized Biography of Frank Sinatra*, Bantam Books, 1986, p. 418.

[27] Telephone interview of Edwin Stier, September 14, 2015.

[28] Ibid.

[29] Lahr, John, *Sinatra: The Artist and the Man*, Random House, 1997, p. 72.

[30] Kelly, pp. 486-487.

[31] Lahr, p. 73.

[32] Wilson, Earl, *Sinatra: An Unauthorized Biography*, Macmillan Publishing Co., Inc., 1976, p. 270.

[33] Ibid., p. *xi*.

[34] Lahr, p. 72.

[35] Wilson, p. 270.

[36] Lahr, p. 72.

[37] Wilson, pp. 272-273.

[38] Sinatra, Tina, with Jeff Coplon, *My Father's Daughter: A Memoir*, Simon & Schuster, 2000, p. 125.

[39] Summers, Anthony, and Robbyn Swan, *Sinatra: The Life*, Alfred A. Knopf, 2005, p. 344.

[40] Sinatra, Tina, with Jeff Coplon, p. 126.

[41] Wilson, p. 273.

[42] Ibid., p. 274.

[43] Irwin, Lew, Sinatra: *A Life Remembered*, Courage Books, an imprint of Running Press, 1997, p. 118.

[44] Sinatra, Nancy, p. 231.

[45] Kelley, p. 419.

[46] Wilson, p. 277.

[47] Kelley, p. 422.

[48] Ibid., p. 424.

[49] Ibid., pp. 424-425.

[50] Ibid., p. 425.

[51] Ibid., p. 426.

[52] Ibid., p. 427.

[53] Ibid., p. 452.

[54] Summers and Swan, pp. 347-349.

[55] Sinatra, Barbara, with Wendy Holden, *Lady Blue Eyes: My Life With Frank*, Crown Archetype,

an imprint of the Crown Publishing group, 2011, pp. 52, 63.

56 Ibid., p. 107.

57 Ibid., pp. 107-108.

58 Sinatra, Tina, with Jeff Coplon, p. 152

59 Levy, Shawn, *Rat Pack Confidential: Frank, Dean, Sammy, Peter, Joey, and the Last Great Showbiz Party*, Doubleday, 1998, p. 202.

60 Sinatra, Barbara, with Wendy Holden, p. 177.

CHAPTER 21

1 Kelley, Kitty, *His Way: The Unauthorized Biography of Frank Sinatra*, Bantam Books, 1986, p. 361.

2 Ibid., pp. 361-362.

3 Ibid., p. 268.

4 Ibid., p. 459. Reagan's letter to this citizen was later sold at auction for $12,000, the highest amount ever paid for the correspondence of a living person. The winning bid was submitted, secretly, by Frank Sinatra.

5 Ibid., p. 461.

6 Ibid., pp. 461-462.

7 Nancy Sr. obtained an abortion in 1947, when it looked like her marriage to Frank was on the rocks. Nancy Jr. had an abortion at age 19, in 1958 or 1960 — her mother took her for the procedure, which was done with Frank's knowledge. See Taraborrelli, J. Randy, *Sinatra: Behind the Legend*, A Birch Lane Press Book, published by Carol Publishing Group, 1997, p. 451. Tina had an abortion in late 1970, at age 22. See Sinatra, Tina, with Jeff Coplon, *My Father's Daughter: A Memoir*, Simon & Schuster, 2000, pp. 129-130.

8 Sinatra, Nancy, *Frank Sinatra: An American Legend*, W. Quay Hays, Publisher, 1995, 1998, p. 250.

9 Sinatra, Barbara, with Wendy Holden, *Lady Blue Eyes: My Life with Frank*, Crown Archetype, an imprint of the Crown Publishing Group, 2011, p. 204.

10 Sinatra, Tina, with Jeff Coplon, p. 168.

11 Sinatra, Barbara, with Wendy Holden, p. 205.

12 Sinatra, Tina, with Jeff Coplon, p. 172. Frank and Barbara Sinatra were married in a Catholic ceremony at the home of Irish tenor Morton Downey in Palm Beach, Florida, soon after the annulment became official. Later, they would repeat those religious vows in St. Patrick's Cathedral in New York. See Sinatra, Barbara, with Wendy Holden, pp. 205-206.

13 Sinatra, Tina, with Jeff Coplon, p. 174.

14 Sinatra, Barbara, with Wendy Holden, p. 207.

15 Sinatra, Tina, with Jeff Coplon, pp. 166-167.

16 Ibid., p. 167.

17 Ibid., pp. 167-168.

18 Ibid., p. 169.

19 Ibid., p. 175.

20 Ibid., p. 177.

21 Reagan would be highly successful in that endeavor, all over the country, when blue-collar Democrats rallied to his support and created a phalanx of Republican supporters known to this

day as "Reagan Democrats."

[22] Interview on May 19, 2015, of Pat Politis, who cooked President Reagan's dinner that night in Hoboken, under the watchful eyes of the Secret Service; see also, Kelley, pp. 503-504.

[23] Sinatra, Barbara, with Wendy Holden, p. 276.

[24] Sinatra, Tina, with Jeff Coplon, p. 191.

[25] Ibid., pp. 194-195.

[26] Ibid., p. 196.

[27] Ibid., pp. 108-109, 203.

[28] Ibid., pp. 204-206.

[29] Sinatra, Barbara, with Wendy Holden, pp. 322-323.

[30] Charlie Callas, as told to Albert Wunsch III

[31] Sinatra, Tina, with Jeff Coplon, pp. 229-230.

[32] MacLaine, Shirley, *My Lucky Stars: A Hollywood Memoir*, Bantam Books, 1995, pp. 101, 107-108.

[33] Sinatra, Barbara, with Wendy Holden, p. 333.

[34] Petkov, Steven, and Leonard Mustazza, Editors, *The Frank Sinatra Reader*, Oxford University Press, 1995, p. 179. from a *New York Newsday* article by Murray Kempton, June 17, 1993, titled "The Lion in Winter."

[35] Sinatra, Tina, with Jeff Coplon, p. 240.

[36] Ibid., pp. 243-246.

[37] Ibid., p. 253.

[38] Ibid., p. 259.

[39] Ibid., pp. 268-268.

[40] Ibid. p. 279.

[41] Sinatra, Barbara, with Wendy Holden, pp. 355-357.

[42] Sinatra, Tina, with Jeff Coplon, p. 286.

EPILOGUE

[1] Iowa voters select their preferred candidate before New Hampshire does, but Iowa is a caucus state, as opposed to a primary state.

[2] Zehme, Bill, *The Way You Wear Your Hat: Frank Sinatra and the Lost Art of Livin'*, Harper Collins, 1997, pp. 73-74.

[3] MacLaine, Shirley, *My Lucky Stars: A Hollywood Memoir*, Bantam Books, 1995, p. 87.

[4] Quirk, Lawrence J., and William Schoell, *The Rat Pack: The Hey-Hey Days of Frank and the Boys*, Taylor Publishing Company, 1998, pp. 144-145.

[5] Consiglio, Tony, as told to Franz Douskey, *Sinatra and Me: The Very Good Years*, Tantor Media, Inc., 2012, p. 75.

[6] Pugliese, Stanislao G., Editor, *Frank Sinatra: History, Identity, and Italian American Culture*, Palgrave Macmillan, 2004, p. 54, from the essay "Frank Sinatra and Presidential Politics," by Michael Nelson.

[7] Taken from *Frank Sinatra: Voice of the Century*, a BBC production, which originally aired on May 14, 1998, the day Sinatra died.

[8] Jacobs, George, and William Stadiem, *Mr. S: My Life with Frank Sinatra*, Harper Entertain-

ment, 2003, p. 212.

9 Spada, James, *Peter Lawford: The Man Who Kept The Secrets*, Bantam Books, 1991, p. 209.

10 Petkov, Steven, and Leonard Mustazza, *The Frank Sinatra Reader*, Oxford University Press, 1995, p. 250.

11 Kelley, Kitty, *His Way: The Unauthorized Biography of Frank Sinatra*, Bantam Books, 1986, p. 156.

12 Ibid., p. 289.

13 Frew, Tim, *Sinatra*, élan press, 1998, p. 93.

INDEX